Microsound

Curtis Roads

Microsound

The MIT Press
Cambridge, Massachusetts
London, England

First MIT Press paperback edition, 2004
© 2001 Massachusetts Institute of Technology

This book was set in Times New Roman in '3B2' by Asco Typesetters, Hong Kong and was printed and bound in the United States of America.

Library of Congress Cataloging-in-Publication Data

Roads, Curtis.
  Microsound / Curtis Roads.
    p.   cm.
  Includes bibliographical references and index.
  ISBN 978-0-262-18215-7 (hc. : alk. paper), 978-0-262-68154-4 (pb.)
  1. Music—Acoustics and physics. 2. Electronic music—History and criticism.
3. Computer music—History and criticism. I. Title.
ML3805 .R69 2001
781.2′2—dc21   2001030633

Contents

Introduction

Beneath the level of the note lies the realm of microsound, of sound particles. Microsonic particles remained invisible for centuries. Recent technological
advances let us probe and explore the beauties of this formerly unseen world.
Microsonic techniques dissolve the rigid bricks of music architecture—the notes
—into a more fluid and supple medium. Sounds may coalesce, evaporate, or
mutate into other sounds.

The sensations of point, pulse (regular series of points), line (tone), and surface (texture) appear as the density of particles increases. Sparse emissions leave
rhythmic traces. When the particles line up in rapid succession, they induce the
illusion of tone continuity that we call pitch. As the particles meander, they
flow into streams and rivulets. Dense agglomerations of particles form swirling
sound clouds whose shapes evolve over time.

In the 1940s, the Nobel prize winning physicist Dennis Gabor proposed that
any sound could be decomposed into acoustical quanta bounded by discrete
units of time and frequency. This quantum representation formed the famous
Gabor matrix. Like a sonogram, the vertical dimension of the Gabor matrix
indicated the location of the frequency energy, while the horizontal dimension
indicated the time region in which this energy occurred. In a related project,
Gabor built a machine to granulate sound into particles. This machine could
alter the duration of a sound without shifting its pitch.

In these two projects, the matrix and the granulator, Gabor accounted for
both important domains of sound representation. The matrix was the original
windowed frequency-domain representation. "Windowed" means segmented in
time, and "frequency-domain" refers to spectrum. The granulation machine, on
the other hand, operated on a *time-domain representation*, which is familiar to
anyone who has seen waveforms in a sound editor. This book explores microsound from both perspectives: the windowed frequency-domain and the micro

time-domain. Both concern microacoustic phenomena lasting less than one-tenth of a second.

This book is the fruit of a lengthy period of activity involving synthesis experiments, programming, and composition dating back to the early 1970s. I started writing the text in 1995, after completing my textbook *The Computer Music Tutorial* (The MIT Press 1996). Beginning with a few strands, it eventually grew into a lattice of composition theory, historical accounts, technical overviews, acoustical experiments, descriptions of musical works, and aesthetic reflections. Why such a broad approach? Because at this stage of development, the musical, technical, and aesthetic problems interweave. We are inventing particles at the same time that we are learning how to compose with them. In numerous "assessment" sections I have tried to summarize the results, which in some cases are merely preliminary. More experimentation is surely needed.

Microsound records this first round of experimentation, and thus serves as a diary of research. Certain details, such as the specific software and hardware that I used, will no doubt become obsolete rapidly. Even so, I decided to leave them in for the historical record.

The experimentation and documentation could go on indefinitely. One could imagine, for example, a kind of synthesis "cookbook" after the excellent example of Jean-Claude Risset (1969). His text provided detailed recipes for making specific sounds from a variety of synthesis techniques. This would be a worthy project, and I would encourage others in this direction. As for myself, it is time to compose.

A Note on The Paperback Edition (2004)

Much has happened since *Microsound* was first published in March 2002. In particular, I supervised a graduate project on real-time wavelet transformations by Sekhar Ramakrishnan, and became aware of the research of Stephan Mallat and his colleagues in signal analysis based on the matching pursuit algorithm (Mallat and Zhang 1993; Mallat 1998). My student Garry Kling and I have been exploring this avenue of research for the past two years. Our first publications will appear by the time that this edition is released (Kling and Roads 2004). I would like to also thank David Thall for his efforts over the past year in developing a new generation of real-time microsonic instruments. Finally, the collection *POINT LINE CLOUD*, which gathers together thirteen of my electronic music compositions, is being released in a CD+DVD package by Asphodel (San Francisco), with videos realized by Brian O'Reilly.

Acknowledgments

This book derives from a doctoral thesis written for the Université de Paris VIII (Roads 1999). It would never have started without strong encouragement from Professor Horacio Vaggione. I am deeply indebted to him for his patient advocacy, as well as for his inspired writings and pieces.

The congenial atmosphere in the Département Musique at the Université de Paris VIII was ideal for the gestation of this work. I would also like to extend my sincere appreciation to Jean-Claude Risset and Daniel Arfib. Despite much pressure on their time, these pioneers and experts kindly agreed to serve on the doctoral committee. Their commentaries on my text resulted in major improvements.

I owe a debt of thanks to my colleague Gérard Pape at the Centre de Création Musicale «Iannis Xenakis» (CCMIX) for his support of my research, teaching, and composition. I must also convey appreciation to Iannis Xenakis for his brilliant example and for his support of our work in Paris. My first contact with him, at his short course in Formalized Music in 1972, started me on this path.

I completed this book while teaching in the Center for Research in Electronic Art Technology (CREATE) in the Department of Music and in the Media Arts and Technology Program at the University of California, Santa Barbara. I greatly appreciate the friendship and support of Professor JoAnn Kuchera-Morin, Director of CREATE, during this productive period. I would also like to extend my thanks to the rest of the CREATE team, including Stephen T. Pope for his collaboration on pulsar synthesis in 1997. It was a great pleasure to work with Alberto de Campo, who served as CREATE's Research Director in 1999–2000. Together we developed the PulsarGenerator software and the Creatovox synthesizer. I consider these engaging musical instruments to be among the main accomplishments of this research.

Allow me to remember my late colleague Professor Aldo Piccialli of the Department of Physics at the University of Naples «Federico II.» His intense fascination with the subject of microsound inspired me to dive deeper into the theory of musical signal processing, and led to the notion of pulsar synthesis. This exploration has been most rewarding. I also appreciate the discussions and correspondence with my friends in Naples, including Sergio Cavaliere, Gianpaolo Evangelista, and Giancarlo Sica.

Many other colleagues provided information and advice, including Clifton Kussmaul, Corey Cheng, Tom Erbe, Christopher Weare, and Jean de Reydellet. Brigitte Robindoré, Pierre Roy, Jakub Omsky, Luca Lucchese, and Thom Blum kindly read parts of the manuscript and provided much valuable feedback. Their comments are most appreciated. The MIT Press arranged for three anonymous reviews of the book. These critiques led to many improvements. I would also like to thank Douglas Sery of The MIT Press for his enthusiastic sponsorship of this project.

Parts of this book were written during vacations at the family home in Illinois. I will always be grateful to my mother, Marjorie Roads, for the warm atmosphere that I enjoyed there during sabbaticals.

Overview

Chapter 1 projects a view of nine time scales of musical sound structure. It examines this hierarchy from both aesthetic and technical viewpoints. Major themes of this chapter include: the boundaries between time scales, the particularities of the various time scales, and the size of sounds.

Chapter 2 traces the history of the idea of microsound, from the ancient philosophy of atomism to the recent analog era. It explains how particle models of sound emerged alongside wave-oriented models. It then presents the modern history of microsound, beginning with the Gabor matrix. It follows the writings of a diverse collection of authors, including Ezra Pound, Henry Cowell, Werner Meyer-Eppler, Iannis Xenakis, Abraham Moles, Norbert Wiener, and Karlheinz Stockhausen. It also looks at the viability of a microsonic approach in analog synthesis and instrumental music.

Chapter 3 presents the theory and practice of digital granular synthesis in its myriad manifestations. It examines the different methods for organizing the grains, and looks at the effects produced in each parameter of the technique. It then surveys the various implementations of computer-based granular synthesis, beginning with the earliest experiments in the 1970s.

Chapter 4 is a catalog of experiments with newer particles, featuring glissons, grainlets, pulsars, and trainlets. We also examine sonographic and formant particles, transient drawing, particle cloning, and physical and abstract models of particle synthesis.

Chapter 5 surveys a broad variety of microsonic sound transformations. These range from audio compression techniques to micromontage and granulations. The brief presentation on the Creatovox instrument emphasizes real-time performance with granulated sound. The chapter then covers transformations on a micro scale, including pitch-shifting, pitch-time changing, filtering, dynamics processing, frequency-domain granulation, and waveset transformations.

The final sections present techniques of spatialization with sound particles, and convolution with microsounds.

Chapter 6 explores a variety of sound transformations based on windowed spectrum analysis. After a theoretical section, it presents the main tools of windowed spectrum transformation, including the phase vocoder, the tracking phase vocoder, the wavelet transform, and Gabor analysis.

Chapter 7 turns from technology to compositional applications. It begins with a description of the first studies realized with granular synthesis on a digital computer. It then looks at particle techniques in my recent compositions, as well as those by Barry Truax, Horacio Vaggione, and other composers.

Chapter 8, on the aesthetics of composing with microsound, is the most philosophical part of the book. It highlights both specific and general aesthetic issues raised by microsound in composition.

Chapter 9 concludes with a commentary on the future of microsound in music.

Microsound

1   Time Scales of Music

Time Scales of Music

Boundaries between Time Scales

Zones of Intensity and Frequency

Infinite Time Scale

Supra Time Scale

Macro Time Scale

    Perception of the Macro Time Scale

    Macroform

        Design of Macroform

Meso Time Scale

    Sound Masses, Textures, and Clouds

        Cloud Taxonomy

Sound Object Time Scale

    The Sensation of Tone

    Homogeneous Notes versus Heterogeneous Sound Objects

    Sound Object Morphology

Micro Time Scale

    Perception of Microsound

        Microtemporal Intensity Perception

        Microtemporal Fusion and Fission

The evolution of musical expression intertwines with the development of musical instruments. This was never more evident than in the twentieth century. Beginning with the gigantic Telharmonium synthesizer unveiled in 1906 (Weidenaar 1989, 1995), research ushered forth a steady stream of electrical and electronic instruments. These have irrevocably molded the musical landscape.

The most precise and flexible electronic music instrument ever conceived is the digital computer. As with the pipe organ, invented centuries earlier, the computer's power derives from its ability to emulate, or in scientific terms, to model phenomena. The models of the computer take the form of symbolic code. Thus it does not matter whether the phenomena being modeled exist outside the circuitry of the machine, or whether they are pure fantasy. This makes the computer an ideal testbed for the representation of musical structure on multiple time scales.

This chapter examines the time scales of music. Our main focus is the micro time scale and its interactions with other time scales. By including extreme time scales—the infinite and the infinitesimal—we situate musical time within the broadest possible context.

Time Scales of Music

Music theory has long recognized a temporal hierarchy of structure in music compositions. A central task of composition has always been the management of the interaction amongst structures on different time scales. Starting from the topmost layer and descending, one can dissect layers of structure, arriving at the bottom layer of individual notes.

This hierarchy, however, is incomplete. Above the level of an individual piece are the cultural time spans defining the oeuvre of a composer or a stylistic period. Beneath the level of the note lies another multilayered stratum, the microsonic hierarchy. Like the quantum world of quarks, leptons, gluons, and bosons, the microsonic hierarchy was long invisible. Modern tools let us view and manipulate the microsonic layers from which all acoustic phenomena emerge. Beyond these physical time scales, mathematics defines two ideal temporal boundaries—the infinite and the infinitesimal—which appear in the theory of musical signal processing.

Taking a comprehensive view, we distinguish nine time scales of music, starting from the longest:

1. *Infinite* The ideal time span of mathematical durations such as the infinite sine waves of classical Fourier analysis.

2. *Supra* A time scale beyond that of an individual composition and extending into months, years, decades, and centuries.

3. *Macro* The time scale of overall musical architecture or form, measured in minutes or hours, or in extreme cases, days.

4. *Meso* Divisions of form. Groupings of sound objects into hierarchies of phrase structures of various sizes, measured in minutes or seconds.

5. *Sound object* A basic unit of musical structure, generalizing the traditional concept of note to include complex and mutating sound events on a time scale ranging from a fraction of a second to several seconds.

6. *Micro*   Sound particles on a time scale that extends down to the threshold of auditory perception (measured in thousandths of a second or milliseconds).

7. *Sample*   The atomic level of digital audio systems: individual binary samples or numerical amplitude values, one following another at a fixed time interval. The period between samples is measured in millionths of a second (microseconds).

8. *Subsample*   Fluctuations on a time scale too brief to be properly recorded or perceived, measured in billionths of a second (nanoseconds) or less.

9. *Infinitesimal*   The ideal time span of mathematical durations such as the infinitely brief delta functions.

Figure 1.1 portrays the nine time scales of the time domain. Notice in the middle of the diagram, in the frequency column, a line indicating "Conscious time, the present (∼600 ms)." This line marks off Winckel's (1967) estimate of the "thickness of the present." The thickness extends to the line at the right indicating the physical NOW. This temporal interval constitutes an estimate of the accumulated lag time of the perceptual and cognitive mechanisms associated with hearing. Here is but one example of a disparity between *chronos*—physical time, and *tempus*—perceived time (Küpper 2000).

The rest of this chapter explains the characteristics of each time scale in turn. We will, of course, pay particular attention to the micro time scale.

Boundaries between Time Scales

As sound passes from one time scale to another it crosses perceptual boundaries. It seems to change quality. This is because human perception processes each time scale differently. Consider a simple sinusoid transposed to various time scales (1 μsec, 1 ms, 1 sec, 1 minute, 1 hour). The waveform is identical, but one would have difficulty classifying these auditory experiences in the same family.

In some cases the borders between time scales are demarcated clearly; ambiguous zones surround others. Training and culture condition perception of the time scales. To hear a flat pitch or a dragging beat, for example, is to detect a temporal anomaly on a micro scale that might not be noticed by other people.

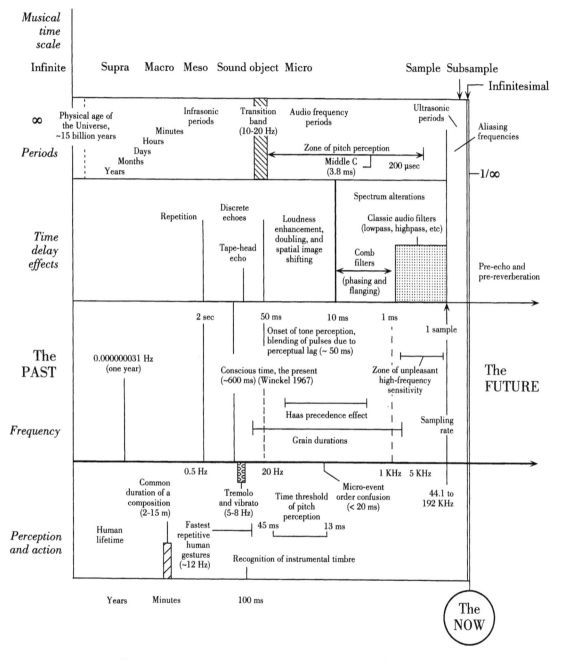

Figure 1.1   The time domain, segmented into periods, time delay effects, frequencies, and perception and action. Note that time intervals are not drawn to scale.

Digital audio systems, such as compact disc players, operate at a fixed sampling frequency. This makes it easy to distinguish the exact boundary separating the sample time scale from the subsample time scale. This boundary is the Nyquist frequency, or the sampling frequency divided by two. The effect of crossing this boundary is not always perceptible. In noisy sounds, aliased frequencies from the subsample time domain may mix unobtrusively with high frequencies in the sample time domain.

The border between certain other time scales is context-dependent. Between the sample and micro time scales, for example, is a region of transient events—too brief to evoke a sense of pitch but rich in timbral content. Between the micro and the object time scales is a stratum of brief events such as short staccato notes. Another zone of ambiguity is the border between the sound object and meso levels, exemplified by an evolving texture. A texture might contain a statistical distribution of micro events that are perceived as a unitary yet time-varying sound.

Time scales interlink. A given level encapsulates events on lower levels and is itself subsumed within higher time scales. Hence to operate on one level is to affect other levels. The interaction between time scales is not, however, a simple relation. Linear changes on a given time scale do not guarantee a perceptible effect on neighboring time scales.

Zones of Intensity and Frequency

Sound is an alternation in pressure, particle displacement, or particle velocity propagated in an elastic material. (Olson 1957)

Before we continue further, a brief discussion of acoustic terminology might be helpful. In scientific parlance—as opposed to popular usage—the word "sound" refers not only to phenomena in air responsible for the sensation of hearing but also "whatever else is governed by analogous physical principles" (Pierce 1994). Sound can be defined in a general sense as mechanical radiant energy that is transmitted by pressure waves in a material medium. Thus besides the airborne frequencies that our ears perceive, one may also speak of underwater sound, sound in solids, or structure-borne sound. Mechanical vibrations even take place on the atomic level, resulting in quantum units of sound energy called phonons. The term "acoustics" likewise is independent of air and of human perception. It is distinguished from *optics* in that it involves mechanical—rather than electromagnetic, wave motion.

Corresponding to this broad definition of sound is a very wide range of transient, chaotic, and periodic fluctuations, spanning frequencies that are both higher and lower than the human ear can perceive. The *audio* frequencies, traditionally said to span the range of about 20 Hz to 20 kHz are perceptible to the ear. The specific boundaries vary depending on the individual.

Vibrations at frequencies too low to be heard as continuous tones can be perceived by the ear as well as the body. These are the infrasonic impulses and vibrations, in the range below about 20 Hz. The infectious rhythms of the percussion instruments fall within this range.

Ultrasound includes the domain of high frequencies above the range of human audibility. The threshold of ultrasound varies according to the individual, their age, and the test conditions. Science and industry use ultrasonic techniques in a variety of applications, such as acoustic imaging (Quate 1998) and highly directional loudspeakers (Pompei 1998).

Some sounds are too soft to be perceived by the human ear, such as a caterpillar's delicate march across a leaf. This is the zone of *subsonic* intensities.

Other sounds are so loud that to perceive them directly is dangerous, since they are destructive to the human body. Sustained exposure to sound levels around 120 dB leads directly to pain and hearing loss. Above 130 dB, sound is felt by the exposed tissues of the body as a painful pressure wave (Pierce 1983). This dangerous zone extends to a range of destructive acoustic phenomena. The force of an explosion, for example, is an intense acoustic shock wave.

For lack of a better term, we call these *perisonic* intensities (from the Latin *periculos* meaning "dangerous"). The *audible* intensities fall between these two ranges. Figure 1.2 depicts the zones of sound intensity and frequency. The α zone in the center is where audio frequencies intersect with audible intensities, enabling hearing. Notice that the α zone is but a tiny fraction of a vast range of sonic phenomena.

Following this discussion of acoustical terms, let us proceed to the main theme of this chapter, the time scales of music.

Infinite Time Scale

Complex Fourier analysis regards the signal sub specie aeternitatis.   (Gabor 1952)

The human experience of musical time is linked to the ticking clock. It is natural to ask: when did the clock begin to tick? Will it tick forever? At the

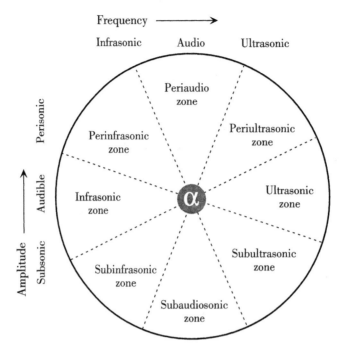

Figure 1.2   Zones of intensities and frequencies. Only the zone marked α is audible to the ear. This zone constitutes a tiny portion of the range of sound phenomena.

extreme upper boundary of all time scales is the mathematical concept of an infinite time span. This is a logical extension of the infinite series, a fundamental notion in mathematics. An infinite series is a sequence of numbers $u_1, u_2, u_3 \ldots$ arranged in a prescribed order and formed according to a particular rule. Consider this infinite series:

$$\sum_{i=1}^{\infty} u_i = u_1 + u_2 + u_3 + \cdots$$

This equation sums a set of numbers u_i, where the index i goes from 1 to ∞. What if each number u_i corresponded to a tick of a clock? This series would then define an infinite duration. This ideal is not so far removed from music as it may seem. The idea of infinite duration is implicit in the theory of Fourier analysis, which links the notion of frequency to sine waves of infinite duration. As chapter 6 shows, Fourier analysis has proven to be a useful tool in the analysis and transformation of musical sound.

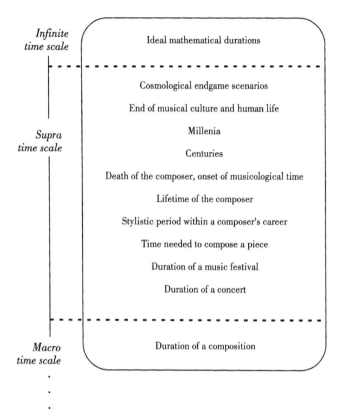

Infinite time scale

Ideal mathematical durations

Supra time scale

Cosmological endgame scenarios

End of musical culture and human life

Millenia

Centuries

Death of the composer, onset of musicological time

Lifetime of the composer

Stylistic period within a composer's career

Time needed to compose a piece

Duration of a music festival

Duration of a concert

Macro time scale

Duration of a composition

Figure 1.3   The scope of the supratemporal domain.

Supra Time Scale

The supra time scale spans the durations that are beyond those of an individual composition. It begins as the applause dies out after the longest compositions, and extends into weeks, months, years, decades, and beyond (figure 1.3). Concerts and festivals fall into this category. So do programs from music broadcasting stations, which may extend into years of more-or-less continuous emissions.

Musical cultures are constructed out of supratemporal bricks: the eras of instruments, of styles, of musicians, and of composers. Musical education takes years; cultural tastes evolve over decades. The perception and appreciation of a single composition may change several times within a century. The entire history of music transpires within the supratemporal scale, starting from the earliest known musical instrument, a Neanderthal flute dating back some 45,000 years (Whitehouse 1999).

Composition is itself a supratemporal activity. Its results last only a fraction of the time required for its creation. A composer may spend a year to complete a ten-minute piece. Even if the composer does not work every hour of every day, the ratio of 52,560 minutes passed for every 1 minute composed is still significant. What happens in this time? Certain composers design a complex strategy as prelude to the realization of a piece. The electronic music composer may spend considerable time in creating the sound materials of the work. Either of these tasks may entail the development of software. Virtually all composers spend time experimenting, playing with material in different combinations. Some of these experiments may result in fragments that are edited or discarded, to be replaced with new fragments. Thus it is inevitable that composers invest time pursuing dead ends, composing fragments that no one else will hear. This backtracking is not necessarily time wasted; it is part of an important feedback loop in which the composer refines the work. Finally we should mention documentation. While only a few composers document their labor, these documents may be valuable to those seeking a deeper understanding of a work and the compositional process that created it. Compare all this with the efficiency of the real-time improviser!

Some music spans beyond the lifetime of the individual who composed it, through published notation, recordings, and pedagogy. Yet the temporal reach of music is limited. Many compositions are performed only once. Scores, tapes, and discs disappear into storage, to be discarded sooner or later. Music-making presumably has always been part of the experience of *Homo sapiens*, who it is speculated came into being some 200,000 years ago. Few traces remain of anything musical older than a dozen centuries. Modern electronic instruments and recording media, too, are ephemeral. Will human musical vibrations somehow outlast the species that created them? Perhaps the last trace of human existence will be radio waves beamed into space, traveling vast distances before they dissolve into noise.

The upper boundary of time, as the concept is currently understood, is the age of the physical universe. Some scientists estimate it to be approximately fifteen billion years (Lederman and Scramm 1995). Cosmologists continue to debate how long the universe may expand. The latest scientific theories continue to twist the notion of time itself (see, for example, Kaku 1995; Arkani-Hamed et al. 2000).

Macro Time Scale

The macro level of musical time corresponds to the notion of form, and encompasses the overall architecture of a composition. It is generally measured in minutes. The upper limit of this time scale is exemplified by such marathon compositions as Richard Wagner's *Ring* cycle, the Japanese Kabuki theater, Jean-Claude Eloy's evening-long rituals, and Karlheinz Stockhausen's opera *Licht* (spanning seven days and nights). The literature of opera and contemporary music contains many examples of music on a time scale that exceeds two hours. Nonetheless, the vast majority of music compositions realized in the past century are less than a half-hour in duration. The average duration is probably in the range of a kilosecond (16 min 40 sec). Complete compositions lasting less than a hectosecond (1 min 40 sec) are rare.

Perception of the Macro Time Scale

Unless the musical form is described in advance of performance (through program notes, for example), listeners perceive the macro time scale in retrospect, through recollection. It is common knowledge that the remembrance of things past is subject to strong discontinuities and distortions. We cannot recall time as a linearly measured flow. As in everyday life, the perceived flow of musical time is linked to reference events or memories that are tagged with emotional significance.

Classical music (Bach, Mozart, Beethoven, etc.) places reference events at regular intervals (cadences, repetition) to periodically orient the listener within the framework of the form. Some popular music takes this to an extreme, reminding listeners repeatedly on a shorter time base.

Subjective factors play into a distorted sense of time. Was the listener engaged in aesthetic appreciation of the work? Were they paying attention? What is their musical taste, their training? Were they preoccupied with stress and personal problems? A composition that we do not understand or like appears to expand in time as we experience it, yet vanishes almost immediately from memory.

The perception of time flow also depends on the objective nature of the musical materials. Repetition and a regular pulse tend to carry a work efficiently through time, while an unchanging, unbroken sound (or silence) reduces the flow to a crawl.

The ear's sensitivity to sound is limited in duration. Long continuous noises or regular sounds in the environment tend to disappear from consciousness and are noticed again only when they change abruptly or terminate.

Macroform

Just as musical time can be viewed in terms of a hierarchy of time scales, so it is possible to imagine musical structure as a tree in the mathematical sense. Mathematical trees are inverted, that is, the uppermost level is the root symbol, representing the entire work. The root branches into a layer of macrostructure encapsulating the major parts of the piece. This second level is the form: the arrangement of the major sections of the piece. Below the level of form is a syntactic hierarchy of branches representing mesostructures that expand into the terminal level of sound objects (Roads 1985d).

To parse a mathematical tree is straightforward. Yet one cannot parse a sophisticated musical composition as easily as a compiler parses a computer program. A compiler references an unambiguous formal grammar. By contrast, the grammar of music is ambiguous—subject to interpretation, and in a perpetual state of evolution. Compositions may contain overlapping elements (on various levels) that cannot be easily segmented. The musical hierarchy is often fractured. Indeed, this is an essential ingredient of its fascination.

Design of Macroform

The design of macroform takes one of two contrasting paths: *top-down* or *bottom-up*. A strict top-down approach considers macrostructure as a preconceived global plan or template whose details are filled in by later stages of composition. This corresponds to the traditional notion of form in classical music, wherein certain formal schemes have been used by composers as molds (Apel 1972). Music theory textbooks catalog the generic classical forms (Leichtentritt 1951) whose habitual use was called into question at the turn of the twentieth century. Claude Debussy, for example, discarded what he called "administrative forms" and replaced them with fluctuating mesostructures through a chain of associated variations. Since Debussy, composers have written a tremendous amount of music not based on classical forms. This music is full of local detail and eschews formal repetition. Such structures resist classification within the catalog of standard textbook forms. Thus while musical form has continued to evolve in practice in the past century, the acknowledged catalog of generic forms has hardly changed.

This is not to say that the use of preconceived forms has died away. The practice of top-down planning remains common in contemporary composition. Many composers predetermine the macrostructure of their pieces according to a more-or-less formal scheme before a single sound is composed.

By contrast, a strict bottom-up approach conceives of form as the result of a process of internal development provoked by interactions on lower levels of musical structure. This approach was articulated by Edgard Varèse (1971), who said, "Form is a result—the result of a process." In this view, macrostructure articulates processes of attraction and repulsion (for example, in the rhythmic and harmonic domains) unfolding on lower levels of structure.

Manuals on traditional composition offer myriad ways to project low-level structures into macrostructure:

Smaller forms may be expanded by means of external repetitions, sequences, extensions, liquidations and broadening of connectives. The number of parts may be increased by supplying codettas, episodes, etc. In such situations, derivatives of the basic motive are formulated into new thematic units. (Schoenberg 1967)

Serial or germ-cell approaches to composition expand a series or a formula through permutation and combination into larger structures.

In the domain of computer music, a frequent technique for elaboration is to time-expand a sound fragment into an evolving sound mass. Here the unfolding of sonic microstructure rises to the temporal level of a harmonic progression.

A different bottom-up approach appears in the work of the conceptual and chance composers, following in the wake of John Cage. Cage (1973) often conceived of form as arising from a series of accidents—random or improvised events occurring on the sound object level. For Cage, form (and indeed sound) was a side-effect of a conceptual strategy. Such an approach often results in discontinuous changes in sound structure. This was not accidental; Cage disdained continuity in musical structure, always favoring juxtaposition:

Where people had felt the necessity to stick sounds together to make a continuity, we felt the necessity to get rid of the glue so that sounds would be themselves. (Cage 1959)

For some, composition involves a mediation between the top-down and bottom-up approaches, between an abstract high-level conception and the concrete materials being developed on lower levels of musical time structure. This implies negotiation between a desire for orderly macrostructure and imperatives that emerge from the source material. Certain phrase structures cannot be encapsulated neatly within the box of a precut form. They mandate a container that conforms to their shape and weight.

The debate over the emergence of form is ancient. Musicologists have long argued whether, for example, a fugue is a template (form) or a process of variation. This debate echoes an ancient philosophical discourse pitting form against flux, dating back as far as the Greek philosopher Heraclitus. Ultimately, the dichotomy between form and process is an illusion, a failure of language to bind two aspects of the same concept into a unit. In computer science, the concept of *constraints* does away with this dichotomy (Sussman and Steele 1981). A form is constructed according to a set of relationships. A set of relationships implies a process of evaluation that results in a form.

Meso Time Scale

The mesostructural level groups sound objects into a quasi hierarchy of phrase structures of durations measured in seconds. This *local* as opposed to *global* time scale is extremely important in composition, for it is most often on the meso level that the sequences, combinations, and transmutations that constitute musical ideas unfold. Melodic, harmonic, and contrapuntal relations happen here, as do processes such as theme and variations, and many types of development, progression, and juxtaposition. Local rhythmic and metric patterns, too, unfold on this stratum.

Wishart (1994) called this level of structure the *sequence*. In the context of electronic music, he identified two properties of sequences: the *field* (the material, or set of elements used in the sequence), and the *order*. The field serves as a lexicon—the vocabulary of a piece of music. The order determines thematic relations—the grammar of a particular piece. As Wishart observed, the field and the order must be established quickly if they are to serve as the bearers of musical code. In traditional music, they are largely predetermined by cultural norms.

In electronic music, the meso layer presents timbre melodies, simultaneities (chord analogies), spatial interplay, and all manner of textural evolutions. Many of these processes are described and classified in Denis Smalley's interesting theory of *spectromorphology*—a taxonomy of sound gesture shapes (Smalley 1986, 1997).

Sound Masses, Textures, and Clouds

To the sequences and combinations of traditional music, we must add another principle of organization on the meso scale: the sound mass. Decades ago,

Edgard Varèse predicted that the sounds introduced by electronic instruments would necessitate new organizing principles for mesostructure.

When new instruments will allow me to write music as I conceive it, taking the place of the linear counterpoint, the movement of sound masses, or shifting planes, will be clearly perceived. When these sound masses collide the phenomena of penetration or repulsion will seem to occur. (Varèse 1962)

A trend toward shaping music through the global attributes of a sound mass began in the 1950s. One type of sound mass is a cluster of sustained frequencies that fuse into a solid block. In a certain style of sound mass composition, musical development unfolds as individual lines are added to or removed from this cluster. György Ligeti's *Volumina* for organ (1962) is a masterpiece of this style, and the composer has explored this approach in a number of other pieces, including *Atmosphères* (1961) and *Lux Aeterna* (1966).

Particles make possible another type of sound mass: statistical clouds of microevents (Xenakis 1960). Wishart (1994) ascribed two properties to cloud textures. As with sequences, their field is the set of elements used in the texture, which may be constant or evolving. Their second property is density, which stipulates the number of events within a given time period, from sparse scatterings to dense scintillations.

Cloud textures suggest a different approach to musical organization. In contrast to the combinatorial sequences of traditional meso structure, clouds encourage a process of statistical evolution. Within this evolution the composer can impose specific morphologies. Cloud evolutions can take place in the domain of amplitude (crescendi/decrescendi), internal tempo (accelerando/rallentando), density (increasing/decreasing), harmonicity (pitch/chord/cluster/noise, etc.), and spectrum (high/mid/low, etc.).

Xenakis's tape compositions *Concret PH* (1958), *Bohor I* (1962), and *Persepolis* (1971) feature dense, monolithic clouds, as do many of his works for traditional instruments. Stockhausen (1957) used statistical form-criteria as one component of his early composition technique. Since the 1960s, particle textures have appeared in numerous electroacoustic compositions, such as the remarkable *De natura sonorum* (1975) of Bernard Parmegiani.

Varèse spoke of the interpenetration of sound masses. The diaphanous nature of cloud structures makes this possible. A crossfade between two clouds results in a smooth mutation. Mesostructural processes such as disintegration and coalescence can be realized through manipulations of particle density (see chapter 6). Density determines the transparency of the material. An increase in density lifts a cloud into the foreground, while a decrease causes evaporation, dissolving a continuous sound band into a pointillist rhythm or vaporous background texture.

Cloud Taxonomy

To describe sound clouds precisely, we might refer to the taxonomy of cloud shapes in the atmosphere:

Cumulus   well-defined cauliflower-shaped cottony clouds

Stratocumulus   blurred by wind motion

Stratus   a thin fragmented layer, often translucent

Nimbostratus   a widespread gray or white sheet, opaque

Cirrus   isolated sheets that develop in filaments or patches

   In another realm, among the stars, outer space is filled with swirling clouds of cosmic raw material called *nebulae*.

The cosmos, like the sky on a turbulent summer day, is filled with clouds of different sizes, shapes, structures, and distances. Some are swelling cumulus, others light, wispy cirrus—all of them constantly changing colliding, forming, and evaporating.   (Kaler 1997)

   Pulled by immense gravitational fields or blown by cosmic shockwaves, nebulae form in great variety: dark or glowing, amorphous or ring-shaped, constantly evolving in morphology. These forms, too, have musical analogies. Programs for sonographic synthesis (such as MetaSynth [Wenger and Spiegel 1999]), provide airbrush tools that let one spray sound particles on the time-frequency canvas. On the screen, the vertical dimension represents frequency, and the horizontal dimension represents time. The images can be blurred, fragmented, or separated into sheets. Depending on their density, they may be translucent or opaque. Displacement maps can warp the cloud into a circular or spiral shape on the time-frequency canvas. (See chapter 6 on sonographic transformation of sound.)

Sound Object Time Scale

The sound object time scale encompasses events of a duration associated with the elementary unit of composition in scores: the note. A note usually lasts from about 100 ms to several seconds, and is played by an instrument or sung by a vocalist. The concept of sound object extends this to allow any sound, from any source. The term *sound object* comes from Pierre Schaeffer, the pioneer of *musique concrète*. To him, the pure *objet sonore* was a sound whose origin a listener could not identify (Schaeffer 1959, 1977, p. 95). We take a broader view here. Any sound within stipulated temporal limits is a sound object. Xenakis (1989) referred to this as the "ministructural" time scale.

The Sensation of Tone

The sensation of tone—a sustained or continuous event of definite or indefinite pitch—occurs on the sound object time scale. The low-frequency boundary for the sensation of a continuous sound—as opposed to a fluttering succession of brief microsounds—has been estimated at anywhere from 8 Hz (Savart) to about 30 Hz. (As reference, the deepest sound in a typical orchestra is the open E of the contrabass at 41.25 Hz.) Helmholtz, the nineteenth century German acoustician, investigated this lower boundary.

In the first place it is necessary that the strength of the vibrations of the air for very low tones should be extremely greater than for high tones. The increase in strength ... is of especial consequence in the deepest tones.... To discover the limit of the deepest tones it is necessary not only to produce very violent agitations in the air but to give these a simple pendular motion. (Helmholtz 1885)

Helmholtz observed that a sense of continuity takes hold between 24 to 28 Hz, but that the impression of a definite pitch does not take hold until 40 Hz.

Pitch and tone are not the same thing. Acousticians speak of *complex tones* and *unpitched tones*. Any sound perceived as continuous is a tone. This can, for example include noise.

Between the sensation of a continuous tone and the sensation of metered rhythm stands a zone of ambiguity, an infrasonic frequency domain that is too slow to form a continuous tone but too fast for rhythmic definition. Thus continuous tone is a possible quality, but not a necessary property, of a sound object. Consider a relatively dense cloud of sonic grains with short silent gaps on the order of tens of milliseconds. Dozens of different sonic events occur per second, each unique and separated by a brief intervals of zero amplitude, yet such a cloud is perceived as a unitary event—a single sound object.

A sense of regular pulse and meter begins to occur from approximately 8 Hz down to 0.12 Hz and below (Fraisse 1982). Not coincidentally, it is in this rhythmically apprensible range that the most salient and expressive vibrato, tremolo, and spatial panning effects occur.

Homogeneous Notes versus Heterogeneous Sound Objects

The sound object time scale is the same as that of traditional notes. What distinguishes sound objects from notes? The note is the homogeneous brick of conventional music architecture. *Homogeneous* means that every note can be described by the same four properties:

- *pitch*, generally one of twelve equal-tempered pitch classes
- *timbre*, generally one of about twenty different instruments for a full orchestra, with two or three different attack types for each instrument
- *dynamic marking*, generally one of about ten different relative levels
- *duration*, generally between ∼100 ms (slightly less than a thirty-second note at a tempo of 60 M.M.) to ∼8 seconds (for two tied whole notes)

These properties are static, guaranteeing that, in theory, a note in one measure with a certain pitch, dynamic, and instrumental timbre is functionally equivalent to a note in another measure with the same three properties. The properties of a pair of notes can be compared on a side-by-side basis and a distance or interval can be calculated. The notions of equivalence and distance lead to the notion of *invariants*, or intervallic distances that are preserved across transformations.

Limiting material to a static homogeneous set allows abstraction and efficiency in musical language. It serves as the basis for operations such as transposition, orchestration and reduction, the algebra of tonal harmony and counterpoint, and the atonal and serial manipulations. In the past decade, the MIDI protocol has extended this homogeneity into the domain of electronic music through standardized note sequences that play on any synthesizer.

The merit of this homogeneous system is clear; highly elegant structures having been built with standard materials inherited from centuries past. But since the dawn of the twentieth century, a recurring aesthetic dream has been the expansion beyond a fixed set of homogeneous materials to a much larger superset of heterogeneous musical materials.

What we have said about the limitations of the European note concept does not necessarily apply to the musics of other cultures. Consider the shakuhachi music of Japan, or contemporary practice emerging from the advanced developments of jazz.

Heterogeneity means that two objects may not share common properties. Therefore their percept may be entirely different. Consider the following two examples. Sound A is a brief event constructed by passing analog diode noise through a time-varying bandpass filter and applying an exponentially decaying envelope to it. Sound B lasts eight seconds. It is constructed by granulating in multiple channels several resonant low-pitched strokes on an African slit drum, then reverberating the texture. Since the amplitudes and onset times of the grains vary, this creates a jittering sound mass. To compare A and B is like comparing apples and oranges. Their microstructures are different, and we can only understand them through the properties that they do not have in common.

Thus instead of homogeneous notes, we speak of *heterogeneous sound objects*. The notion of sound object generalizes the note concept in two ways:

1. It puts aside the restriction of a common set of properties in favor of a heterogeneous collection of properties. Some objects may not share common properties with other objects. Certain sound objects may function as unique singularities. Entire pieces may be constructed from nothing but such singularities.
2. It discards the notion of static, time-invariant properties in favor of time-varying properties (Roads 1985b).

Objects that do not share common properties may be separated into diverse classes. Each class will lend itself to different types of manipulation and musical organization. Certain sounds layer well, nearly any mixture of elongated sine waves with smooth envelopes for example. The same sounds organized in a sequence, however, rather quickly become boring. Other sounds, such as isolated impulses, are most effective when sparsely scattered onto a neutral sound canvas.

Transformations applied to objects in one class may not be effective in another class. For example, a time-stretching operation may work perfectly well on a pipe organ tone, preserving its identity and affecting only its duration. The same operation applied to the sound of burning embers will smear the crackling transients into a nondescript electronic blur.

In traditional western music, the possibilities for transition within a note are limited by the physical properties of the acoustic instrument as well as frozen by theory and style. Unlike notes, the properties of a sound object are free to vary over time. This opens up the possibility of complex sounds that can mutate from one state to another within a single musical event. In the case of synthesized sounds, an object may be controlled by multiple time-varying envelopes for pitch, amplitude, spatial position, and multiple determinants of timbre. These variations may take place over time scales much longer than those associated with conventional notes.

We can subdivide a sound object not only by its properties but also by its temporal states. These states are composable using synthesis tools that operate on the microtime scale. The micro states of a sound can also be decomposed and rearranged with tools such as time granulators and analysis-resynthesis software.

Sound Object Morphology

In music, as in other fields, the organization is conditioned by the material. (Schaeffer 1977, p. 680)

The desire to understand the enormous range of possible sound objects led Pierre Schaeffer to attempt to classify them, beginning in the early 1950s (Schaeffer and Moles 1952). Book V of his *Traité des objets musicaux* (1977), entitled *Morphologie and typologie des objets sonores* introduces the useful notion of *sound object morphology*—the comparison of the shape and evolution of sound objects. Schaeffer borrowed the term *morphology* from the sciences, where it refers to the study of form and structure (of organisms in biology, of word-elements in linguistics, of rocks in geology, etc.). Schaeffer diagrammed sound shape in three dimensions: the harmonic (spectrum), dynamic (amplitude), and melodic (pitch). He observed that the elements making up a complex sound can be perceived as either merged to form a *sound compound*, or remaining separate to form a *sound mixture*. His typology, or classification of sound objects into different groups, was based on acoustic morphological studies.

The idea of sound morphology remains central to the theory of electroacoustic music (Bayle 1993), in which the musical spotlight is often shone on the sound object level. In traditional composition, transitions function on the mesostructural level through the interplay of notes. In electroacoustic music, the morphology of an individual sound may play a structural role, and transitions can occur within an individual sound object. This ubiquity of mutation means that every sonic event is itself a potential transformation.

Micro Time Scale

The micro time scale is the main subject of this book. It embraces transient audio phenomena, a broad class of sounds that extends from the threshold of timbre perception (several hundred microseconds) up to the duration of short sound objects (~100 ms). It spans the boundary between the audio frequency range (approximately 20 Hz to 20 kHz) and the infrasonic frequency range (below 20 Hz). Neglected in the past owing to its inaccessibility, the microtime domain now stands at the forefront of compositional interest.

Microsound is ubiquitous in the natural world. Transient events unfold all around in the wild: a bird chirps, a twig breaks, a leaf crinkles. We may not take notice of microacoustical events until they occur en masse, triggering a global statistical percept. We experience the interactions of microsounds in the sound of a spray of water droplets on a rocky shore, the gurgling of a brook, the pitter-patter of rain, the crunching of gravel being walked upon, the snapping of burning embers, the humming of a swarm of bees, the hissing of rice grains poured into a bowl, and the crackling of ice melting. Recordings of dolphins reveal a language made up entirely of high-frequency clicking patterns.

One could explore the microsonic resources of any musical instrument in its momentary bursts and infrasonic flutterings, (a study of traditional instruments from this perspective has yet to be undertaken). Among unpitched percussion, we find microsounds in the angled rainstick, (shaken) small bells, (grinding) ratchet, (scraped) guiro, (jingling) tambourine, and the many varieties of rattles. Of course, the percussion roll—a granular stick technique—can be applied to any surface, pitched or unpitched.

In the literature of acoustics and signal processing, many terms refer to similar microsonic phenomena: *acoustic quantum, sonal atom, grain, glisson, grainlet, trainlet, Gaussian elementary signal, Gaussian pulse, short-time segment, sliding window, microarc, voicel, Coiflet, symmlet, Gabor atom, Gabor wavelet, gaborette, wavelet, chirplet, Liénard atom, FOF, FOG, wave packet, Vosim pulse, time-frequency atom, pulsar, waveset, impulse, toneburst, tone pip, acoustic pixel,* and *window function pulse* are just a few. These phenomena, viewed in their mathematical dual space—the frequency domain—take on a different set of names: *kernel, logon,* and *frame,* for example.

Perception of Microsound

Microevents last only a very short time, near to the threshold of auditory perception. Much scientific study has gone into the perception of microevents. Human hearing mechanisms, however, intertwine with brain functions, cognition, and emotion, and are not completely understood. Certain facts are clear.

One cannot speak of a single time frame, or a *time constant* for the auditory system (Gordon 1996). Our hearing mechanisms involve many different agents, each of which operates on its own time scale (see figure 1.1). The brain integrates signals sent by various hearing agents into a coherent auditory picture. Ear-brain mechanisms process high and low frequencies differently. Keeping high frequencies constant, while inducing phase shifts in lower frequencies, causes listeners to hear a different timbre.

Determining the temporal limits of perception has long engaged psychoacousticians (Doughty and Garner 1947; Buser and Imbert 1992; Meyer-Eppler 1959; Winckel 1967; Whitfield 1978). The pioneer of sound quanta, Dennis Gabor, suggested that at least two mechanisms are at work in microevent detection: one that isolates events, and another that ascertains their pitch. Human beings need time to process audio signals. Our hearing mechanisms impose minimum time thresholds in order to establish a firm sense of the identity and properties of a microevent.

In their important book *Audition* (1992), Buser and Imbert summarize a large number of experiments with transitory audio phenomena. The general result from these experiments is that below 200 ms, many aspects of auditory perception change character and different modes of hearing come into play. The next sections discuss microtemporal perception.

Microtemporal Intensity Perception

In the zone of low amplitude, short sounds must be greater in intensity than longer sounds to be perceptible. This increase is about +20 dB for tone pips of 1 ms over those of 100 ms duration. (A tone pip is a sinusoidal burst with a quasi-rectangular envelope.) In general, subjective loudness diminishes with shrinking durations below 200 ms.

Microtemporal Fusion and Fission

In dense portions of the Milky Way, stellar images appear to overlap, giving the effect of a near-continuous sheet of light ... The effect is a grand illusion. In reality ... the nightime sky is remarkably empty. Of the volume of space only 1 part in 10^{21} [one part in a quintillion] is filled with stars.   (Kaler 1997)

Circuitry can measure time and recognize pulse patterns at tempi in the range of a gigahertz. Human hearing is more limited. If one impulse follows less than 200 ms after another, the onset of the first impulse will tend to mask the second, a time-lag phenomenon known as *forward masking*, which contributes to the illusion that we call a *continuous tone*.

The sensation of tone happens when human perception reaches attentional limits where microevents occur too quickly in succession to be heard as discrete events. The auditory system, which is nonlinear, reorganizes these events into a group. For example, a series of impulsions at about 20 Hz fuse into a continuous tone. When a fast sequence of pitched tones merges into a continuous "ripple," the auditory system is unable to successfully track its rhythm. Instead, it simplifies the situation by interpreting the sound as a continuous texture. The opposite effect, *tone fission*, occurs when the fundamental frequency of a tone descends into the infrasonic frequencies.

The theory of *auditory streams* (McAdams and Bregman 1979) aims to explain the perception of melodic lines. An example of a streaming law is: the faster a melodic sequence plays, the smaller the pitch interval needed to split it into two separately perceived "streams." One can observe a family of streaming effects between two alternating tones A and B. These effects range from *coherence* (the tones A and B form a single percept), to *roll* (A dominates B), to *masking* (B is no longer perceived).

The theory of auditory streaming was an attempt to create a psychoacoustic basis for contrapuntal music. A fundamental assumption of this research was that "several musical dimensions, such as timbre, attack and decay transients, and tempo are often not specified exactly by the composer and are controlled by the performer" (McAdams and Bregman 1979). In the domain of electronic music, such assumptions may not be valid.

Microtemporal Silence Perception

The ear is quite sensitive to intermittencies within pure sine waves, especially in the middle range of frequencies. A 20 ms fluctuation in a 600 Hz sine wave, consisting of a 6.5 ms fade out, a 7 ms silent interval, and a 6.5 ms fade in, breaks the tone in two, like a double articulation. A 4 ms interruption, consisting of a 1 ms fade out, a 2 ms silent interval, and a 1 ms fade in, sounds like a transient pop has been superimposed on the sine wave.

Intermittencies are not as noticeable in complex tones. A 4 ms interruption is not perceptible in pink noise, although a 20 ms interruption is.

In intermediate tones, between a sine and noise, microtemporal gaps less than 10 ms sound like momentary fluctuations in amplitude or less noticeable transient pops.

Microtemporal Pitch Perception

Studies by Meyer-Eppler show that pitch recognition time is dependent on frequency, with the greatest pitch sensitivity in the mid-frequency range between 1000 and 2000 Hz, as the following table (cited in Butler 1992) indicates.

Frequency in Hz	100	500	1000	5000
Minimum duration in ms	45	26	14	18

Doughty and Garner (1947) divided the mechanism of pitch perception into two regions. Above about 1 kHz, they estimated, a tone must last at least 10 ms to be heard as pitched. Below 1 kHz, at least two to three cycles of the tone are needed.

Microtemporal Auditory Acuity

We feel impelled to ascribe a temporal arrangement to our experiences. If β is later than α and γ is later than β, then γ is also later than α. At first sight it appears obvious to assume that a temporal arrangement of events exists which agrees with the temporal arrangement of experiences. This was done unconsciously until skeptical doubts made themselves felt. For example, the order of experiences in time obtained by acoustical means can differ from the temporal order gained visually . . . (Einstein 1952)

Green (1971) suggested that temporal auditory acuity (the ability of the ear to detect discrete events and to discern their order) extends down to durations as short as 1 ms. Listeners hear microevents that are less than about 2 ms in duration as a click, but we can still change the waveform and frequency of these events to vary the timbre of the click. Even shorter events (in the range of microseconds) can be distinguished on the basis of amplitude, timbre, and spatial position.

Microtemporal Preattentive Perception

When a person glimpses the face of a famous actor, sniffs a favorite food, or hears the voice of a friend, recognition is instant. Within a fraction of a second after the eyes, nose, ears, tongue or skin is stimulated, one knows the object is familiar and whether it is desirable or dangerous. How does such recognition, which psychologists call preattentive perception, *happen so accurately and quickly, even when the stimuli are complex and the context in which they arise varies?* (Freeman 1991)

One of the most important measurements in engineering is the response of a system to a unit impulse. It should not be surprising to learn that auditory neuroscientists have sought a similar type of measurement for the auditory system. The impulse response equivalents in the auditory system are the *auditory evoked potentials*, which follow stimulation by tone pips and clicks.

The first response in the auditory nerve occurs about 1.5 ms after the initial stimulus of a click, which falls within the realm of *preattentive perception* (Freeman 1995). The mechanisms of preattentive perception perform a rapid analysis by an array of neurons, combining this with past experience into a wave packet in its physical form, or a percept in its behavioral form. The neural activities sustaining preattentive perception take place in the cerebral cortex. Sensory stimuli are preanalyzed in both the pulse and wave modes in intermediate stations of the brain. As Freeman noted, in the visual system complex operations such as adaptation, range compression, contrast enhancement, and motion detection take place in the retina and lower brain. Sensory stimuli activate *feature extractor* neurons that recognize specific characteristics. Comparable operations have been described for the auditory cortex: the final responses to a click occur some 300 ms later, in the medial geniculate body of the thalamus in the brain (Buser and Imbert 1992).

Microtemporal Subliminal Perception

Finally, we should mention *subliminal perception*, or perception without awareness. Psychological studies have tested the influence of brief auditory stimuli on various cognitive tasks. In most studies these take the form of verbal hints to some task asked of the listener. Some evidence of influence has been shown, but the results are not clear-cut. Part of the problem is theoretical: how does subliminal perception work? According to a cognitive theory of Reder and Gordon (1997), for a concept to be in conscious awareness, its activation must be above a certain threshold. Magnitude of activation is partly a function of the exposure duration of the stimulus. A subliminal microevent raises the activation of the corresponding element, but not enough to reach the threshold. The brain's "production rules" cannot fire without the elements passing threshold, but a subliminal microevent can raise the current activation level of an element enough to make it easier to fire a production rule later.

The musical implications are, potentially, significant. If the subliminal hints are not fragments of words but rather musical cues (to pitch, timbre, spatial position, or intensity) then we can embed such events at pivotal instants, knowing that they will contribute to a percept without the listener necessarily being aware of their presence. Indeed this is one of the most interesting dimensions of microsound, the way that subliminal or barely perceptible variations in the properties of a collection of microevents—their onset time, duration, frequency, waveform, envelope, spatial position, and amplitude—lead to different aesthetic perceptions.

Viewing and Manipulating the Microtime Level

Microevents touch the extreme time limits of human perception and performance. In order to examine and manipulate these events fluidly, we need digital audio "microscopes"—software and hardware that can magnify the micro time scale so that we can operate on it.

For the serious researcher, the most precise strategy for accessing the micro time scale is through computer programming. Beginning in 1974, my research was made possible by access to computers equipped with compiler software and audio converters. Until recently, writing one's own programs was the only possible approach to microsound synthesis and transformation.

Many musicians want to be able to manipulate this domain without the total immersion experience that is the lifestyle of software engineering. Fortunately, the importance of the micro time scale is beginning to be recognized. Any sound editor with a zoom function that proceeds down to the sample level can view and manipulate sound microstructure (figure 1.4).

Programs such as our Cloud Generator (Roads and Alexander 1995), offer high-level controls in the micro time domain (see appendix A). Cloud Generator's interface directly manipulates the process of particle emission, controlling the flow of many particles in an evolving cloud. Our more recent PulsarGenerator, described in chapter 4, is another example of a synthetic particle generator.

The perceived result of particle synthesis emerges out of the interaction of parameter evolutions on a micro scale. It takes a certain amount of training to learn how operations in the micro domain translate to acoustic perceptions on higher levels. The grain duration parameter in granular synthesis, for example, has a strong effect on the perceived spectrum of the texture.

This situation is no different from other well-known synthesis techniques. *Frequency modulation synthesis*, for example, is controlled by parameters such as carrier-to-modulator ratios and modulation indexes, neither of which are direct terms of the desired spectrum. Similarly, *physical modeling synthesis* is controlled by manipulating the parameters that describe the parts of a virtual instrument (size, shape, material, coupling, applied force, etc.), and not the sound.

One can imagine a musical interface in which a musician specifies the desired sonic result in a musically descriptive language which would then be translated

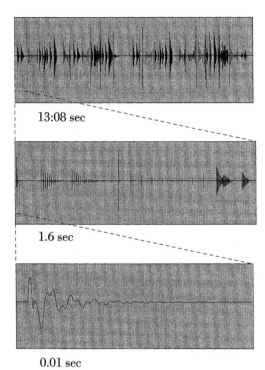

13:08 sec

1.6 sec

0.01 sec

Figure 1.4   Viewing the micro time scale via zooming. The top picture is the waveform of a sonic gesture constructed from sound particles. It lasts 13.05 seconds. The middle image is a result of zooming in to a part of the top waveform (indicated by the dotted lines) lasting 1.5 seconds. The bottom image is a microtemporal portrait of a 10 millisecond fragment at the beginning of the top waveform (indicated by the dotted lines).

into particle parameters and rendered into sound. An alternative would be to specify an example: "Make me a sound like this (soundfile), but with less vibrato." This is a challenging task of *parameter estimation*, since the system would have to interpret how to approximate a desired result. For more on the problems of parameter estimation in synthesis see Roads (1996).

Do the Particles Really Exist?

In the 1940s, the physicist Dennis Gabor made the assertion that all sound—even continuous tones—can be considered as a succession of elementary particles of acoustic energy. (Chapter 2 summarizes this theory.) The question then arises: do sound particles really exist, or are they merely a theoretical construction? In certain sounds, such as the taps of a slow drum roll, the individual particles are directly perceivable. In other sounds, we can prove the existence of a granular layer through logical argument.

Consider the whole number 5. This quantity may be seen as a sum of sub-quantities, for example $1+1+1+1+1$, or $2+3$, or $4+1$, and so on. If we take away one of the subquantities, the sum no longer is 5. Similarly, a continuous tone may be considered as a sum of subquantities—as a sequence of overlapping grains. The grains may be of arbitrary sizes. If we remove any grain, the signal is no longer the same. So clearly the grains exist, and we need all of them in order to constitute a complex signal. This argument can be extended to explain the decomposition of a sound into any one of an infinite collection of orthogonal functions, such as wavelets with different basis functions, Walsh functions, Gabor grains, and so on.

This logic, though, becomes tenuous if it is used to posit the preexistence (in an ideal Platonic realm) of all possible decompositions within a whole. For example, do the slices of a cake preexist, waiting to be articulated? The philosophy of mathematics is littered with such questions (Castonguay 1972, 1973). Fortunately it is not our task here to try to assay their significance.

Heterogeneity in Sound Particles

The concept of heterogeneity or diversity of sound materials, which we have already discussed in the context of the sound object time scale, also applies to other time scales. Many techniques that we use to generate sound particles assign to each particle a unique identity, a precise frequency, waveform, duration, amplitude morphology, and spatial position, which then distinguishes it from every other particle. Just as certain sound objects may function as singularities, so may certain sound particles.

Sampled Time Scale

Below the level of microtime stands the sampled time scale (figure 1.5). The electronic clock that drives the sampling process establishes a time grid. The spacing of this grid determines the temporal precision of the digital audio medium. The samples follow one another at a fixed time interval of $1/f_S$, where f_S is the sampling frequency. When $f_S = 44.1$ kHz (the compact disc rate), the samples follow one another every 22.675 millionths of a second (μsec).

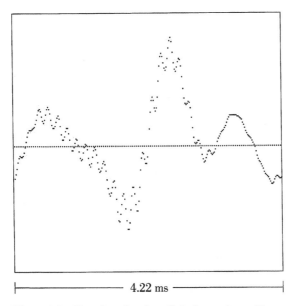

|—————————— 4.22 ms ——————————|

Figure 1.5   Sample points in a digital waveform. Here are 191 points spanning a 4.22 ms time interval. The sampling rate is 44.1 kHz.

The atom of the sample time scale is the *unit impulse*, the discrete-time counterpart of the continuous-time Dirac delta function. All samples should be considered as time-and-amplitude-transposed (delayed and scaled) instances of the unit impulse.

The interval of one sample period borders near the edge of human audio perception. With a good audio system one can detect the presence of an individual high-amplitude sample inserted into a silent stream of zero-valued samples. Like a single pixel on a computer screen, an individual sample offers little. Its amplitude and spatial position can be discerned, but it transmits no sense of timbre and pitch. Only when chained into sequences of hundreds do samples float up to the threshold of timbral significance. And still longer sequences of thousands of samples are required to represent pitched tones.

Sound Composition with Individual Sample Points

Users of digital audio systems rarely attempt to deal with individual sample points, which, indeed, only a few programs for sound composition manipulate directly. Two of these are G. M. Koenig's Sound Synthesis Program (SSP) and

Herbert Brün's Sawdust program, both developed in the late 1970s. Koenig and Brün emerged from the Cologne school of serial composition, in which the interplay between macro- and microtime was a central aesthetic theme (Stockhausen 1957; Koenig 1959; Maconie 1989). Brün wrote:

For some time now it has become possible to use a combination of analog and digital computers and converters for the analysis and synthesis of sound. As such a system will store or transmit information at the rate of 40,000 samples per second, even the most complex waveforms in the audio-frequency range can be scanned and registered or be recorded on audio tape. This . . . allows, at last, the composition of timbre, instead of with timbre. In a sense, one may call it a continuation of much which has been done in the electronic music studio, only on a different scale. The composer has the possibility of extending his compositional control down to elements of sound lasting only 1/20,000 of a second. (Brun 1970)

Koenig's and Brün's synthesis programs were conceptually similar. Both represented a pure and radical approach to sound composition. Users of these programs stipulated sets of individual time and amplitude points, where each set was in a separate file. They then specified logical operations such as *linking, mingling,* and *merging,* to map from a time-point set to an amplitude-point set in order to construct a skeleton of a waveform fragment. Since these points were relatively sparse compared to the number of samples needed to make a continuous sound, the software performed a linear interpolation to connect intermediate amplitude values between the stipulated points. This interpolation, as it were, fleshed out the skeleton. The composer could then manipulate the waveform fragments using logical set theory operations to construct larger and larger waveforms, in a process of hierarchical construction.

Koenig was explicit about his desire to escape from the traditional computer-generated sounds:

My intention was to go away from the classical instrumental definitions of sound in terms of loudness, pitch, and duration and so on, because then you could refer to musical elements which are not necessarily the elements of the language of today. To explore a new field of sound possibilities I thought it best to close the classical descriptions of sound and open up an experimental field in which you would really have to start again. (Roads 1978b)

Iannis Xenakis proposed a related approach (Xenakis 1992; Hoffmann 1994, 1996, 1997). This involves the application of *sieve theory* to the amplitude and time dimensions of a sound synthesis process. As in his Gendyn program, the idea is to construct waveforms from fragments. Each fragment is bounded by two breakpoints. Between the breakpoints, the rest of the waveform is filled in by interpolation. Whereas in Gendyn the breakpoints are calculated from a nonlinear stochastic algorithm, in sieve theory the breakpoints would be calculated according to a partitioning algorithm based on sieved amplitude and time dimensions.

Assessment of Sound Composition with Samples

To compose music by means of logical operations on samples is a daunting task. Individual samples are subsymbolic—perceptually indistinguishable from one another. It is intrinsically difficult to string together samples into meaningful music symbols. Operations borrowed from set theory and formal logic do not take into account the samples' acoustical significance. As Koenig's statement above makes clear, to compose intentionally a graceful melodic figure, a smooth transition, a cloud of particles, or a polyphonic texture requires extraordinary effort, due to the absence of acoustically relevant parameters for building higher-level sound structures. Users of sample-based synthesis programs must be willing to submit to the synthesis algorithm, to abandon local control, and be satisfied with the knowledge that the sound was composed according to a logical process. Only a few composers took up interest in this approach, and there has not been a great deal of experimentation along these lines since the 1970s.

Subsample Time Scale

A digital audio system represents waveforms as a stream of individual samples that follow one another at a fixed time interval ($1/f_S$, where f_S is the sampling frequency). The subsample time scale supports fluctuations that occur in less than two sampling periods. Hence this time scale spans a range of minuscule durations measured in nanoseconds and extending down to the realm of infinitesimal intervals.

To stipulate a sampling frequency is to fix a strict threshold between a subsample and the sample time scale. Frequencies above this threshold—the *Nyquist frequency* (by definition: $f_S/2$)—cannot be represented properly by a digital audio system. For the standard compact disc sampling rate of 44.1 kHz, the Nyquist frequency is 22.05 kHz. This means that any wave fluctuation shorter than two samples, or 45 μsec, is relegated to the subsample domain. The 96 kHz sampling rate standard reduces this interval to 20.8 μsec.

The subsample time scale encompasses an enormous range of phenomena. Here we present five classes of subsample phenomena, from the real and perceptible to the ideal and imperceptible: aliased artefacts, ultrasounds, atomic sounds, and the Planck interval.

Aliased Artefacts

In comparison with the class of all time intervals, the class of perceptible audio periods spans relatively large time intervals. In a digital audio system, the sample period is a threshold separating all signal fluctuations into two classes: those whose frequencies are low enough to be accurately recorded and those whose frequencies are too high to be accurately recorded. Because a frequency is too high to be recorded does not mean that it is invisible to the digital recorder. On the contrary, subsample fluctuations, according to the theorem of Nyquist (1928), record as aliased artefacts. Specifically, if the input frequency is higher than half the sampling frequency, then:

aliased frequency = sampling frequency − input frequency

Thus if the sampling rate is 44.1 kHz, an input frequency of 30 kHz is reflected down to the audible 11.1 kHz. Digital recorders must, therefore, attempt to filter out all subsample fluctuations in order to eliminate the distortion caused by aliased artefacts.

The design of antialiasing filters has improved in the past decade. Current compact disc recordings are effectively immune from aliasing distortion. But the removal of all information above 22.05 kHz poses problems. Many people hear detail (referred to as *air*) in the region above 20 kHz (Koenig 1899; Neve 1992). Rigorous scientific experiments have confirmed the effects, from both physiological and subjective viewpoints, of sounds above 22 kHz (Oohashi et al. 1991; Oohashi et al. 1993). Furthermore, partials in the ultrasonic region interact, resulting in audible subharmonics and air. When the antialiasing filter removes these ultrasonic interactions, the recording loses detail.

Aliasing remains a pernicious problem in sound synthesis. The lack of *frequency headroom* in the compact disc standard rate of 44.1 kHz opens the door to aliasing from within the synthesis algorithm. Even common waveforms cause aliasing when extended beyond a narrow frequency range. Consider these cases of aliasing in synthesis:

1. A band-limited square wave made from sixteen odd-harmonic components causes aliasing at fundamental frequencies greater than 760 Hz.

2. An additive synthesis instrument with thirty-two harmonic partials generates aliased components if the fundamental is higher than 689 Hz (approximately E5).

3. The partials of a sampled piano tone A-sharp2 (116 Hz) alias when the tone is transposed an octave and a fifth to F4 (349 Hz).

4. A sinusoidal frequency modulation instrument with a carrier-to-modulator ratio of 1:2 and a fundamental frequency of 1000 Hz aliases if the modulation index exceeds 7. If either the carrier or modulator is a non-sinusoidal waveform then the modulation index must typically remain less than 1.

As a consequence of these hard limits, synthesis instruments require preventative measures in order to eliminate aliasing distortion. Commercial instruments filter their waveforms and limit their fundamental frequency range. In experimental software instruments, we must introduce tests and constrain the choice of waveforms above certain frequencies.

The compact disc sampling rate of 44.1 kHz rate is too low for high-fidelity music synthesis applications. Fortunately, converters operating at 96 kHz are becoming popular, and sampling rates up to 192 kHz also are available.

Ultrasonic Loudspeakers

Even inaudible energy in the ultrasonic frequency range can be harnessed for audio use. New loudspeakers have been developed on the basis of *acoustical heterodyning* (American Technology Corporation 1998; Pompei 1998). This principle is based on a phenomenon observed by Helmholtz. When two sound sources are positioned relatively closely together and are of a sufficiently high amplitude, two new tones appear: one lower and one higher than either of the original tones. The two new combination tones correspond to the sum and the difference of the two original tones. For example, if one were to emit 90 kHz and 91 kHz into the air, with sufficient energy, one would produce the sum (181 kHz) and the difference (1 kHz), the latter being in the range of human hearing. Reporting that he could also hear summation tones (whose frequency is the sum, rather than the difference, of the two fundamental tones), Helmholtz argued that the phenomenon had to result from a nonlinearity of air molecules. Air molecules begin to behave nonlinearly (to *heterodyne*) as amplitude increases. Thus, a form of acoustical heterodyning is realized by creating difference frequencies from higher frequency waves. In air, the effect works in such a way that if an ultrasonic carrier is increased in amplitude, a difference frequency is created. Concurrently, the unused sum frequency diminishes in loudness as the carrier's frequency increases. In other words, the major portion of the ultrasonic energy transfers to the audible difference frequency.

Unlike regular loudspeakers, acoustical heterodyning loudspeakers project energy in a collimated sound beam, analogous to the beam of light from a flashlight. One can direct an ultrasonic emitter toward a wall and the listener will perceive the sound as coming from a spot on that wall. For a direct sound beam, a listener standing anywhere in an acoustical environment is able to point to the loudspeaker as the source.

Atomic Sound: Phonons and Polarons

As early as 1907, Albert Einstein predicted that ultrasonic vibration could occur on the scale of atomic structure (Cochran 1973). The atoms in crystals, he theorized, take the form of a regular lattice. A one-dimensional lattice resembles the physical model of a taut string—a collection of masses linked by springs. Such a model may be generalized to other structures, for example three-dimensional lattices. Lattices can be induced to vibrate ultrasonically, subjected to the proper force, turning them into high-frequency oscillators. This energy is not continuous, however, but is quantized by atomic structure into units that Einstein called phonons, by analogy to photons—the quantum units of light. It was not until 1913 that regular lattices were verified experimentally as being the atomic structure of crystals. Scientists determined that the frequency of vibration depends on the mass of the atoms and the nature of the interatomic forces. Thus the lower the atomic weight, the higher the frequency of the oscillator (Stevenson and Moore 1967). Ultrasonic devices can generate frequencies in the trillions of cycles per second.

Complex sound phenomena occur when phononic energy collides with other phonons or other atomic particles. When the sources of excitation are multiple or the atomic structure irregular, phonons propagate in cloud-like swarms called *polarons* (Pines 1963). Optical energy sources can induce or interfere with mechanical vibrations. Thus optical photons can scatter acoustic phonons. For example, laser-induced lattice vibrations can change the index of refraction in a crystal, which changes its electromagnetic properties. On a microscopic scale, optical, mechanical, and electromagnetic quanta are interlinked as elementary excitations.

Laser-induced phonic sound focuses the beams from two lasers with a small wavelength difference onto a crystal surface. The difference in wavelength causes interference, or beating. The crystal surface shrinks and expands as this oscillation of intensity causes periodic heating. This generates a wave that propagates through the medium. The frequency of this sound is typically in the gigahertz range, with a wavelength of the order of 1 micron. Because of the small dimensions of the heated spot on the surface, the wave in the crystal has the shape of a directional beam. These sound beams can be used as probes, for example, to determine the internal features of semiconductor crystals, and to detect faults in their structure.

One of the most important properties of laser-induced phononic sound is that it can be made *coherent* (the wave trains are phase-aligned), as well as mono-chromatic and directional. This makes possible such applications as *acoustic holography* (the visualization of acoustic phenomena by laser light). Today the study of phononic vibrations is an active field, finding applications in *surface acoustic wave* (SAW) filters, waveguides, and condensed matter physics.

At the Physical Limits: The Planck Time Interval

Sound objects can be subdivided into grains, and grains into samples. How far can this subdivision of time continue? Hawking and Penrose (1996) have suggested that time in the physical universe is not infinitely divisible. Specifically, that no signal fluctuation can be faster than the quantum changes of state in subatomic particles, which occur at close to the *Planck scale*. The Planck scale stands at the extreme limit of the known physical world, where current concepts of space, time, and matter break down, where the four forces unify. It is the exceedingly small distance, related to an infinitesimal time span and extremely high energy, that emerges when the fundamental constants for gravitational attraction, the velocity of light, and quantum mechanics join (Hawking and Penrose 1996).

How much time does it take light to cross the Planck scale? Light takes about 3.3 nanoseconds (3.3×10^{-10}) to traverse 1 meter. The *Planck time interval* is the time it takes light to traverse the Planck scale. Up until recently, the Planck scale was thought to be 10^{-33} meter. An important new theory puts the figure at a much larger 10^{-19} meter (Arkani-Hamed et al. 2000). Here, the Planck time interval is 3.3×10^{-28} seconds, a tiny time interval. One could call the Plank time interval a kind of "sampling rate of the universe," since no signal fluctuation can occur in less than the Planck interval.

If the flow of time stutters in discrete quanta corresponding to fundamental physical constants, this poses an interesting conundrum, recognized by Iannis Xenakis:

Isn't time simply an epiphenomenal notion of a deeper reality? ... The equations of Lorentz-Fitzgerald and Einstein link space and time because of the limited velocity of light. From this it follows that time is not absolute ... It "takes time" to go from one point to another, even if that time depends on moving frames of reference relative to the observer. There is no instantaneous jump from one point to another in space, much less spatial ubiquity—that is, the simultaneous presence of an event or object everywhere in space. To the contrary, one posits the notion of displacement. Within a local reference frame, what does displacement signify? If the notion of displacement were more fundamental than that of time, one could reduce all macro and micro cosmic transformations to weak chains of displacement. Consequently ... if we were to adhere to quantum mechanics and its implications, we would perhaps be forced to admit the notion of quantified space and its corollary, quantified time. But what could a quantified time and space signify, a time and space in which contiguity would be abolished. What would the pavement of the universe be if there were gaps between the paving stones, inaccessible and filled with nothing? (Xenakis 1989)

Infinitesimal Time Scale

Besides the infinite-duration sinusoids of Fourier theory, mathematics has created other ideal, infinite-precision boundary quantities. One class of ideal phenomena that appears in the theory of signal processing is the mathematical impulse or delta (∂) function. Delta functions represent infinitely brief intervals of time. The most important is the *Dirac delta function*, formulated for the theory of quantum mechanics. Imagine the time signal shown in figure 1.6a, a narrow pulse of height $1/b$ and width b, centered on $t = 0$. This pulse, $x(t)$, is zero at all times $|t| > b/2$. For any nonzero value of b, the integral of $x(t)$ is unity. Imagine that b shrinks to a duration of 0. Physically this means that the pulse's height grows and the interval of integration (the pulse's duration) becomes very narrow. The limit of $x(t)$ as $b \to 0$ is shown in figure 1.6b. This shows that the pulse becomes an infinitely high spike of zero width, indicated as $\partial(t)$, the Dirac delta function. The two significant properties of the ∂ function are: (1) it is zero everywhere except at one point, and (2) it is infinite in amplitude at this point, but approaches infinity in such a way that its integral is unity—a curious object!

(a)

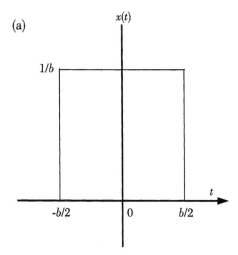

(b)

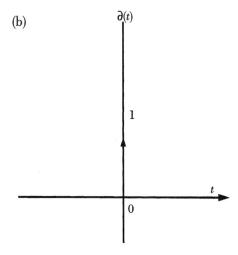

Figure 1.6   Comparison of a pulse and the Dirac delta function. (a) A narrow pulse of height $1/b$ and width b, centered on $t = 0$. (b) The Dirac delta function.

The main application of the ∂ function in signal processing is to bolster the mathematical explanation of the process of sampling. When a ∂ function occurs inside an integral, the value of the integral is determined by finding the location of the impulse and then evaluating the integrand at that location. Since the ∂ is infinitely brief, this is equivalent to sampling the function being integrated. Another interesting property of the ∂ function is that its Fourier transform,

$$\left| e^{-j2\pi ft} \right| = 1$$

for any real value of t. In other words, the spectrum of an infinitely brief impulse is infinite (Nahin 1996).

We see here a profound law of signal processing, which we will encounter repeatedly in this thesis, that duration and spectrum are complementary quantities. In particular, the shorter a signal is, the broader is its spectrum. Later we will see that one can characterize various signal transformations by how they respond to the ∂ function and its discrete counterpart, the unit impulse.

The older *Kronecker delta* is an integer-valued ideal impulse function. It is defined by the properties

$$\partial_{m,n} = \begin{cases} 0 & m \neq n \\ 1 & m = n \end{cases}$$

The delta functions are defined over a continuous and infinite domain. The section on *aliased artefacts* examines similar functions in the discrete sampled domain.

Outside Time Music

Musical structure can exist, in a sense, "outside" of time (Xenakis 1971, 1992). By this, we mean abstract structuring principles whose definition does not imply a temporal order. A scale, for example, is independent of how a composer uses it in time. Myriad *precompositional* strategies, and databases of material could also be said to be outside time.

A further example of an outside time structure is a musical instrument. The layout of keys on a piano gives no hint of the order in which they will be played. *Aleatoric* compositions of the 1950s and 1960s, which left various parameters, including the sequence of events to chance, were also outside time structures.

Today we see installations and virtual environments in which sounds occur in an order that depends on the path of the person interacting with the system. In all of these cases, selecting and ordering the material places it in time.

The Size of Sounds

Sounds form in the physical medium of air—a gaseous form of matter. Thus, sound waves need space to form. Just as sounds exist on different time scales, so they take shape on different scales of space. Every sound has a three-dimensional shape and size, which is its diffusion or dispersion pattern over time. Since the wavelength of a high frequency sound is short, high frequencies form in small spaces. A low frequency waveform needs several meters to unfold. The temporal and the spatial morphologies of a sound intertwine. A sound's duration, frequency, amplitude, and pattern of radiation from its source all contribute to its physical form, as does the space in which the sound manifests.

The duration of a sound is an important determinant of physical shape, especially in the open air. A long-duration sound is long in spatial extent, spanning the entire distance from the source to the point at which its energy is completely absorbed. Short-duration sounds, on the contrary, are thin in spatial extent, disappearing from their point of origin quickly. The wave of a short-duration sound occupies a thin band of air, although the fluctuations that it carries may travel great distances if it is loud enough.

Today we have accurate measurements of the speed of sound waves in a variety of media (Pierce 1994). The accepted value for the speed of sound in dry air is 331.5 meters/second. Thus a 20 Hz acoustical wave requires no less than 16.5 meters (54.13 feet) to unfold without obstruction. Obstructions such as walls cause the wave to reflect back on itself, creating phase cancellation effects. A high-frequency waveform at 20 kHz has a period of only 1/20,000th of a second. This takes only 1.65 cm to form. The ear is very sensitive to the time of arrival of sounds from different spatial positions. Thus, even a minor difference in the distance of the listener from two separate sources will skew the spatial images.

The most important determinant of a sound's size is its amplitude. Very loud sounds (such as atmospheric thunder and other explosions) travel far. As they travel, the air gradually absorbs the high frequencies, so that only the low frequencies reach great distances.

Summary

Particle physics seeks to find a simple and orderly pattern to the behavior of matter on the atomic and subatomic level. To this end, large particle accelerators are built, acting like giant microscopes that zoom down through the atom ... Astronomers build equally complex devices—telescopes and observatories. These gather data from distant clusters of galaxies, all the way out to the rim of the cosmos ... We are seeing here a convergence between particle physics and cosmology. The instruments, and even the stated objectives, are different, but the languages draw closer. The laws of nature that control and order the microscopic world, and those that determined the creation and evolution of the universe,... are beginning to look identical.   (Lederman and Schramm 1995)

Projecting time horizontally, and amplitude vertically, the concept of nil duration corresponds to a zero-dimensional point on the time-amplitude plane. This point zero is mute: no flux of energy can occur in the absence of a time window. In that ideal world experienced only by the gods of mathematics, the delta function $\partial(t)$ breaks the monotony with an instantaneous impulse that is born and dies within the most infinitesimal window beyond point zero.

Our mundane digital domain is a discrete approximation to the ideal realm of infinitesimal time. In the digital domain, the smallest event has a duration equivalent to the period of the sampling frequency. This sound atom, the sample period, is the grid that quantizes all time values in an audio signal. Any curve inscribed on the amplitude-versus-time plane must synchronize to this grid. Individual samples remain subsymbolic. Like the woven threads of canvas holding paint in place, their presence is a necessity, even if we can see them only in the aggregate.

As the window of time expands, there is a possibility for chaotic fluctuation, periodic repetition, echoes, tone, noise, and measured silence. Each additional instant of time accrues new possibilities.

Microsonic particles can be likened to molecules built from atomic samples. To view this level of detail, we rely on the tools of sound analysis and display. Under this scrutiny, remarkable patterns emerge and we gain new insight into sound structure. These images show the hidden morphologies of elementary sound molecules (figure 1.7).

Molecular materials alter the terrain of composition. Pliant globules can be molded into arbitrary object morphologies. The presence of mutating sound objects suggests a fluid approach to compositional mesostructure, spawning rivulets, streams, and clouds as well as discrete events. The package for all these

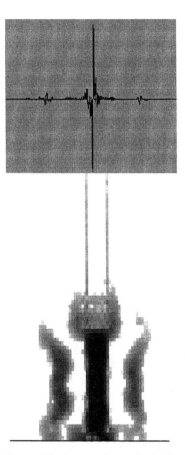

Figure 1.7 Image of a grain in the time-domain (top) and its frequency-domain counterpart (bottom).

musical structures, the macroform, can be tailored with high flexibility and precision in a sound mixing program.

It is necessary to see music over a broad range of time scales, from the infinitesimal to the supra scale (Christensen 1996). Not all musicians are prepared to view musical time from such a comprehensive perspective, however, and it may well take decades for this perspective to filter into our general musical vocabulary.

2 The History of Microsound from Antiquity to the Analog Era

Microsound in the Instrumental Domain

Summary

Musical ideas are prisoners, more than one might believe, of musical devices.
—Schaeffer (1977, pp. 16–17)

The evolution of sound synthesis has always been interwoven with the engines of acoustic emission, be they mechanoacoustic, electromechanical, electro-optical, analog electronic, or digital. The current state of music technology has been arrived at through decades of laboratory experimentation. If we are to benefit from this legacy, we must revisit the past and recover as much knowledge as we can.

Table 2.1 lists electric and electronic music instruments developed in the period 1899–1950. The first column names each instrument. The second column shows the date of their first public demonstration (rather than the date of their conception). Before 1950, almost all instruments were designed for live performance. After 1950, the technology of recording changed the nature of electronic music, ushering in the era of the tape-based electronic music studio.

Electronic instruments invented before 1950 represented a wave-oriented approach to synthesis, as opposed to a particle-oriented approach. Gabor's experiments in the late 1940s signaled the beginning of a new era in synthesis.

This chapter explores the ancient philosophical debate between waves and particles. It then presents the modern history of microsound synthesis, continuing through the era of analog electronics. Chapter 7 continues this story by recounting the history of early experiments in microsound synthesis by digital computer.

Waves versus Particles: Early Concepts of Microsound

To view the microacoustical domain is to confront a scientific dilemma that has confounded physicists for centuries: the wave versus the particle nature of signal energy. Debates concerning electromagnetic signals (such as light) have motivated most scientific inquiries. But much of what has been discovered about these signals applies to sound—the domain of mechanoacoustic vibrations as well. We will briefly look at the debate in both domains, optics and acoustics.

Table 2.1 Electric and electronic musical instruments: 1899–1950

Instrument	Date of demonstration	Inventor	Notes
Singing Arc	1899	W. Duddell	Early electric keyboard instrument
Choralcello Electric Organ	1903	Farrington, C. Donahue, and A. Hoffman	Electromagnetic instrument
Telharmonium	1906	T. Cahill	Rotating tone generators, massive synthesizer
Audio oscillator and Audion Piano	1915	L. De Forest	First vacuum-tube instrument
Synthetic Tone Musical Instrument	1918	S. Cabot	Rotating tone wheels to generate current, the current drove metallic resonating bars
Thereminovox	1920	L. Theremin	Antenna instrument played with hands in air; based on heterodyne tone generator
Electrophon	1921	J. Mager	Heterodyne tone generator with filter
Staccatone	1923	H. Gernsback	Sharp attack, inductance-controlled keyboard instrument
Sphaerophon	1926	J. Mager	Improved Electrophon with keyboard
Electronic Harmonium	1926	L. Theremin and ?. Rzhevkin	1200 divisions per octave, designed for studies in melody and harmony
Pianorad	1926	H. Gernsback	Polyphonic, based on vacuum-tube oscillators
Violen	c. 1926	W. Gurov and ?. Volynken	
Light Siren	c. 1926	Kovakenko	Rotating optical disks and photocell detectors
Illuminovox	1926	L. Theremin	Electro-optical projector with rotating disc
SuperPiano	1927	E. Spielmann	"Light-chopper" instrument
Electric guitar prototype	1927	Les Paul	Solid body construction with electromagnetic pickups
Electronic Violin	1927	E. Zitzmann-Zirini	Space control of pitch like the Theremin, but switched control of volume
Spielman Electric Piano Harp	1928	J. Bethenod	Microphone and speaker feedback to sustain oscillations
Ondes Martenot	1928	M. Martenot	First of many versions
Dynaphon	1928	R. Bertrand	Multivibrator oscllator
Hellertion	1929	B. Helberger and P. Lertes	Vacuum-tube oscillator with feedback, continuous linear controllers
Crea-tone	1930	S. Cooper	Electric piano with feedback circuits for sustain
Givelet-Coupleaux organ	1930	J. Givelet and E. Coupleaux	Automated additive synthesis, oscillators controlled by paper tape

Table 2.1   (continued)

Instrument	Date of demon- stration	Inventor	Notes
Trautonium	1930	F. Trautwein	Neon-tube sawtooth tone generators, resonance filters to emphasize formants
Magnetoelectric organ	1930	R. H. Ranger	
Westinghouse organ	1930	R. Hitchcock	Research instrument based on vacuum tube oscillators
Ondium Pechadre	1930	?	Theremin-like instrument with a volume key instead of antenna
Hardy-Goldwaithe organ	1930	A. Hardy and S. Brown	Electro-optical tone generators
Neo-Bechstein piano	1931	W. Nernst	Physics Institute, Berlin, piano with electrical pickups instead of soundboard
Radiopiano	1931	Hiller	Amplified piano
Trillion-tone Organ	1931	A. Lesti and F. Sammis	Electro-optical tone generators
Radiotone	1931	Boreau	String-induced radio-receiver tone generator with filter circuits
Rangertone Organ	1931	R. Ranger	Rotating tone wheels
Emicon	1932	N. Langer and Hahnagyi	Gas-discharge tube oscillator, controlled by keyboard
Gnome	1932	I. Eremeef	Rotating electromagnetic tone wheels
Miessner Electronic Piano	1932	B. F. Miessner	88 electrostatic pickups
Rhythmicon (I)	1932	H. Cowell, L. Theremin	Complex rhythm machine with keyboard
Rhythmicon (II)	1932	W. Miessner	Not the same as previous device; Rotating "rhythm sounder" (U.S. Patent 1,887,857)
Mellertion	1933	?	10-division octave
Electronde	1933	L. or M. Taubman	Battery-powered, space control of pitch like the Theremin, with volume pedal
Cellulophone	1933	P. Toulon	Electro-optical tone generators
Elektroakustische Orgel	1934	O. Vierling and Kock	12 vacuum-tube master oscillators, other pitches derived by frequency division
La Croix Sonore	1934	N. Oboukhov	Heterodyning oscillator
Ethonium	1934	G. Blake	Emulation of the Theremin heterodyne oscillator
Keyboard Theremin	1934	L. Theremin	Bank of tone generators controlled by traditional organ keyboard
Loar Vivatone	1934	L. Loar	A modified acoustic/electric guitar

Table 2.1   (continued)

Instrument	Date of demon- stration	Inventor	Notes
Polytone	1934	A. Lesti and F. Sammis	Electro-optical tone generators
Syntronic Organ	1934	I. Eremeef and L. Stokowski	Electro-optical tone generators; one-hour of continuous variation
Everett Orgatron	1934	F. Hoschke and B. Miessner	Amplified vibrating brass reeds
Partiturphon	1935	J. Mager	Five-voice Sphaerophon with three keyboards
Hammond electric organ	1935	L. Hammond and B. Miessner	Rotating tone generators
Photona	1935	I. Eremeef	12 electro-optical tone generators, developed at WCAU radio, Philadelphia
Variophone	1935	Y. Sholpo	Photo-electric instrument in which the musician draws the sound on sprocketed film
Electrone	1935	Compton Organ Company	Based on design of L. Bourn; electrostatic rotary generators
Foerster Electrochord	1936	O. Vierling	Electromechanical piano
Sonothèque	1936	L. Lavalée	Coded performance instrument using photoelectric translation of engraved grooves
Kraft-durch-Freude Grosstonorgel	1936	O. Vierling and staff of Heinrich-Hertz-Institut, Berlin	Played at 1936 Olympic games
Welte Light-Tone organ	1936	E. Welte	Electro-optical tone generators
National Dobro VioLectric Violin and Supro Guitar	1936	J. Dopyera	Commercial instruments with electromagnetic pickups
Electric Hawaiian guitar	1936	L. Fender	Commercial instrument with electromagnetic pickups
Singing Keyboard	1936	F. Sammis	Played electro-optical recordings, precursor of samplers
Warbo Formant organ	1937	H. Bode and C. Warnke	Four-voice polyphonic, envelope shaping, key assignment, two filters
Oscillion	1937	W. Swann and W. Danforth	Gas-discharge tube oscillator
Krakauer Electone	1938	B. F. Miessner	Early electric piano
Melodium	1938	H. Bode	Touch-sensitive solo keyboard
Robb Wave organ	c. 1938	M. Robb	Rotating electromagnetic tone generators

Table 2.1   (continued)

Instrument	Date of demon-stration	Inventor	Notes
Sonor	c. 1939	?. Ananyev	Moscow, ribbon controller on a horizontal fingerboard; violin-like sound
Kaleidaphon	1939	J. Mager	"Kaleidoscopic" tone mixtures
Allen organ	1939	Jerome Markowitz	Vacuum-tube oscillators
Neo Bechstein piano	1939	O. Vierling and W. Nernst	First commercial version of the electric piano
Amplified piano	1939	B. Miessner	Variable tonal quality depending on the position of the pickups
Novachord	1939	Hammond Company	Several tube oscillators, divide-down synthesis, formant filters
Parallel Bandpass Vocoder	1939	H. Dudley, Bell Laboratories	Analysis and cross-synthesis
Dynatone	1939	B. Miessner, A. Amsley	Electric piano
Voder speech synthesizer	1939	H. Dudley	Voice model played by a human operator
Violena	1940	W. Gurov	
Emiriton	1940	A. Ivanov and A. Rimsky-Korsakov	Neon-tube oscillators
Ekvodin	1940	A. Volodin, Russia	
V-8	c. 1940	A. Volodin, Russia	
Solovox	1940	L. Hammond	Monophonic vacuum-tube oscillator with divide-down circuitry
Univox	c. 1940	Univox Company	Vacuum-tube sawtooth generator with diode waveform shaper circuit
Multimonika	1940	Hohner GmbH	Lower manual is wind-blown, upper manual has sawtooth generator
Ondioline	1941	Georges Jenny	Multistable vibrator and filters, keyboard mounted on springs for vibrato
Melotone	c. 1944	Compton Organ Company	Electrostatic rotary generators
Hanert Electrical Orchestra	1945	J. Hanert	Programmable performance controlled by punched paper cards
Joergensen Clavioline	1947	M. Constant Martin	Monophonic, three-octave keyboard
Rhodes Pre-Piano	1947	H. Rhodes	Metal tines amplified by electrostatic pickups

Table 2.1   (continued)

Instrument	Date of demonstration	Inventor	Notes
Wurlitzer electronic organ	1947	Wurlitzer Company	Based on the Orgatron reed design, later modified according to B. Miessner's patents
Conn Organ	1947	Conn Organ Company	Individual oscillators for each key
Electronic Sackbut	1948	Hugh LeCaine	Voltage-controlled synthesizer, pitch, waveform, and formant controllers
Free Music Machine	1948	B. Cross and P. Grainger	Electronic oscillators and continuous automated control
Mixturtrautonium	1949	O. Sala	Trautonium with noise generator, "circuit-breaker" sequencer, frequency dividers
Heliophon	1949	B. Helberger	
Mastersonic organ	1949	J. Goodell and E. Swedien	Rotating pitch wheels
Connsonata	1949	Conn Organ Company	Oscillators designed by E. L. Kent
Melochord	1947–9	H. Bode	Later installed at North West German Radio, Cologne
Bel Organ	c. 1947	Bendix Electronics	12 vacuum-tube oscillators, other pitches obtained by divide-down circuit
Elektronium Pi	1950	Hohner GmbH	Monophonic vacuum-tube oscillator with divide-down circuitry
Radareed organ	1950	G. Gubbins	Amplified reeds fitted with resonators
Dereux organ	c. 1950	Société Dereux	Electrostatic rotary generators, waveforms derived from oscillogram photographs

What is a wave? In acoustics it is defined as a disturbance (wavefront) that propagates continuously through a medium or through space. A wave oscillation moves away from a source and transports no significant amount of matter over large distances of propagation.

Optical Wave versus Particle Debate

The wave–particle debate in optics began in the early eighteenth century, when Isaac Newton, in his *Opticks* (published in 1704), described light as a stream of particles, partly because "it travels in a straight line." Through experiments with color phenomena in glass plates he also recognized the necessity of ascribing certain wavelike properties to light beams. Newton was careful not to speculate further, however, and the *corpuscular* or particle theory of light held sway for a century (de Broglie 1945; Elmore and Heald 1969).

A competing wave theory began to emerge shortly afterward with the experiments in reflection and refraction of Christian Huygens, who also performed experiments on the wave nature of acoustical signals. The early nineteenth century experiments of Thomas Young reinforced the wave view. Young observed that a monochromatic beam of light passing through two pinholes would set up an interference pattern resembling "waves of water," with their characteristic patterns of reinforcement and cancellation at points of intersection, depending on their phase. Experiments by Augustin Fresnel and others seemed to confirm this point of view. The theory of electromagnetic energy proposed by the Scottish physicist James Clerk Maxwell (1831–1879) described light as a wave variation in the electromagnetic field surrounding a charged particle. The oscillations of the particle caused the variations in this field.

Physicists resolved the optical wave–particle controversy in the first two decades of the twentieth century. This entailed a unified view of matter and electromagnetic energy as manifestations of the same phenomena, but with different masses. The wave properties of polarization and interference, demonstrated by light, are also exhibited by the atomic constituents of matter, such as electrons. Conversely, light, in its interaction with matter, behaves as though composed of many individual units (called *photons*), which exhibit properties usually associated with particles, such as energy and momentum.

Acoustical Wave versus Particle Debate

What Atomes make Change
Tis severall Figur'd Atomes that make Change,
When severall Bodies meet as they do range.
For if they sympathise, and do agree,
They joyne together, as one Body bee.
But if they joyne like to a Rabble-rout,
Without all order running in and out;
Then disproportionable things they make,
Because they did not their right places take.
(Margaret Cavendish 1653)

The idea that a continuous tone could be decomposed into smaller quantities of time emerges from ancient atomistic philosophies. The statement that all matter is composed of indivisible particles called atoms can be traced to the ancient city of Abdera, on the seacoast of Thrace. Here, in the latter part of the fifth century BC, Leucippus and Democritus taught that all matter consists only of atoms and empty space. These Greek philosophers are the joint founders of atomic theory. In their opinion, atoms were imperceptible, individual particles differing only in shape and position. The combination of these particles causes the world we experience. They speculated that any substance, when divided into smaller and smaller pieces, would eventually reach a point where it could no longer be divided. This was the atom.

Another atomist, Epicurus (341–270 BC), founded a school in Athens in 306 BC and taught his doctrines to a devoted body of followers. Later, the Roman Lucretius (55) wrote *De Rerum Natura* (*On the Nature of the Universe*) delineating the Epicurean philosophy. In Book II of this text, Lucretius characterized the universe as a fortuitous aggregation of atoms moving in the void. He insisted that the soul is not a distinct, immaterial entity but a chance combination of atoms that does not survive the body. He further postulated that earthly phenomena are the result of purely natural causes. In his view, the world is not directed by divine agency; therefore fear of the supernatural is without reasonable foundation. Lucretius did not deny the existence of gods, but he saw them as having no impact upon the affairs of mortals (Cohen 1984, p. 177).

The atomistic philosophy was comprehensive: both matter and energy (such as sound) were composed of tiny particles.

Roughness in the voice comes from roughness in its primary particles, and likewise smoothness is begotten of their smoothness.   (Lucretius 55, Book IV, verse 524)

At the dawn of early modern science in the seventeenth century, the French natural philosophers Pierre Gassendi (1592–1655) and René Descartes (1596–1650) revived atomism. Descartes' theory of matter was based on particles and their motion. Gassendi (1658) based his system on atoms and the void. The particles within these two systems have various shapes, weights, or other qualities that distinguish them. From 1625 until his death, Gassendi occupied himself with the promulgation of the philosophy of Epicurus.

During the same period, the science of acoustics began to take shape in western Europe. A confluence of intellectual energy, emanating from Descartes, Galileo, Beekman, Mersenne, Gassendi, Boyle, and others, gradually forced a paradigm shift away from the Aristotelian worldview toward a more experimental perspective. It is remarkable how connected was this shift in scientific thinking to the analysis of musical sound (Coelho 1992). Problems in musical acoustics motivated experiments that were important to the development of modern science.

The Dutch scholar Isaac Beekman (1588–1637) proposed in 1616 a "corpuscular" theory of sound. Beekman believed that any vibrating object, such as a string, cuts the surrounding air into spherical particles of air that the vibrations project in all directions. When these particles impinge on the eardrum, we perceive sound.

The very same air that is directly touched and affected by a hard thing is violently shocked and dispersed [by a vibrating object] and scattered particle-wise everywhere, so that the air itself that had received the impulse strikes our ear, in the way that a candle flame spreads itself through space and is called light. (Cohen 1984)

In Beekman's theory, the particles emitted by a vibrating string derive their velocity from the force with which the string hits them. Every particle flies off on its own, is homogeneous, and represents in its particular shape and size the properties of the resulting sound. If a particle does not hit the ear, it finally comes to rest, according to the laws of projectile motion, and is then reintegrated into the surrounding air. Beekman ascribed differences in timbre to variations in the size, shape, speed, and density of sound particles. Gassendi also argued that sound is the result of a stream of particles emitted by a sounding body. The velocity of sound is the speed of the particles, and frequency is the number of particles emitted per unit time.

Almost two centuries later, in 1808, an English school teacher, John Dalton (1766–1844), formulated an atomic theory of matter. Unlike the speculations of Beekman and Gassendi, Dalton based his theory on experimental evidence (Kargon 1966). Dalton stated that all matter is composed of extremely small atoms that cannot be subdivided, created, or destroyed. He further stated that all atoms of the same element are identical in mass, size, and chemical and physical properties, and that the properties of the atom of one element, differ from those of another. What differentiates elements from one another, of course, are their constituent particles. Eighty-nine years after Dalton, the first elementary particle—the electron—was discovered by another Englishman, J. J. Thomson (Weinberg 1983).

As the particle theory of matter emerged, however, the particle theory of sound was opposed by increasing evidence. The idea of sound as a wave phenomenon grew out of ancient observations of water waves. That sound may exhibit analogous behavior was emphasized by a number of Greek and Roman philosophers and engineers, including Chrysippus (c. 240 BC), Vetruvius

(c. 25 BC), and Boethius (480–524). The wave interpretation was also consistent with Aristotle's (384–322 BC) statement to the effect that air motion is generated by a source, "thrusting forward in like manner the adjoining air, so that the sound travels unaltered in quality as far as the disturbance of the air manages to reach."

By the mid-1600s, evidence had begun to accumulate in favor of the wave hypothesis. Robert Boyle's classic experiment in 1640 on the sound radiation of a ticking watch in a partially evacuated glass vessel gave proof that the medium of air was necessary for the production or transmission of audible sound.

Experiments showed the relation between the frequency of air motion and the frequency of a vibrating string (Pierce 1994). Galileo Galilei's book *Mathematical Discourses Concerning Two New Sciences*, published in 1638, contained the clearest statement given until then of frequency equivalence, and, on the basis of accumulated experimental evidence, René Descartes rejected Beekman's corpuscular theory of sound (Cohen 1984, p. 166).

Marin Mersenne's description in his *Harmonie Universelle* (1636) of the first absolute determination of the frequency of an audible tone (at 84 Hz) implies that he had already demonstrated that the absolute-frequency ratio of two vibrating strings, radiating a musical tone and its octave, is as $1:2$. The perceived harmony (*consonance*) of two such notes could be explained if the ratio of the air oscillation frequencies is also $1:2$, which is consistent with the wave theory of sound.

Thus, a continuous tone could be decomposed into small time intervals, but these intervals would correspond to the periods of a waveform, rather than to the rate of flow of sonic particles.

The analogy with water waves was strengthened by the belief that air motion associated with musical sounds is oscillatory and by the observation that sound travels with a finite speed. Another matter of common knowledge was that sound bends around corners, suggesting diffraction, also observed in water waves (figure 2.1). Sound diffraction occurs because variations in air pressure cannot go abruptly to zero after passing the edge of an object. They bend, instead, into a shadow zone in which part of the propagating wave changes direction and loses energy. This is the diffracted signal. The degree of diffraction depends on the wavelength (short wavelengths diffract less), again confirming the wave view.

While the atomic theory of matter became the accepted viewpoint in the nineteenth century, the wave theory of sound took precedence. New particle-based acoustic theories were regarded as oddities (Gardner 1957).

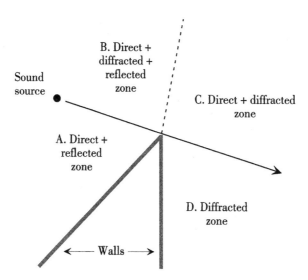

Figure 2.1 Zones of audition with respect to a sound ray and a corner. Listeners in zone A hear the direct sound and also the sound reflected on the wall. Those in zone B hear a combination of direct, reflected, and diffracted sound. In zone C they hear a combination of direct and diffracted sound. Listeners in zone D hear only diffracted sound (after Pierce 1994).

Waves versus Particles: a Contemporary Perspective

The wave theory of sound dominated the science of acoustics until 1907, when Albert Einstein predicted that ultrasonic vibration could occur on the quantum level of atomic structure, leading to the concept of *acoustical quanta* or *phonons*. Einstein's theory of phonons was finally verified in 1913.

Writing about the music of Edgard Varèse, Dane Rudyar (quoted in Miller 1945) recognized the significance of this discovery:

Every tone is a complex entity made up of elements ordered in various ways ... In other words, every tone is a molecule of music, and as such can be dissociated into component sonal atoms.... [These] may be shown to be but waves of the all-pervading sonal energy radiating throughout the universe, like the recently discovered cosmic rays which Dr. Milliken calls, interestingly enough, the birth cries of the simple elements: helium, oxygen, silicon, and iron. (Varèse 1940)

The scientific development of acoustical quantum theory in the domain of audible sounds was left to the physicist Dennis Gabor (1946, 1947, 1952). Gabor proposed that all sound could be decomposed into a family of functions obtained by time and frequency shifts of a single Gaussian particle. Gabor's pioneering ideas have deeply affected signal processing and sound synthesis. (See chapters 3 and 6.) Later in this chapter, we present the basic idea of the Gabor matrix, which divides time and frequency according to a grid.

Today we would say that the wave and particle theories of sound are not opposed. Rather, they reflect complementary points of view. In matter, such as water, waves move on a macro scale, but water is composed of molecules moving on a micro scale. Sound can be seen in a similar way, either wavelike or particle-like, depending upon the scale of measurement, the density of particles, and the type of operations that we apply to it.

The Modern Concept of Microsound

Fundamental to microsound synthesis is the recognition of the continuum between rhythm (the infrasonic frequencies) and pitch (the audible frequencies). This idea was central to what the poet and composer Ezra Pound called the theory of the "Great Base" (Pound 1934). In 1910 he wrote:

Rhythm is perhaps the most primal of all things known to us ... Music is, by further analysis, pure rhythm; rhythm and nothing else, for the variation of pitch is the variation in rhythms of the individual notes, and harmony, the blending of these varied rhythms. (Pound 1910, in Schafer 1977)

Pound proposed the Great Base theory in 1927:

You can use your beat as a third or fourth or Nth note in the harmony. To put it another way; the percussion of the rhythm can enter the harmony exactly as another note would. It enters usually as a Bassus ... giving the main form to the sound. It may be convenient to call these different degrees of the scale the megaphonic and microphonic parts of the harmony. Rhythm is nothing but the division of frequency plus an emphasis or phrasing of that division. (Pound 1927, in Schafer 1977)

In this theory, Pound recognized the rhythmic potential of infrasonic frequencies. The composer Henry Cowell also describes this relationship:

Rhythm and tone, which have been thought to be entirely separate musical fundamentals ... are definitely related through overtone ratios. (Cowell 1930)

Later in his book he gives an example:

Assume that we have two melodies in parallel to each other, the first written in whole notes and the second in half-notes. If the time for each note were to be indicated by the tapping of a stick, the taps for the second melody would recur with double the rapidity of those of the first. If now the taps were to be increased greatly in rapidity without changing the relative speed, it will be seen that when the taps for the first melody reach sixteen to the second, those for the second melody will be thirty-two to the second. In other words, the vibrations from the taps of one melody will give the musical tone C, while those of the other will give the tone C one octave higher. Time has been translated, as it were, into musical tone. Or, as has been shown above, a parallel can be drawn between the ratio of rhythmical beats and the ratio of musical tones by virtue of the common mathematical basis of both musical time and musical tone. The two times, in this view, might be said to be "in harmony," the simplest possible. . . . There is, of course, nothing radical in what is thus far suggested. It is only the interpretation that is new; but when we extend this principle more widely we begin to open up new fields of rhythmical expression in music.   (Cowell 1930)

Cowell formulated this insight two decades before Karlheinz Stockhausen's temporal theory, explained later in this chapter.

Temporal Continuity in Perception

Inherent in the concept of microsound is the notion that sounds on the object time scale can be broken down into a succession of events on a smaller time scale. This means that the apparently continuous flow of music can be considered as a succession of frames passing by at a rate too fast to be heard as discrete events. This ideal concept of time division is ancient (consider Zeno of Elea's four paradoxes). It could not be fully exploited by technology until the modern age.

In the visual domain, the illusion of cinema—motion pictures—is made possible by a perceptual phenomenon known as *persistence of vision*. This enables a rapid succession of discrete images to fuse into the illusion of a continuum. Persistence of vision was first explained scientifically by P. M. Roget in 1824 (Read and Welch 1977). W. Fritton demonstrated it with images on the two sides of a card: one of a bird, the other of a cage. When the card was spun rapidly, it appeared that the bird was in the cage (de Reydellet 1999).

The auditory analogy to persistence of vision is the phenomenon of tone fusion induced by the forward masking effect, described in chapter 1.

Throughout the nineteenth century, slow progress was made toward the development of more sophisticated devices for the display of moving images. (See Read and Welch 1977 for details.) A breakthrough, however, did come in 1834 with W. G. Horner's Zoetrope (originally called the Daedelum). The Zoetrope took advantage of persistence of vision by rotating a series of images around a fixed window fitted with a viewing lens. Depending on the speed of rotation, the image appeared to move in fast or slow motion.

After the invention of celluloid film for photography, the ubiquitous Thomas Alva Edison created the first commercial system for motion pictures in 1891. This consisted of the Kinetograph camera and the Kinetoscope viewing system. Cinema came into being with the projection of motion pictures onto a large screen, introduced by the Lumière brothers in 1895.

In 1889 George Eastman demonstrated a system which synchronized moving pictures with a phonograph, but the "talking picture" with optical soundtrack did not appear until 1927. An optical sound track, however, is not divided into frames. It appears as a continuous band running horizontally alongside the succession of vertical image frames.

In music, automated mechanical instruments had long quantized time into steps lasting as little as a brief note. But it was impossible for these machines to operate with precision on the time scale of microsound. Electronics technology was needed for this, and the modern era of microsound did not dawn until the acoustic theory and experiments of Dennis Gabor in the 1940s.

The Gabor Matrix

Inherent in the concept of a continuum between rhythm and pitch is the notion that tones can be considered as a succession of discrete units of acoustic energy. This leads to the notion of a granular or quantum approach to sound, first proposed by the British physicist Dennis Gabor in a trio of brilliant papers. These papers combined theoretical insights from quantum physics with practical experiments (1946, 1947, 1952). In Gabor's conception, any sound can be decomposed into a family of functions obtained by time and frequency shifts of a single Gaussian particle. Another way of saying this is that any sound can be decomposed into an appropriate combination of thousands of elementary grains. It is important to emphasize the analytical orientation of Gabor's theory. He was interested in a general, invertible method for the analysis of waveforms. As he wrote in 1952:

The orthodox method [of analysis] starts with the assumption that the signal s is a function s(t) of time t. This is a very misleading start. If we take it literally, it means that we have a rule of constructing an exact value of s(t) to any instant of time t. Actually we are never in a position to do this. . . . If there is a bandwidth W at our disposal, we cannot mark time any more exactly than by a time-width of the order 1/W; hence we cannot talk physically of time elements smaller than 1/W. (Gabor 1952, p. 6)

Gabor took exception to the notion that hearing was well represented by Fourier analysis of infinite signals, a notion derived from Helmholtz (1885). As he wrote:

Fourier analysis is a timeless description in terms of exactly periodic waves of infinite duration. On the other hand it is our most elementary experience that sound has a time pattern as well as a frequency pattern.... A mathematical description is wanted which ab ovo *takes account of this duality.*   (Gabor 1947, p. 591)

Gabor's solution involved the combination of two previously separated dimensions: frequency and time, and their correlation in two new representations: the mathematical domain of acoustic quanta, and the psychoacoustical domain of hearing. He formed a mathematical representation for acoustic quanta by relating a time-domain signal $s(t)$ to a frequency-domain spectrum $S(f)$. He then mapped an energy function from $s(t)$ over an "effective duration" Δt into an energy function from $S(f)$ over an "effective spectral width" Δf to obtain a characteristic cell or acoustic quantum. Today one refers to analyses that are limited to a short time frame as *windowed analysis* (see chapter 6). One way to view the Gabor transform is to see it as a kind of collection of localized Fourier transforms. As such, it is highly useful for the analysis of time-varying signals, such as music.

Gabor recognized that any windowed analysis entails an uncertainty relation between time and frequency resolution. That is, a high resolution in frequency requires the analysis of a large number of samples. This implies a long time window. It is possible to pinpoint specific frequencies in an analyzed segment of samples, but only at the cost of losing track of when exactly they occurred. Conversely, it is possible to pinpoint the temporal structure of audio events with great precision, but only at the cost of giving up frequency precision. This relation is expressed in Gabor's formula:

$$\Delta t \times \Delta f \geq 1$$

For example, if the uncertainty product is 1 and Δt is 10 ms (or 1/100 Hz), then Δf can be no less than 100 Hz. Another way of stating this is: to resolve frequencies to within a bandwidth of 100 Hz, we need a time window of at least 10 ms.

Time and frequency resolution are bound together. The more precisely we fix one magnitude, the more inexact is the determination of the other.

Gabor's quanta are units of elementary acoustical information. They can be represented as elementary signals with oscillations at any audible frequency f, modulated by a finite duration envelope (a Gaussian curve). Any audio signal fed into a Gabor analyzer can be represented in terms of such signals by expanding the information area (time versus frequency) into unit cells and associating with each cell an amplitude factor (figure 2.2). His formula for sound quanta was:

$$g(t) = e^{-a^2(t-t_0)^2} \times e^{2\pi j f_0 t} \tag{1}$$

where

$$\Delta t = \pi^{1/2}/a \quad \text{and} \quad \Delta f = a/\pi^{1/2}$$

The first part of equation 1 defines the Gaussian envelope, while the second part defines the complex sinusoidal function (frequency plus initial phase) within each quantum.

The geometry of the acoustic quantum $\Delta t\, \Delta f$ depends on the parameter a, where the greater the value of a, the greater the time resolution at the expense of the frequency resolution. (For example, if $a = 1.0$, then $\Delta t = 1.77245$, and $\Delta f = 0.56419$. Setting the time scale to milliseconds, this corresponds to a time window of 1.77245 ms, and a frequency window of 564.19 Hz. For $a = 2.0$, Δt would be 0.88 ms and Δf would be 1128.38 Hz.) The extreme limiting cases of the Gabor series expansion are a time series (where Δt is the delta function δ), and the Fourier series (where $\Delta t = \infty$).

Gabor proposed that a quantum of sound was a concept of significance to the theory of hearing, since human hearing is not continuous and infinite in resolution. Hearing is governed by quanta of difference thresholds in frequency, time, and amplitude (see also Whitfield 1978). Within a short time window (between 10 and 21 ms), he reasoned, the ear can register only one distinct sensation, that is, only one event at a specific frequency and amplitude.

Gabor gave an iterative approximation method to calculate the matrix. By 1966 Helstrom showed how Gabor's analysis/resynthesis approximation could be recast into an exact identity by turning the elementary signals into orthogonal functions. Bacry, Grossman, and Zak (1975) and Bastiaans (1980, 1985) verified this hypothesis. They developed analytic methods for calculating the matrix and resynthesizing the signal.

A similar time-frequency lattice of functions was also proposed in 1932 in a different context by the mathematician John von Neumann. It subsequently became known as the *von Neumann lattice* and lived a parallel life among quantum physicists (Feichtinger and Strohmer 1998).

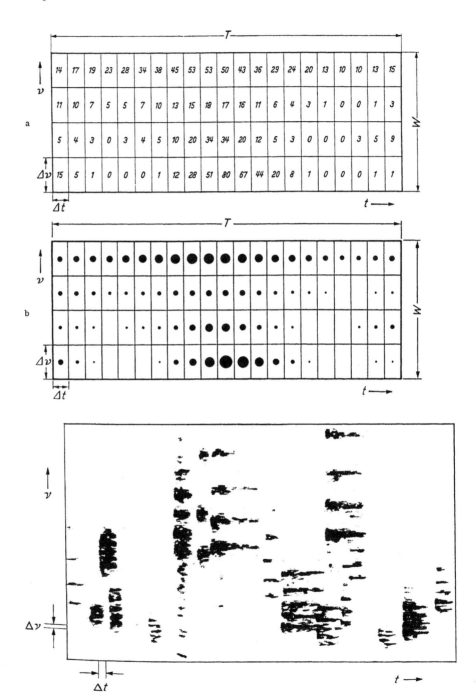

Electro-optical and Electromechanical Sound Granulation

Gabor was also an inventor, and indeed, he won the Nobel Prize for the invention of holography. In the mid-1940s, he constructed a sound granulator based on a sprocketed optical recording system adapted from a 16 mm film projector (Gabor 1946). He used this "Kinematical Frequency Convertor" to make *pitch-time changing* experiments—changing the pitch of a sound without changing its duration, and vice versa.

Working with Pierre Schaeffer, Jacques Poullin constructed another spinning-head device, dubbed the Phonogène, in the early 1950s (Schaeffer 1977, pp. 417–9, 427–8; Moles 1960). (See also Fairbanks, Everitt, and Jaeger 1954 for a description of a similar invention.) Later, a German company, Springer, made a machine based on similar principles, using the medium of magnetic tape and several spinning playback heads (Morawaska-Büngler 1988; Schaeffer 1977, pp. 427–8). This device, called the Zeitregler or Tempophon, processed speech sounds in Herbert Eimert's 1963 electronic music composition *Epitaph für Aikichi Kuboyama* (recorded on Wergo 60014).

The basic principle of these machines is time-granulation of recorded sounds. In an electromechanical pitch-time changer, a rotating head (the sampling head) spins across a recording (on film or tape) of a sound. The sampling head spins in the same direction that the tape is moving. Because the head only contacts the tape for a short period, the effect is that of *sampling* the sound on the tape at regular intervals. Each of these sampled segments is a grain of sound.

In Gabor's system, the grains were reassembled into a continuous stream on another recorder. When this second recording played back, the result was a more-or-less continuous signal but with a different time base. For example, shrinking the duration of the original signal was achieved by slowing down the rotation speed of the sampling head. This meant that the resampled recording contained a joined sequence of grains that were formerly separated. For time expansion, the rotating head spun quickly, sampling multiple copies (clones) of the original signal. When these samples were played back as a continuous signal, the effect of the multiple copies was to stretch out the duration of the

Figure 2.2 The Gabor matrix. The top image indicates the energy levels numerically. The middle image indicates the energy levels graphically. The lower image shows how the cells of the Gabor matrix (bounded by Δv, where v is frequency, and Δt, where t is time) can be mapped into a sonogram.

resampled version. The local frequency content of the original signal and in particular of the pitch, is preserved in the resampled version.

To effect a change in pitch without changing the duration of a sound, one need only to change the playback rate of the original and use the timescale modification just described to adjust its duration. For example, to shift the pitch up an octave, play back the original at double speed and use time-granulation to double the duration of the resampled version. This restores the duration to its original length. Chapter 5 looks at sound granulation using digital technology.

Meyer-Eppler

The acoustician Werner Meyer-Eppler was one of the founders of the West Deutscher Rundfunk (WDR) studio for electronic music in Cologne (Morawska-Büngler 1988). He was well aware of the significance of Gabor's research. In an historic lecture entitled *Das Klangfarbenproblem in der elektronischen Musik* ("The problem of timbre in electronic music") delivered in August 1950 at the Internationale Ferienkurse für Neue Musik in Darmstadt, Meyer-Eppler described the Gabor matrix for analyzing sounds into acoustic quanta (Ungeheuer 1992). He also presented examples of Oskar Fischinger's animated films with their optical images of waveforms as the "scores of the future." In his later lecture *Metamorphose der Klangelemente,* presented in 1955 at among other places, Gravesano, Switzerland at the studio of Hermann Scherchen, Meyer-Eppler described the Gabor matrix as a kind of score that could be composed with a "Mosaiktechnik." In his textbook, Meyer-Eppler (1959) described the Gabor matrix in the context of measuring the information content of audio signals. He defined the "maximum structure content" of a signal as a physical measurement

$$K = 2 \times W \times T$$

where W is the bandwidth in Hertz and T is the signal duration. Thus for a signal with a full bandwidth of 20 kHz and a duration of 10 seconds, the maximum structure content is $2 \times 20000 \times 10 = 400,000$, which is—by the sampling theorem—the number of samples needed to record it. He recognized that aural perception was limited in its time resolution, and estimated that the lower boundary on perception of parameter differences was of the order of 15 ms, about 1/66th of a second.

The concept of time-segmentation was central to his notion of *systematic sound transformation* (Meyer-Eppler 1960). For example, he described experiments with speech in which grains from one word could be interpolated into another to change its sense.

Moles

The physicist Abraham Moles (1960, 1968) was interested in applying Shannon's information theory to aesthetic problems, particularly in new music (Galante and Sani 2000). Pierre Schaeffer hired him to work at the Groupe de Recherches Musicale (GRM). Significantly, this coincided with Iannis Xenakis's residencies in the GRM studios (Orcalli 1993). Moles had read Meyer-Eppler's book. He sought a way to segment sound objects into small units for the purpose of measuring their information content. Following the Gabor matrix, he set up a three-dimensional space bounded by quanta in frequency, loudness, and time. He described this segmentation as follows:

We know that the receptor, the ear, divides these two dimensions [pitch and loudness] into quanta. Thus each sonic element may be represented by an elementary square. A pure sinusoidal sound, without any harmonics, would be represented by just one of these squares. . . . Because thresholds quantize the continua of pitch and loudness, the repertoire is limited to some 340,000 elements. Physically, these elements are smaller and denser toward the center of the sonic domain, where the ear is more acute. . . . In most cases each symbol [in a sonic message] is a combination of elements, that is, of a certain number of these squares. (Moles 1968)

Wiener

The MIT mathematician Norbert Wiener (the founder of cybernetics) was well aware of Gabor's theory of acoustic quanta, just as Gabor was well aware of Wiener's work. In 1951, Gabor was invited to present his acoustical quantum theory in a series of lectures at MIT (Gabor 1952).

Like Gabor, Wiener rejected the view (expounded by Leibniz in the eighteenth century) that time, space, and matter are infinitely subdivisible or continuous. He supported Planck's quantum theory principle of discontinuity in light and in matter. Wiener noted that Newton's model of deterministic physics was being replaced by Gibbsian statistical mechanics—a "qualified indeterminism." And like Gabor, he was skeptical of Fourier analysis as the best representation for music.

The frequency and timing of a note interact in a complicated manner. To start and stop a note involves an alteration of its frequency content which may be small but very real. A note lasting only a finite time is to be analyzed as a band of simple harmonic motions, no one of which can be taken as the only simple harmonic motion present. The considerations are not only theoretically important but correspond to a real limitation of what a musician can do. You can't play a jig in the lowest register of an organ. If you take a note oscillating at sixteen cycles per second and continue it only for one twentieth of a second, what you get is a single push of air without any noticeable periodic character. Just as in quantum theory, there is in music a difference of behavior between those things belonging to small intervals of time and what we accept on the normal scale of every day. (Wiener 1964a, 1964b)

Going further, Wiener stressed the importance of recognizing the time scale of a model of measurement:

The laws of physics are like music notation—things that are real and important provided that we do not take them too seriously and push the time scale down below a certain level. (Wiener 1964a, 1964b)

Theory and Experiments of Xenakis

Iannis Xenakis leaves many legacies. Besides his remarkably inventive compositional output, he was one of the great free-thinkers in the history of music theory. He expanded the mathematical foundations of music in all its dimensions: pitch and scale, rhythm, timbre, sound synthesis, composition strategy, and form. Unlike most musicians, Xenakis constantly kept aware of developments in science and engineering. This knowledge fed his musical theories.

A fascination for statistical and particulated sound textures is apparent in his first orchestral composition *Metastasis* (1954). This interest carries through to his 1958 electroacoustic composition *Concret PH*, realized at the Groupe de Recherches Musicale (GRM) studios in Paris and premiered at the Philips Pavilion at the Brussels World's Fair. To create the granular texture for this work, he mixed recordings of burning wood-embers, cut into one-second fragments (Solomos 1997). These crackling sound mixtures were manipulated slightly in the studio of the GRM. Describing this work, he said:

Start with a sound made up of many particles, then see how you can make it change imperceptibly, growing and developing, until an entirely new sound results. . . . This was in defiance of the usual manner of working with concrète sounds. Most of the musique concrète which had been produced up to the time of Concret PH *is full of many abrupt changes and juxtaposed sections without transitions. This happened because the original recorded sounds used by the composers consisted of a block of one kind of sound, then a block of another, and did not extend beyond this. I seek extremely rich sounds (many high over-*

tones) that have a long duration, yet with much internal change and variety. Also, I explore the realm of extremely faint sounds highly amplified. There is usually no electronic alteration of the original sound, since an operation such as filtering diminishes the richness. (Xenakis program notes, Nonesuch recording H-71246)

The main techniques employed in *Concret PH* are the splicing of numerous bits of magnetic tape, tape speed change, and mixing to obtain varying densities. This work was not the result of mathematical operations, but was approached by the composer intuitively, in the manner of sound sculpture.

Organization of Analogique B

A year after *Concret PH*, Xenakis tried working more systematically with sound grains. He proposed the hypothesis that every sound could be understood as the assembly of a number of elementary particles. In *Analogique B*, completed in 1959 and premiered in Gravesano later that year, he drew from Moles's research at the GRM, and from Meyer-Eppler's (1959) book on information theory, which describes the Gabor matrix.

Analogique B consists of granular sounds produced by recording sine tones emitted by analog tone generators onto analog tape, and then cutting the tones into fragments. This brief composition (2 minute 25-sec) was meant to be played after *Analogique A*, a stochastically composed score for two violins, two cellos, and two contrabasses. Chapter 3 of *Formalized Music* (Xenakis 1971, 1992) describes how he organized the synthetic grains in *Analogique B* (1959, Éditions Salabert). See also Di Scipio (1995, 1997a, 1998), and Harley (forthcoming). The graphic score of *Analogique B* appears in the front matter of *Formalized Music*.

Analogique B was designed by scattering grains onto time-grids, called *screens* by Xenakis. The screens represented elementary sonic quanta in three dimensions: difference thresholds in frequency, amplitude, and time. He coined the term "grains of sound" (Xenakis 1960), and was the first musician to explicate a compositional theory for sound grains. He proposed the following lemma:

All sound, even continuous musical variation, is conceived as an assemblage of a large number of elementary sounds adequately disposed in time. In the attack, body, and decline of a complex sound, thousands of pure sounds appear in a more or less short interval of time Δt. (Xenakis 1992, p. 43)

Synchronized with the advancing time interval Δt, the screens are snapshots of sound bounded by frequency and amplitude grids, each screen subdivided into elementary squares of sonic energy, according to the resolution of the Gabor matrix. Xenakis goes on to specify a mesostructural unit describing a sequence of screens, which he calls a *book*. A book of screens could constitute the entirety of a complex sound—a cloud of points in evolution.

How should the grains be distributed on the screen? For a given density, Xenakis turned to probability theory for the answer. He proposed an exponential distribution to determine the duration of the strands, which were divided up between a succession of screens. This formula is as follows:

$$P_x = ce^{-cx}\,dx$$

where c is the mean duration and x is the time axis. This equation describes the probability P that an event of duration x_i between x and $x + dx$ will occur. (See Lorrain 1980.) For the frequency, amplitude, and density parameters of the grains he proposed the *linear distribution* rule:

$$P_\gamma = 2/a(1 - [\gamma/a])\,d\gamma$$

which gives the probability that a segment (or interval) of length a will have a length included within γ and $(\gamma + d\gamma)$, for $0 \leq \gamma \leq a$. Such a formula favors smaller intervals. Setting $a = 10$, for example, the probability of the small interval 2 is 0.16, while for the larger interval 9 it is 0.02.

Xenakis observed how sound particles could be viewed as short vectors within a three-dimensional space bounded by frequency, amplitude, and time. The Gabor grain, with its constant frequency and amplitude, is a special case of this view. It could also be possible to create grains that were short glissandi, for example (Xenakis 1960, p. 100). (I have implemented this idea in the technique of glisson synthesis, described in chapter 4.)

After defining the framework, Xenakis proposed a set of transformations that could be applied to the screens in order to create new screens. New screens could be generated, for example, by taking the logical intersection of two screens. He also proposed other Boolean operations, such as set union, complement, and difference.

His next theoretical elaboration scrutinized the *ataxy* or degree of order versus disorder in a succession of screens. Maximum disorder, for example, would correspond to extreme changes in the distribution of frequency and amplitude energy, creating a sonic effect akin to white noise. Perfect order would correspond to a solitary sine wave extending across multiple screens.

The flow of ataxy could be regulated via a matrix of transition probabilities, otherwise known as a *Markov chain* (Roads 1996). A Markov chain lets one encode transitions from order to disorder as a set of weighted probabilities, where the probability at time t depends on the history at times $t - 1$, $t - 2$, etc. Here is a simple transition matrix for a first-order Markov chain. It is called first-order because it only looks back one step.

	A	B	C
A	0.1	0.9	0
B	0.33	0.33	0.34
C	0.8	0.1	0.1

This matrix indicates the probabilities of three outcomes A, B, C, given three possible previous states A, B, C. For a given previous state, indicated by the columns, we read across the rows to determine the probabilities for the next state. The probabilities in a row add up to 1. Given the previous state A, for example, we see that A has a 0.1 chance of occurring again, while B has a 0.9 chance, and C has a probability of 0. Thus C will never follow A, and it is very likely that B will follow A. In granular synthesis, the states could be grain frequencies, amplitudes, or densities.

At the same time Xenakis recognized that ataxy as a compositional principle was incomplete. For example, certain configurations of grains on the plane of frequency-versus-amplitude engage the listener, while others do not, even if both measure the same in terms of ataxy.

Problems with a Constant Microtime Grid

In Xenakis's theory of screens, the assumption is that the frame rate and the grain duration are constant. The frame rate would determine the smallest grain size. The idea that all grains have the same duration is aesthetically limiting. Experiments (described in chapter 3) show that grain size is one of the most important time-varying parameters of granular synthesis.

The constant microtemporal grid or frame rate Δt of the screens poses technical problems. The main problem being that such a frame rate will tend to cause audible artefacts (a constant modulation or comb filtering effect, depending on the precise rate) unless countermeasures are taken. Consider a single stream of grains, one following the next, each lasting 40 ms, each with a Gaussian envelope. The attack of each grain takes 5–10 ms, as does its decay. This creates a regular amplitude modulation effect, producing sidebands around the carrier frequency.

If one were to implement Xenakis's screens, one would want to modify the theory to allow Δt to be less than the grain duration. This measure would allow grain attacks and decays to overlap, thereby smoothing over the perception of the frame rate. Similar problems of frame rate and overlap are well known in windowed analysis-resynthesis techniques such as the *short-time Fourier transform* (STFT). Frame-based representations are fragile, since any transformation of the frames that perturbs the perfect summation criteria at the boundaries of each frame leads to audible distortions (see chapter 6).

We face the necessity for a synchronous frame rate in any real-time implementation of granular synthesis. Ideally, however, this frame rate should operate at a speed as close as possible to the audio sampling rate.

Analog Impulse Generators

The most important sound particle of the 1950s, apart from those identified in Xenakis's experiments, was the analog impulse. An impulse is a discrete amplitude-time fluctuation, producing a sound that we hear as a click. Although the impulse is ideally a narrow rectangular shape, in practice it may be band-limited or have a ramped attack and decay. An *impulse generator* emits a succession of impulses at a specified frequency. Impulse generators serve many functions in a laboratory, such as providing a source for testing the *impulse response* (IR) of a circuit or system. The IR is an important system measurement (see chapter 5).

The common analog circuit for impulse and square wave generation is the *multivibrator* (figure 2.3). Multivibrators can be built using many electronic technologies: vacuum tubes, transistors, operational amplifiers, or logic gates. Although sometimes referred to as an oscillator, a multivibrator is actually an automatic switch that moves rapidly from one condition to another, producing a voltage impulse which can be positive, negative, or a combination of the two. The multivibrator circuit has the advantage that it is easily tuned to a specific frequency and duty cycle by adjusting a few circuit elements—either resistance or capacitance values (Douglas 1957).

The multivibrator was used in electronic music instruments as early as 1928, in René Bertrand's Dynaphone (Rhea 1972). Musicians appropriated laboratory impulse generators in the electronic music studios of the 1950s. Karlheinz Stockhausen and Gottfried Michael Koenig worked extensively with impulse generators at the Cologne studio. As Koenig observed:

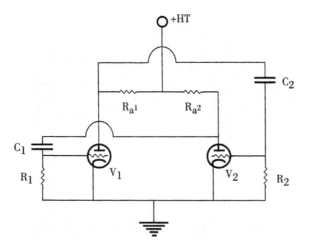

Figure 2.3   A multivibrator circuit, after Douglas (1957). Suppose that when switching on, a small positive voltage appears at V1. This increases the anode current of V1, and in so doing increases the anode potential of V1, which is communicated to the grid of V2. As the voltage of V2 falls, so will the anode current of V2, causing a rise in the anode potential of V1, making it more positive. The process continues until it reaches the cutoff voltage of the vacuum tube. The circuit stays in this condition while the grid of V2 leaks away at a rate depending on the time constant of C1 and R1. As soon as the anode potential of V2 reaches a point where anode current can flow again, the anode potential of V2 will fall again since the current is increasing, which drives the grid of V1 negative. The whole process is continued in the opposite direction until V1 is cut off, and so on continuously. If C1 = C2 and R1 = R2 the waveform is symmetrical (square) and has only odd harmonics.

[The pure impulse] has no duration, like sinus and noise, but represents a brief energy impetus, comparable to a leaping spark. Consequently it has neither pitch nor timbre. But it encounters an object and sets it vibrating; as pitch, noise, or timbre of the object which has been impelled.   (Koenig 1959)

Stockhausen's great 1960 composition *Kontakte*, realized with assistance from Koenig (Supper 1997), is based entirely on filtered impulses. Figure 2.4 shows the patch interconnections used in its realization, all of which begin with impulse generation. The technique of *recirculating tape feedback loops*, seen in many of the patches, was developed in 1951 by Werner Meyer-Eppler, Stockhausen's teacher (Ungeheuer 1992, p. 121).

Kaegi (1967) describes applications of impulse generators in electronic music. Chapter 4 presents applications of impulse generators (trainlets and pulsars) in digital synthesis.

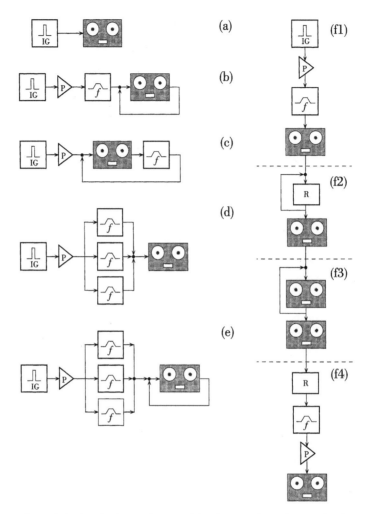

Figure 2.4 Synthesis patches used in the creation of *Kontakte* by Stockhausen. The components include impulse generators (IG), preamplifiers (P), analog tape recorders, bandpass filters (f), and plate reverberators (R). Feedback loops appears as arrows pointing backwards. (a) Simple impulse generation and recording. (b) Impulse generation with preamplification, filtering, and tape feedback. (c) Impulse generation with preamplification and filtered feedback. (d) Impulse generation with preamplification, and multiband filtering. (e) Impulse generation with preamplification, multiband filtering, and tape feedback. (f) A four-stage process involving (f1) Impulse generation, preamplification, filtering, and recording. (f2) Reverberation with feedback and recording. (f3) Tape feedback and recording. (f4) Reverberation, filtering, preamplification, and recording.

Stockhausen's Temporal Theory

In the 1950s, the Cologne school of electronic music emerged from the studios of the West Deutscher Rundfunk (WDR). It posited that a composition could be assembled out of a small number of elementary signals, such as sine waves, impulses, and filtered noise. In the first issue of the influential journal *die Reihe*, published in Cologne in 1955, this concept is championed by Karlheinz Stockhausen, Gottfried Michael Koenig, Herbert Eimert, Karel Goeyvaerts, and Paul Gredinger. In the same issue, Pierre Boulez, who later turned against purely electronic music, could not resist this tide of enthusiasm for electronic sound materials:

Electronic music compels us to assemble each note as we require it.   (Boulez 1955)

Ernst Krenek, one of the first composers to own an electronic music synthesizer, seemed to anticipate the notion of sound quanta when he mused:

The next step might be the splitting of the atom (that is, the sine tone).   (Krenek 1955)

Could he, perhaps, have been thinking of the Gabor quanta?

The Cologne composers were optimistic about synthesizing interesting forms of musical sound through combinations of sine waves (Eimert 1955; Goeyvaerts 1955). Many fascinating sounds, however, have transient fluctuations that are not well modelled with sinusoids. Stockhausen's sinusoidal *Electronic Etude I* of 1953 was important in its day, but now sounds like a sterile exercise. The initial enthusiasm for composition using only sine waves soon evaporated. By the time of *Gesang der Jünglinge* (1956), Stockhausen had moved ahead to identify eleven sound sources:

1. Sine tones

2. Sine tones in which the frequency modulates periodically

3. Sine tones in which the frequency modulates statistically

4. Sine tones in which the amplitude modulates periodically

5. Sine tones in which the amplitude modulates statistically

6. Periodic combinations of both frequency and amplitude modulation

7. Statistical combinations of both frequency and amplitude modulation

8. Colored noise with constant density

9. Colored noise with statistically varying density

10. Periodic sequences of filtered clicks (impulses)

11. Statistical sequences of filtered clicks

He also formulated a theory of the continuum between rhythm and pitch, that is, between infrasonic frequencies and the audible frequencies of impulses.

If the rate of beat is gradually increased beyond the time constant of the filter and the limits beyond which the ear can no longer differentiate, what started as a rhythmically repeated note becomes continuous. . . . We see a continuous transition between what might be called durational intervals which are characterized as rhythmic intervals and durational intervals characterized as pitch levels.   (Stockhausen 1955)

Stockhausen used an impulse generator to create a regular pulse train. To the output of this generator he applied a narrow bandpass filter, giving each pulsation a sharp resonance. If the band was narrow enough, the impulse resonated around a specific pitch or interval. If the pulse train was irregular, the infrasonic frequencies generated ametrical rhythms. By transposing these rhythms into the audible frequency range, Stockhausen could build unpitched noises from aperiodic sequences of impulses.

Further development of this approach led to a pair of landmark papers on the composition of microsound, discussed in the next two sections.

How Time Passes

Stockhausen's text ". . . . . *How time passes* . . . . ." was one of many controversial pronouncements made by the composer (Stockhausen 1957). Written over two months in 1956, when he was 28, and published immediately, it is a raw outpouring of intellectual reflection. The text clearly could have been improved by critical editing: goals are not stated at the outset, the text unfolds as one long rambling discourse, and the composer poses problems offering differing solutions. As his exposition proceeds, new criteria are introduced making previous solutions inadequate, so the argument is constantly shifting. Despite these flaws, ". . . . . *How time passes* . . . . ." stands as an ingeniously detailed analysis of certain relationships between different musical time scales, summarized here.

Stockhausen's article has been criticized for its non-standard acoustical terminology, found in both the original German as well as the English translation by Cornelius Cardew. (The republication of the German edition, in Stockhausen (1963), contains a statement acknowledging the use of nonstandard terminology.) For example, instead of the common term "period," denoting the time interval spanning one cycle of a waveform, Stockhausen uses the term "phase" (*Phasen*), referring not to a "fundamental period" but to a "fundamental phase." He substitutes the term "formant" for "harmonic," so a harmonic spectrum built up of a fundamental and integer-multiple frequencies is called a "formant spectrum." He applies the term "field" (*Feld*) to denote an uncertainty region (or band) around a time interval or a central frequency. As long as one understands these substitutions of terms, however, one can follow Stockhausen's arguments. In the representation of his article below, I replace Stockhausen's neologisms with standard acoustical terminology. Page numbers refer to the English translation.

The most important insight of ". . . . . *How time passes* . . . . ." is a unified view of the relationship between the various time scales of musical structure. Stockhausen begins by noting the generality of the concept of period, an interval between two cycles. Period appears in both rhythm (from 6 sec to 1/16th of a sec) and pitch (from about 1/16th sec to about 1/3200th sec). The key here is that pitch and rhythm can be considered as one and the same phenomenon, differing only in their respective time scales. Taking this argument deeper into the microtemporal domain, the *tone color* or steady-state spectrum of a note can also be seen as a manifestation of microrhythm over a fundamental frequency. This point of view can also be applied in the macrotemporal domain. Thus, an entire composition can be viewed as one time spectrum of a fundamental duration. (As noted earlier, this idea was proposed by Ezra Pound in the 1920s, and by Henry Cowell in 1930.)

The bulk of Stockhausen's text applies this viewpoint to a problem spawned by serial composition theory; that of creating a scale of twelve durations corresponding to the chromatic scale of pitches in the twelve-tone system. The problem is exacerbated by Stockhausen's desire to notate the result for performance on traditional instruments. Later, after the composer has developed a method for generating some of the most arcane rhythmic notation ever devised (see, for example, the scores of *Zeitmasse* or the *Klavierstücken*), he turns to the difficulties of indeterminate notation. Let us now look in more detail at these arguments.

Stockhausen begins by observing a contradiction in twelve-tone composition theory, which rigorously organizes pitch but not, in any systematic way, rhythm. Since pitch and rhythm can both be considered as dimensions of time, Stockhausen proposes that they should both be organized using twelve-element scales. Constructing a scale of durations that makes sense logically and makes sense perceptually, however, is not simple. Stockhausen presents several strategies. The first, adopted by unnamed composers, builds a twelve-element scale by multiplying a small unit, for example, $1 \times \eighthnote, 2 \times \eighthnote, 3 \times \eighthnote, \ldots 12 \times \eighthnote$. Clearly, if serial selection order is maintained (i.e., if an element can be chosen a second time only after all other elements in the series have been chosen), the long durations will overshadow the short durations. Why is this? The total duration of a twelve-element series is $78 \times \eighthnote$. If we add up the time taken by the first four members of the series, their total duration is $10 \times \eighthnote$. This, however, is only about 13% of the total duration of the series. At the other extreme, the last four notes $9 \times \eighthnote, 10 \times \eighthnote, 11 \times \eighthnote, 12 \times \eighthnote$, take up $42 \times \eighthnote$, or more than 53% of the total duration of the series. Nonetheless, this scheme has been used by (unnamed) composers, with the obvious added constraint that the tempo be kept constant in order for the duration series to be perceptible.

To inject this scheme with more flexibility composers superimposed series on top of one another. This led to irregular rhythms that could only be perceived through what Stockhausen calls *statistical form-criteria*. A corresponding procedure was adopted with pitch, when "flocks of notes" sounding in a short time period, blurred the pitch structure. Stockhausen was uncomfortable with this forced agreement between pitch and duration series.

This discomfort led to another strategy for constructing a duration scale. By subdividing a whole into a series of fractional intervals of the form: $1, 1/2, 1/3, 1/4, \ldots 1/12$. Stockhausen observed that the rhythmic tuplet series (duplet, triplet, quadruplet, ...) could be considered as analogous to the harmonic series (of pitches). An eighth-note triplet, for example, might correspond to the third harmonic duration of a quarter note. One can speak of a fundamental rhythm with harmonically-related rhythms superimposed. A periodic tone can be seen as having a rhythmic microstructure, with waveform peaks corresponding to its internal rhythmic intervals. The difference between meter and rhythm corresponds to the distinction on the microtime scale between fundamental tone and tone color, and one could just as well speak of "harmonic rhythm" (my term) as of tone color.

For Stockhausen, the next stage was to relate this harmonic duration scale to the equal-tempered pitch scale according to the principles of twelve-tone serial composition. This, however, revealed a new problem: the harmonic scale and the chromatic scale have little in common. So using a harmonic scale for duration and a chromatic scale for pitch countermands the search for a single time scale for both domains, the point of which is to unify duration and pitch through a single set of serial intervallic operations.

So Stockhausen took on the task of constructing a tempered chromatic scale of durations corresponding to the equal-tempered scale. He divided the ratio 2:1 into 12 equal intervals, according to the logarithmic relationship of the 12th root of 2. These 12 do not translate directly into the common symbols of music notation, an essential requirement for Stockhausen. He adopted a notational solution wherein all time durations would be represented by the same symbol, a whole note, for example, adjusted by a tempo indication. So to create a scale from $\mathbf{o} = 60$ M.M. to $\mathbf{o} = 120$, the note's values are set successively to tempi of 60, 63.6, 67.4, 71.4, 75.6, 80.1, 84.9, 89.9, 95.2, 100.9, 106.9, 113.3, 120. The interval between each of these numbers corresponds to the standard 6% minor second difference of the equal-tempered scale. The final value corresponds to $\downarrow = 60$ M.M., and the scale can be transposed easily. In this scheme, pitch and time are equal under the regime of the twelve-tone system.

In a sleight-of-hand, Stockhausen then translates an arbitrary duration series from the equal-tempered notation just described into a list of harmonic proportions, without explaining the procedure. Presumably he multiplies tempo and note value, rounds off the result to integers, and compares subsequent integers in the series to obtain a list of harmonic (integer) proportions. This is merely an exercise, for he then returns to insisting on equal-tempered notation, which, he observes, remains precise and will not be affected by transposition.

His argument veers off course at this point. While insisting on consistently equal-tempered proportions for pitch and duration, Stockhausen switches to harmonic proportions for the organization of higher-level groups of rhythmic phrases. This is clearly inconsistent with his previous argument.

With this harmonically related hierarchy as his premise, Stockhausen proposes that other serial operations be used to create elaborate networks of harmonic proportions. By deleting some notes and tying others, for example, ever more complicated relationships can arise. Such transformations lend a sense of aperiodicity to the rhythmic structure, which Stockhausen compares to the aperiodic microstructure of noise.

Addressing a practicality of performance, Stockhausen writes that if certain rhythms cannot be realized by instrumentalists synchronized by a single conductor, then the instrumentalists can be divided into groups and synchronized by separate conductors (a procedure employed in his, *Gruppen* for three orchestras). He also confronts the problem for performers of accurately playing the complicated rhythms generated by the manipulations described above. Notational ambiguity adds to the difficulty, since one and the same rhythmic formula may be written in different ways, some harder than others for performers to realize. Stockhausen tries to allow for such imprecisions in his theory by assigning an "uncertainty band" (*time-field*) to the different notations. These time-fields could be derived by recording expert instrumentalists playing different figures while measuring the precision of their interpretation. (Obviously it would be impractical if every rhythmic formula in a composition had to be notated in multiple ways and tested in such a way.) Stockhausen then proposes that one could serialize the degree of inaccuracy of performance (!).

The degree of notational complexity and the exactness of performance are inversely related. If metronome markings are changing from measure to measure, the uncertainty factor increases. Multiple simultaneous tempi and broad uncertainty bands lead to general confusion. At this point, Stockhausen switches the direction of his argument to the organization of statistical groups. All parameters of time can be turned into ranges, for example, leaving it to the performers to select from within a specified range. Stockhausen points out that John Cage, in his proportional notation was not interested in proportional relationships, depending, as they do, on memories of the past. In Cage's compositions, temporal events are not intentionally linked to the past; always one is in the present.

Stockhausen prefers a system in which determinacy and indeterminacy stand at opposite poles of a continuum. He seeks a way to notate structural indeterminacy in a determinate way. This involves "time smearing" the music by interpolating grace notes and articulations (staccato, legato, etc.) that "fade" into or out of a central note. Indeterminate notation can also be extended to meso and macrostructure.

The structure of a piece is presented not as a sequence of development in time but as a directionless time-field . . . The groups are irregularly distributed on paper and the general instructions are: Play any group, selected at random. . . .   (p. 36)

The important principle in this gamut between determinacy and indeterminacy is the interplay between the rational counting of time and the "agitation of time" by an instrumentalist. The score is no longer the reference for time.

Instead of mechanically quantifying durations that conflict with the regularity of metronomic time, [the performer] now measures sensory quanta; he feels, discovers the time of the sounds; he lets them take their time. (pp. 37–8)

The domain of pitch can also be notated aleatorically, and the gamut between pitch and noise can be turned into a compositional parameter.

To fully realize the pitch-noise continuum, he argues, a new keyboard instrument could be built in which a certain key-pressure produces a constant repetition of waveform periods (a continuous pitched tone), but a stronger pressure causes aleatoric modulation leading into noise. This "ideal instrument" would be able to move from duration to pitch, from tone to noise, and also be able to alter the timbre and amplitude of the oscillations. Several instruments playing together would be able to realize all of the riches of Stockhausen's temporal theory. After lamenting on how long one might have to wait for such an instrument, Stockhausen finishes his article by asserting:

It does not seem very fruitful to founder on a contradiction between, on the one hand, a material that has become useless—instruments that have become useless—and, on the other, our compositional conception.

He leaves this thought hanging as the article ends.

It is evident from his voluminous output of pieces for traditional instruments since 1957 that Stockhausen did not want to wait for such instruments. For obvious social and economic reasons he chose to stay within traditional instrumental practice, albeit with many creative extensions. The technology of synthesis has greatly advanced since 1957. Stockhausen's ideal instrument is realizable today using real-time sound synthesis and modern controllers although, sadly, Stockhausen himself has all but ignored such developments. The Creatovox, described in chapter 5, is one such solution.

The Unity of Musical Time

Stockhausen based his article *"The unity of musical time"* (Stockhausen 1962) on a radio broadcast he gave in 1961. This concise text summarizes the basic principles of Stockhausen's integrated approach to electronic music composition.

[In working with an impulse generator], one must proceed from a basic concept of a single unified musical time; and the different perceptual categories such as color, harmony and melody, meter and rhythm, dynamics, and form must be regarded as corresponding to the different components of this unified time.   (p. 217)

Stockhausen distinguishes twenty-one time octaves spanning the durations from 1/16th of a second to 3600 seconds (one hour), which constitute the range of perceivable events in a music composition. Finally, he describes the procedure by which he crossed over the boundaries of rhythm and pitch in his composition *Kontakte*, with specific reference to the pivotal section between 16:56 and 18:26.

Assessment of Stockhausen's Temporal Theory

The important thing ... is that tone-color is the result of time structure. (Stockhausen 1957, p. 19)

When it was published, "..... *How time passes .....*" presented a new viewpoint on musical time. This viewpoint is more familiar to us now, yet we can still appreciate the depth of Stockhausen's insight. Few articles on music from the 1950s ring with such resonance today.

The quest for a scale of durations for serial composition is no longer a compelling musical problem. Even in the heyday of serial composition, Stockhausen's solution never entered the repertory of common practice. The most prominent American exponent of serial techniques, Milton Babbitt (1962), explicitly rejected the idea of constructing a duration scale from multiples of an elementary unit. For Babbitt, the temporal order of the pitches in the row was more important than the actual durations of the notes. Thus he reduced the problem of serial organization of time to the organization of the instants at which notes started, which he called the *time point set*. (See also Morris 1987.)

Stockhausen's arguments managed to resolve temporarily one of the many contradictions and inconsistencies of serial theory. At the same time, they left unresolved a host of major problems involving perception, notation, traditional instrumental timbre, and higher-level organization. To untangle and examine these issues in detail would require another book. Even if these problems could somehow be magically resolved, it would not automatically "validate" compositions made with these techniques, for music will always be more than a game of logic.

Today it is easier than ever before to compose on all time scales. Yet we must continue to respect the differences between them. In his essay on aesthetic questions in electronic music, the musicologist Carl Dahhaus (1970) criticized the use of identical methodologies for macro and micro composition. As he wisely pointed out, serial methods that are already barely decipherable on the level of notes and phrases disappear into invisibility when applied on the micro-level of tone construction. (See the discussion in chapter 8.)

Henry Cowell's (1930) ideas concerning the relationship between musical time scales precede those of Stockhausen by almost thirty years. Cowell pointed out that rhythms, when sped up, become tones. He introduced the concept of *undertones* at fractional intervals beneath a fundamental tone, leading to the notion of a *rhythmic undertone*. In order to represent divisions of time not easily handled by traditional music notation, Cowell proposed a shape note scheme. He observed that a series of partial frequencies, as seen in spectra, could be used to build a scale of meters or a scale of tempi, with different tempi running simultaneously and various rates of accelerando and ritardando notated graphically. He proposed a scale of dynamic stress:

In spite of its importance, there is no adequate notation for dynamics, and the fine distinctions are left to the performer, although such distinctions might well be considered an essential part of composition. . . . Science can measure the loudness of sound by a number of well-known means. Since we have a familiar instrument for measuring so delicate a thing as rate of speed—namely, a metronome—it would seem that we should also have some simple instrument for the measurement of stress. Then we could devise scales of degrees of stress. This could be done on an additional staff, if desired. (Cowell 1930, pp. 82–3)

Cowell's writings prove that a comprehensive multiscale view of time can be formulated quite independently of serial theory.

". . . . . *How time passes* . . . . ." exemplifies the disadvantages of discussing microtemporal composition within the limits of traditional instrumental writing. It is hard to imagine how certain acoustic instruments could be made to cross between the infrasonic and audio frequencies, where, for example, rhythm turns into pitch and timbre. Stockhausen does not address the question of timbre until the end of the article, when he muses on the possibility of an "ideal instrument."

As noted earlier the technology of synthesis has greatly advanced since Stockhausen wrote in 1957. Another technology that has changed dramatically is that of sound editing and spectrum analysis. Today one can easily probe and alter the inner microrhythm of musical timbre. Stockhausen's spectral view of rhythm can be measured now by applying the short-time Fourier transform to signals in the range ~0.06 Hz to 30 Hz, in order to obtain frequency analyses of rhythm (figure 2.5). Pulsar synthesis, presented in chapter 4, blurs the boundary between the infrasonic and the audio frequency domains, since the fundamental frequency envelope can cross between them to create either rhythm or continuous tone.

After *Kontakte*, Stockhausen discarded impulse generation and processing techniques. He realized only three more works in the electronic music studio. Both *Telemusik* (1966), composed at the studios of the NHK in Tokyo, and *Hymnen* (1967) composed in Cologne, reflected the composer's interest in intermodulation based on recordings of world music. Then, after a hiatus of twenty-three years, *Oktophonie* (1990) realized in collaboration with his son,

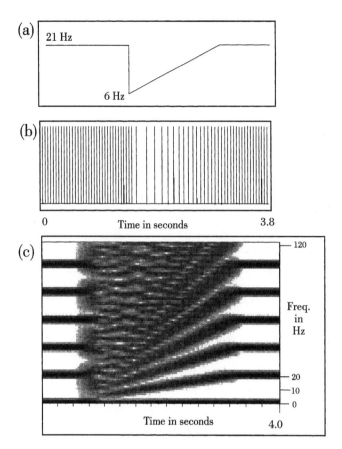

Figure 2.5 Spectrum analysis of infrasonic (rhythmic) frequencies. (a) Fundamental frequency envelope of a pulsar train. (b) Time-domain view of pulsar train. (c) Infraspectrum of pulsar train.

focused on the movement in space of long sustained tones produced by commercial synthesizers. None of these works, however, continues or extends the theoretical principles underlying *Kontakte*.

Other Assessments of Stockhausen's Temporal Theory

Christopher Koenigsberg (1991) presented a balanced analysis of Stockhausen's temporal theory and of its critics. His review prompted me to revisit these contemporaneous critiques. The most heated seem to have been provoked by Stockhausen's nonstandard terminology. The American acoustician John Backus wrote:

In physics, a quantum is an undivisible unit; there are no quanta in acoustical phenomena. (Backus 1962, p. 18; see also Backus 1969, p. 280)

Backus had probably not read Gabor's papers. And while certain of his criticisms concerning terminology are valid, they tend to focus on the details of a much broader range of musical ideas. The same can be said of Adriaan Fokker's (1962) comments. G. M. Koenig's (1962) response to Fokker's critique attempts to re-explicate Stockhausen's theories. But Koenig manages to be even more confusing than the original because of his insistence on defending its nonstandard terminology. This leads him to some arcane arguments, such as the convoluted attempt to explain the word "phase" (Koenig 1962, pp. 82–5). (See also Davies 1964, 1965.)

Milton Babbitt's (1962) proposal on *time-point sets*, which we have already mentioned, was published in the same issue of *Perspectives of New Music* as the Backus attack on Stockhausen's article. This might have been intentional, since Babbitt's theory was an alternative proposal for a set-theory approach to rhythmic structure. The theory of time-point sets, however, left open the question of which durations to use, and was not concerned with creating a unique scale of equal-tempered durations. Babbitt broached the possibility of microrhythms, but never followed up on this concept.

Microsound in the Analog Domain

The wave model of sound informed the design of early analog electronic instruments (table 2.1). The Thereminovox, for example, operated in continuous wave emission—always oscillating—with one hand controlling the amplitude of the emitted tone. In the hands of a virtuoso, such as Clara Rockmore or Lydia Kavina, these instruments produce expressive tones, although the duration and density of these tones never approaches the microsonic threshold.

Further examples of a timeless wave model include the sine and pulse generators of the pioneering electronic music studios. These devices were designed for precise, repeatable, and unchanging output, not for real time performance. A typical generator might have a vernier dial for frequency, but with the sweepable frequency range broken into steps. This meant that a continuous sweep, say from 1 Hz to 10 kHz, was not possible. The amplitude and waveform controls typically offered several switchable settings.

Analog magnetic tape offered a breakthrough for microsound processing. In discussing the musique concrète of the early 1950s, M. Chion wrote:

Soon the tape recorder, which was used in the musique concrète, would replace the turntable. It allowed editing, which was difficult with the vinyl disc. The possibility of assembling tight mosaics of sound fragments with magnetic tape definitively launched electroacoustic music. The first pieces for tape were "micro-edited," using as their basis sounds that were reduced to the dust of temporal atoms (Pierre Henry's Vocalises, *Boulez's* Etudes, *Stockhausen's* Étude Concrète*). In this "analytic" period, one sought the atomic fission of sound, and magnetic tape (running at the time at 76 cm/s) was seen as having a tangible duration that could be cut up ad infinitum, up to one hundred parts per second, allowing the realization of abstract rhythmic speculations that human performers could never play, as in the* Timbres-Durées *(1953) of Olivier Messaien.*   (Chion 1982)

Composers could record the emissions from laboratory generators on tape, using a potentiometer in the recording chain to vary the amplitude manually. The duration of the tones could be rearranged by tape cutting and splicing, and the spectrum could be altered by filtering. Even so, the precision of these operations was, as G. M. Koenig explained, limited:

If the frequency of tuning is 440 cycles per second . . . The individual vibration period thus lasts 1/440th of a second. But the studio has not a device at its disposal which makes it possible to open a generator for this length of time, should one want to use a single period. Even if such a device were available, the tape would still have to be cut off 0.068 of an inch. . . . It has become possible to assemble timbres from components in the studio, but on the other hand it is impossible determine their absolute duration at will, because of the limitations of the "instrument," namely the apparatus in the electronic studio.   (Koenig 1959)

Presaging the advent of digital particle synthesis, he goes on:

If one could get around this obstacle, composition of timbre could be transposed to a time region in which individual elements would hardly be audible any longer. The sound would last not seconds ... but only milliseconds.... Instead of five sounds, we should compose fifty, so that the number of points in the timetable would radically increase. But these points would not be filled out with sinus tones perceptible as such, but single periods, which would only be audible en masse, as a fluctuating timbre. (Koenig 1959)

Only by the mid 1970s, through the introduction of digital technology, was it feasible to experiment with microsound in the manner predicted by Koenig. (See chapter 3.) Digital editing on any time scale did not become possible until the late 1980s.

The novel sound of analog circuitry was used brilliantly in early works by Stockhausen, Koenig, and Xenakis to create a new musical world based on microsonic fluctuations. The acoustical signature of analog generators and filters remains a useful resource for twenty-first century composers. At the same time, one must recognize the constraints imposed by analog techniques, which can be traced to a finite class of waveforms and the difficulty of controlling their evolution on a micro level. New analog synthesizers have been introduced into the marketplace, but they are no more than variations on a well-established theme. There is little room for further evolution in analog technology.

Microsound in the Instrumental Domain

In his early orchestral pieces *Metastasis, Pithoprakta,* and *Achorripsis,* Iannis Xenakis creates sparse or dense clouds made of brief, irregular notes, especially string pizzicati. Similar techniques abound in certain compositions of Ligeti and Penderecki, among others, from the 1960s and 1970s. During this period the "stochastic cloud" was sometimes reduced to a special effect. Although this was taken up by many other composers, little new has been added.

Detailed micro control of intricate multipart acoustic music is not practical. Technical, social, and economic obstacles have to be overcome in order to pursue this path, and those who try to coax unwilling institutions, performers, and instruments to realize microtemporal music go against the grain of the music establishment.

A composer whose instrument is the computer does not face these limitations. Thus a more practical strategy for the composer who seeks a link to traditional sonorities seems to be a mixed approach, combining instrumental performance with electronic processing (granulation, for example, see chapter 5) and synthetic sound.

Summary

The notion that apparently continuous phenomena can be subdivided into particles can be traced to the atomistic philosophers of Greek antiquity. Debates between proponents of the "wave" and "particle" views in optics and acoustics have occupied scientists for centuries. These debates were central to the formation of early modern science.

The contemporary scientific view of microsound dates back to Dennis Gabor, who applied the concept of an acoustic quantum (already introduced by Einstein) to the threshold of human hearing. With Meyer-Eppler as intermediary, the pioneering composers Xenakis, Stockhausen, and Koenig injected this radical notion into music. Xenakis's theory of granular synthesis has proven to be an especially inspiring paradigm. It has directly influenced me and many other composers who have employed granular techniques in their works. Over decades, a microsonic perspective has gradually emerged from the margins of musical thought to take its present place as a valuable fountain of compositional ideas.

3   Granular Synthesis

Theory of Granular Synthesis
    Anatomy of a Grain
    The Grain Generator
    Global Organization of the Grains
        Matrices and Screens on the Time-Frequency Plane
        Pitch-Synchronous Granular Synthesis
        Synchronous and Quasi-Synchronous Granular Synthesis
        Pitch and Noise Perception in Synchronous Granular Synthesis
        Asynchronous Granular Synthesis
        Physical and Algorithmic Models
        Streams and Clouds of Granulated Samples
    Spectra of Granular Streams
    Parameters of Granular Synthesis
        Grain Envelope Shape Effects
        Experiments in Time Reversal
        Grain Duration Effects
        Grain Waveform Effects
        Frequency Band Effects
        Density and Fill Factor
        Granular Spatial Effects
    Granular Clouds as Sound Objects
    Cloud Mixtures

Implementations of Granular Synthesis

    The Author's Implementations of Granular Synthesis

    Other Implementations of Granular Synthesis

Summary

To stubbornly conditioned ears, anything new in music has always been called noise. But after all, what is music but organized noises?
—Edgard Varèse (1962)

Digital sound synthesis techniques inhabit a virtual world more pure and precise than the physical world, and purity and precision have an undeniable charm in music. In the right hands, an unadorned sine wave can be a lush and evocative sonority. A measured pulsation can invite emotional catharsis. Synthesis, however, should be able to render expressive turbulence, intermittency, and singularity; the overuse of precision and purity can lead to sterile music. Sonic grains, and techniques used to scatter the grains in evocative patterns, can achieve these results.

This chapter is devoted entirely to granular synthesis (GS). I present its theory, the history of its implementations, a report on experiments, and an assessment of its strengths and weaknesses. A thorough understanding of the principles of granular synthesis is fundamental to understanding the other techniques presented in this book. This chapter focuses on synthesis with synthetic waveforms. Since granulation transforms an existing sound, I present the granulation of sampled sound in chapter 5 with other particle-based transformations.

Theory of Granular Synthesis

The seeds of granular synthesis can be traced back to antiquity, although it was only after the papers of Gabor and Xenakis that these seeds began to take root (see chapter 2). A grain of sound is a brief microacoustic event, with a duration near the threshold of human auditory perception, typically between one thousandth of a second and one tenth of a second (from 1 to 100 ms). Each grain contains a waveform shaped by an amplitude envelope (figure 3.1).

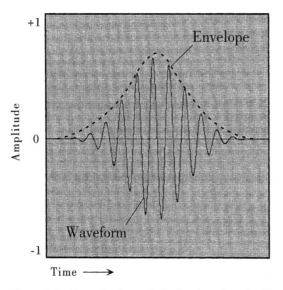

Figure 3.1   Portrait of a grain in the time domain. The duration of the grain is typically between 1 and 100 ms.

A single grain serves as a building block for sound objects. By combining thousands of grains over time, we can create animated sonic atmospheres. The grain is an apt representation of musical sound because it captures two perceptual dimensions: time-domain information (starting time, duration, envelope shape) and frequency-domain information (the pitch of the waveform within the grain and the spectrum of the grain). This stands in opposition to sample-based representations that do not capture frequency-domain information, and abstract Fourier methods, which account only for the frequency domain.

Granular synthesis requires a massive amount of control data. If n is the number of parameters per grain, and d is the density of grains per second, it takes n times d parameter values to specify one second of sound. Since n is usually greater than ten and d can exceed one thousand, it is clear that a global unit of organization is necessary for practical work. That is, the composer specifies the sound in global terms, while the granular synthesis algorithm fills in the details. This greatly reduces the amount of data that the composer must supply, and certain forms of granular synthesis can be played in real time with simple MIDI controllers. The major differences between the various granular techniques are found in these global organizations and algorithms.

Anatomy of a Grain

A grain of sound lasts a short time, approaching the minimum perceivable event time for duration, frequency, and amplitude discrimination (Whitfield 1978; Meyer-Eppler 1959; Winckel 1967). Individual grains with a duration less than about 2 ms (corresponding to fundamental frequencies > 500 Hz) sound like clicks. However one can still change the waveform and frequency of grains and so vary the tone color of the click. When hundreds of short-duration grains fill a cloud texture, minor variations in grain duration cause strong effects in the spectrum of the cloud mass. Hence even very short grains can be useful musically.

Short grains withhold the impression of pitch. At 5 ms it is vague, becoming clearer by 25 ms. The longer the grain, the more surely the ear can hear its pitch.

An amplitude envelope shapes each grain. In Gabor's original conception, the envelope is a bell-shaped curve generated by the Gaussian method (figure 3.2a).

$$p(x) = \frac{1}{\sqrt{2^{\pi}}} e^{-x^2/2} \, dx$$

A variation on the pure Gaussian curve is a *quasi-Gaussian envelope* (Roads 1978a, 1985), also known as a *cosine taper* or *Tukey window* (Harris 1978). This envelope can be imagined as a cosine lobe convolved with a rectangle (figure 3.2b). It transitions smoothly at the extrema of the envelope while maximizing the effective amplitude. This quality persuaded me to use it in my earliest experiments with granular synthesis.

In the early days of real-time granular synthesis, it was necessary to use simple line-segment envelopes to save memory space and computation time (Truax 1987, 1988). Gabor (1946) also suggested line-segment envelopes for practical reasons (figure 3.2c and d). Keller and Rolfe (1998) have analyzed the spectral artefacts introduced by a line-segment trapezoidal window. Specifically, the frequency response is similar to that of a Gaussian window, with the addition of comb-shaped spectral effects. Null points in the spectrum are proportional to the position of the corners of the window.

Figure 3.2e portrays another type of envelope, the band-limited pulse or sinc function. The sidelobes (ripples) of this envelope impose a strong modulation effect. The percussive, exponentially decaying envelope or *expodec grain*

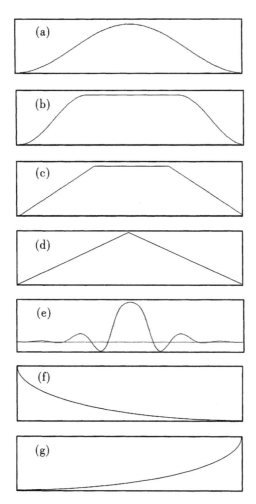

Figure 3.2   Grain envelopes. (a) Gaussian. (b) Quasi-Gaussian. (c) Three-stage line segment. (d) Triangular. (e) Sinc function. (f) Expodec. (g) Rexpodec.

(figure 3.2f) has proven to be effective in transformations such as convolution (described in chapter 5). Figure 3.2g depicts the reversed expodec or *rexpodec* grain. Later we study the strong effect the grain envelope imposes on the spectrum.

The grain envelope and duration can vary in a frequency-dependent manner (shorter envelopes for high frequency sounds); such a correlation is characteristic of the wavelet transform (see chapter 6), and of the grainlet synthesis technique described in chapter 4.

The waveform within the grain is an important grain parameter. It can vary from grain to grain, be a fixed waveform that does not change over the grain's duration, or it can be a time-varying waveform. Typical fixed waveforms include the sine wave and sums of sine waves with increasing harmonic content up to a bandlimited pulse. A time-varying waveform can be generated by frequency modulation or another mathematical technique (Jones and Parks 1988). The grain waveform can also be a single period extracted from a recorded sound. This differs from granulation (chapter 5), which scans across a long sampled waveform, extracting many different grains over time.

Other parameters of the grain include its duration, the frequency of its waveform, its amplitude coefficient, and its spatial location. We examine these parameters later.

The Grain Generator

In its most basic form, the grain generator is a simple digital synthesis instrument. Its circuit consists of a wavetable oscillator whose amplitude is controlled by a Gaussian envelope. The output of the oscillator goes to a spatial panner (figure 3.3).

As a general principle of synthesis, we can trade off instrument complexity for score complexity. A simple instrument suffices, because the complexity of the sound derives from the changing combinations of many grains. Hence we must furnish a massive stream of control data for each parameter of the instrument.

Despite the simplicity of the instrument, we gain two spectral controls for free, owing to the specific properties of the micro time scale. Specifically, variations in the grain duration and the grain envelope affect the spectrum of the resulting signal (as a later of this book section clarifies).

Of course, we can always make the granular synthesis instrument more complex, for instance by adding a local frequency control, per-grain reverberation,

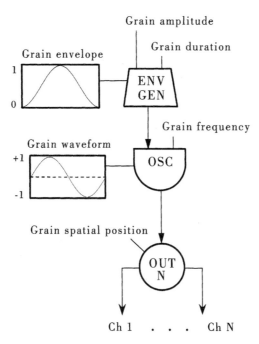

Figure 3.3 The simplest grain generator, featuring a Gaussian grain envelope and a sinusoidal grain waveform. The grains can be scattered to a position in *N* channels of output.

multichannel output, etc. Chapter 4 describes several extensions to the basic granular instrument.

Global Organization of the Grains

The main forms of granular synthesis can be divided into six types, according to how each organizes the grains. They are:

- Matrices and screens on the time-frequency plane
- Pitch-synchronous overlapping streams
- Synchronous and quasi-synchronous streams
- Asynchronous clouds
- Physical or abstract models
- Granulation of sampled sound

Matrices and Screens on the Time-Frequency Plane

The Gabor matrix, shown in chapter 2, is the original time-frequency matrix for sound, based on the analysis of an existing sound. In the same general family are the analyses produced by the short-time Fourier transform (STFT) and the wavelet transform (WT), presented in chapter 6. These operations transform a time-domain signal into a frequency-domain representation that is quantized in both the time and frequency dimensions, creating a two-dimensional matrix. Frequency-domain matrices offer many opportunities for sound transformation.

A related organizational scheme is Xenakis's (1960, 1971) notion of screens (also described in chapter 2). Each screen is like a snapshot of a microsound. It represents a Gabor matrix at a specific moment, divided into cells of amplitude and frequency. Like the frames of a film, a synchronous sequence of screens constitutes the evolution of a complex sound. Rather than starting from an analyzed sound, Xenakis proposed to fill the screen with grains by means of stochastic algorithms. Another proposal suggested that the grains be generated from the interaction of cellular automata (Bowcott 1989; Miranda 1998).

Pitch-Synchronous Granular Synthesis

Pitch-synchronous granular synthesis (PSGS) is an efficient analysis-synthesis technique designed for the generation of pitched sounds with one or more formant regions in their spectra (De Poli and Piccialli 1991). It begins with a spectrum analysis of a sound. Each time-frequency cell corresponds to a grain. As a preparation for resynthesis, at each grain boundary along the frequency axis, a standard algorithm derives the coefficients for a filter. The impulse response of this filter corresponds to the frequency response of the cell. At each grain boundary along the time axis, a pitch detection algorithm determines the fundamental pitch period. In resynthesis, a pulsetrain at the detected frequency drives a bank of parallel minimum-phase finite impulse response filters. The musical signal results from the excitation of the pulsetrain on the weighted sum of the impulse responses of all the filters. At each grain time frame, the system emits a waveform that is overlapped with the previous grain to create a smoothly varying signal. An implementation of PSGS by De Poli and Piccialli features several transformations that can create variations of the original sound. A focus of their implementation was the use of data reduction techniques to save computation and memory space. See De Poli and Piccialli (1991), and Cavaliere and Piccialli (1997) for details.

Synchronous and Quasi-Synchronous Granular Synthesis

Granular streams appear naturally from iterative sound production—any kind of roll or trill on drums, percussion, or any sounding material. They are produced vocally by rolled "r" sounds. (Wishart 1994)

In *synchronous granular synthesis* (SGS), sound results from one or more streams of grains. Within each stream, one grain follows another, with a delay period between the grains. "Synchronous" means that the grains follow each other at regular intervals.

An excellent use of SGS is to generate metric rhythms, particularly when the grain emissions are sparse per unit of time. The density parameter controls the frequency of grain emission, so *grains per second* can be interpreted as a frequency value in Hertz. For example, a density of 1 grain per second indicates that a grain is produced every second. Synchronous densities in the range of about 0.1 to 20 grains per second will generate metrical rhythms. When densities change over time, the listener hears accelerandi and rallentandi.

At higher densities, the grains fuse into continuous tones. Here is found the sweeter side of granular synthesis. These tones have a strong fundamental frequency, and depending on the grain envelope and duration, may also exhibit sidebands. The sidebands may sound like separate pitches or they may blend into a formant peak. At certain settings, these tones exhibit a marked vocal-like quality. In these cases, SGS resembles other techniques such as FOF and Vosim synthesis. Chapter 4 describes these particle-based formant synthesis methods.

The formant shape and strength depend greatly on the grain duration and density which also, under certain conditions, affect the perceived fundamental frequency. We explore this in more detail in the next section.

In *quasi-synchronous granular synthesis* (QSGS), the grains follow each other at unequal intervals, where a random deviation factor determines the irregularity. If the irregularity is great, the sounds produced by this method become similar to those produced by asynchronous granular synthesis. SGS and QSGS are well-adapted to real-time implementations.

Pitch and Noise Perception in Synchronous Granular Synthesis

The fragility of the illusion of pitch is made apparent in SGS. The perceived pitch of a granular stream depends primarily on interactions among three periodicities:

a is the period corresponding to the frequency of the waveform in the grain

b is the period corresponding to the grain envelope

c is the period corresponding to the density, or rate of synchronous grain emission

One or another of these factors may override the others in determining the perceived pitch. In certain cases, modulations caused by their interaction may render the pitch—and especially the specific octave—ambiguous.

Figure 3.4 illustrates these effects. Consider a tone made up of a series of 10 ms grains, where each grain contains two periods of a 200 Hz sine wave. Assume, as in figure 3.4a, that the density of the grains is 50 per second. Here we have:

$a = 5$ ms

$b = 10$ ms

$c = 20$ ms

As figure 3.4a shows, the 10 ms gap between *b* and *c* means that there is a *dead interval* between successive grains, leading to a modulation effect with its associated sidebands. The perceived pitch is a buzzy 100 Hz.

A linear increase in grain density (from 50 to 100 grains per second in the above case) causes a pitch doubling effect. The perceived pitch is now 200 Hz. Here the three variables take the values:

$a = 5$ ms

$b = 10$ ms

$c = 10$ ms

In figure 3.4c, the grain density is 200 grains per second. The variables take these values:

$a = 5$ ms

$b = 10$ ms

$c = 5$ ms

Now we have a pure sinusoidal tone. Only one period of the waveform can unfold within the grain repetition period *c*, and the influence of the grain envelope *b* is diminished.

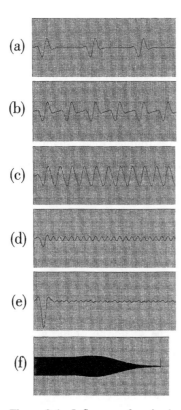

Figure 3.4 Influence of grain density on pitch. The waveforms in (a) through (e) last 59 ms. (a) 50 grains/sec. (b) 100 grains/sec. (c) 200 grains/sec. (d) 400 grains/sec. (e) 500 grains/sec. (f) Plot of a granular stream sweeping from the infrasonic frequency of 10 grains/sec to the audio frequency of 500 grains/sec over thirty seconds.

When the grain density increases to 400 grains per second (figure 3.4d), the perceived pitch doubles to 400 Hz. This is due to the increasing frequency of wavefronts (as in the well-known Doppler shift effect). Notice that the amplitude of tone diminishes after beginning, however, because the density period c is less than the waveform period a. Only the first few samples of the product of the sine wavetable and the grain envelope are being repeated, resulting in a low-amplitude signal.

Finally, at a density of 500 grains per second (figure 3.4e), the signal has almost no amplitude. It is reading only the first few samples of the sinusoid, which are near zero.

Figure 3.4f shows the amplitude profile of a granular stream that sweeps from 10 grains per second to 500 grains per second over thirty seconds. Notice the diminution of amplitude due to the effect shown in figure 3.4e.

Besides pitch changes, other anomalies, such as phase cancellation, can occur when the grain density and envelope duration are at odds with the frequency of the grain waveform.

Even the impression of synchronicity can be undermined. If we widen the frequency limits of a dense synchronous stream slightly, the result quickly truns into a noiseband. The fact that the grain emissions are regular and the frequency changes at regular intervals (for example, every 1 ms), does not alter the general impression of noise. The effect is similar to that produced by asynchronous granular synthesis, described next.

Asynchronous Granular Synthesis

Asynchronous granular synthesis (AGS) abandons the concept of linear streams of grains. Instead, it scatters the grains over a specified duration within regions inscribed on the time-frequency plane. These regions are clouds—the units with which the composer works. The scattering of the grains is irregular in time, being controlled by a stochastic or chaotic algorithm. The composer may specify a cloud with the following parameters:

1. Start-time and duration of the cloud

2. Grain duration—may vary over the duration of the cloud

3. Density of grains per second, with a maximum density depending upon the implementation; density can vary over the duration of the cloud

4. Frequency band of the cloud; specified by two curves forming high and low frequency boundaries within which grains are scattered; alternatively, the frequency of the grains in a cloud can be restricted to a specific set of pitches

5. Amplitude envelope of the cloud

6. Waveform(s) within the grains

7. Spatial dispersion of the cloud, where the number of output channels is implementation-specific

The grain duration (2) can be a constant (in milliseconds), or a variable that changes over the course of a cloud. (It can also be correlated to other parameters, as in the grainlet synthesis described in chapter 4.) Grain duration can also be derived as a random value between an upper and a lower boundary set by the user. The next section explains the effects of different grain durations in more detail.

Parameter (3), grain density, specifies the number of grains per unit of time. For example, if the grain density is low, then only a few grains are scattered at random points within the cloud. If the grain density is high, grains overlap to create rich, complex spectra.

Parameter (6) is one of the most flexible cloud parameters, since each grain may have a its own waveform.

Physical and Algorithmic Models

Physical modeling (PhM) synthesis starts from a mathematical description of acoustic sound production (Roads 1996; Fletcher and Rossing 1991). That is, the equations of PhM describe the mechanical and acoustical behavior of an instrument as it is played. An example of physical modeling applied to granular synthesis is Perry Cook's Physically Informed Stochastic Event Modeling (PhISEM). This suite of programs simulates the sounds of shaken and scraped percussion such as maracas, sekere, cabasa, bamboo windchime, tambourine, sleighbells, and guiro (Cook 1996, 1997). See more about this technique in chapter 4. Going beyond traditional instruments, Keller and Truax created sound models of such physical processes as the bounce of a metallic ball and the rush of a stream of water (Keller and Truax 1998). Physical models of granular processes could be taken still further. A large body of scientific literature centers on granular processes such as grain mixing, granular flow, grain vibration patterns, and grain and fluid interactions. This literature appears in research periodicals such as *Granular Matter, Powders and Grains, Powder Technology, Journal of Fluid Mechanics, Physical Review, Journal of Applied Mechanics*, as well as such Internet web sites as www.granular.com.

Going beyond emulations of the natural world, one can also develop models of virtual worlds through abstract algorithms. To cite an example, Alberto de Campo (1998) proposed a method of grain scattering in time based on a recursive substitution algorithm. Another idea would be using *chaotic functions* to scatter the grains in time (Gleick 1988; Holden 1986; Moon 1987). Chaotic functions produce different results from scattering algorithms based on pseudorandom algorithms. The values produced by pseudorandom number generators tend to be uniform and adirectional, tending toward the mean. To make them directional, they must be filtered through stochastic weightings. In contrast, chaotic functions vacillate between stable and unstable states, between intermittent transients and full turbulence (Di Scipio 1990, 1997b; Gogins 1991, 1995; Miranda 1998). The challenge is to set up a musically compelling mapping between chaotic behavior and the synthesis parameters.

Streams and Clouds of Granulated Samples

The granulation of sampled sounds is a powerful means of sound transformation. To granulate means to segment (or window) a sound signal into grains, to possibly modify them in some way, and then to reassemble the grains in a new time order and microrhythm. This might take the form of a continuous stream or of a statistical cloud of sampled grains.

The exact manner in which granulation occurs will vary from implementation to implementation. Chapter 5 includes a major section on granulation so here we shall limit the discussion to noting, that granulation can be controlled by any of the global control structures described above.

Spectra of Granular Streams

When the intervals between successive grains are equal, the overall envelope of a stream of grains forms a periodic function. Since the envelope is periodic, the signal generated by SGS can be analyzed as a case of *amplitude modulation* or AM. AM occurs when the shape of one signal (the *modulator*) determines the amplitude of another signal (the *carrier*). From a signal processing standpoint, we observe that for each sinusoidal component in the carrier, the periodic envelope function contributes a series of *sidebands* to the final spectrum. (Sidebands are additional frequency components above and below the frequency of the carrier.) The sidebands separate from the carrier by a distance corresponding to the inverse of the period of the envelope function. For grains lasting 20 ms, therefore, the sidebands in the output spectrum will be spaced at 50 Hz intervals. The shape of the grain envelope determines the precise number and amplitude weighting of these sidebands.

The result of modulation by a periodic envelope is that of a formant surrounding the carrier frequency. That is, instead of a single line in the spectrum (a single frequency), the spectrum looks like a sloping peak (a group of frequencies around the carrier). In the case of a bell-shaped Guassian envelope, the spectrum is similarly bell-shaped. In other words, for a Gaussian envelope, the spectrum is an *eigenfunction* of the time envelope.

When the delay interval between the grains is irregular, perfect grain synchronization disappears. The randomization of the onset time of each grain leads to a controllable thickening of the sound spectrum—a "blurring" of the formant structure (Truax 1988).

In its simplest form, the variable-delay method is similar to amplitude modulation using low-frequency colored noise as a modulator. In itself, this is not particularly new or interesting. The granular representation, however, lets us move far beyond simple noise-modulated AM. We can simultaneously vary several other parameters on a grain-by-grain basis, such as grain waveform, amplitude, duration, and spatial location. On a global level, we can also dynamically vary the density of grains per second, creating a variety of scintillation effects.

Parameters of Granular Synthesis

Research into sound synthesis is governed by aesthetic goals as much as by scientific curiosity. Some of the most interesting synthesis techniques have resulted from applied practice, rather than from formal theory. Sound design requires taste and skill and at the experimentation stage, musical intuition is the primary guide.

Grain Envelope Shape Effects

Of Loose Atomes

In every Braine loose Atomes there do lye,
Those which are Sharpe, from them do Fancies flye.
Those that are long, and Aiery, nimble be.
But Atomes Round, and Square, are dull, and sleepie.
(Margaret Cavendish 1653)

This section presents empirical reports on the effects caused by manipulating the grain envelope, duration, waveform, frequency, band, density, and spatial parameters.

Referring back to figure 3.2, the classical grain envelope is the bell-shaped Gaussian curve (figure 3.2a). This is the smoothest envelope from a mathematical point of view. A quasi-Gaussian (Tukey) envelope retains the smooth attack and decay but has a longer sustain portion in the envelope and so increases its perceived amplitude (figure 3.2b). Compared to a pure Gaussian of the same duration, the quasi-Gaussian broadens the spectrum. Its highest sidelobe is only −18 dB down, as opposed to −42 dB for a pure Gaussian curve (Harris 1978). The band-limited pulse or sinc function imposes a strong modulation effect (figure 3.2e). I have used it myself to create "bubbling" or "frying" clouds.

I have carried out numerous experiments using grain envelopes with a sharp attack (typically less than 10 ms) and an exponential decay. These are the expodec grains (figure 3.2f). The percussive attack of the expodec articulates the rhythmic structure. As chapter 5 describes, clouds of expodec grains can be especially useful as impulse responses for convolution with other sounds. Reversed expodec or rexpodec grains feature a long attack envelope with a sudden decay (figure 3.2g). Granulated concrète sounds appear to be "reversed" when they are played with rexpodec grains, even though they are not.

While keeping the envelope shape constant, a change in the grain duration has a strong effect on the spectrum. Furthermore, the grain envelope and duration can vary in a frequency-dependent manner (shorter envelopes for high frequency sounds); such a correlation is characteristic of the wavelet transform and the grainlets.

Experiments in Time Reversal

The concept of time has been thoroughly twisted by modern theoretical physics (Kaku 1995). Barry Truax (1990b) drew an analogy between the world of particle physics—in which time appears to be reversible at the quantum level—and granular synthesis. According to his hypothesis, if a grain is reversed in time, it should sound the same. Moreover, granular synthesis textures should also be reversible. Such a position would also follow on from Trevor Wishart's assertion:

Although the internal structure of sounds is the cause of what we hear, we do not resolve this internal structure in our perception. The experience of a grain is indivisible.   (Wishart 1994)

Under special circumstances, all of this is quite true. But if we loosen any one of a number of constraints, time reversibility does not hold. For it to hold at the micro scale, the grain envelope must be symmetrical. This, then, excludes asymmetric techniques such as FOF grains (Rodet 1980), trainlets (chapter 4), expodec, or rexpodec grains. The grain waveform must not alter in time, so excluding techniques such as the time-varying FM grains (Jones and Parks 1988), long glissons (chapter 4), or grains whose waveform derives from a time-varying sampled sound. With texture a grain stream or cloud is time-reversible only if it is stationary in the statistical sense, meaning that its overall amplitude and spectral envelopes are symmetrical, its internal density is constant, and the waveform of all the grains is similar.

Grain Duration Effects

The duration of the grains inside a cloud has profound effects on the resulting audio signal. Within clouds, there are four classes of grain durations:

1. *Constant duration*   the duration of every grain in the cloud is the same.
2. *Time-varying duration*   the grain duration varies as a function of time.
3. *Random duration*   the duration of a grain is random between an upper and lower duration boundaries.
4. *Parameter-dependent duration*   the duration of a grain is tied to its fundamental frequency period, as it is in synthesis with wavelets, or any other parameter, as in the grainlet synthesis.

Regarding constant durations, early estimates of the optimum grain duration varied from 10 ms (Gabor 1946, 1947) to 60 ms (Moles 1968).

The grain envelope contributes an amplitude modulation (AM) effect. The modulation spawns sidebands around the carrier frequency of the grain at intervals of the envelope period. If the grain duration is D, the center frequency of the AM is $1/D$. In an asynchronous cloud, the AM sounds like an aperiodic fluttering tremolo when D is around 100 ms (table 3.1).

Table 3.1   Effects of grain durations in asynchronous granular synthesis

Grain duration	Frequency of modulation	Perceived effect
200 μsec	5 KHz	Noisy particulate disintegration
500 μsec	2 KHz	
1 ms	1 KHz	Loss of pitch
10 ms	100 Hz	Fluttering, gurgling
50 ms	20 Hz	Stable pitch formation
100 ms	10 Hz	
200 ms	5 Hz	Aperiodic tremolo, jittering

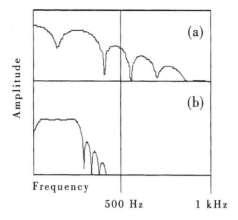

Figure 3.5 Comparison of grain spectra produced by a 7 ms grain duration (top) versus a 29 ms grain duration (bottom). Notice the narrowing of the spectrum as the duration lengthens.

The laws of micro-acoustics tell us that the shorter the duration of a signal, the greater its bandwidth. Thus the width of the frequency band B caused by the sidebands is inversely proportional to the duration of the grain D (figure 3.5).

A dramatic effect occurs when the grain duration is lowered to below the period of the grain waveform. This results in a signal that is entirely unipolar in energy, which is a byproduct of the ratio of the grain duration to the fundamental frequency period P_f of the grain waveform, or D/P_f. The effect is caused by an incomplete scan of the wavetable, where the waveform starts in either the positive or the negative quadrant. It occurs whenever D/P_f is less than 1.0. In the specific case of a 1 ms grain with a fundamental frequency of 500 Hz, the ratio is $0.001/0.002 = 1/2$.

To completely represent one period of a given frequency, the grain duration must be at least equal to the frequency period. If we took this criterion as a standard, grains could last no less than 50 ms (corresponding to the period of 20 Hz) for low frequency signal energy to be captured completely. As it happens however, much shorter grains can represent low frequency signals, but this short grain duration introduces modulation products. Our experiments show that grains shorter than 5 ms tend to generate particulated clouds in which a sense of center-pitch is still present but is diffused by noise as the frequency descends.

Grain Waveform Effects

One of the most interesting features of granular synthesis is that one can insert any waveform into a grain. The waveform can vary on a grain-by-grain basis. This makes possibile micro-animated textures that evolve directionally over time or simply scintillate from the effects of constantly changing grain waveforms.

The simplest grain waveforms are the fixed synthetic types: the sine, saw, square, and sinc (band-limited impulse). In early experiments, I used ten synthetic waveforms created by adding one to ten sine waves in a harmonic relationship.

Interspersing different waveforms in a single cloud leads to cloud *color type* (Roads 1991). Three possibilities for cloud color type are:

- *monochrome*   containing a single waveform
- *polychrome*   containing two or more waveforms
- *transchrome*   the grain waveform evolves from one waveform to another over the duration of the cloud

For a monochrome cloud, we stipulate a single wavetable for the entire cloud. For a polychrome cloud, we specify two or more waveforms which can scatter uniformly in time or according to a time-varying tendency curve. For a transchrome cloud, if we specify a list of N waveforms, the cloud mutates from one to the next, through all N over its duration.

So far we have discussed waveform variations on the time scale of clouds. But even within a single grain, the waveform may be varying in time. The grain waveform could be generated by time-varying frequency modulation, for example. Since the duration of the grain is brief, however, such techniques tend to result in noisy, distorted textures unless the modulating frequencies and the amount of modulation are strictly controlled.

As a practical aside, it has been necessary to use the standard 44.1 or 48 kHz sampling rates for software and hardware compatibility in recording, synthesis, and playback. These sampling rates provide little "frequency headroom," and one must be aware that when the fundamental frequency of a grain is high and the waveform is complex, aliasing can occur. To avoid this, one can constrain the choice of waveform depending on the fundamental frequency, particularly in the region above half of the Nyquist frequency (11.025 or 12 kHz, depending on the sampling rate). Above these limits, waveforms other than sine cause foldover. For this reason, higher sampling rates are better for digital synthesis.

The grain waveform can also be extracted from a sampled sound. In this case, a single extracted waveform is fed to an oscillator, which reads the waveform repetitively at different frequencies. In Cloud Generator, for example, the extracted waveform constitutes the first 2048 samples (46 ms) of a selected sound file (see the appendix). This differs from granulation, which extracts many different segments of a long sample file. See chapter 5.

Frequency Band Effects

Frequency band parameters limit the fundamental frequencies of grain waveforms. Within the upper and lower boundaries of the band, the grain generator scatters grains. This scattering can be aligned to a frequency scale or to random frequencies. When the frequency distribution is random and the band is greater than a small interval, the result is a complex texture, where pitch is ambiguous or unidentifiable. The combined AM effects of the grain envelope and grain density strongly influence pitch and spectrum.

To generate harmonic texture, we can constrain the choice of fundamental frequency to a particular set of pitches within a scale. We distinguish two classes of frequency specifications:

Cumulus   The frequencies of the grains scatter uniformly within the upper and lower bounds of a single band specified by the composer.

Stratus   The frequencies of the grains align to a set of specified frequencies.

Figure 3.6 depicts a variety of frequency band specifications for granular clouds. When the band centers on a single frequency (figure 3.6a), the cloud produces a single pitch. The frequency can be changed to create a glissando (figure 3.6b). A stratus cloud contains multiple frequency specifications (figure 3.6c). With sampled soundfiles, one can achieve the harmonic effect of a stratus cloud by keeping a database of tones at all the pitches from a desired scale, or by pitch-shifting in conjunction with granulation. When the band is wider than a single pitch, grains scatter randomly between the upper and lower boundaries of a cumulus cloud (figure 3.6d). When the initial and final bands are different, the shape of the cumulus band changes over time (figure 3.6e). In the most flexible case, two time-varying curves shape the bandlimits of the cloud (figure 3.6f).

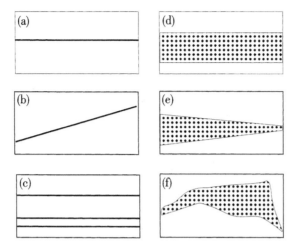

Figure 3.6 Frequency band specifications. (a) The band centers on a single frequency. (b) The center frequency changes over time, creating a glissando effect. (c) Stratus cloud with several frequencies. (d) Cumulus cloud where the grains scatter randomly between the upper and lower boundaries. (e) The shape of the cumulus band changes over time. (f) Time-varying curves shape the bandlimits of the cumulus cloud.

Density and Fill Factor

"Density" is the number of grains per second. If this specification is not linked with the grain duration, however, it tells us little about the resulting texture. Grain duration and density combined produce texture.

A one-second cloud containing twenty 100 ms grains is continuous and opaque, whereas a cloud containing twenty 1 ms grains is sparse and transparent. The difference between these two cases is their *fill factor* (*FF*). The fill factor of a cloud is the product of its density and its grain duration in seconds (*D*). In the cases just cited, the fill factor of the first cloud is $20 \times 0.1 = 2$, and of the second cloud $20 \times 0.01 = 0.2$. These are simple cases, where the density and grain duration are constants, in practice grain density and grain duration can vary over the duration of the cloud. In this case we derive the *average density* and the *average fill factor*, calculated as the mean between any two extremes. These measurements provide these descriptors of fill factor:

- *Sparse FF* < 0.5, more than half the cloud is silence
- *Covered FF* ~ 1.0, the cloud is more-or-less filled by sonic grains
- *Packed FF* > 1.0, the cloud is filled with overlapping grains

In asynchronous granular synthesis, the starting time of a grain is random. One cannot guarantee that fifty 20 ms grains will completely fill a one-second cloud. Some grains may overlap, leaving silences at other points in the cloud. To create what we hear as a solid cloud, a good rule of thumb is to set the density per second of the cloud to at least $2/D$. Hence, for 20 ms grains, it takes about 100 to cover a one-second cloud. Tiny gaps (less than about 50 ms) do not sound as silences, but rather as momentary fluctuations of amplitude.

For a typical grain duration of 25 ms, we can make the following observations concerning grain density as it crosses perceptual thresholds:

<15 grains per sec—Rhythmic sequences.

15–25 grains per sec—Fluttering, sensation of rhythm disappears. If the cloud is asynchronous, we hear intermittencies.

25–50 grains per sec—Grain order disappears. Upper and lower frequency bounds can be inferred. In a synchronous cloud, the perception of synchronicity evaporates if the upper and lower frequency bounds extend beyond several semitones. As the density increases, we no longer perceive an acceleration of tempo in the grain emissions, but rather we feel an increase in the flow of grains.

50–100 grains per sec—Texture band. If the bandwidth is greater than a semitone, we cannot discern individual frequencies.

>100 grains per sec—Continuous sound mass. No space between grains. In some cases resembles reverberation.

Density and frequency band effects are also synergistic, and, depending on the grain density, the musical results of the band parameter will differ. For sparse, pointillist effects, for example, where each grain is heard as a separate event, keep the grain density to less than $0.5/D$, where D is grain duration in seconds. So, for a grain duration of 20 ms, the density should be less than 25 grains per sec (0.5/0.02).

By increasing the grain density, we enrich the texture, creating effects that depend on the bandwidth.

- Narrow bands and high densities generate pitched streams with formant spectra.
- Medium bands (e.g., intervals of several semitones) and high densities generate turgid colored noise.

▪ Wide bands (e.g., an octave or more) and high densities generate massive clouds of sound.

As we have seen, in the section on grain duration effects, another way to modify the bandwidth of a cloud is by changing the grain duration parameter.

Granular Spatial Effects

Granular synthesis calls for multichannel output, with an individual spatial location for each grain. If the cloud is monaural, with every grain in the same spatial position, it is spatially flat. In contrast, when each grain scatters to a unique location, the cloud manifests a vivid three-dimensional spatial morphology, evident even in a stereophonic configuration.

From a psychoacoustical point of view, the listener's perception of the spatial position of a grain or series of grains is determined by both the physical properties of the signal and the *localization blur* introduced by the human auditory system (Blauert 1997). Localization blur means that a point source sound produces an auditory image that spreads out in space. For Gaussian tonebursts, the horizontal localization blur is in the range of 0.8° to 3.3°, depending on the frequency of the signals (Boerger 1965). The localization blur in the median plane (starting in front, then going up above the head and down behind) is greater, on the order of 4° for white noise and becoming far greater (i.e. less accurate) for purer tones. (See Boerger 1965 for a study of the spatial properties of Gaussian grains.)

Taking localization blur into account, one can specify the spatial distribution of the grains in one of two ways: as an envelope that pans across N channels, or as a random dispersion of grains among N channels. Random dispersion is especially effective in the articulation of long grains at low densities.

Chapter 5 presents more on the spatial effects made possible through particle scattering and other techniques.

Granular Clouds as Sound Objects

A cloud of grains may come and go within a short time span, for example, less than 500 ms. In this case, a cloud of grains forms a tiny sound object. The inner structure of the cloud determines its timbral evolution. I have conducted numerous experiments in which up to fifty grains were generated within a time span of 20 to 500 ms. This is an effective way to construct singular events that cannot be created by other means.

Cloud Mixtures

A granular composition is a flow of multiple overlapping clouds. To create such textures, the most flexible strategy is first to generate each individual cloud. Then to mix the clouds to precisely order and balance their flow in time. To create a polychrome cloud texture, for example, several monochrome clouds, each with a different grain waveform are superimposed in a mixing program.

It is easy to granulate a sound file and take the results "as is." A more sophisticated strategy is to take the granulation as a starting point. For example, one can create a compound cloud—one with an interesting internal evolution—by carefully mixing several granulated sound files.

Mixing is also effective in creating rhythmic structures. When the density of a synchronous cloud is below about 20 Hz, it creates a regular metric pulse. To create a polyrhythmic cloud, one can generate several clouds at different densities, amplitudes, and in different frequency regions to stratify the layers.

Implementations of Granular Synthesis

This section surveys the history of implementations of granular synthesis on computers. It begins with my own first experiments, going on to cover a variety of implementations since.

The Author's Implementations of Granular Synthesis

My involvement with granular synthesis dates back to May of 1972, when I participated in Iannis Xenakis's workshop on music and mathematics at Indiana University. The workshop was based on his book *Formalized Music* (Xenakis 1971, 1992). One chapter of this book described a theoretical approach to sound synthesis based on "elementary sonic particles:"

A complex sound may be imagined as a multicolored firework in which each point of light appears and instantaneously disappears against a black sky ... A line of light would be created by a sufficiently large multitude of points appearing and disappearing instantaneously. (Xenakis 1992 pp. 43–4)

This description intrigued me, but there were no sounds to hear. Granular synthesis remained a theoretical topic at the workshop. Maestro Xenakis took us to the campus computing center to show us experiments in stochastic waveform generation (also described in his book), but he never realized granular synthesis on a computer.

Later that year, I enrolled as a student in music composition at California Institute of the Arts. During this period, I also studied mathematics and computer programming with Leonard Cottrell. For the next two years, I wrote many programs for the Data General Nova 1200, a minicomputer at the Institute. Thus included software for stochastic processes and algorithmic composition based on Xenakis's formulas (Roads 1992a). I spent much time testing the formulas, which fostered in me a deeper understanding of probability theory. The Nova 1200 was limited, however. It lacked memory and had no digital audio converters. Its only peripheral was a teletype with a paper tape punch for storing and reading programs. Digital sound synthesis was out of the question.

In March 1974, I transferred to the University of California, San Diego (UCSD), having learned of its computer sound synthesis facilities. Bruce Leibig, a researcher at UCSD, had recently installed the Music V program (Mathews 1969) on a mainframe computer housed in the UCSD Computer Center. The dual-processor Burroughs B6700 was an advanced machine for its day, with a 48-bit wordlength, virtual memory, digital tape storage, and support for parallel processing. A single language, Extended Algol, provided access to all levels of the system, from the operating system to the hardware. This is not to say that music synthesis was easy; because of the state of input and output technology, the process was laborious.

The Burroughs machine could not produce sound directly. It could, however, write a digital tape that could be converted to sound on another computer, in this case a Digital Equipment Corporation (DEC) PDP-11/20, housed on campus at the Center for Music Experiment (CME). Bruce Leibig wrote the PAL-11 assembly language code that performed the digital-to-analog conversion. This important programming work laid the foundation for my research. I enrolled in an Algol programming course offered by the computer science department. There were no courses in computer sound synthesis, but with help from Bruce Leibig, I learned the Music V language. We programmed on punched paper cards, as there were no interactive terminals.

Owing to storage limitations, my sound synthesis experiments were limited to a maximum of one minute of monaural sound at a sampling rate of 20 kHz. It took several days to produce a minute of sound, because of the large number of steps involved. The UCSD Computer Center scheduled sound calculations for the overnight shift. So I would submit a box of punched cards to a computer operator and return the next day to collect a large digital tape reel containing the previous evening's data. In order to convert this data into sound, I had first to transfer it from the tape to a disk cartridge. This transfer involved setting up an appointment at the Scripps Institute of Oceanography. Surrounded by the pungent atmosphere of the squid tanks of the Neurology Computing Laboratory, I transferred the contents of the tape. Then I would take the disk cartridge to CME and mount it on the DEC minicomputer. This small computer, with a total of 28 kbytes of magnetic-core RAM, had a single-channel 12-bit digital-to-analog converter (DAC) designed and built by Robert Gross. The digital-to-analog converter truncated the four low-order bits of the 16-bit samples.

After realizing a number of short études with Music V, in December 1974 I tested the first implemention of asynchronous granular synthesis. For this experiment, called *Klang-1*, I typed each grain specification (frequency, amplitude, duration) onto a separate punched card. A stack of about eight hundred punched cards corresponded to the instrument and score for thirty seconds of granular sound. Following this laborious experience, I wrote a program in Algol to generate grain specifications from compact, high-level descriptions of clouds. Using this program, I realized an eight-minute study in granular synthesis called *Prototype*. Chapter 7 describes these studies in detail. (See also Roads 1975, 1978a, 1985c, 1987.)

In 1980, I was offered a position as a Research Associate at the Experimental Music Studio at the Massachusetts Institute of Technology. The computing environment centered on a Digital Equipment Corporation PDP-11/50 minicomputer (16-bit word length) running the UNIX operating system. There I implemented two forms of granular synthesis in the C programming language. These programs generated data that could be read by the Music 11 sound synthesis language. The Csound language (Boulanger 2000; Dodge and Jerse 1997; Vercoe 1993) is a superset of Music 11. The initial tests ran at a 40 kHz sampling rate, and used 1024-word function tables for the waveforms and envelopes. The 1980 implementation generated a textual score or note-list for a sinusoidal granular synthesis oscillator. The second, 1981, implementation at MIT granulated sampled sound files using the soundin unit generator of Music 11. I implemented gestures such as percussion rolls by granulating a single stroke on a snare drum or cymbal. Due to the limitations of the Music 11 language, however, this version was constrained to a maximum density of thirty-two simultaneous grains.

An important transition in technology took place in the 1980s with the introduction of personal computers. By 1988, inexpensive computers (less than

$5000 for a complete system including audio converters) had become powerful enough to support stereo 16-bit, 44.1 kHz audio synthesis. In 1988, I programmed new implementations of granular synthesis and granulation of sampled soundfiles for the Apple Macintosh II computer in my home studio (Roads 1992c, d). I called these C programs Synthulate and Granulate, respectively. For playback, I used the Studer Dyaxis, a digital audio workstation with good 16-bit converters attached to the Macintosh II. My synthesis programs worked with a version of the Music 4C language, which I modified to handle the large amounts of data associated with granular synthesis. Music 4C (Gerrard 1989) was a C-language variant of the venerable Music IVBF language developed in the 1960s (Mathews and Miller 1965; Howe 1975). I revised the synthesis programs in 1991 while I was at the Kunitachi College of Music in Tokyo. After moving to Paris in 1992, I modified the grain generator to work with instruments that I wrote for the Csound synthesis language (Boulanger 2000). The revised programs ran on a somewhat faster Macintosh Quadra 700 (25 MHz), but it still took several minutes to calculate a few hundred grains of sound.

Working at Les Ateliers UPIC in 1995, John Alexander and I developed the Cloud Generator program (Roads and Alexander 1995). Cloud Generator is a stand-alone synthesis and granulation program for MacOS computers. The Appendix documents this program. Our implementation of Cloud Generator merged the C code from several of my previous programs (Synthulate, Granulate, etc.) into a single interactive application. Since then, Cloud Generator has served as a teaching aid in the basics of granular synthesis. It has also been used in compositions by many musicians around the world. It provides a variety of options for synthesis and sound processing. I have used it extensively for research purposes, and in composition.

Although Synthulate and its cousins have no graphical interface, they are extensible. For this reason, I have continued to use them when I needed to try an experiment that could not be realized in Cloud Generator. In early 1999, I revised and recompiled Synthulate and its cousins for the Metrowerks C compiler on the Apple Power Macintosh computer.

Between 1996 and 2000, my CREATE colleagues and I also implemented a variety of particle synthesis and sound processing programs using versions 1 and 2 of the SuperCollider language (McCartney 1996, 1998). SuperCollider provides an integrated environment for synthesis and audio signal processing, with gestural, graphical envelope, or algorithmic control. SuperCollider is my synthesis environment of choice at the present time.

Other Implementations of Granular Synthesis

The number of implementations of granular synthesis has increased greatly in recent years. They are happening all over the world, running on different platforms. Although I try here to be comprehensive, this survey is inevitably incomplete.

Working at the Oberlin Conservatory, Gary Nelson carried out an experiment with something similar to granular synthesis in 1974. Beyond a brief mention in (Nelson 1997), there seems to be no further documentation.

According to Clarke (1996), Michael Hinton implemented a type of granular synthesis for a hybrid computer music system called IMPAC, at EMS Stockholm as early as 1984. When launched, the program generated a sequence of short notes with pseudorandom variations on a number of parameters. These included the upper and lower boundaries of a frequency region within which the program scattered the notes. The synthesis was carried out by a combination of custom-made digital frequency modulation oscillators and analog oscillators. A user could control various parameters in real time with either a joystick or a digital pen. By 1988, Clarke had implemented FOF synthesis (a granular technique; see chapter 4), on Atari computers and within the Csound language (Clarke 1996). (See also Clarke 1998.)

The Canadian composer Barry Truax developed a series of important implementations of granular synthesis. In 1986, he wrote a real-time application on the Digital Music Systems DMX-1000 signal processor, controlled by a DEC LSI-11 microcomputer (Truax 1986). By 1987, he had modified his software to granulate a brief sampled sound. He achieved a technical breakthrough in 1990, making it possible to perform real-time granulation on an incoming sound source, such as the live sound of an instrumentalist. This technique enabled him to realize a number of pioneering compositions (see chapter 7). Truax later worked with engineers to develop the Quintessence Box for real-time granular synthesis, using a Motorola DSP 56001 chip for signal processing. A prototype of this box was demonstrated at the 1991 International Computer Music Conference. An operational unit was installed in 1993 at the studios of Simon Fraser University, where the composer teaches.

Working at the University of Naples «Federico II,» Cavaliere, Evangelista, and Piccialli (1988) constructed a circuit called the PSO Troll that could realize up to sixteen voices of granular synthesis in real time at sampling rates up to 62.5 kHz.

In the early 1990s, the Marseilles team of Daniel Arfib and Nathalie Delprat created the program Sound Mutations for time-frequency analysis of sound. After analyzing a sound, the program modified and resynthesized it using granular techniques. It could also perform transformations including time-stretching, transposition, and filtering (Arfib and Delprat 1992, 1993).

James McCartney included a granular instrument in his Synth-O-Matic program for MacOS (McCartney 1990, 1994). Users could draw envelopes on the screen of the computer to control synthesis parameters.

Mara Helmuth realized two different implementations of granular synthesis techniques. StochGran was a graphical interface to a Cmix instrument (Helmuth 1991). StochGran was originally developed for NeXT computers, and later ported to the Silicon Graphics Incorporated IRIX operating system. Helmuth also developed Max patches for granular sampling in real time on the IRCAM Signal Processing Workstation (Helmuth 1993).

A group at the University of York implemented granular synthesis with graphical control (Orton, Hunt, and Kirk 1991). A novel feature was the use of cellular automata to modify the output by mapping the automata to the tendency masks produced by the drawing program. Csound carried out the synthesis.

In 1992 and 1993, I presented several lectures at IRCAM on granular synthesis and convolution techniques, After I left the institute, a number of people who had attended these lectures launched granular synthesis and convolution research of their own as extensions of other long-standing projects, namely Chant synthesis and Max on the IRCAM Musical Workstation. The Granular Synthesis Toolkit (GIST) consisted of a set of external objects for the Max programming language, including a sinusoidal FOF grain generator, and a FOG object for granulation (Eckel, Rocha-Iturbide, and Becker 1995; Rocha 1999). (See the description of FOF synthesis in chapter 4, and the description of granulation in chapter 5.) Also at IRCAM, Cort Lippe (1993), developed another Max application for granulation of sound files and live sound.

Recent versions of the Csound synthesis language (Boulanger 2000) provide four unit generators for granular synthesis: fof, fof2, grain, and granule. Another unit generator, fog, was implemented in versions of Csound from the universities of Bath and Montréal. The fof generator reads a synthetic waveform function table and is oriented toward generating formant tones. The fof2 generator adds control over the initial phase increment in the waveform function table. This means that one can use a recorded sound and perform time-stretching, or extract segments. The grain unit generator begins reading a waveform function table from a random point. The granule unit generator handles up to four different grain streams with individual pitches. However, most parameters (including a time-stretch factor) must be set at initialization time (the beginning of each note in Csound), so the only parameter that can be controlled during performance is grain density. The fog generator extracts grains from a sound file. Lee (1995) also implemented a granular unit generator for the Csound language.

The CDP GrainMill granular synthesis program runs on Windows. It derives from Trevor Wishart's command line program Granula, a part of the Composer's Desktop Project System since 1996. The parameters affect each grain individually as it is created. The parameters include size of the grain, density control, time expansion and compression, pitch placement, amplitude, the portion of soundfile from which the grain is extracted, spatial placement, and time placement. The envelope of the grains is variable.

Tom Erbe's Cornbucket (1995) generated a granular synthesis score for Csound. It offered envelope control for all synthesis parameters and was distributed in the form of source code in the C language.

Ross Bencina's Audiomulch is an audio signal processing application also for Windows (Bencina 2000). It includes two modules for granulation of sampled sounds. The Barcelona group of López, Martí, and Resina (1998) developed real-time granular synthesis (again, for Windows), featuring envelope, fader, and MIDI control.

In 1995, R. De Tintis presented a paper to the Italian Computer Music Association (AIMI) on his implementation of granular synthesis and sampling on the IRIS-MARS workstation. The same year, Schnell (1995) and Todoroff (1995) implemented variants of granular synthesis on the IRCAM Musical Workstation.

Kyma (Windows or MacOS) is a commercial package that offers real-time granular synthesis. It is a graphical sound design environment in which one interconnects graphical modules to construct synthesis patches. A synthesizer called the Capybara renders the sound. The 1997 version of Kyma included modules for granular synthesis, granular time expansion, and granular frequency scaling. The parameters of the grains (frequency, pitch deviation, rate of emission, deviation in emission rate, waveform, grain envelope) are controllable in real time through MIDI continuous controllers or faders displayed on the screen, which also allow a source signal to be time-stretched and frequency-scaled.

SuperCollider 2 (McCartney 1996, 1998; De Campo 1999) is a powerful software environment for real-time audio synthesis that runs on MacOS computers. The SuperCollider 2 programming language offers an object-oriented class system, a graphical interface builder for creating a patch control panel, a graphical interface for creating wavetables and breakpoint envelopes, MIDI control, a library of signal processing and synthesis functions, and a library of functions for list processing of musical data. Users can write both the synthesis and compositional algorithms for their pieces in the same high level language. This allows the creation of synthesis instruments with considerably more flexibility than is possible in other synthesis languages. SuperCollider can read and write audio in real time or stream audio to or from a file. The new version, SuperCollider 3, optimizes and extends these capabilities.

Gerhard Behles's real-time Granular program (Technical University Berlin) runs on Silicon Graphics computers. The program reads a sound file and manipulates it in real time. The user moves onscreen faders to change the effects settings. The same author's Stampede allows composers to explore a continuum of sound transformations under MIDI control. It performs granulation operations similar to those in Cloud Generator, but operates in real time. Andre Bartetzki, at the electronic music studio of the Hochschule für Musik Berlin, has written a granular event generator called CMask that generates grain specifications for Csound (Bartetzki 1997a, 1997b). CMask provides numerous options for scattering grains according to probabilistic functions, sieves, and analogies to simple physical processes.

Damiàn Keller and Barry Truax (1998) developed Cmask models for bouncing, breaking, scraping, and filling. The Cmask control functions determine where to scatter the grains in time and frequency. For example, a recursive equation approximated a bouncing pattern. By changing a damping parameter, one could obtain a family of exponential curves with different rates of damping or grain rate acceleration. Starting from samples of water drops, Keller and Truax developed models of droplet patterns and streams, allowing for a smooth transition between discrete droplets and denser aqueous sounds. Chris Rolfe and Damiàn Keller (1999) developed a standalone MacOS program for soundfile granulation called MacPOD.

William Mauchly of the company Waveboy created a granular synthesis plugin for the Ensoniq ASR-10 and EPS-16 Plus samplers. Working as a signal processor, users can granulate any sampled sound or live audio input. This software offers time-scrambling, pitch-shifting, and adjustment of grain duration. Any MIDI controller can modulate the granulation parameters.

Michael Norris (1997) provided four granulation processes in his Sound-MagicFX package, which works with the SoundMaker program for MacOS. Entitled Brassage Time Stretch, Chunk Munger, Granular Synthesis, and Sample Hose, these flexible procedures allow multiple-file input, time-varying parameters, and additional signal processing to be applied to soundfiles, resulting in a wide range of granular textures.

Eduardo Miranda developed a Windows application called ChaosSynth for granular synthesis using cellular automata (CA) control functions (Miranda 1998). Depending on how the CA are configured, they calculate the details of the grains. A difficulty posed by this approach is the conceptual rift between the CA controls (number of cell values, resistances of the potential divider, capacitance of the electrical capacitor, dimension of the grid, etc.) and the acoustical results (Correa, Miranda, and Wright 2000).

In 1999, Arboretum Systems offered a scattering granulator effect in its popular Hyperprism effects processing software. The user controls grain size, randomization, speed, as well as density and spread.

Can a standard MIDI synthesizer realize granular synthesis? Yes, in a limited form. The New York–based composer Earl Howard has done so on a Kurzweil K2500 sampling synthesizer. The K2500 lets one create short samples, which can repeat by internal signals as fast as 999 bpm, or about every 10 ms. Howard created granular textures by layering several streams operating at different rates, with each stream having a random delay. Another MIDI-based approach to granular synthesis is found in Clarence Barlow's *spectastics* (spectral stochastics) technique. This generates up to two hundred notes per second to approximate the spectrum of a vocal utterance (Barlow 1997).

Even with all these implementations, there is still a need for an instrument optimized with controllers for the virtuoso performance of granular textures. Apropos of this, see the description of the Creatovox project in chapter 5.

Summary

As regards electric instruments for producing sound, the enmity with which the few musicians who know them is manifest. They judge them superficially, consider them ugly, of small practical value, unnecessary. . . . [Meanwhile, the inventors] undiscerningly want the new electric instruments to imitate the instruments now in use as faithfully as possible and to serve the music that we already have. What is needed is an understanding of the . . . possibilities of the new instruments. We must clearly evaluate the increase they bring to our own capacity for expression ... The new instruments will produce an unforeseen music, as unlooked for as the instruments themselves.   (Chavez 1936)

Granular synthesis is a proven method of musical sound synthesis, and is featured in important compositions (see chapter 7). Implementations of granular techniques are widespread. Most focus on the granulation of sampled sound files. Pure granular synthesis using synthetic waveforms is available only in a few packages.

At low densities, synchronous GS serves as a generator of metrical rhythms and precise accelerandi/rallentandi. A high-density cloud set to a single frequency produces a stream of overlapping grains. This forms sweet pitched tones with strong formants, whose position and strength depend greatly on the grain envelope and duration.

Asynchronous GS sprays thousands of sonic grains into cloudlike formations across the audio spectrum. At high densities the result is a scintillating sound complex that varies over time. In musical contexts, these types of sounds can act as a foil to the smoother, more sterile sounds emitted by digital oscillators. Granulation of sampled sound—a popular technique—produces a wide range of extraordinary variations, explored in chapter 5. The destiny of granular synthesis is linked both to graphics and to real-time performance.

A paint program offers a fluid interface for granular synthesis. The Meta-Synth program (Wenger and Spiegel 1999), for example, provides a spray brush with a variable grain size. A further extension would be a multicolored spray jet for sonic particles, where the color palette corresponds to a collection of waveform samples. (In MetaSynth, the color of the grains indicates their spatial location.)

Analysis/resynthesis systems, such as the phase vocoder, have an internal granular representation that is usually hidden from the user. As predicted (in Roads 1996), the interfaces of analysis/resynthesis systems—which resemble sonograms—have merged with interactive graphics techniques. This merger—sonographic synthesis—is a direct and intuitive approach to sound sculpture. (See chapters 4 and 6 for more on sonographic synthesis and transformation.) One can scan a sound image (sonogram), touch it up, paint a new image, or erase it, with the algorithmic brushes of computer graphics.

My colleagues and I continue to refine our instrument for real-time virtuoso performance of granular synthesis (Roads 1992–1997). The Creatovox research project at the University of California, Santa Barbara has resulted in a prototype of a granular synthesis instrument, playable on a standard musical keyboard and other controllers. (See the description in chapter 5.)

Granular synthesis offers unique opportunities to the composer and suggests new ways of organizing musical structure—as clouds of evolving sound spectra. Indeed, granular representation seems ideal for representing statistical processes of timbral evolution. Time-varying combinations of clouds lead to such dramatic effects as evaporation, coalescence, and mutations created by cross-fading overlapping clouds. A striking similarity exists between these processes and those created in computer graphics by *particle synthesis* (Reeves 1983), often used to create images of fire, water, clouds, fog, and grasslike textures, analogous to some of the audio effects possible with asynchronous granular synthesis.

4   Varieties of Particle Synthesis

Glisson Synthesis

    Magnetization Patterns of Glisson Clouds

    Implementation of Glisson Synthesis

    Experiments with Glisson Synthesis

    Assessment of Glisson Synthesis

Grainlet Synthesis

    Parameter Linkage in Grainlet Synthesis

    Frequency-Duration Experiments

    Amplitude-Duration Experiments

    Space-Duration Eperiments

    Frequency-Space Experiments

    Amplitude-Space Experiments

    Assessment of Grainlet Synthesis

Trainlet Synthesis

    Impulse Generation

    Theory and Practice of Trainlets

    Assessment of Trainlet Cloud Synthesis

Pulsar Synthesis

    Basic Pulsar Synthesis

        Pulsaret-Width Modulation

        Synthesis across Time Scales

        Spectra of Basic Pulsar Synthesis

There are two kinds of experimentalists. One kind talks to theorists. The theorist makes predictions and the experimentalist then does the experiments. To do this is important, but then all you do is follow the theory. Another type designs his own experiments, and in this way is ahead of the theorists.
—Samuel C. C. Ting (Nobel Prize in Physics 1988)

Unlike particles probed by physicists, synthetic particles inhabit a virtual world. This world is invented, and the waveforms produced by the particles are algorithmically derived. They may be simple and regular in structure, forming smooth pitched tones, or complex and irregular, forming crackling noisy masses.

The engines of particle synthesis are not especially complicated. It is the combination of many simple elements that forms a complex time-varying sound. We shape the sound's evolution by controlling this combination from a high musical level. High-level controls imply the existence of algorithms that can interpret a composer's directives, translating them into low-level particle specifications. (See chapter 8's discussion of simplicity versus complexity in microsound synthesis.)

This chapter presents a catalog of particle synthesis techniques. These include glissons, grainlets, trainlets, pulsars, graphic and sonographic particles, formant particles, transient drawing, particle cloning, and physical and abstract models of particles.

Glisson Synthesis

Glisson synthesis is an experimental technique of particle synthesis. It derives from the technique of granular synthesis, presented in the previous chapter. I implemented glisson synthesis after revisiting Iannis Xenakis's original paper on the theory of granular synthesis (Xenakis 1960). In this article, Xenakis described each grain as a vector within a three-dimensional space bounded by time, frequency, and amplitude. Since the grain is a vector, not a point, it can vary in frequency, creating a short glissando. Such a signal is called a *chirp* or *chirplet* in digital signal processing (Mann and Haykin 1991). Jones and Parks implemented frequency-modulated grains with a variable chirp rate in 1988. My implementation of glisson synthesis dates to 1998.

In glisson synthesis, each particle or glisson has an independent frequency trajectory—an ascending or descending glissando. As in classic granular synthesis, glisson synthesis scatters particles within cloud regions inscribed on the time-frequency plane. These clouds may be synchronous (metric) or asynchronous (ametric). Certain parameters of glisson synthesis are the same as for granular synthesis: start time and duration of the cloud, particle duration, density of particles per second, frequency band of the cloud, amplitude envelope of the cloud, waveform(s) within the particles, and spatial dispersion of the cloud. (See the description in the previous chapter.)

Magnetization Patterns of Glisson Clouds

The *magnetization pattern*—a combination of several parameters—determines the frequency direction of the glissons within a cloud. First, the glissandi may be deep (wide frequency range) or shallow (small frequency range) (figure 4.1a, b). Second, they may be unidirectional (uniformly up or down) or bidirectional (randomly up or down) (figure 4.1c, d, e). Third, they may be diverging (starting from a common center frequency and diverging to other frequencies), or converging (starting from divergent frequencies that converge to a common center frequency). The center frequency can be changing over time.

Implementations of Glisson Synthesis

Stephen Pope and I developed the first implementation of *glisson synthesis* in February 1998. The software was coded in the SuperCollider 1 synthesis language (McCartney 1996, Pope 1997). Later, I modified the glisson program and carried out systematic tests. In the summer of 1999, Alberto de Campo and I reimplemented glisson synthesis in the SuperCollider 2 language (McCartney 1998).

Experiments with Glisson Synthesis

Short glissons ($<$ 10 ms) with a large frequency variation ($>$ 100 Hz) resemble the classic chirp signals of digital signal processing; sweeping over a wide frequency range in a short period of time. An individual glisson of this type in the starting frequency range of 400 Hz sounds like a tap on a wood block. When the starting frequency range is around 1500 Hz, the glissons sound more like the tapping of claves. As the density of glissons increases and the deviation randomizes in direction, the texture tends quickly toward colored noise.

Medium-length (25–100 ms) glissons "tweet" (figure 4.2a), so that a series of them sounds like birdsong.

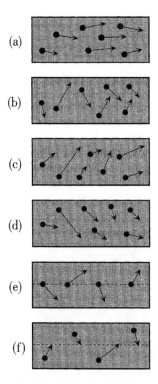

Figure 4.1 Magnetization patterns in glisson synthesis. The vertical axis is frequency and the horizontal axis is time. (a) Shallow (small frequency deviation) bidirectional. (b) Deep (large frequency deviation) bidirectional. (c) Upwards unidirectional. (d) Downwards unidirectional. (e) Diverging from center frequency. (f) Converging to center frequency.

Long glissons (> 200 ms) result in dramatic cascades of sound (figure 4.2b). At certain densities, they are reminiscent of the massed glissandi textures heard in such orchestral compositions as Xenakis's *Metastasis* (1954). A striking effect occurs when the glissandi diverge from or converge upon a common central frequency. By constraining the glissandi to octaves, for example, it is possible to generate sounds similar to the Shepard tones (Risset 1989a, 1997), which seem to spiral endlessly upward or downward.

Assessment of Glisson Synthesis

Glisson synthesis is a variant of granular synthesis. Its effects segregate into two categories. At low particle densities, we can perceive each glissando as a sepa-

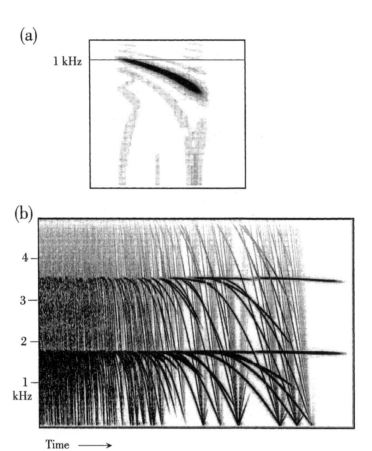

Figure 4.2   Glissons. (a) Sonogram of a single 25-ms glisson. Notice the gray artefacts of the analysis, reflecting the time-frequency uncertainty at the beginning and end of the particle. (b) Glisson cloud generated by a real-time performance. The glisson durations increase over the 16-second duration of the cloud.

rate event in a micro-melismatic chain. When the glissons are short in duration (< 50 ms), their internal frequency variation makes it difficult to determine their pitch. Under certain conditions—such as higher particle densities with greater particle overlap—glisson synthesis produces second-order effects that we perceive on the time scale of sound objects. In this case, the results tend toward a mass of colored noise, where the bandwidth of the noise is proportional to the frequency variation of the glissandi. Several factors can contribute to the sensation of a noise mass, the most important being density, wide frequency variations, and short glisson durations.

Grainlet Synthesis

Grainlet synthesis combines the idea of granular synthesis with that of wavelet synthesis. (See chapter 6.) In granular synthesis, the duration of a grain is unrelated to the frequency of its component waveform. In contrast, the wavelet representation scales the duration of each particle according to its frequency. Short wavelets represent high frequencies, and long wavelets represent low frequencies. Grainlet synthesis generalizes this linkage between synthesis parameters. The fundamental notion of grainlet synthesis is that any parameter of synthesis can be made dependent on (or linked to) any other parameter. One is not, for example, limited to an interdependence between frequency and duration.

I implemented grainlet synthesis in 1996 as an experiment in parameter linkage within the context of granular cloud synthesis (described in the previous chapter). Grainlet synthesis imposes no constraints on the choice of waveform, particle envelope, or any other parameter, except those that we introduce through parameter linkage.

Parameter Linkage in Grainlet Synthesis

Parameter linkage is the connecting of one parameter with a dependent parameter. As parameter *A* increases, for example, so does its dependent parameter *B*. One can also stipulate inverse linkages, so that an increase in *A* results in a decrease in *B*.

Parameter linkages can be drawn as patch diagrams connecting one parameter to another (figure 4.3). An arrow indicates a direct influence, and a gray

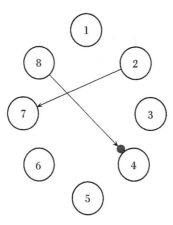

Figure 4.3 Parameter linkage in grainlet synthesis. Each circle represents a parameter of grainlet synthesis. An arrow from one parameter to another indicates a dependency. Here parameter 7 is dependent on parameter 2. If parameter 7 is spatial depth and parameter 2 is grainlet start time, then later grainlets have more reverberation. Notice that parameter 4 is inversely dependent on parameter 8, as indicated by the gray dot. If parameter 4 was grainlet duration and parameter 8 was grainlet frequency, then higher frequency grainlets are shorter in duration (as in wavelet resynthesis).

circle an inverse linkage. I wrote a program in the C language to realize these parameter linkages. In the first version, grainlet duration could be specified in terms of the number of cycles of the fundamental period. If the number of cycles is ten, for example, a grainlet at 100 Hz lasts 10×0.01 sec $= 0.1$ sec, while a grainlet at 1000 Hz lasts 10×0.001 Hz $= 0.01$ sec.

After initial tests, I generalized the parameter linkage from frequency and duration to dependencies between any two synthesis variables. The grainlet synthesis program generates a data file. A Csound program for granular synthesis interprets this file and synthesizes the sound. The synthesis parameters include the following:

- Cloud density (number of grainlets per second)
- Grainlet amplitude
- Grainlet start-time
- Grainlet frequency
- Grainlet duration

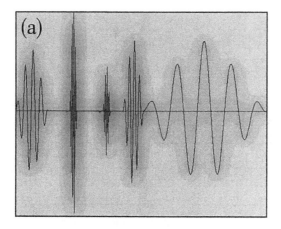

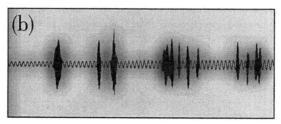

Figure 4.4   Collections of grainlets. (a) These grainlets are scaled in duration according to their frequency. (b) Superposition of short high-frequency grainlets over a long low-frequency grainlet.

- Grainlet waveform
- Grainlet position in the stereo field
- Grainlet spatial depth (amount of reverberation)

Frequency-Duration Experiments

The first experiments with grainlet synthesis simulated the relationship between grain duration and grain frequency found in wavelet representation (figure 4.4a and b). I later generalized this to allow any frequency to serve as a *point of attraction* around which certain durations (either very long or very short) could gravitate (figure 4.5).

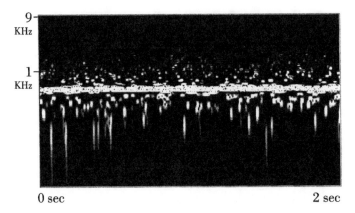

Figure 4.5   Inverse sonogram plotted on a logarithmic frequency scale, showing a frequency point of attraction around the grainlet spectrum. The grainlets whose frequencies are close to the point of attraction (700 Hz) are long in duration, creating a continuous band centered at this point.

Amplitude-Duration Experiments

These experiments linked grain duration with the amplitude of the grains. In the case of a direct link, long grains resulted in louder grains. In an inverse relationship, shorter grains had higher amplitudes.

Space-Duration Experiments

These experiments positioned grains in space according to their duration. Grains of a stipulated duration always appeared to emanate from a specific location, which might be any point in the stereo field. Grains whose duration was not stipulated scattered randomly in space.

Frequency-Space Experiments

These experiments positioned grains in space according to their frequency. Grains of a stipulated frequency appeared to always emanate from a specific location, which might be any point in the stereo field. Other grains whose frequency was not stipulated scattered randomly in space.

Amplitude-Space Experiments

These experiments assigned grains a spatial location according to their amplitude. Grains of a stipulated amplitude appeared to always emanate from a specific location, which might be any point in the stereo field. Other grains whose amplitude was not stipulated scattered randomly in space.

Assessment of Grainlet Synthesis

Grainlet synthesis is an experimental technique for realizing linkages among the parameters of microsonic synthesis. It appears to be a good technique for forcing high-level organizations to emerge from microstructure. Specifically, the clouds generated by grainlet synthesis stratify, due to the internal constraints imposed by the parameter linkages. This stratification is seen in textures such as a dense cloud of brief, high-frequency grains punctuated by low and long grains. Other clouds stratify by spatial divisions. Many parameter linkages are easy to discern, conveniently serving as articulators in music composition.

Trainlet Synthesis

A *trainlet* is an acoustic particle consisting of a brief series or train of impulses. Like other particles, trainlets usually last between 1 to 100 ms. To create time-varying tones and textures, an algorithm is needed that can spawn thousands of trainlets from a few high-level specifications. The main parameters of trainlet synthesis are the density of the trainlets, their attack time, pulse period, harmonic structure, and spectral energy profile. Before explaining the theory of trainlets, let us summarize the basics of impulse generation.

Impulse Generation

An *impulse* is an almost instantaneous burst of energy followed by an immediate decline in energy. In its ideal form, an impulse is infinitely narrow in the time dimension, creating a single vertical line in its time-domain profile. In practice, however, impulses always last a finite time; this is their *pulse width*. Electronic impulses in the real world vary greatly, exhibiting all manner of attack shapes, decay shapes, and transition times. These variations only make them more interesting from a musical point of view.

Table 4.1 Technical specifications of the Hewlett-Packard HP8005B pulse generator

Repetition rate	0.3 Hz to 20 mHz in five ranges; Vernier control within each range
Attack and decay transition times	<10 ns to 2 s in five ranges; Verniers for leading and trailing edges
Overshoot, preshoot, and ringing	<5% of pulse amplitude each
Pulse width	<25 ns to 3 s in five ranges; Vernier controls within each range
Width jitter	<0.1% + 50 ps of any width setting
Pulse delay	<100 ns to 3 s, in five ranges
Delay jitter	<0.1% + 50 ps of any delay setting
Period jitter	<0.1% of any period setting

Impulse generation is one of the most venerable methods of electronic sound synthesis. At infrasonic frequencies, we perceive impulses separately and notice their rhythmic pattern. At audio frequencies the impulses fuse into continuous tones. Electronic music studios of the 1950s were equipped with laboratory impulse generators (IGs). The IGs installed in the WDR Cologne studio had a pulse frequency range that extended from the infrasonic frequencies (1.1 Hz, corresponding to a pulse duration of 900 ms) to the high audio frequencies (10 kHz, or pulse duration of 0.1 ms).

Laboratory impulse generators have evolved considerably since the 1950s. Modern IGs are solid-state analog devices. Table 4.1 lists the specifications of a low-voltage IG in the price range of $600. Notice the wide frequency range, from 0.15 Hz (one impulse every 6.6 seconds) to 20 MHz. The spectrum of an impulse with a period of 50 nanoseconds (corresponding to a frequency of 20 MHz) is very broad. More expensive IGs, costing up to $25,000, extend the fundamental frequency range beyond 3 gHz. The main parameters of an IG are the shape of the impulse, the fundamental period of repetition, and the duty cycle of the pulse wave relative to the period. These parameters affect the rhythm or pitch of the output signal, and its overall spectrum.

Industrial impulse generators are not designed for flexible performance in real time. Notice the specifications in table 4.1, where repetition rate, transition time, pulse width, and pulse delay are broken into five or six ranges. This means that they cannot sweep continuously from one setting to another. They are also not designed for automated operation.

Moreover, the raw output of an IG is a series of clicks, not sufficient in themselves for music synthesis. Since a click has a broad bandwidth, a common synthesis technique is to filter the impulses with a bandpass characteristic to carve out a specific peak in the spectrum. When the filter is very narrow, a single impulse causes the filter to resonate at a specific frequency, yielding the sensation of pitch. Another processing trick is to pass the impulse train through a variable delay and feedback loop, so that the density of impulses accumulates under the control of the composer. Karlheinz Stockhausen and Gottfried Michael Koenig used these kinds of techniques in the synthesis of *Kontakte* in 1960. (See also Kaegi 1967.)

Ultimately, all electronic signals, whether analog or digital, are bandlimited. An analog IG has an obvious advantage over a digital IG, which is strictly bandlimited by the Nyquist theorem. As is clear from the specifications in table 4.1, the bandwidth of analog IGs is much broader.

Theory and Practice of Trainlets

A *trainlet cloud* contains one or more trainlets. The main variables in the synthesis of a trainlet cloud are:

- Density per second of trainlets
- Trainlet pulse period
- Trainlet harmonic structure
- Trainlet spectral energy profile

An *amplitude envelope* shapes each trainlet, and the generator projects each trainlet to a specific location in space. The parameters vary for each trainlet, so each trainlet may be unique.

Since trainlet synthesis operates in the digital domain, it is important that the impulses be bandlimited to avoid aliasing. A standard bandlimited impulse generator for modern synthesis languages is Godfrey Winham's buzz unit generator and its variant, gbuzz (Winham 1966; Winham and Steiglitz 1970; Howe 1975; Steiglitz 1996). Buzz emits a set of N harmonic partials of equal amplitude. As the number of harmonics N increases, the pulse width becomes narrower (figure 4.6). Gbuzz emits a set of N harmonic partials with more flexible control of the spectrum.

In the 1998 prototype implementation of trainlet synthesis, I wrote the synthesis engine in the Csound language (Boulanger 2000). Csound's gbuzz unit generator emits harmonic cosines aligned to a fundamental frequency. It scales the amplitudes of the cosines so their sum equals a stipulated peak value. One

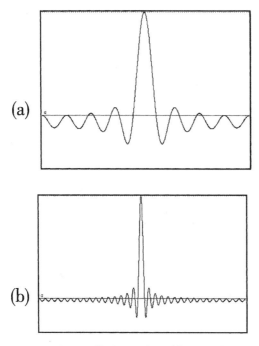

Figure 4.6 Bandlimited pulses. (a) Sum of eight harmonics. (b) Sum of thirty-two harmonics. Notice the narrowing of the pulse.

can stipulate the lowest harmonic, the total number of harmonics starting from the lowest, and the chroma of the harmonic series (see below).

Chroma is a spectral brightness factor. Figure 4.7 shows the relationship between chroma and spectra. Chroma determines the relative strength of the harmonic series. If the lowest harmonic partial has a strength coefficient of A, the lowest harmonic $+ n$th partial will have a coefficient of $A \times (\text{chroma}^n)$, an exponential curve. The chroma may be positive, zero, or negative, and is not restricted to integers. If chroma $= 1$, the harmonics are of equal strength. If chroma < 1, the higher harmonics are attenuated, as though the signal had been sent through a lowpass filter. As the value of chroma tends toward 0, they attenuate more rapidly. If chroma > 1, the highest harmonic has the greatest amplitude (as though a highpass filter had processed it), while each lower harmonic stepping down from the highest has a progressively lower amplitude. As the chroma value increases, the signal is brighter in timbre.

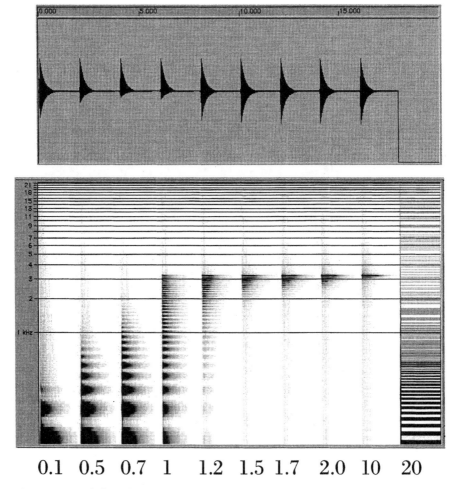

Figure 4.7 Relationship between chroma and spectra. We see time-domain waveforms and sonogram spectra (on a logarithmic frequency scale) of trainlets with increasing chroma. All trainlets have a pulse frequency of 100 Hz, with thirty-two harmonics, and the lowest harmonic is always 1. The chroma values are indicated at the bottom of the figure. In the last example, chroma = 20, the algorithm explodes.

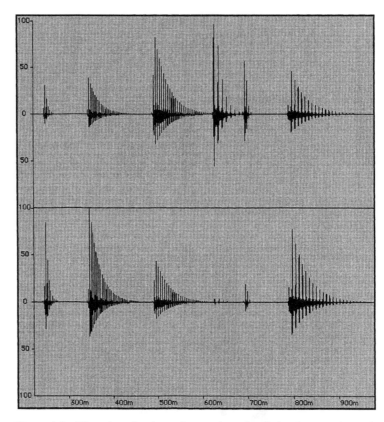

Figure 4.8 Time-domain view of scattering of trainlets in two channels. The trainlets are at various frequencies and have various durations. The amplitude of each trainlet (the sum of both channels) is constant.

Trainlet clouds are musical units on the sound object time scale. As in granular synthesis, synchronous clouds spawn a regular series of trainlets. A linear accelerando or rallentando can also be realized in this mode. Asynchronous clouds spawn trainlets at random intervals according to the stipulated density. Figure 4.8 provides a time-domain view of a trainlet cloud, while figure 4.9 shows the sonogram of two trainlet clouds, one with long trainlets, the other with short trainlets. Notice their characteric spectral pattern.

Table 4.2 enumerates the rest of the cloud parameters. The values in brackets are typical ranges.

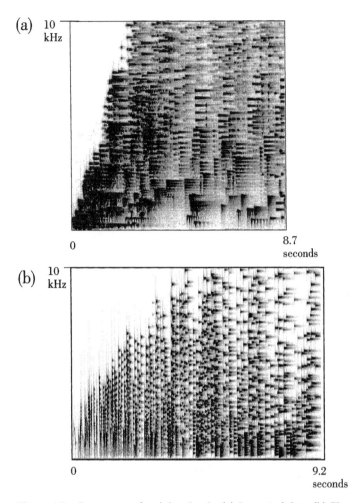

Figure 4.9   Sonogram of trainlet clouds. (a) Long trainlets. (b) Short trainlets.

Table 4.2   Trainlet cloud parameters

---

1. Cloud start time, in seconds
2. Cloud duration, in seconds
3. Random duration flag. If set, interpret the initial and final trainlet durations as maximum and minimum trainlet durations, respectively. The actual durations are generated randomly between these limits.
4. Trainlet durations at start of cloud (0.001–0.8 sec)
5. Trainlet durations at end of cloud
6. Density of trainlets per second at start of cloud (1–300)
7. Density of trainlets per second at end of cloud
8. Upper frequency bandlimit of the cloud at start (20 Hz–20 KHz)
9. Lower frequency bandlimit of the cloud at start
10. Upper frequency bandlimit of the cloud at end
11. Lower frequency bandlimit of the cloud at end
12. Amplitude at start of cloud (1–96 dB)
13. Amplitude at end of cloud
14. Number of harmonics per trainlet at start of cloud (1–64)
15. Number of harmonics per trainlet at end of cloud
16. Lowest sounding harmonic at start of cloud
17. Lowest sounding harmonic at end of cloud
18. Chroma at start of cloud. If chroma < 0 then the effect is lowpass. If chroma $= 1$ all harmonics are equal in strength. If chroma > 1 then the effect is highpass.
19. Chroma at end of cloud,
20. Initial waveform, usually sine
21. Final waveform, usually sine
22. Spatial position of trainlets in the stereo field at the start of the cloud, either fixed $(0 = L, 0.5 = \text{middle}, 1 = \text{right})$ or random
23. Spatial position of trainlets in the stereo field at the end of the cloud
24. Initial attack time (5–50 ms)
25. Final attack time

Note: Initial and final values refer to the beginning of the cloud and the end of the cloud, respectively.

We have also implemented a version of trainlet synthesis in the real-time Creatovox synthesizer, described in chapter 5. One hand can play the trainlet clouds on the keyboard of the instrument, while the other manipulates the cloud parameters with joysticks and other MIDI controllers.

Assessment of Trainlet Cloud Synthesis

I conducted numerous tests with the trainlet cloud technique focussing primarily on trainlets with exponential attacks, linear sustains, and linearly decaying envelopes. The gbuzz unit generator, stamps the trainlet sonority with its "brittle" signature (Schindler 1998). This brittleness derives from gbuzz's fixed waveform and unnatural spectrum. Long trainlets in sparse clouds revisit a sound quality that was characteristic of early computer music studies.

My best results involved trainlets with durations of 40 ms to 100 ms, where the characteristic timbre of the trainlets had just enough time to manifest. Fundamental frequencies greater than 500 Hz tend to sound metallic, fundamentals under 500 Hz are darker and more effective. In any case, with trainlets having up to thirty-two harmonics, the fundamental must remain under 600 Hz in order to avoid aliasing. A 32-harmonic trainlet at 600 Hz with a chroma of 1.0 is very bright.

With over twenty parameters to vary, a wide range of sound material can be produced by trainlet cloud synthesis, which seems to have considerable musical potential. More research is needed, however. As with any technique, the output of trainlet synthesis can be taken as a starting point for further signal processing. I have, for example, tested configurations in which a trainlet generator connects to a constant-Q bandpass filter. The filter lets one accentuate a particular formant in the partial spectrum.

Pulsar Synthesis

Pulsar synthesis (PS), named after the spinning neutron stars that emit periodic signals in the range of 0.25 Hz to 642 Hz, is a powerful method of digital sound synthesis with links to past analog techniques. Coincidentally, this range of frequencies—between rhythm and tone—is of central importance in pulsar synthesis.

PS melds established principles within a new paradigm. In its basic form, it generates electronic pulses and pitched tones similar to those produced by analog instruments such as the Ondioline (Jenny 1958; Fourier 1994) and the Hohner Elektronium (1950), which were designed around the principle of filtered pulse trains. Pioneering electronic music composers including Stockhausen (1955, 1957, 1961, 1963) and Koenig (1959, 1962) used filtered impulse generation as a staple in their studio craft. Pulsar synthesis is a digital technique, however, and so it accrues the advantages of precise programmable control, waveform flexibility, graphical interface, and extensibility. In its advanced form, pulsar synthesis generates a world of rhythmically structured crossbred sampled sounds.

This section first presents the basic theory of pulsars and pulsar graphs. We then move on to the more advanced technique of using pulsars to transform sampled sounds through cross-synthesis, presenting musical applications of pulsar synthesis in compositions by the author. At the end of this section, we describe the features of a new interactive program called PulsarGenerator (Roads 2001).

Basic Pulsar Synthesis

Basic pulsar synthesis generates a family of classic electronic music timbres akin to those produced by an impulse generator connected to a bandpass filter. Unlike this classic technique, however, there is no filter in the basic PS circuit.

A single pulsar is a particle of sound. It consists of an arbitrary *pulsaret* waveform w with a period d followed by a silent time interval s (figure 4.10a). The total duration of a pulsar is $p = d + s$, where p is the *pulsar period*, d is the *duty cycle*, and s is silent. Repetitions of the pulsar signal form a *pulsar train*. Let us define the frequency corresponding to the repetition period as $f_p = 1/p$ and the frequency corresponding to the duty cycle as $f_d = 1/d$. Typical ranges of f_p are between 1 Hz and 5 kHz, the typical range of f_d is from 80 Hz to 10 kHz.

In PS, both f_p and f_d are continuously variable quantities. They are controlled by separate envelope curves that span a train of pulsars. The train is the unit of musical organization on the time scale of notes and phrases, and can last anywhere from a few hundred milliseconds to a minute or more.

Notice in figure 4.10b that the *duty ratio* or *d:s ratio* varies while p remains constant. In effect, one can simultaneously manipulate both fundamental frequency (the rate of pulsar emission) and what we could call a *formant frequency* (corresponding to the duty cycle), each according to separate envelopes. A

(a)

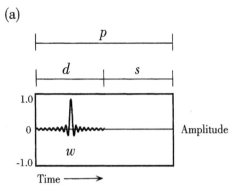

(b)

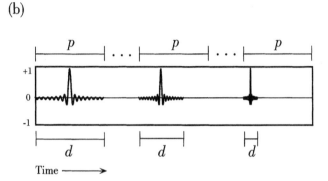

Figure 4.10   Anatomy of a pulsar. (a) A pulsar consists of a brief burst of energy called a *pulsaret w* of a duration *d* followed by a silent interval *s*. The waveform of the pulsaret, here shown as a band-limited pulse, is arbitrary. It could also be a sine wave or a period of a sampled sound. The total duration $p = d + s$, where p is the fundamental period of the pulsar. (b) Evolution of a pulsar train, time-domain view. Over time, the pulsar period p remains constant while the pulsaret period d shrinks. The ellipses indicate a gradual transition period containing many pulsars between the three shown.

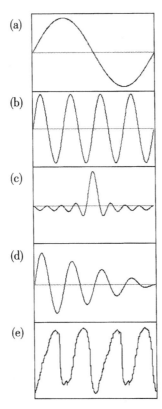

Figure 4.11 Typical pulsaret waveforms. In practice, any waveform can be used. (a) Sine. (b) Multicycle sine. (c) Band-limited pulse. (d) Decaying multicycle sinusoid. (e) Cosmic pulsar waveform emitted by the neutron star Vela X-1.

formant is a peak region in a spectrum. Lowering the fundamental means increasing s, and raising the fundamental means decreasing s.

So far, the structure we have described is similar to that of a standard impulse generator. Pulsar synthesis generalizes this configuration in several ways. First, it allows the pulsaret w to be any waveform. Figure 4.11 shows some typical pulsaret waveforms, including those with multiple subperiods within their duty cycle (figure 4.11b, d, and e).

Let us assume that w is a single cycle of a sine wave. From a signal processing point of view, this can be seen as a sine wave that has been limited in time by a rectangular function v, which we call the *pulsaret envelope*. An important

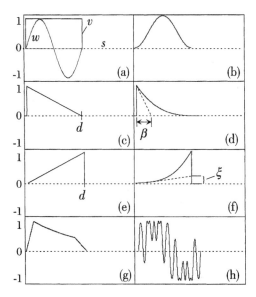

Figure 4.12 Typical pulsaret envelopes. (a) Rectangular. (b) Gaussian. (c) Linear decay. (d) Exponential decay. The term β determines the steepness of the exponential curve. (e) Linear attack, with duty cycle d. (f) Exponential attack. The term ξ determines the steepness of the exponential curve. (g) FOF envelope. (h) Bipolar modulator.

generalization is that v can also be any shape. As we show later, the envelope v strongly affects the spectrum of the pulsar train.

Figure 4.12 shows some typical pulsaret envelopes. A rectangular envelope (figure 4.12a) produces a broad spectrum with strong peaks and nulls for any pulsaret. Figure 4.12g depicts a well-known configuration for formant synthesis, an envelope with a sharp attack followed by an exponential decay. This corresponds to the FOF and Vosim techniques described later in this chapter. Such a configuration can be seen as a special case of pulsar synthesis. As figure 4.12h shows, the envelope can also be a bipolar ring modulator.

Keeping p and w constant and varying d on a continuous basis creates the effect of a resonant filter swept across a tone. There is, of course, no filter in this circuit. Rather, the frequency corresponding to the duty cycle d appears in the spectrum as a formant peak. By sweeping the frequency of this peak over time, we obtain the sonic equivalent of a time-varying bandpass filter applied to a basic impulse train.

Pulsaret-Width Modulation

Pulse-width modulation (PWM) is a well-known analog synthesis effect occuring when the duty cycle of a rectangular pulse varies while the fundamental frequency remains constant (figure 4.13a). This produces an edgy "sawing" quality as the upper odd harmonics increase and decrease over the course of the modulation. At the extremes of PWM, the signal is silent. For example, when $d = 0$, PWM results in a signal of zero amplitude (figure 4.13b). When $d = p$, PWM produces a signal of a constant amplitude of 1 (figure 4.13c).

Pulsaret-width modulation (PulWM) extends and improves this model. First, the pulsaret waveform can be any arbitrary waveform. Second, it allows the duty cycle frequency to pass through and below the fundamental frequency. Here $f_d \leq f_p$. Notice in figure 4.13 how the duty cycle of the sinusoid increases from (d) to (e). In (f), $p = d$. Finally, in (g) $p < d$. That is, the duty cycle is longer than the fundamental period. Only the first quadrant of the sine wave repeats. The fundamental period cuts off the duty cycle of the pulsaret in mid-waveform. In our implementation, we apply a user-controlled crossfade time around this cutoff point, which we call the *edge* factor. When there is no crossfade, the edge factor is high.

   We have also tested an alternative approach to pulsar-width modulation, designed by Alberto de Campo, which produces a different sound. In this method, *overlapped pulsaret-width modulation* or OPulWM, the fundamental frequency corresponds to the rate of pulsar emission, independent of the pulsaret duty cycle. That is, the duty cycle of an individual pulsar always completes, even when it crosses below the fundamental frequency. Whenever the fundamental period expires, our algorithm spawns a new pulsar. Thus, when $d > p$ several pulsars overlap with others whose duty cycle has not yet completed. As d increases, the generator spawns more and more overlapping pulsars. For practical reasons, then, we stipulate an arbitrary overlap limit. OPulWM results in a great deal of phase cancellation and so tends to be a more subtle effect than regular PulWM.

Synthesis across Time Scales

PS operates within and between musical time scales. It generates a stream of microsonic particles at a variable rate across the continuum spanning infrasonic pulsations and audio frequencies. When the distance between successive

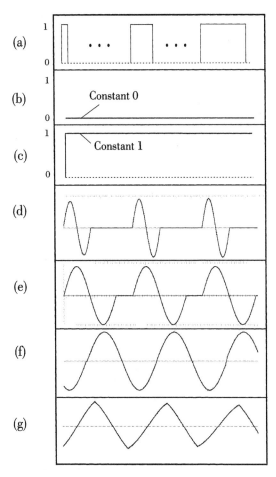

Figure 4.13 Pulsaret-width modulation. (a) Classical PWM with a rectangular pulse shape. The ellipses indicate a gradual transition between the pulses. (b) PWM when the duty cycle $d = 0$ results in a signal of zero amplitude. (c) PWM when the duty cycle $d = p$ (the fundamental period), the result is a signal with a constant amplitude of 1. (d) Pulsar train with a sinusoidal pulsaret. (e) Same period as (d), but the duty cycle is increasing. (f) The duty cycle and the period are equal, resulting in a sinusoid. (g) The duty cycle is greater than the fundamental period, which cuts off the final part of the sine waveform.

impulses is less than about one twentieth of a second, the human hearing mechanism causes them to fuse into a continuous tone. This is the *forward masking effect* (Buser and Imbert 1992). As Helmholtz (1885) observed, in the range between 20 and 35 Hz, it is difficult to distinguish the precise pitch of a sustained tone; reliable pitch perception takes hold at about 40 Hz, depending on the waveform. So listeners hear pitch in a periodic sustained tone for p between approximately 25 ms (corresponding to $f_p = 40$ Hz) and 200 µsec (corresponding to $f_p = 5$ kHz).

As the rate of pulsar emission slows down and crosses through the threshold of the infrasonic frequencies ($f_p < 20$ Hz), the sensation of continuous tone evaporates, and we can perceive each pulsar separately. When the fundamental f_p falls between 62.5 ms (corresponding to the time span of a thirty-second note at quarter note = 60 MM) and 8 sec (corresponding to the time span of two tied whole notes at quarter note = 60 MM), we hear rhythm. The fundamental frequency envelope becomes a graph of rhythm. This takes the form of a function of time that a user draws on the screen of a computer. Such a *pulsar graph* can serve as an alternative form of notation for one dimension of rhythmic structure, namely the onset time of events. The correspondence between the musical units of rhythmic structure (note values, tuplets, rests, etc.) can be made clear by plotting note values on the vertical or frequency scale. For example, assuming a tempo of 60 MM, a frequency of 5 Hz corresponds to a quintuplet figure. Note that the two-dimensional pulsar graph does not indicate the duration of the events. This could be represented by adding a third dimension to the plot.

To interpret the rhythm generated by a function inscribed on a pulse graph, one has to calculate the duration of the grain emission curve at a given fixed frequency rate. For example, a grain emission at 4 Hz lasting 0.75 seconds emits three grains. When grain emission switches from one value to the next, the pulsar corresponding to the new duration plays immediately followed by a silence equal to the period of grain emission. Figure 4.14 plots a rhythm that alternates between fixed-rate pulses, accelerandi, and silence.

Spectra of Basic Pulsar Synthesis

Many time-varying parameters interact to produce the pulsar timbre, including the pulsaret, the pulsaret envelope, the fundamental frequency, multiple formant frequencies, and the burst masking ratio. The spectrum of a single pulsar stream is the convolution product of w and v, biased in frequency by f_d and f_p.

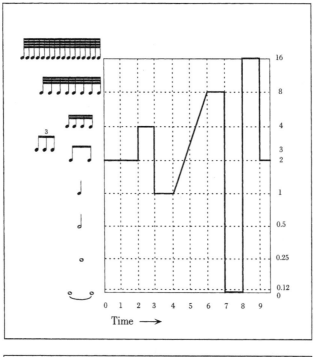

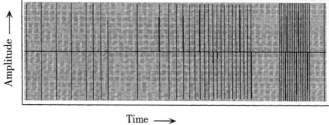

Figure 4.14 Pulsar rhythms. (Top) Pulse graph of rhythm showing rate of pulsar emission (vertical scale) plotted against time (horizontal scale). The left-hand scale measures traditional note values, while the right-hand scale measures frequencies. (Bottom) Time-domain image of generated pulsar train corresponding to the plot above.

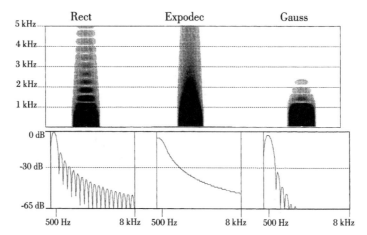

Figure 4.15   Effect of the pulsaret envelope on the spectrum. The top row presents frequency-versus-time sonograms of an individual pulsar with a sinusoidal pulsaret, a fundamental frequency of 12 Hz, and a formant frequency of 500 Hz. The sonograms use 1024-point fast Fourier transform plots with a Von Hann window. They are plotted on a linear frequency scale. From left to right, we see the sonogram produced by a rectangular envelope, an expodec envelope, and a Gaussian envelope. The lower row plots the spectra of these pulsars on a dB scale.

Since w and v can be arbitrary waveforms, and f_d and f_p can vary continuously, the range of spectra produced by PS is quite large.

When the formant frequency is set at a specific frequency energy spreads in that region of the spectrum. Precisely how the energy spreads depends on w and v. The pulsaret waveform w can be considered a template of spectrum shape that repeats at the stipulated fundamental frequency f_p and is time-scaled by the duty cycle or formant frequency f_d. If, for example, the ratio of the amplitudes of the first five harmonics of w is $5:4:3:2:1$, this ratio prevails, independent of the specific values of p and d, when $f_p \leq f_d$.

The pulsaret envelope's contribution to the spectrum is significant. Figure 4.15 shows the spectra of individual pulsars where the waveform w is a sinusoid, and the pulsaret envelope v varies among three basic shapes. In the case of figure 4.15a, v is rectangular. Consequently, the formant spectrum takes the form of a broad sinc $(\sin[x]/x)$ function in the frequency domain. The spectrum shows strong peaks at factors of $1.5f_d$, $2.5f_d$, etc., and nulls at harmonics of f_d. This is characteristic of the sinc function. An exponential decay or *expodec* envelope (such as in figure 4.15d) tends to smooth the peaks and valleys in the spectrum (figure 4.15b). The bell-shaped Gaussian envelope compresses the spectral energy, centering it around the formant frequency (figure 4.15c).

Thus by modifying the pulsaret envelope, one can alter the profile of the pulsar spectrum. The appendix presents a mathematical analysis of the spectra of simple pulsaret envelopes.

Advanced Pulsar Synthesis

Advanced pulsar synthesis builds upon basic pulsar synthesis by adding several features that take it beyond the realm of vintage electronic sonorities. Three methods are of particular importance:

1. Multiple pulsar generators sharing a common fundamental frequency but with individual formant and spatial trajectories
2. Pulse-masking to shape the rhythm of the pulsar train
3. Convolution of pulsar trains with sampled sounds

Figure 4.16 outlines the schema of advanced pulsar synthesis. The following sections explain the different parts of this schema.

Multiple Pulsar Generators

A pulsar generator has seven parameters:

- Pulsar train duration
- Pulsar train fundamental frequency envelope f_p
- Pulsaret formant frequency envelope f_d
- Pulsaret waveform w
- Pulsaret envelope v
- Pulsar train amplitude envelope a
- Pulsar train spatial path s

The individual pulsar train is the simplest case. To synthesize a complex sound with several resonance peaks, we can add several pulsar trains with the same fundamental frequency but with different time-varying formant frequencies f_d. One envelope controls their common fundamental frequency, while two or more separate envelopes control their formant trajectories f_{d1}, f_{d2}, etc.

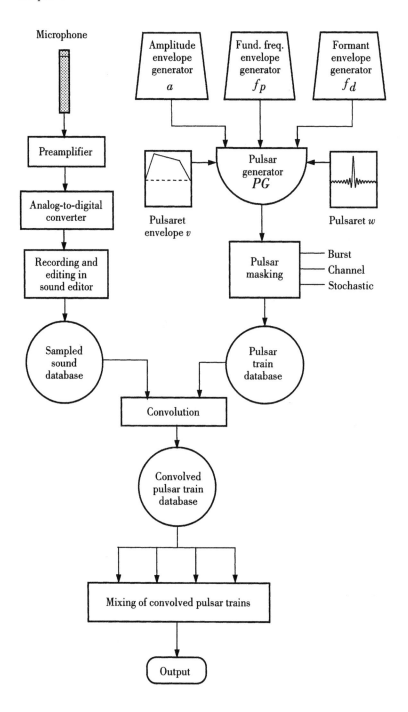

A unique feature of pulsar synthesis is that each formant can follow its own spatial path. This leads to complex spatial interplay within a single tone or rhythmic phrase.

Pulsar Masking, Subharmonics, and Long Tonepulses

A pulsar generator emits a metronomic sequence of pulsars, where the rate of emission can vary over time according to the fundamental frequency envelope function f_p. *Pulsar masking* breaks up the stream by introducing intermittancies (regular or irregular) into the metronomic sequence. It deletes individual pulsarets, leaving an interval of silence in their place. This takes three forms: *burst, channel,* and *stochastic masking*.

Burst masking (figure 4.17a) models the burst generators of the classic electronic music studios. It produces a regular pattern of pulsarets that are interrupted at regular intervals. The on/off pattern can be stipulated as the *burst ratio* $b{:}r$, where b is the burst length in pulsaret periods and r is the rest length in pulsaret periods. For example, a $b{:}r$ ratio of 4:2 produces an alternating sequence of four pulsarets and two silent periods: 111100111100111100111100, etc. If the fundamental frequency is infrasonic, the effect is rhythmic.

When the fundamental is in the audio frequency range, burst masking imposes an amplitude modulation effect on the timbre (figure 4.18), dividing the fundamental frequency by a subharmonic factor $b + r$. With the Pulsar-Generator program (described later), we can alter the burst ratio in real time, producing a gamut of subharmonic permutations.

When $b + r$ is large, the subharmonic crosses through the threshold separating tone and rhythm. The result is a series of alternating long tonepulses (at the fundamental pitch) and silent intervals.

Channel masking (figure 4.17b) selectively masks pulsars in two channels, creating a dialog within a phrase by articulating each channel in turn. Figure 4.17b shows two channels only, but we can generalize this scheme to N channels.

Figure 4.16 Schema of pulsar synthesis. A pulsar generator with separate envelope controls for fundamental frequency, formant frequency, amplitude, stochastic masking, and spatial position. In advanced pulsar synthesis, several generators may be linked with separate formant and spatial envelopes. A pulsar stream may be convolved with a sampled sound.

(a)

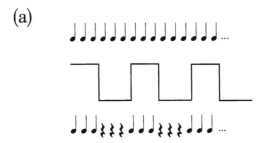

(b)

(c)

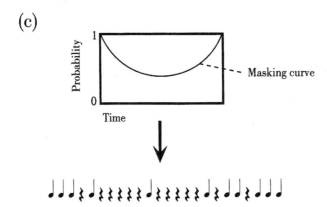

Figure 4.17   Pulsar masking turns a regular train into an irregular train. Pulsars are illustrated as quarter notes, and masked pulsars are indicated as quarter rests. (a) Burst masking. The burst ratio here is 3:3. (b) Channel masking. (c) Stochastic masking according to a probability table. When the probability is 1, there is no masking. When the probability is 0, there are no pulsars. In the middle, the pulsar train is intermittent. Notice the thinning out of the texture as the probability curve dips in the center.

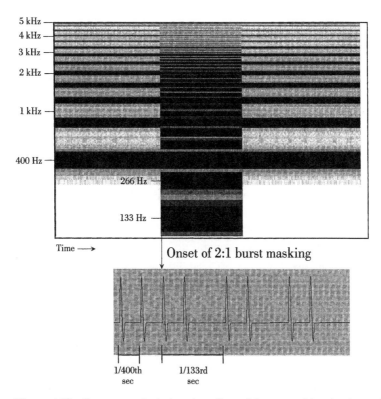

Figure 4.18 Sonogram depicting the effect of burst masking in the audio frequency range. The pulsaret is one cycle of a sinusoid, and the pulsaret envelope is rectangular. The $b:r$ ratio is 2:1. The fundamental frequency is 100 Hz and the formant frequency is 400 Hz. Notice the subharmonics at 133 Hz and 266 Hz caused by the extended periodicity of the pulse masking interval (400 Hz/3).

Stochastic masking introduces random intermittancy into the regular stream of pulsars. We have implemented stochastic masking as a weighted probability that a pulsar will be emitted at a particular point in a pulsar train. The probability is expressed as an envelope over the duration of the pulsar train. When the value of the envelope is 1, a pulsar is emitted. If the value is less than 1, it has less possibility. A value of 0 results in no pulsar emissions. Values between 0.9 and 0.8 produces an interesting analog-like intermittancy, as if there were an erratic contact in the synthesis circuit (figure 4.17c).

Convolution of Pulsars with Samples

Pulsar synthesis can be harnessed as a method of sound transformation through convolution. Convolution is fundamental to the physics of waves (Rabiner and Gold 1975). It "crosses" two signals, creating a new signal that combines the time structures and spectra of both inputs. Many transformations emerge from convolution, including exotic filters, spatializers, models of excitation/resonance, and a gamut of temporal transformations (echoes, reverberation, attack-smoothing, rhythm-mapping). Pure convolution, however, has no control parameters, that is, the type of effect achieved depends entirely on the nature of the input signals. See Roads (1992b, 1993a, 1997) for applications of convolution in musical sound transformation.

Sophisticated transformations involving rhythm- and spatial-mapping can be achieved through convolution. It is well known that any series of impulses convolved with a brief sound maps that sound into the time pattern of the impulses. These impulses can be emitted by a pulsar generator. If the pulsar train frequency is in the infrasonic range, then each pulsar is replaced by a copy of the sampled sound object, creating a rhythmic pattern. The convolution of a rhythmic pattern with a sound object causes each impulse to be replaced by a filtered copy of the sound object. Each instance of the sampled object is projected in space according to the spatial location of a specific pulsar's position.

In convolution, each pulsar represents the impulse response of a filter. Thus timbral variations can derive from two factors: (1) filtering effects imposed by the time-varying pulsar train, and (2) overlapping effects caused by convolution with pulsar trains whose fundamental period is shorter than the duration of the sampled sound.

Figure 4.19 shows the temporal and filtering effects of convolution in the form of sonograms. The input signal (b) is the Italian word *qui* (pronounced "kwee"). It convolves with the pulsar train (a) with a variable infrasonic fundamental frequency and a variable audio formant frequency. The resulting convolution (c) combines the time structure and the spectra of the two signals.

The composer can stockpile a database of sampled sound objects for crossing with trains selected from the pulsar database. If the goal of the synthesis is to retain the time structure of the pulsar train (e.g., to maintain a specific rhythm), the sampled sound objects should be of short duration (less than the fundamental period of the pulsar train) and have a sharp attack (a rise time of less than 100 ms). These constraints minimize the time-smearing effects of convolution (Roads 1992b, 1993a, 1997). A good starting point for a sound database

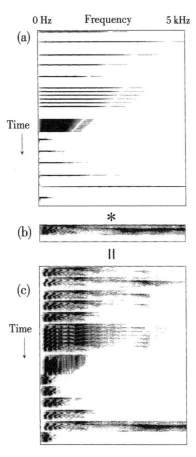

Figure 4.19 Effect of convolution with pulsar train. (a) Infrasonic pulsar train with a variable fundamental and formant frequency. (b) Sampled sound, the Italian word *qui* (pronounced "kwee"). (c) Convolution of (a) and (b).

is a collection of percussion samples. If one seeks a smoother and more continuous texture the constraints can be relaxed. Samples with long durations superimpose multiple copies of the sampled object, creating a rippling sound stream. Samples with slow attacks blur the onset of each sample copy, smearing the stream into a continuum. Thus by controlling the attack shape of the sample one can affect the sonic texture.

Implementations of Pulsar Synthesis

My original implementation of PS dates to 1991, using James McCartney's Synth-O-Matic, a programmable sound synthesis environment for Apple Macintosh computers (McCartney 1990, 1994). In 1996, Mr. McCartney replaced Synth-O-Matic with SuperCollider 1—an object-oriented programming language with a Power Macintosh runtime system (McCartney 1996). Using SuperCollider 1, Stephen T. Pope and I created a new implementation of basic PS in 1997.

With the improved SuperCollider 2 (McCartney 1998), Alberto de Campo and I developed a new realization of pulsar synthesis, presented in a 1999 summer course at the Center for New Music and Audio Technology, University of California, Berkeley. Further refinement of this prototype has led to the PulsarGenerator application, distributed by CREATE. Figure 4.20 shows the graphical interface of PulsarGenerator, version 1. Notice the control envelopes for the synthesis variables. Users can design these envelopes in advance of synthesis, or manipulate them in real time as the instrument plays. We have implemented a scheme for saving and loading these envelopes in groups called *settings*. The program lets one crossfade at a variable rate between settings, which takes performance with PulsarGenerator to another level of musical complexity.

In wave-oriented synthesis techniques, an algorithm loops through a wavetable and varies the signal according to relatively slowly-updated control functions. Thus the efficiency of synthesis corresponds to the number of simultaneous unit generators (oscillators, filters, etc.). In contrast, particle synthesis is more demanding, since the synthesis algorithm must also handle the task of scheduling possibly thousands of events per second, each of which may be unique. The efficiency of pulsar synthesis is therefore related to the rate of particle emission. At infrasonic rates (< 20 pulsars per second), the PulsarGenerator application uses less than 3.6% of the processor on a single-processor Apple G4 running at a 500 MHz clock speed. At high audio rates (such as a three-formant instrument emitting six thousand pulsars per second, corre-

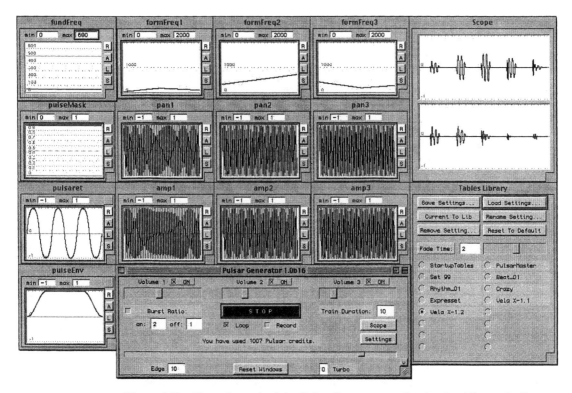

Figure 4.20 Control panel of the PulsarGenerator application by Alberto de Campo and Curtis Roads. Copyright Alberto de Campo, Curtis Roads, and the Regents of the University of California 2000.

sponding to the fundamental frequency of 2 kHz), the application requires approximately 45% of the processor. It is a testimony to SuperCollider 2 that the entire implementation, including the graphical interface, needed less than one thousand and five hundred lines of code and comments. Our code builds the interface, defines the synthesis algorithm, schedules the pulsars, and handles file input and output. McCartney's SCPlay, an efficient real-time sound engine, calculates the samples.

Composing with Pulsars

To interact with PulsarGenerator in real time is to experiment directly with sonic ideas. While experimenting, a composer can save settings and plan how these will be used within a composition. The PulsarGenerator program can also record the sounds produced in a real-time session. The composer can then edit the session or convolve and mix it with other material.

A final stage of pulsar composition is to merge multiple trains to form a composite texture. This is a question of montage, and is best handled by editing and mixing software designed for this purpose. Each layer of the texture may have its own rhythmic pattern, formant frequency envelope, choice of convolved objects, and spatial path. Working on a variety of time scales, a composer can apply signal processing transformations such as mixing with other sounds, filtering, modulations, and reverberation to individual pulsars, pulsar trains, and pulsar textures.

Musical Applications of Pulsar Synthesis

I developed pulsar synthesis while realizing *Clang-Tint* (Roads 1993b), an electronic music composition commissioned by the Japanese Ministry of Culture (Bunka-cho) and the Kunitachi College of Music, Tokyo. The second movement of this work, entitled *Organic*, focuses on expressive phrasing. It combines bursts of insect noise and animal and bird calls with electronic pulse-tones. The electronic sound palette utilizes pulsar synthesis in many forms: pulsating blips, elongated formant tones, and clouds of asynchronous pulsars. For the latter, I first generated multiple infrasonic pulsar trains, each one beating at a different frequency in the range of 6 to 18 Hz. I then mixed these together to obtain the asynchronous pulsar cloud.

The raw material of my electronic music composition *Half-life*, composed in 1998 and 1999, is a one-minute pulsar train that is wildly varied. Most of the sounds in the rest of the work are derived from this source. *Half-life* extends the pulsar material through processes of granulation, microfiltration, granular pitch-shifting, recirculating feedback echo, individual pulsar amplitude shaping, and selective reverberation. *Tenth vortex* (2000) and *Eleventh vortex* (2001) continue in this direction.

Assessment of Pulsar Synthesis

Music unfolds on multiple time scales, from high-level macrostructure down to a myriad of individual sound objects or notes. Below this level is another hierarchy of time scales. Here are the microsonic particles such as the classical rectangular impulses, grains, wavelets, and pulsars (Roads 1999). Musicians proved the effectiveness of analog impulse generation decades ago. In comparison, digital pulsar synthesis offers a flexible choice of waveforms and envelopes, increased precision, and graphical programmable control.

Unlike wave-oriented synthesis techniques, the notion of rhythm is built into techniques based on particles. Rhythm, pitch, and timbre are all interrelated but can be separately controlled. Pulsar synthesis offers a seamless link between the time scales of individual particle rhythms, periodic pitches, and the meso or phrase level of composition. A novel feature of this technique is the generation of multiple independent formant trajectories, each following its own spatial path.

As we have shown, basic pulsar technique can create a broad family of musical structures: singular impulses, rhythmic sequences, continuous tones, time-varying phrases, and beating textures. Pulsar microevents produce rhythmic sequences or, when the density of events is sufficiently high, sustained tones, allowing composition to pass directly from microstructure to mesostructure.

Graphic and Sonographic Synthesis of Microsound

Graphic and sonographic sound synthesis employ visual means to translate images into sound. Here we look at two approaches to interpreting graphical images as sound waveforms: time-domain or graphic, and frequency-domain or sonographic.

Graphic Synthesis in the Time-Domain and Frequency-Domain

Electro-optical synthesizers read waveforms inscribed on rotating tone wheels as in a recent implementation of *photosonic synthesis* using a rotating optical disc with its inscribed time-domain waveform (Duden and Arfib 1990; Arfib, Duden, and Sanchez 1996). In this approach to graphic synthesis, a short waveform repeats many times per second to form a tone.

Another approach is to draw a waveform over an extended period of time. A sound editor presents an image of sound waveforms in a time domain, some programs providing an onscreen pencil for drawing waveforms or smoothing over discontinuities. The time-domain approach to graphic synthesis can be effective on the micro time scale, but requires a great deal of labor. In the era of optical film soundtracks, a few dedicated souls made short pieces using a similar technique. A prime example is Norman McLaren's 1948 *Dots Points*, a 2-minute 47-second film in which both sound and visuals are drawn directly on the film with pen and ink. (See also the transient drawing technique presented later in this chapter, which creates individual particles by sculpting waveforms in a sound editor.)

Time-domain graphic synthesis lets one design the microstructure of each sound event in detail. However, this approach does not scale well to higher time spans. Acoustical microstructure is delicate. The ear is extremely sensitive to even minor alterations in transient morphology and envelope shape, such as the slope or duration of an attack. Even a slight amplitude discontinuity may cause an audible click or thump. At the same time, the ear tends to ignore permutations in the phase of partials that cause dramatic changes in the shape of the waveform.

Waveform drawing loses usefulness as one zooms out from a waveform display to take in a larger time view. One gains a global view of the sound object envelope, but can no longer see the inner structure of the sound (waveshape, number of iterations, microvariations, etc.), which largely determine its identity.

Another approach to graphic synthesis, which is more powerful on larger time scales, is based on a sonogram frequency-domain representation. To produce a sonogram, a sound is passed through a bank of filters and the output energy from each filter is traced as a function of frequency and time. The sonogram projects frequency on the vertical axis and time on the horizontal axis. The amplitude appears as darkness on a white background, where a darker trace means more energy.

Any visual representation that captures the basic idea of a frequency-versus-time plane is a sonographical notation. Now available are a number of systems, where graphical traces which one can inscribe on a frequency-time grid can be converted directly into sound. In effect one can paint the sound, erase it, or touch it up with all the flexibility of a software paint program. Indeed, several systems let one import images that have been prepared with visual software. The next sections survey three sonographic systems, with emphasis on their microsonic capabilities.

Micro-Arc Synthesis with the UPIC

The UPIC (Unité Polyagogique Informatique de CEMAMu) is a sound synthesis system conceived by Iannis Xenakis and built by engineers at the Centre d'Études de Mathématique et Automatique Musicales (CEMAMu) in Paris (Xenakis 1992). The UPIC system offers both graphical (time-domain) and sonographical (frequency-domain) interfaces for sound composition. In an initial version, dating from 1977, the user interacted by way of a large graphics tablet, mounted vertically like a painter's easel. The first composition realized with the UPIC was Xenakis's *Mycenae-Alpha* (1980). A major breakthrough for the system was the development of a real-time version, based on a 64-oscillator synthesis engine (Raczinski and Marino 1988). By 1991, engineers had coupled this engine to a personal computer running the Windows operating system, permitting a sophisticated graphical interface (Marino, Raczinski, and Serra 1990; Raczinski, Marino, and Serra 1991). The program now runs stand-alone, with no additional hardware.

At the level of sound microstructure, waveforms and event envelopes can be drawn directly onto the tablet and displayed onscreen. At a higher level of organization, composers can draw the sonographical frequency/time structure of a score page. Lines—called *arcs*—appear on the display screen as one draws with the mouse. Individual arcs can then be moved, stretched or shrunk, cut, copied, or pasted. The arcs on the page can also represent sampled sounds.

In the 1991 version of the UPIC, a page can have sixty-four simultaneous arcs, with four thousand arcs per page. Most importantly, the duration of each page can last from 6 ms to more than two hours. This temporal flexibility lets the user zoom in to the micro time scale. When a page lasts only a second, say, any arcs written onto it will be microsounds. These *micro-arcs* can also be cut, copied, and pasted, as well as stretched or compressed in time and frequency. Moreover, the rate at and direction in which the score is read can be controlled in real time with a mouse. This allows discontinuous jumps from one region of the score to another, for example. The sequence of control motions as it plays a score can be recorded and later the same performance can be replayed or edited.

The UPIC system is an especially pliable musical tool since it integrates many levels of composition within a common user interface. Graphic functions created onscreen can function equally as envelopes, waveforms, pitch-time scores, tempo curves, or performance trajectories. This uniform treatment of composition data at every level should be extended to more computer music systems.

Synthesis of Microsound in Phonogramme

Vincent Lebros developed Phonogramme in 1993 at the Université de Paris VIII (Lesbros 1995, 1996). Phonogramme offers an approach to graphical synthesis with some similarities to the UPIC, but offering a number of extensions. First, the program can generate sound directly from a MacOS computer, or it can generate MIDI data to be sent to a bank of synthesizers. Second, the program offers a *harmonic pen*, which draws a number of harmonically related partials above the arc inscribed by the user. Users can adjust the number and strength of these partials before drawing. The harmonic pen solves a common problem of sonographic synthesis: a single arc is not a complete description of a sound object. As a sonogram of a concrète sound clearly indicates, it takes many traces on the sonographic plane to create a sound object with a fundamental frequency, formant structure, harmonic/inharmonic partials, and inner variations. Finally, unlike the 1991 UPIC system, Phonogramme can analyze a sound and generate an editable sonographic representation.

Phonogramme's score page can be interpreted on any time scale chosen by the user. A line or arc inscribed can be interpreted as a microsonic particle. It is also possible to turn the drawing pencil into a kind of dot spray where a fast gesture made with the mouse leaves behind not a continuous line but a series of microsonic dots (figure 4.21).

Synthesis of Microsound in MetaSynth

The MetaSynth program by (Wenger and Spiegel 1999) is a recent implementation of sonographical synthesis. It operates on a MacOS computer with real-time playback (or delayed playback for complex scores). Although it does not incorporate every feature of predecessors such as UPIC and Phonogramme, it does offer unique features that take graphical synthesis to a new level of power and expressivity.

Among the drawing implements included with MetaSynth are some tools for microsound synthesis, including a granular spray brush (figure 4.22). The spray brush determines the time and frequency span of the grains. The grain envelope is fixed as a triangle. In another mode, it can play back a line drawing with a granular instrument. The waveform of the grains is variable on a per-page basis, from a synthetic waveform to a sampled waveform.

MetaSynth is a major contribution to sonographic synthesis in that it greatly expands the palette of brushes and other implements to paint sound color. It also permits nongraphical granulation of sound files in its Effects window. (See chapter 5 for more on granulation of sound files.)

Assessment of Graphic and Sonographic Synthesis of Microsound

Graphic and sonographic synthesis share a common interface: drawing. What their drawings represent are quite different, however. Graphic synthesis depicts

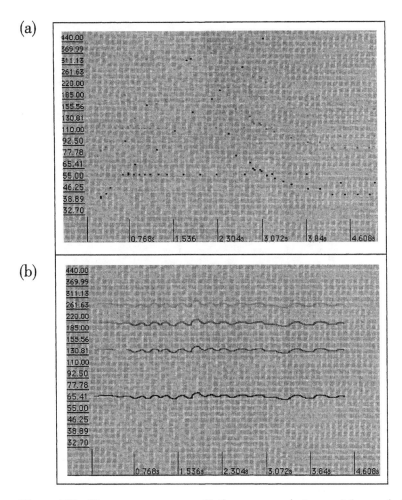

Figure 4.21 Phonogramme scores. Both scores are just over 4.6 seconds in length. (a) Fast horizontal gestures leave behind a stream of micro-arcs. Notice the four harmonics superimposed over the original low-frequency gestures by the harmonic pencil. (b) Slow hand movements create continuous tones.

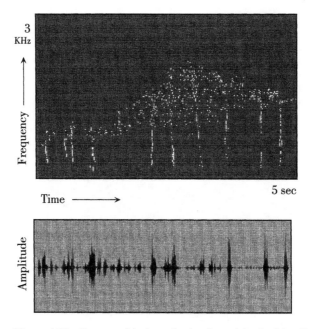

Figure 4.22   Sonographical synthesis of particles in MetaSynth. (a) The particles were drawn by hand with a spray brush tool. This particle score can be played back with many different waveforms, including sampled sounds. (b) Time-domain view of the waveform.

time-domain envelopes and waveforms. To draw pitch curves and envelope shapes with graphic tools is a supple and efficient procedure. It is easy to create shapes and phrases that would be difficult to achieve by other means.

To draw time-domain waveforms, however, is problematic. It is difficult to infer a sound directly from a view of its waveform. This is further complicated by the fact that the same sound can be represented graphically by innumerable ways whose only differences are in the phase relationships among the frequency components. Furthermore, any waveform repeated without variation takes on a static quality. So, as in other approaches to synthesis, waveform generation in graphic synthesis systems has shifted from individual fixed waveforms to evolving sources such as sampled sounds or groups of time-varying waveforms.

Sonographic sound synthesis is a direct and intuitive approach to sound sculpture. Interaction with sonographical synthesis can be either precise or imprecise, depending on how the user treats the process. A composer who plans each line and its mapping into sound can obtain precise results. It is just as worthwhile to treat the medium as a sketch pad, where initial drawings are later refined into a finished design.

Unlike traditional notation, which requires serious study for a long period of time, a child can learn the relationship between drawn gestures and sound in minutes. This initial simplicity hides a deeper complexity, however. As with any technique, the best results demand a long period of study and experimentation.

As mentioned earlier, a single arc is not a description of a complete sound object. An arc is only one component of a complex time-varying sound. Such sounds require many arcs. We can see this complex nature in the sonograms of relatively simple instrumental tones, such as a cello. Noiser timbres, such as a cymbal or gong, display enormous complexity. They seem to be composed of globules of energy that sometimes connect and at other times break apart.

As such representations become more commonplace, a long process of codification—from complex sonographic patterns into abstract iconic notation—seems to be inevitable. The Acousmagraphe system, developed at the Groupe de Recherches Musicale (Paris), points in this direction (Desantos 1997).

Particle-Based Formant Synthesis

A *formant* is a peak of energy in a spectrum, which can include both harmonic and inharmonic partials as well as noise. Formant peaks are a characteristic of the spoken vowel sounds and the tone color of many musical instruments. Within the range of 0 to 5000 Hz, the vocal tract has five formant regions. Formant regions act as a kind of "spectral signature" or "timbral cue" to the source of many sounds. The formants of a voice or an instrument are not fixed, however, they drift according to the frequency of the fundamental (Luce 1963). Furthermore, formants are only one clue the ear uses to identify the source of a tone.

Fully understanding the nature of formants in human speech has long been a goal of scientific research. Ingenious methods for synthesizing the formants of vowel-like tones have been developed (Tyndall 1875; Miller 1916), and it is not surprising that this research has served as a wellspring of ideas for musical formant synthesis.

The rest of this section presents concise descriptions of three particle synthesis techniques: formant wave-function or FOF synthesis, Vosim, and window-function (WF) synthesis. FOF and Vosim evolved from attempts to simulate human speech, whereas WF was developed to emulate the formants of traditional musical instruments. For more detailed descriptions, see the references and Roads (1996).

FOF Synthesis

Formant wave-function synthesis (*fonction d'onde formantique* or FOF) generates a stream of grains, each separated by a quantum of time, corresponding to the period of the fundamental frequency. So a single note produced by this technique contains hundreds of FOF grains. The definitive FOF grain is a sine wave with either a steep or smooth attack and a quasi-exponential decay.

The envelope of a FOF grain is local, that of the entire note is global. The local envelope of a FOF grain is defined as follows. For the attack portion of the FOF grain, $0 \leq t \leq tex$, the envelope is:

$$env_t = 1/2 \times [1 - \cos(\pi_t/tex)] \times \exp(-atten_t)$$

For the decay portion, $t \geq tex$, the envelope is:

$$env_t = \exp(-atten_t)$$

π is the initial phase of the FOF signal, *tex* is the attack time of the local envelope, and *atten* is the decay time (D'Allessandro and Rodet 1989). The effect is that of a damped sinusoidal burst, each FOF grain lasting just a few milliseconds. The convolution of the brief FOF envelope with the sinusoid contributes audible sidebands around the sine wave, creating a formant spectrum. The spectrum of the damped sine generator is equivalent to the frequency response curve of one of the bandpass filters and the result of summing several FOF generators is a spectrum with several formant peaks.

Each FOF generator is controlled by many parameters. Among these are the formant parameters $p1$ through $p4$:

$p1$ is the center frequency of the formant.

$p2$ is the formant bandwidth, defined as the width between the points that are −6 dB from the peak of the formant.

$p3$ is the peak amplitude of the formant.

$p4$ is the width of the *formant skirt*. The formant skirt is the lower part of the formant peak, about 40 dB below the peak, akin to the foothills of a mountain. The skirt parameter is independent of the formant bandwidth, which specifies the breadth at the peak of the mountain.

The inherent connection between time-domain and frequency-domain operations is exemplified in the way FOF parameters are specified. Two of the main formant parameters are specified in the time domain as properties of the envelope of the FOF grain. First, the duration of the FOF attack controls parameter $p4$, the width of the formant skirt, that is, as the duration of the attack lengthens, the skirtwidth narrows. Second, the duration of the FOF decay determines $p2$, the formant bandwidth. Hence a long decay length translates into a sharp resonance peak, while a short decay widens the bandwidth of the signal.

The basic sound production model embedded in FOF synthesis is the voice. However, users can tune many parameters to move beyond vocal synthesis toward synthetic effects and emulations of instruments (Bennett and Rodet 1989).

Typical applications of FOF synthesis configure several FOF generators in parallel. Some implementations are very complicated, with over 60 parameters to be specified for each sound event. The CHANT program, developed in the 1980s, was proposed as a response to this complexity, providing a collection of rules for controlling multiple FOF streams in parallel (Rodet, Potard, and Barrière 1984).

Vosim

Like FOF synthesis, the Vosim technique generates a series of short-duration particles in order to produce a formant effect. Vosim synthesis was developed by Werner Kaegi and Stan Tempelaars at the Institute of Sonology in Utrecht during the early 1970s (Kaegi 1973, 1974; Tempelaars 1976, 1977, 1996). Vosim generates a series of tonebursts, producing a strong formant component. Like FOF, it was originally designed for vowel sounds, and later extended to model vocal fricatives—consonants such as [sh]—and quasi-instrumental tones (Kaegi and Tempelaars 1978).

The Vosim waveform approximates the signal generated by the human voice in the form of a series of pulsetrains, where each pulse is the square of a sine function. The parameter A sets the amplitude of the highest pulse. Each of the pulsetrains contains $N \sin^2$ pulses in series decreasing in amplitude by a decay factor b. The width (duration) of each pulse T determines the position of the formant spectrum. A variable-length delay M follows each pulse train, which contributes to the pulsetrain's overall period, and thus determines the fundamental frequency period. The period is $(N \times T) + M$, so for seven pulses of

Table 4.3 VOSIM parameters

Name	Description
T	Pulsewidth
δT	Increment or decrement of T
M	Delay following a series of pulses
δM	Increment or decrement of M
D	Maximum deviation of M
A	Amplitude of the first pulse
δA	Increment or decrement of A
b	Attentuation constant for the series of pulses
N	Number of pulses per period
S	Type of modulation (sine or random)
NM	Modulation rate
NP	Number of periods

200 μsec duration and a delay equal to 900 μsec, the total period is 3 ms and the fundamental frequency is 333.33 Hz. The formant centers at 5000 Hz.

Two strong percepts emerge from the typical Vosim signal: a fundamental corresponding to the repetition frequency of the entire signal, and a formant peak in the spectrum corresponding to the pulsewidth of the $\sin^2$ pulses. A Vosim oscillator produces one formant. In order to create a sound with several formants, it is necessary to mix the outputs of several Vosim oscillators.

Table 4.3 lists the set of parameters that control the Vosim oscillator. T, M, N, A, and b are the primary parameters. By modulating the delay period M, one can produce vibrato, frequency modulation, and noise sounds. Kaegi and Tempelaars introduced three additional variables: S, D, and NM, corresponding respectively to the type of modulation (sine or random), the maximum frequency deviation, and the modulation rate. They wanted also to be able to provide for "transitional" sounds, which led to the introduction of the variables NP, δT, δM, and δA. These are the positive and negative increments of T, M, and A, respectively, within the number of periods NP.

By changing the value of the pulsewidth T, the formant changes in time. This is *formant shifting*, a different effect than the progressive spectral enrichment which occurs in, for example, frequency modulation synthesis. The Vosim signal is not bandlimited, but spectral components are greater than 60 dB down at six times the fundamental frequency (Tempelaars 1976).

Window Function Synthesis

Window function (WF) synthesis generates pulsestreams that result in formants of purely harmonic content (Bass and Goeddel 1981). It begins with the creation of a broadband harmonic signal. Then a weighting stage emphasizes or attenuates different harmonics in this signal to create time-varying formant regions which can emulate the harmonic spectra of traditional instruments.

The building block of WF synthesis is a particle known as a *window function pulse*. A typical window function is a smooth pulse with a bell-shaped envelope. Window spectra exhibit a characteristic center lobe and side lobes. The center lobe is typically much higher in amplitude than the side lobes, meaning that the signal is bandlimited. In the Blackman-Harris window function chosen by Bass and Goeddel, the frequencies in the side lobes are down at least 60 dB.

Bass and Goeddel created a broadband signal by linking a periodic series of WF pulses separated by a period of zero amplitude. For different fundamental frequencies, the duration of the WF pulse stays the same; only the interpulse silence varies. In this use of a pulse followed by a period of deadtime, the WF technique is similar to pulsar synthesis, Vosim, and the FOF method explained earlier. In other respects, however, the techniques are not similar.

In WF synthesis, the number of harmonics increases as the fundamental frequency decreases. This is because the higher harmonics fall outside the center lobe of the WF pulse's spectrum. Thus, low tones are timbrally rich, while high tones are less so. This is characteristic of some traditional instruments such as pipe organs and pianos, which Bass and Goeddel wanted to simulate. Note that not all instruments—for example, the harpsichord—exhibit this behavior. Furthermore, some instruments do not have a purely harmonic spectrum and so make poor models for the WF technique.

To create formant regions in the spectrum requires a further processing called *slot weighting*. A *time slot* is defined as the duration of a single WF pulse plus a portion of its deadtime. The timbre of the sound can be altered by weighting the slots (i.e., multiplying a slot by a value) with a periodic sequence of *N* slot weights. This feeds a stream of WF pulses to a multiplier as an input signal, along with a periodic stream of slot weights. The multiplier computes the product of each input pulse with a specific weight, making an output stream of WF pulses at different amplitudes. The spectrum of such a stream exhibits peaks and valleys at various frequencies. For time-varying timbres, each slot weight can be specified as a time-varying function.

WF synthesis requires an amplitude compensation scheme, because low frequencies contain few pulses and much zero-amplitude deadtime or silence, while high frequencies contain many pulses and almost no deadtime. A quasi-linear scaling function adjusts the amplitude as an inverse function of frequency. That is, low tones are emphasized and high tones are attentuated for equal balance throughout the frequency range.

Assessment of Particle-Based Formant Synthesis Techniques

Particle-based formant synthesis models a class of natural mechanisms which resonate when excited, and are quickly damped by physical forces. A typical example would be a stroke on a woodblock—a sound which cuts off almost immediately. The result is a grain-like "pop." Another example is the glottal pulse, which the vocal tract filters. Continuous tones string together a series of such particles.

FOF synthesis has been available within the widely distributed Csound language for some time (Boulanger 2000). The Common Lisp Music language (Schottstaedt 2000) includes a wavetrain object able to realize both FOF and Vosim synthesis. Window Function synthesis technique was experimental, and since its original realization, has not continued.

Vocal-like tones can be simulated by mimicking the fast impulses that continuously excite resonance in the vocal tract. Realistic simulation from a particle technique, however, requires an enormous investment of time. In the 1980s, vocal synthesis using the FOF technique performed the "Queen of the Night" aria from Mozart's *Magic Flute*. The realization of this 30-second fragment took months of effort.

In the simulation of vocal and instrumental tone, the particle representation should be invisible. If we divorce these techniques from their original uses, we can see that particle-based formant synthesis remains a rich resource for synthetic timbres, both at the infrasonic frequency level—where it produces a wide variety of rhythmic pops—and also at the audio frequency level, where it generates expressive resonant tones.

Synthesis by Transient Drawing

Synthesis by *transient drawing* is a direct method. It takes two forms: *synthetic* and *transformational*. Synthetic transient drawing requires a graphical sound

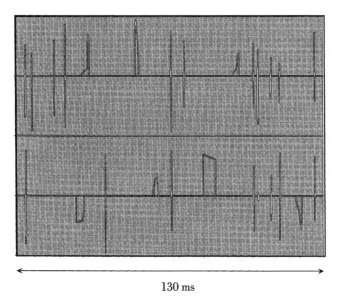

130 ms

Figure 4.23   Transient wave writing in a sound editor. Notice the hand-drawn transients interspersed with narrow computer-generated impulses.

editor which provides a waveform pencil that can be used to manually inscribe the waveform of a transient. These transients can be interspersed with waveforms produced by other means (figure 4.23).

Transformational transient drawing also uses a sound editor, after beginning with an existing low-level audio signal, such as background noise or the tail of a reverberant envelope. A brief extract of this nonstationary signal is selected and rescaled to a much higher amplitude, creating a transient particle (figure 4.24). This particle can be reshaped using the implements of the editor, such as narrowband filtering, envelope reshaping, phase inversion, and spatialisation. The following frequency bands are especially important in filtering the transient particles.

1. Direct current (DC) cut—removal of frequencies below 20 Hz

2. Deep bass cut or boost—80 Hz

3. Mid-bass boominess cut—200 Hz

4. Low-mid boost—500–700 Hz resonances

5. Mid harshness cut—1–2 kHz

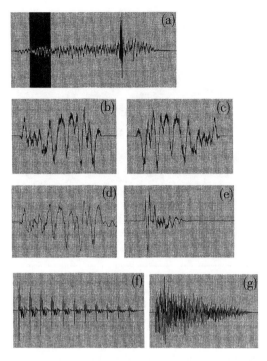

Figure 4.24 Manipulations of a transient wave extracted from an ambient texture. (a) Ambient noise texture. The darkened part is a 120-ms transient that we extract as a transient wave. (b) Detail of the extracted transient. (c) Reversal of (b). (d) Lowpass filtered (smoothed) version of (b). (e) Re-enveloped and pitch-shifted copy of (b), now lasting less than 50 ms. (f) Ten-fold replication (cloning) of (e) to form a decaying sound object. (g) Copy of (b) that has been passed through a bank of narrow filters to form a pitched tone. The attack was edited to create a sharper onset.

6. Crackle boost—notches at 3 kHz and 6 kHz

7. High harshness removal—lowpass at 5 kHz

8. Brilliance boost—12 kHz

Filters 2, 4, 6, and 8 accentuate the particle, while filters 1, 3, 5, and 7 attenuate it in the harsh frequency zones. Successive micro operations can radically transform the original signal. For example, a sharp narrow filter applied to a brief noise particle transforms it into a resonating pure tone (figure 4.24g). If we apply advanced techniques such as time-stretching, there comes a point at which we can transform any transient into a myriad of sounds on any time scale.

Assessment of Transient Drawing

Transient drawing takes compositional decision-making down to a microscopic level, starting from almost nothing and obliging the composer to handcraft each individual particle in a phrase. The extreme differentiation resulting from this approach leads to a high probability of *singularities* or unique sound events. In this sense, transient drawing maximizes the information content of the musical signal.

Both the synthetic and the transformational approaches to transient drawing are labor-intensive, relying on manual editing. In effect, the composer works in a manner similar to a Pointillist painter such as Georges Seurat, building an image from thousands of tiny brush strokes. In Seurat's later paintings (for example, *La Luzerne, Saint-Denis*) the particles can be scattered within dense masses. When one of these particles appears isolated by silence, its singularity conveys a striking impact.

As we saw in the section on graphic synthesis, waveform drawing makes sense only on a micro time scale. It does not translate well to higher time scales. This is because zooming out on a waveform display provides a global view of the sound object envelope at the expense of the inner microstructure (waveform shape, number of iterations, etc.).

Transient drawing has become an integral part of my compositional practice. Many examples of it appear in *Clang-Tint*, especially in the movement *Organic*. I also made extensive use of the technique in the first movement of *Half-life*, in which a number of singularities appear. Perhaps the most practical use of transient drawing is for fabricating such singularities to be scattered over sparse textures. In order to build continuous tones from a single transient, I used transient drawing in conjunction with particle cloning (described next).

Particle Cloning Synthesis

In particle cloning synthesis, a brief tone pip, or a longer continuous or fluttering tone, is made by repeatedly cloning a single sound particle. This particle may derive from any synthesis technique, including transient drawing. Figures 4.24f and 4.25 illustrate particle cloning. Here is a recipe for particle cloning:

1. Generate a single particle by any means.

2. Sculpt the particle to the desired shape and duration in a waveform editor.

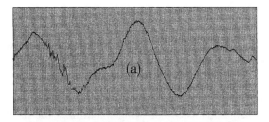

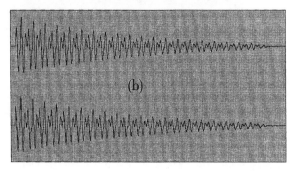

Figure 4.25 Particle cloning synthesis. (a) Solo particle, lasting 35 ms, extracted from an acoustic sample of a drum sound. (b) A 200 ms sound object formed by cloning (a) 50 times, pitch-shifting it up two octaves, creating another channel slightly delayed, and applying an exponentially decaying amplitude curve.

3. Clone the particle and repeat it over a specified duration to form a tone pip. The number of particles cloned corresponds to the total duration divided by the duration of the particle. The resulting pitch depends on the period of the particle.

4. Shape the amplitude envelope of the resulting tone pip.

5. Pitch-shift the tone pip to the desired pitch, with or without time correction.

6. Apply one or more bandpass filters. The important bands to control are the low (50–150 Hz), low-mid (150–300 Hz, narrowband), mid (500–900 Hz), mid-high (3–4 kHz, wide bandwidth), and high (9–12 kHz, wide bandwidth) ranges.

In stage 3, we used a Replicate function in a sound editor to automate the process. Replicate fills an arbitrary duration with the contents of the clipboard. Thus it is possible to copy a particle, select a 3-second region, and fill the region with a sequence of cloned particles. Obviously, the frequency of the tone pip depends on the period of the particle, and so a 10-ms particle produces a tone pip at a pitch of 100 Hz. By selecting some of the silent samples around a particle, one can shift the fundamental frequency downward. The resulting tone can then be transposed to any desired pitch. If the period of the particle is greater than about 50 ms, the texture is no longer continuous, but flutters.

Stages 4, 5, and 6 foster heterogeneity among tones cloned from the same particle. Each tone can have a unique duration, amplitude envelope, pitch, and spectrum weighting.

Assessment of Particle Cloning Synthesis

The construction of tones by particle cloning elevates the time scale of a particle from the micro level to the sound object level, and so fosters the emergence of singularities on the sound object time scale. As we have implemented it, it is a manual technique, carried out with a sound editor. I developed the particle cloning method in the course of composing *Half-life* (1998–99), in which the initial particles derive from pulsar synthesis or transient drawing. These particles stand out prominently in part 1 of the piece, in the melodic section at time 2:04–2:11.

Physical Models of Particles

Computer sound synthesis rests on the premise that a software program can model a sound-generating process. *Physical modeling* (PhM) synthesis starts from a mathematical description of acoustic sound production (Roads 1996). That is, the equations of PhM describe the mechanical and acoustic behavior of an instrument as it is played. The goals of physical modeling synthesis are both scientific and artistic. PhM investigates the extent to which equations and algorithms can simulate the sound-producing mechanisms of existing instruments. In this sense, a physical model embodies the Newtonian ideal of a mathematical model of a complicated mechanico-acoustic process. PhM can also create sounds of fancifully imaginary instruments, otherwise impossible to realize.

PhM synthesis can be traced back to the mathematical descriptions of John William Strutt (Lord Rayleigh). His insightful volume *The Theory of Sound* (1894/1945) laid the foundation for a century of research. For many years, efforts in physical modeling focused on synthesis of continuous tones. Only

```
/************************* MARACA ****************************/

#define MARA_SOUND_DECAY 0.95
#define MARA_SYSTEM_DECAY 0.999
#define MARA_NUM_BEANS 25

void maraca_setup() {
  num_objects = MARA_NUM_BEANS;
  gain = log(num_objects) / log(4.0) * 40.0 / (MY_FLOAT)
num_objects;
  coeffs[0] = -0.96 * 2.0 * cos(3200.0 * TWO_PI / SRATE);
  coeffs[1] = 0.96*0.96;
  soundDecay = MARA_SOUND_DECAY;
  systemDecay = MARA_SYSTEM_DECAY;
}

MY_FLOAT maraca_tick() {
  MY_FLOAT data;
  shakeEnergy *= systemDecay;          // Exponential system decay
  if (my_random(1024) < num_objects)   // If collision
    sndLevel += gain * shakeEnergy;    //   add energy
  input = sndLevel * noise_tick();     // Actual Sound is Random
  sndLevel *= soundDecay;              // Exponential Sound decay
  input -= output[0]*coeffs[0];        // Do gourd
  input -= output[1]*coeffs[1];        //   resonance
  output[1] = output[0];               //     filter
  output[0] = input;                   //       calculations
  data = output[0] - output[1];        // Extra zero for shape
  return data;
}
```

Figure 4.26 Perry Cook's model of a maraca, coded using the Synthesis Toolkit in the C++ language. Notice the declaration at the top indicating the number of beans in the shaker. A statement in a score file (not shown) triggers the maraca model.

more recently has attention turned to synthesis using physical models of the particulated sounds of certain percussion instruments and environmental microsounds. Perry Cook's Physically Informed Stochastic Event Modeling (PhISEM) exemplifies this approach. PhISEM is a suite of programs to simulate the sounds of shaken and scraped percussion such as maracas (figure 4.26), sekere, cabasa, bamboo windchime, tambourine, sleighbells, and guiro (Cook 1996, 1997). Cook also developed a model to simulate the sound of water drops based on the same principles, and suggested that this technique could also synthesize the sound of feet crunching on gravel, or ice cubes in a shaken glass. (See also Keller and Truax (1998) and the discussion of physical models for granular synthesis in chapter 3).

The common thread among instruments modeled by PhISEM is that sound results from discrete microevents. At the core of PhISEM are particle models.

Basic Newtonian equations governing the motion and collision of point masses produce the sounds. For shaken percussion instruments, the algorithm assumes multiple individual sound sources, for example, that with maracas each of them contains many beans. It calculates the probability of bean collisions; very high after a shake, and rapidly decaying. If a bean collision occurs, it is simulated by a burst of exponentially decaying noise. All collision noises pass through a sharply tuned bandpass filter, which simulates the resonance of the gourd.

Assessment of Physical Models of Particles

Many percussion instruments create their distinctive timbre through the accumulation of microsounds. In the case of shaken instruments, this can be modeled as a stochastic process. Physical models of such instruments produce granular sounds, either sparse or dense.

My experiences with this technique were based on the MacOS synthesis program Syd (Bumgardner 1997), which realized Cook's maracas model. It allowed control of the resonance frequency, the resonance pole, the probability of bean collisions, the system decay, and the sound decay. Under certain conditions, these sounds can evoke acoustic instruments recorded in an anechoic environment. When the range of parameter settings is extended, sounds that are not particularly realistic, but still interesting are created.

The physical modelling of particles could go much further. As Chapter 3 points out, a vast scientific literature devoted to models of granular processes has yet to be harnessed for sound synthesis.

Abstract Models of Particles

One can take PhM a step further, and bypass simulations of the acoustic instrument world. Software allows one to develop models of abstract systems which can only exist within the memory of the machine. This is a well-established approach to digital synthesis. Several common synthesis techniques arise out of efficient computational models only indirectly related to acoustical tone production. The technique of frequency modulation (FM) synthesis, for example, can readily be seen as an abstract model (Chowning 1973). FM synthesis is based on a familiar equation in the theory of radio communications. After much effort, John Chowning tested it in the audio frequency range and then tuned the synthesis equation to make the results sound somewhat like traditional instruments. Only when the equation is heavily constrained, however, does it resemble a recognizable instrument, otherwise it produces abstract "radiosonic" timbres.

Abstract models can also control particle synthesis. Chapter 3 described control schemes for granular synthesis based on recursive and chaotic algorithms. The next section discusses an even more abstract approach, where the particles are part of the model, and the sound is a side-effect of their interactions.

Abstract Particle Synthesis

To *sonify* is to translate data into sound. Abstract models sonify particle interactions. Thus the abstract model links particle interactions to sound generation. The sound produced by an abstract model may not sound particulated, it may instead be long and continuous, as in the work of Sturm (1999). Sturm programmed a model of atomic particles which acted according to the laws of physics. When the particles interacted in their environment, they created a unique solution which evolved over time. By using de Broglie's equation—stipulating a relationship between particles and waves—this simulation produced long sine waves. In theory, any signal can be represented by a unique set of particles with specific initial conditions and a particular time-variant potential. Sturm hypothesized that granular sounds could be modeled by the motions of a particle within a box with its interior lined with sound samples.

Xenakis's GENDYN system is another example of the abstract approach (Xenakis 1992; Serra 1992). Instead of using a model imported from atomic physics, however, Xenakis invented a nonlinear algorithm for simulating the behavior of a particle bouncing off elastic barriers. The path traced by the particle is interpreted directly as a soundwave. The waveform is the trace of the particle's chaotic path as it bounces back and forth between the barriers while the model's parameters are changing constantly.

We should also mention the Cosmophone project (Calvet, et al. 2000). The Cosmophone is a device for detection and sonification of cosmic ray bombardments which works by coupling particle detectors to a real-time data acquisition and sound synthesis system. The sonic output of the system goes to a multichannel loudspeaker configuration. The information received by the detectors triggers the emission of sounds. The sounds emitted by the system are programmable. Clearly, various methods of particle synthesis would be well worth testing with such a system.

Table 4.4   Sound particles

Name	Envelope type	Waveform	Characteristics
Grains	Gaussian or arbitrary	Arbitrary, including sampled	Can be scattered irregularly or metrically; each grain is potentially unique; Gaussian grains are compatible with analysis systems like the Gabor transform and the phase vocoder
Glissons	Gaussian or arbitrary	Arbitrary	Variable frequency trajectory; synthesizes glissandi or noise textures
Pulsars	(1) Rectangular around pulsaret, then null; (2) Gaussian (3) Expodec (4) Arbitrary	Arbitrary	Independent control of fundamental and formant spectrum; can also be applied in the infrasonic frequencies as a rhythm generator; synchronous distribution of pulsars
Trainlets	Expodec or arbitrary	Impulse	Used to synthesize tones; offers independent control of fundamental and formant spectrum
Wavelets	Gaussian or other, subject to mathematical constraints	Sinusoidal	Particle duration varies with frequency; starts from an analysis of an existing source sound
Grainlets	Gaussian or arbitrary	Sine	Interdependent synthesis parameters
Micro-arcs	Arbitrary	Arbitrary, including sampled	Flexible graphic design; subject to graphical transformations
FOF grains	Attack, sustain, release	Sine	Envelope controls formant spectrum
Vosim grains	Linear attack, exponential decay	$Sine^2$ pulses	Used for pitched tones; flexible control of spectrum
Window-function pulses	Rectangular around pulse then nil	Blackman-Harris pulse	Synthesizes formants with purely harmonic content
Transient drawing	Arbitrary	Hand-drawn	Generally sharp and percussive; each transwave is unique
Particle cloning	Arbitrary	Arbitrary, including sampled	Repeats a particle so that it becomes a continuous tone

Assessment of Abstract Models of Particles

In most implementations, abstract models of particles have been used to produce a pressure wave representing a continuous sound. Most of Sturm's sound examples sound like the additive synthesis of sine waves, where each sine is warping or sweeping in frequency, usually in synchrony with the other sines. Xenakis's compositions using the GENDYN system are quite different in sonic quality from the sound of Sturm's examples: the waveforms are jagged in shape and rich in spectrum, their behavior is obsessive and erratic, always wavering and warbling, often explosive. Xenakis's *S.709* (1992, EMF CD 003) is a classic example, meandering wildly like some atomic insect.

In abstract models, the mapping between the particle model and the process of sound generation may be quite arbitrary. The history of digital sound synthesis contains numerous examples of all manner of algorithmic schemes applied to the control of sound synthesis. Thus one could easily use an abstract model of particles to control the parameters of an arbitrary synthesis technique; frequency modulation or granular synthesis, for example.

Summary

All forms of music composition—from the freely improvised to the formally organized—are constrained by their sound materials. The urge to expand the field of sound comes from a desire to enrich compositional possibilities, and much can be gained from the harvest of synthetic waveforms produced by particle synthesis. In chapter 3 and in this chapter, we have looked at a variety of sound particles. Chapter 6 describes additional particles derived from windowed spectrum analysis. Table 4.4 summarizes the variety of sound particles studied in this book.

Artists are frequently recalled to the belief that the splendors of nature surpass anything that human beings can create. The natural world, however, did not inhibit the first painters, on the contrary, it inspired them. Similarly, for composers, the omnipresence of natural sound does nothing to quash the need to create a virtual sound world. With the sound particles, we cultivate a new strain of culture within the natural order.

5   Transformation of Microsound

Convolution and Pulsar Synthesis

Assessment of Convolution with Microsounds

Spatialization of Sound Particles

Virtual Spaces

Scattering Particles in Virtual Spaces

Per-Grain Reverberation

Spatialization by Modulation with Particles

Convolutions with Clouds of Sonic Particles

Effect of Cloud Amplitude Envelope

Effect of Particle Envelope

Effect of Particle Duration

Effect of Particle Frequency

Effect of Window Type in Sectioned Convolution

Particle Pluriphony in Physical Spaces

Assessment of Spatialization on a Micro Time Scale

Summary

Physical laws interrelate all the properties of sound signals; a transformation of one is bound to affect the others. By the law of convolution, any change to the time or amplitude structure of a sound simultaneously transforms its spectrum. Reciprocally, to transform the spectrum of a sound is to affect its temporal morphology. Time, frequency, phase, spectrum, and amplitude are all interrelated.

The transformation of sound by means of electronic circuits has a distinguished history (Bode 1984). In the 1940s, Pierre Schaeffer's work creating sound effects for radio and film led to the historic breakthrough known as musique concrète (Schaeffer and Moles 1952). In this new approach to music-making, Schaeffer used recordings as the material to be organized in a composition. In musique concrète, one of the principal strategies of variation, and therefore of composition itself is the transformation of the source material. Transformation has now become a central aspect of our sonic art, taking place on many time scales, from global modifications of macrostructure to micro operations on individual particles and samples. Temporal transformations alter the time scale of the original sound through stretching, shrinking, or reversal.

Other operations smear, scramble, or warp the temporal morphology through convolution, granulation, or modulation.

This chapter examines transformations based on microtemporal representations of sound. It begins by looking at frame-based audio data coding, micromontage, and granulation. After granulating a sound, one can make many transformations on a micro scale, including pitch-shifting, pitch-time changing, filtering, dynamics processing, and reverberation. After a presentation of waveset transformations, we introduce the theory of convolution, and lastly the spatialization of sound particles.

Synthesis and Transformation

Synthesis of sound and transformation of sound have always been closely related. To impose an amplitude envelope on a sine wave—a basic technique in synthesis—is to transform the signal: sharp or smooth attack, single or multiple iterations, steady or tremolo sustain, legato or staccato decay. How then can we distinguish between synthesis techniques and the transformations presented in this chapter and in chapter 6?

In general, synthesis begins with raw material on a micro time scale: a single period of a waveform, an impulse, or a burst of uniformly distributed noise. Transformations, on the contrary, usually begin with a relatively long stream of audio samples (greater than 100 ms) on the sound object time scale. Transformations apply to a vast realm of recorded or sampled sounds, including traditional acoustic instruments, electronic instruments, environmental and industrial noises, the cries of birds and animals, insect noises, and the sounds of human beings. The samples to be transformed can be extracted from a sound file or read directly from a real-time source. Often, we can identify the source of microphone-collected samples, and the goal of the transformation may involve preserving this source identity.

The transformations described in this chapter do not involve a stage of windowed spectrum analysis, which, instead, are surveyed in chapter 6.

Micromontage

Certain transformations clearly articulate the granular texture of sound. Micromontage extracts particles from sound files and rearranges them. The term

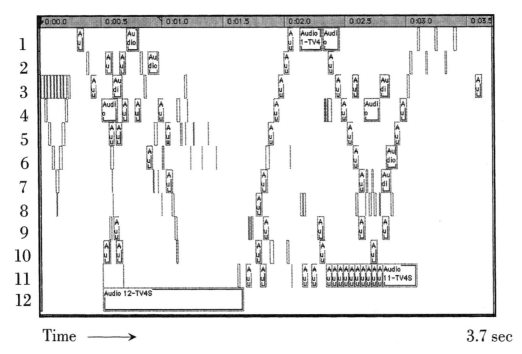

Figure 5.1 Micromontage shown as a display of one hundred and thirty-six sound files organized in a graphical mixing program. The files appear in twelve tracks stacked vertically, while time moves from left to right. Notice that the total duration of this phrase is 3.7 seconds.

"montage" derives from cinema, where it refers to a sequence of rapid images connected through cutting, splicing, dissolving, and other editing operations. With micromontage, a composer can position each particle precisely in time, constructing complex sound patterns by assembling dozens of smaller sounds. Micromontage can be realized by several means: graphical editing, typing a script, or writing a computer program to automate the process.

Micromontage in a Graphical Sound Editing and Mixing Program

A graphical sound editing and mixing program provides a two-dimensional view of sonic structure (figure 5.1). The vertical axis presents multiple rows of tracks, while the horizontal axis presents a time line. An early sound mixing program with a horizontal time-line graphical interface was MacMix (Freed

1987). This interface is now standard in audio workstations, including such popular programs as Digidesign's Pro Tools and many others.

Micromontage requires the following steps:

- Assemble a library of soundfiles, including sounds on several different time scales
- Import the files into the library of the editing and mixing program
- Use the cursor to position each sound at a specific time-point in a track. Most programs allow for multiple positionings, so that a single file can be pasted in repeatedly
- Edit the duration, amplitude, and spatial position of the sounds on all time scales

Each microsound positioned within a track is like a sonic brush stroke, and as in a painting, it may take thousands of strokes to complete the work.

Graphical sound editing and mixing programs offer a multiscale perspective. One can view the innermost details of sonic material, permitting microsurgery on individual sample points. Zooming out to the time scale of objects, one can edit the envelope of a sound until it has just the right weight and shape within a phrase. Zooming out still further one can shape large sound blocks and rearrange macrostructure. The availability of dozens of tracks lets composers work precisely on the micro time scale. A set of sounds that cannot fit on a single track can overlap on several tracks. Multitrack mixing capability also facilitates the construction of dense and variegated textures.

Micromontage by Script

Micromontage by script emerged in the 1980s, when dialects of the Music N synthesis languages were extended to handle input from sampled sound files. In the Csound language developed at MIT, the soundin and loscil unit generators read from a sampled input file (Boulanger 2000). Such a capability made it possible to create arbitrarily complex montages of sound files according to a precise numerical score or script. In these languages, a note statement creates a sound event. In the case of micromontage, each note statement corresponds to a microevent. Thus one must stipulate hundreds or thousands of microevents to create a composition. This process is laborious, but it offers extraordinary control over the montage.

Micromontage by Algorithmic Process

This technique has similarities to micromontage by script. Instead of specifying each particle manually, however, a computer program handles their extraction and time-scattering. The program reads a high-level specification of the montage from the composer. It then generates all the note statements needed to realize the montage. The high-level specifications might include a list of sound files, the location and length of the segments to be extracted, the overall tendencies of the montage, and so on.

Here is a small excerpt of a micromontage text produced by a program that I wrote in 1993. It has the format of a typical note list.

Start	Duration	Soundfile	Amplitude	Location
0.137	0.136	8	0.742	0.985
0.281	0.164	10	0.733	0.899
0.346	0.132	12	0.729	0.721
0.628	0.121	1	0.711	0.178
0.748	0.174	3	0.693	0.555
0.847	0.062	6	0.687	0.159
0.974	0.154	8	0.686	0.031

. . .

Seven events occur in the interval of one second. Each sound file has a number label—from 1 to 12 in this case—shown in the third column. The location parameter indicates spatial location in the stereo field, with 1 corresponding to left, and 0 corresponding to right. The Granulate program generates the score for the micromontage according to high-level instructions stipulated by the composer. The composer specifies the parameters of a cloud, such as which sound files to granulate, the density of particles, their amplitude, shape, and so on. Each cloud may contain hundreds of particles.

The effect of automated micromontage is much the same as granulation. One difference between them is that micromontage is based on a script—a text—that is read by a Music N synthesis program, meaning that the user can edit the script before the montage is rendered into sound.

Composition with Micromontage

Micromontage has been a specialty of the composer Horacio Vaggione for some time, in such works as *Octuor* (1982), *Thema* (1985, Wergo 2026-2), and

Schall (1995, Mnémosyne Musique Média LDC 278-1102). In *Octuor*, the composer began by synthesizing a set of five sound files. He then segmented them into small fragments using the S sound editor, and mixed the fragments into medium-scale and large-scale structures using the MIX program (Moorer 1977b). He further processed these structures and combined them in eight-voice polyphony using an automated mixing program (Vaggione 1984).

Thema explores automated mixing in the Cmusic language (Moore 1990). It features streams of microelements—such as resonant bass saxophone breath-bursts—scattered in both synchronous and asynchronous patterns along the time line.

Figure 5.2 shows time-domain (a) and frequency-domain (b) views of a 120-ms frame, which partitions into five microsections A-E. Microsection A contains 2.5 cycles of a waveform in a space of 34 ms, corresponding to a low fundamental frequency of 73 Hz. Microsection B begins with an impulse of 90 μsec pulse-width, corresponding to a fundamental of 1.1 kHz, followed by decaying bursts in a pattern: 17 ms, 8 ms, 17 ms, 8 ms. Superimposed on these bursts is a waveform with a period of 589 μsec, corresponding to a fundamental of 1.697 Hz. Microsection C lasts 21 ms divided into 2.5 periods, corresponding to a low-frequency fundamental of 116 Hz. Microsection D contains a single 113 μsec click, corresponding to a frequency of 8.894 kHz. Finally, microsection E lasts 13 ms and contains two periods of the frequency 153.8 Hz (slightly south of D-sharp), upon which are superimposed partials in the 8 kHz region.

The raw material of *Schall* consists of sampled piano sounds, granulated and transformed by convolution, waveshaping, and the phase vocoder. According to the composer:

The work plays essentially with tiny textures of feeble intensity, composed of multiple strata, which contrast with some stronger objects of different sizes, in a kind of dialog between the near and the far—as an expression of a concern with a detailed articulation of sound objects at different time scales. (Vaggione 1995 program notes)

For more about this composition, see chapter 7, which also discusses the work of the Princeton-based composer Paul Lansky, another pioneer of micromontage.

Assessment of Micromontage

Micromontage is an open-ended approach, still with many unexploited aesthetic possibilities. Granulation techniques, presented next, have absorbed

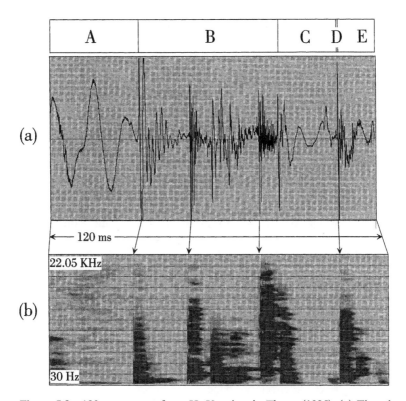

Figure 5.2 120-ms excerpt from H. Vaggione's *Thema* (1985). (a) Time-domain view shows microtemporal variations divided into five sections A-E. See the text for an explanation. The amplitude of the signal has been compressed in order to highlight low-level microvariations. (b) Frequency-domain view plotted on a linear frequency scale.

many of the techniques of micromontage. Perhaps the best way to draw a distinction between granulation and micromontage is to observe that granulation is inevitably an automatic process, whereas a sound-artist can realize micromontage by working directly, point by point. It therefore demands unusual patience.

Granulation

The automatic granulation of sampled sounds is a powerful technique for sound transformation. To *granulate* means to segment a sound signal into tiny grains. (The French term *brassage*, referring to "mashing" or "mixing," is also used.) The sound may be further modified after this segmentation. The granulation algorithm then reassembles the grains in a new time order and microrhythm. The precise manner in which this occurs varies from program to program.

Granulation is a purely time-domain operation. This stands in contrast to techniques such as the Fourier, wavelet, and Gabor transforms, which analyze a signal in both time and frequency. These techniques also granulate, but they then apply spectrum analysis to each grain. In spectrum analysis, the initial stage of granulation is called "windowing." (See chapter 6.)

The parameters of granulation include the following:

- Selection order—from the input stream: sequential (left to right), quasi-sequential, random (unordered)
- Pitch transposition of the grains
- Amplitude of the grains
- Spatial position of the grains
- Spatial trajectory of the grains (effective only on large grains)
- Grain duration
- Grain density—number of grains per second
- Grain envelope shape
- Temporal pattern—synchronous or asynchronous
- Signal processing effects applied on a grain-by-grain basis—filters, reverberators, etc.

Granulation parameters can be controlled by a numerical script, by graphical envelope editing, by physical controllers, or by deterministic or stochastic algorithms. Since granulation accepts any input sound, a truly vast range of sonic textures can emerge from a granulator. The density parameter is key, as it determines the overall texture, whether empty, sparse, gurgling, or continuous.

Granulation from Sound Files with Asynchronous Playback

Asynchronous playback from a sound file allows much more freedom than real-time granulation of a sound coming from a microphone. Because the sound to be granulated resides in a file, we have the flexibility of extracting individual grains in any order: sequential, reversed, random, statistical evolution, or in an arbitrary succession. For example, we can extract a single large grain from a snare drum and clone a periodic sequence of hundreds of grains to create a single-stroke roll. To avoid the repetitious quality of commercial drum machines and samplers, a variation on this method is to select grains from several strokes of a roll and to extract each grain from a different set of samples in the selected sound file.

One can liken granulation to scattering sound particles with a precision spray jet of sampled sound waveforms. Grains sampled from different instruments can be mingled, and grains taken from several sound files can create interwoven fabrics of sound. When the sound files consist of different notes of a scale, the result is a ringing *harmonic cloud*, where the layers stratify at particular pitches. When two harmonic clouds overlap, the sound is a statistical evolution from the first cloud to the second.

It is fascinating to experiment with extracting grains from several different sources, leading to hybrid textures, such as grains from a cello or voice mixed with grains from a cymbal. By controlling the distribution of grains from different sources, we can create clouds which evolve from one texture to another.

In any granulation method, grain duration is an important parameter. As chapter 3 points out, the timbre of a grain correlates strongly with its duration. When the duration of the grain is very short (<40 ms), sampled sound files lose their intrinsic identifiable qualities. For sound files consisting of spoken text or other identifiable material that is to be preserved, longer duration grains (>40 ms) work better.

Implementations of Granulation from Sound Files

Chapters 3 and 7 describe implementations of *granular synthesis* with synthetic waveforms. *Granulation*, on the other hand, implies the existence of analog-to-digital converters and software for sound recording and editing.

In 1981, I was working at the MIT Experimental Music Studio. At the time, we referred to analog-to-digital conversion by the now quaint term "digitizing." The software for digitization and editing was primitive, written by students in short-term research projects. In this fragile environment, I managed to carry out a number of experiments in sound file granulation using a program that I wrote in the C language. This program read a script that I prepared, which described the parameters of a granulated sound cloud. It generated a score consisting of hundreds of note statements in the Music 11 language. I then ran Music 11 with a simple instrument based on the soundin unit generator. The instrument extracted grains from the sample files, applied a quasi-Gaussian envelope to them at a certain amplitude, and wrote each grain to a particular point in the four-channel output sound file.

The primary source material consisted of a collection of monaural percussion sound files digitized by my colleague Christopher Fry, and also some saxophone samples that I digitized (Roads 1985b, 1985c). By extracting grains from these files, I created effects such as cymbal and drum rolls, as well as rolls derived from the grains of alto saxophone tones. Since the studio was quadraphonic, I could send the rolls around the studio.

Working at Simon Fraser University, Barry Truax was the first to implement real-time granulation of a sampled sound (Truax 1986, 1987). The GSAMX program operated on a brief recorded sample, no longer than 170 ms. This limitation was due to the very small memory of the sound processor, a Digital Music Systems DMX-1000 with 4 kwords of memory. This modest configuration nonetheless produced up to twenty simultaneous granular streams, with each stream containing up to one hundred grains per second, resulting in an impressive throughput of two thousand grains per second (Truax 1990a).

In 1990, Truax improved his system to allow extended recording of 16-bit samples to hard disk, with granulation and time stretching. This configuration enabled him to realize a number of pioneering compositions (see chapter 7).

By the late 1980s, it was possible to sample sounds on a personal computer using commercial hardware and software. During a 1991 residency at the Kunitachi College of Music in Tokyo, I wrote the Granulate program in the C language. Designed for the synthesis of complex multicolored textures, Granulate used the engine of Csound to pulverize and scatter up to sixty-four sound files.

Working in Paris at Les Ateliers UPIC in 1995, John Alexander and I developed the Cloud Generator program, which granulates a single sound file at a time (Roads and Alexander 1995). Appendix A documents this program.

Most of my current work with granulation involves programs written in the SuperCollider 2 language, which execute in real time (McCartney 1998).

Many commercial and shareware granulation packages are now available, even excluding those designed solely for time-shrinking and stretching. A typical example is the SoundMagic FX package by Michael Norris (1997), which runs on the MacOS platform. Sound FX includes operations labeled "brassage time-stretch," "sample hose," and "chunk munger" for granulation with multiple effects.

Selective Granulation

An increasing number of signal processing operations analyze and separate different components of a sound signal. One set of components may be retained, while the other is discarded. Alternatively, the components can be treated in different ways and then recombined. The listener recognizes the identity of the original sound, but with an interesting variation in its components.

What are some of the ways of separating a sound into components? One is to send the sound through a bank of filters, where each filter tunes to a different center frequency. This results in a number of output signals that differ in their frequency band. Another technique is to set an amplitude threshold and separate the low level and high level parts of a signal. A third way is to separate the chaotic excitation and the stable resonance parts of a signal. Sounds can be separated by spatial position, by duration, by attack shape, and so on. Generally, there are no limits on the number of ways in which a given sound can be divided.

Selective granulation means granulating one of these separated components. For example, only those sounds that fall above or below a given amplitude threshold. This principle is the foundation of dynamics processing on a micro time scale (see the description later). The granulated sounds can then be combined with the original to create a new hybrid texture.

Granulation in Real Time

Granulation in real time takes two forms. The first is the granulation of an incoming sound source, such as the signal coming from a microphone. The second is the granulation of stored sound files with real-time control. The granulator can be thought of as a delay line. As the sound passes through the delay line, the granulator sets and moves various pointers which identify memory locations in the delay line and extract grains. Several effects are possible:

1. Looping through the incoming samples repeatedly, causes the incoming sound to be time-stretched. The playback or looping rate can vary by changing the speed at which the granulator reads through the samples: from normal speed to a slowed-down rate in which a single grain repeats over and over. Here a brief grain telescopes into a slowly evolving sound object that lasts hundreds of times longer than the original.

2. Overlaying many copies of a grain with different phase delays increases its perceived volume and creates a kind of chorus effect.

3. Varying the size and shape of the granulation window introduces amplitude modulation with its noticeable spectral products—distorting the input sound in a controllable way.

Barry Truax was the pioneer of real-time granulation and is its most inveterate exponent (Truax 1986, 1987, 1988, 1990a, 1990b, 1992, 1994a, 1994b, 1995, 1996a, 1996b; Keller and Truax 1998; see also chapters 3 and 7). Numerous programs now offer granulation in real time, as chapter 3 describes.

Granulation of incoming signals is limited by the forward direction of the arrow of time. As Truax stated:

Granulation may be many things, but it is not omniscient.   (Truax 1994a)

In other words, the read pointer in a real-time system can never peek into the future. This eliminates the possibility of time-shrinking in real time. In contrast, the other form of granulation, reading from stored sound files, has the advantage that it can select grains from any time-point in the sound, making it possible to time shrink and time scramble. Regardless of whether the source is coming in "live" or from a stored sound file, real-time control is especially effective in creating an unending collection of variants of a given sound.

Assessment of Granulation

Granulating and powdering are, strictly speaking, nothing other than mechanical . . . operations, the object of which is to separate the molecules of a material and to reduce them to very fine particles. But . . . they cannot reach the level of the internal structure of the material. . . . Thus every molecule, after granulation, still resembles the original material. This contrasts with the true chemical operations, such as dissolution, which change intimately the structure of the material.   (Antoine Lavoisier 1789, quoted in Vaggione 1996b)

Granulation reduces a continuous sound to a flux of particles. As the great French chemist Lavoisier observed, molecules of grains resemble molecules of the original material. Yet the process of granulation alters their arrangement. This alteration may be subtle, such as a spatial displacement of the grains that leaves the source sound otherwise intact. On the other hand, just as a brilliant multicolored stone may be reduced to an indistinct grey powder, certain granulations render the source unrecognizable by destroying its morphology. The next chapter deals with "chemical" changes in sound composition. These entail alterations in the spectral composition of the sound molecules.

For many years, granulation techniques were available only to those few composers who had implemented them. As new implementations have been made available to a larger circle of musicians, granulation has proven to be popular. To cite an example, at the 1998 Brazilian Computer Music Symposium in the opening concert (featuring composers from Brazil, Italy, Germany, England, and Taiwan) eight out of ten works played used granulation.

With the spread of granulation technology, musical experience has also deepened. Naturally more is known about how to compose with granulated sounds than when they were first invented and recent works show considerable refinement in their manipulation of granulation parameters. Chapter 7 surveys this scene.

The Creatovox Synthesizer: A Brief Description

In the early 1990s, I began a design notebook containing schemes for real-time granular synthesis, including both scheduling algorithms as well as protocols for musical interaction (Roads 1992–1997, 1998b). It seemed to me that the technology had reached a point where it would be possible to build a low-cost synthesizer for granular synthesis. This instrument might look like a standard keyboard, with the addition of a few special controllers and could be compatible with the MIDI protocol. As a guiding principle, I wanted to convey "an illusion of simplicity" to the performing musician by hiding unnecessary technical details.

My original plan was to develop a prototype system based around a dedicated digital signal processor (DSP) chip. It became clear that this approach would require a great deal of time and money. In 1986, a major synthesizer manufacturer solicited my opinion on promising synthesis techniques and I suggested that a granular synthesizer would be a good direction. I did not hear from them again. In 1993, representatives from another synthesizer manufacturer solicited my opinion. I again suggested a granular synthesizer, but apparently, they decided to do something less interesting. The synthesizer project languished.

By the late 1990s, general-purpose microprocessors such as the Apple G3 became fast enough to handle multiple voices of particle synthesis in real time. In 1998, James McCartney released the SuperCollider 2 language (McCartney 1998) which combined musical interaction with synthesis and sound processing, and seemed ideal for prototyping the granular synthesizer. I launched the Creatovox research project at the Center for Research in Electronic Art Technology (CREATE), University of California, Santa Barbara building upon there developments. Its goal was to invent a prototype instrument optimized specifically for expressive performance of particle synthesis and granulation.

The design of the Creatovox has two components: the synthesis engine—how to schedule events, and how to synthesize and process the sound, and the musical performance interface—the controllers and displays manipulated by the musician—and their protocol. The account here is cursory, as the Creatovox continues to evolve.

Synthesis Engine

Many technical issues in the design of the Creatovox's synthesis engine have to do with particle scheduling, setting limits on particle overlap, balancing the amplitudes of the particles, and determining what to do when the performer attempts to exceed computation limits. In this last case, the goal is to degrade performance as gracefully as possible. To generate sufficient grain density, the synthesis engine must be capable of realizing multiple particle streams simultaneously, with individual envelopes and waveforms for each particle.

Current microprocessors have enough speed to implement signal processing operations that transform the particle streams. Fast convolution, for example, allows for cross-synthesis, morphing, and granular reverberation effects (Roads 1993a, 1997).

The prototype Creatovox realizes a variety of particle synthesis techniques, including pure granular synthesis with sinusoidal waveforms and Gaussian envelopes, granular synthesis with other waveforms and envelopes, grainlet and glisson synthesis, trainlet synthesis, pulsar synthesis, and granulation of sampled sound files. These can be combined with real-time signal processing effects running on the same microprocessor.

Musical Interface

The Creatovox is played using standard MIDI keyboard controllers equipped with pitch bend and modulation wheels. To this is added a pedal board, expression (volume) pedal, sustain and sostenuto footswitches, MIDI joysticks, and a fader box. Joysticks are efficient controllers as they let the performer control three separate parameters (left-right, forward-backward, up-down) with one gesture. The mapping between the various controllers and the synthesizer engine, with all the tuning this requires, constitutes a significant portion of our research, and it is here that we have most refined the playability and virtuoso potential of the instrument.

Assessment of the Creatovox

The Creatovox emitted its birth cries on 13 July 1999 in CREATE's Studio Theremin, in the presence of a project team consisting of Alberto de Campo, Ching-Wei Chen, and myself. As of January 2000, another round of development (coded by Alberto de Campo) had produced octophonic output. Demonstrated for the first time at the CREATE symposium on Sound in Space in March 2000, it continues to be the subject of ongoing refinement and musical experimentation (figure 5.3). Its sonic palette is wide, yet its signature is quite distinct, even at first playing. The first composer to use the Creatovox was Bebe Barron, in the summer of 2000. Her fascinating piece, *Mixed Emotions*, was the result.

Pitch Shifting on a Micro Time Scale

Pitch shifting means transposing the fundamental frequency of an audio signal. (Not all sounds, however, have a fundamental frequency.) In the simplest case, this means changing the playback rate. Faster playback shifts the pitch up and shortens the sound, while slower playback shifts the pitch down and lengthens it. (Another effect called pitch-time changing preserves the original duration. The next section looks at this effect.) In the classic electronic music studios of the past, the primary device for pitch shifting was the varispeed reel-to-reel tape recorder. By turning a knob, one could speed up or slow down the playback motor. It took several seconds for the tape recorder to go from one speed to another, but this slow change was sometimes a desired part of the effect.

Digital techniques let us alter the playback speed instantaneously, over any time scale. It is possible, for example, to pitch shift to different intervals on a grain-by-grain basis. The main parameters being the amount of pitch shift (in percent, semitones, or cents, where a 5.9% pitch shift represents one semitone or 100 cents), grain duration, and grain overlap.

Assessment of Pitch Shifting on a Micro Time Scale

The perceptual effect of pitch shifting on a micro time scale depends on the duration of the grains and the frequency variance of the pitch shift. Large grains and large variances result in melodic elaborations of the source. Short

Figure 5.3   The author playing the Creatovox synthesizer in CREATE's Studio Varèse, January 2000. The physical hardware consists of a MIDI keyboard controller, MIDI joystick, and footpedals. A Power Macintosh computer receives the MIDI data. The Creatovox software interprets the MIDI data and synthesizes the sound, with octophonic output through a Digidesign Pro Tools 24 converter.

grains and large variances create noise bands. Large grains and small variances, when combined with overlapping grains, produce a multiple-voice chorus effect. When the grain durations go below about 50 ms, the chorus turns into a ghostly whisper, as the pitch variations become microscopic and the signal dissolves into noise.

Pitch-Time Changing by Granulation

The effect described above, simple pitch transposition, changes the playback sampling rate, with a corresponding change in the duration of the sound. Another effect, pitch-time changing, has been applied extensively in computer music. Pitch-time changing presents two facets. We can stretch the duration of a sound (time expansion) or shrink it (time compression), while the pitch remains unchanged. Alternatively, we can transpose the pitch of the sound up or down, while the duration remains constant. These effects can be achieved, with varying degrees of success, through various strategies. Here we concentrate on time-domain granulation techniques.

To double the duration of a sampled signal, the algorithm segments it into grains, cloning each so that two grains appear for every one in the original. To halve the duration, it deletes every other grain. The grain preserves the local frequency content, while the algorithm alters the time scale by cloning (to stretch duration) or deleting (to shrink duration) grains. To shift the pitch of a sampled signal up an octave but not change its duration, the algorithm doubles the playback sampling rate while cloning every grain to restore the duration to the original. To shift the pitch down an octave but not change the duration, the algorithm halves the playback sampling rate and deletes every other grain to restore the duration to the original length.

These operations double or halve pitch or time, but such operations are not limited to products of two. The frequency and time scale can be altered by arbitrary ratios, by sample rate changing with grain cloning or deleting in corresponding ratios.

Some of the most effective time-stretching happens when applied in a selective, context-sensitive manner. To preserve the identity of an original sound, one might process only the steady-state part of the signal, and not the transient attack. In stretching speech, for example, intelligibility and "naturalness" can be enhanced by stretching vowels more than consonants.

History of Digital Pitch-Time Changing

Chapter 2 described the pioneering role played by Gabor and others in developing sound granulators based on electro-optical technology. This section describes the first attempts to granulate and pitch-time change sound using digital technology.

Pioneering research at the University of Illinois at Urbana-Champaign led to an early digital implementation of pitch-time changing (Otis, Grossman, and Cuomo 1968). This research simulated the effect of rotating-head sampling, it also made plain the flaws in this method. The main problem was that the waveforms at the beginning and end of a sampled grain did not always match in level with preceding and successive resampled grains, creating a transient at the junction of the two grains. Electromechanical time-granulators and some digital implementations exhibited a periodic clicking sound caused by these splicing transients.

Lee (1972) developed the Lexicon Varispeech system as a digital time compressor/expander interfaced with an analog cassette recorder. This design featured an electronic circuit for level matching at splice points to reduce clicking. Scott and Gerber (1972) developed an improved digital version of the Springer Tempophon that used rectangular windows but took pitch into account to determine the optimum window size.

Granular Pitch-Time Changing with a Harmonizer

A *harmonizer* is a real-time transposing device which shifts the pitch of an incoming signal without altering its duration. Based purely on time-domain techniques, the Eventide H910 Harmonizer, released in the mid-1970s, was the first commercially available digital device of this type (Bode 1984).

The following passage describes the Publison, a sampling effects processor developed in France in the early 1980s. The basic notion of a harmonizer is to load a random-access memory with an incoming signal sampled at a rate of SR_{in} and to read out the samples at a rate SR_{out}. The ratio SR_{in}/SR_{out} determines the pitch change. To maintain a continuous output signal, the machine must repeat samples (for upward pitch shifts) or skip samples (for downward pitch shifts). Because the output address pointer repeatedly overtakes the input address pointer (for pitch increases) or is overtaken by the recirculating input address pointer (for pitch decreases), the output address must occasionally jump to a new point in the memory. To make this splice inaudible, the precise size of the jump derives from an estimate of the periodicity (pitch) of the in-coming signal. When the harmonizer decides to splice, a smoothing fade-out envelope ramps the amplitude of the presplice signal to zero and a corre-sponding fade-in envelope ramps to postsplice the signal to full amplitude. Refinements can be added to this basic scheme to improve the audio quality. One is a noise gate connected to the input to the system to ensure that the pitch shifting does not try to shift any ambient noise associated with the input signal.

The sound quality of a simple harmonizer depends on the nature of the input signal and on the ratio of pitch change that it is asked to perform. Small pitch changes tend to generate less audible side effects. Some commercial devices produce undesirable side effects (such as buzzing at the frequency of the splic-ing) when used on material such as vocal sounds.

Granular Time Stretching and Shrinking in Cloud Generator

The Cloud Generator program (Roads and Alexander 1995; see the appendix), can realize a variety of granular time stretching and shrinking effects, some unique to it. Setting the Selection parameter to "Granulate" causes the pro-gram to open a file dialog, requesting a stereo file to process. To time-stretch the file by a factor of two, one sets the cloud duration to be twice the input file's duration. To time-shrink a sound, one sets the cloud duration to be shorter than the selected input sound.

The Selection Order parameter applies only to granulated clouds. It deter-mines in what order grains will be selected from the input sound file. Three options present themselves:

- Random—The program selects input grains from random points in the input sound file.

- Statistical evolution—The program selects input grains in a more-or-less left-to-right order, i.e., at the beginning of the cloud there is a high probability that grains will be selected from the beginning of the input file; at the end of the cloud there is a high probability that grains will be selected from the end of the input file.

- Deterministic progression—The program selects input grains in a strictly left-to-right order.

By experimenting with density and grain duration parameters, one obtains a variety of granular time distortions. With a density of ten grains per second and a grain duration of 0.1, for example, the time-stretching effect is amplitude modulated, since the grain envelope is bell-shaped and there is not enough overlap for a continuous effect. As the density increases to thirty grains per second, overlap increases. The sound is now continuous but the multiple grains overlapping cause a comb filtering effect to become prominent. Another interesting effect is created by stretching the sound with short grains, intentionally leaving gaps between them. The effect can be enhanced by randomizing the spatial position of each grain.

Granular Pitch Shifting: Malah, Jones, and Parks' Methods

Malah (1979) developed a computer-based pitch-synchronous technique with triangular windows called *time-domain harmonic scaling* (TDHS). TDHS achieves pitch synchronization by continuously altering the lengths of the windows so that signals sum in phase. In a related method, Jones and Parks (1988) showed how to smoothly reconstruct the signal by using grain envelopes that overlap slightly, creating a seamless crossfade between grains. In their approach, the duration of the grains (which varies according to the fundamental frequency) is independent of the crossfade point, which is always in phase with its successor grain. A local search and correlation over a window no greater than a 20 ms finds a crossfade point. This calculation operates in real time.

Granular Pitch Shifting with Constant Formants: Lent's Method

We have already seen how it is possible to shift pitch while preserving the duration of a sound by means of a combination of resampling and granulation. A problem with this approach is that pitch-shifting changes not only the fundamental frequency but also shifts the spectrum. For vocal sounds with strong formants, granular pitch shifting by large intervals gives an artificial quality. This artificial quality, which has been called the *chipmunk effect* or *munchkinization*, was addressed by Lent (1989).

Lent's method was designed to work with strongly pitched sources, such as the human voice or monophonic instruments. It begins with a pitch estimation algorithm, in which the signal is first filtered to remove all but the fundamental frequency. Every third zero-crossing boundary thus defines a cycle. Once the pitch period is known, time-shrinking and time-stretching take place. Individual cycles repeat to stretch the duration of a sound, cycles are deleted to shrink it.

To reduce artefacts, individual cycles are windowed by a smooth Hanning function which is twice as long as the cycle. These smooth windows overlap with one another.

Lent introduced a clever trick to this standard and straightforward process. The pitch-shifting algorithm appends zero-valued samples to the cycle. Thus, the fundamental frequency of the signal is lowered, while the spectral relationships in the cycle are maintained—preserving the formants.

Lent does not, however, describe any formant-preserving method for upward pitch shifting. It should also be noted that the zero-crossing pitch-estimation method used in Lent's method is easily confused if the input frequency is not dominated by a fundamental frequency. As our analysis of wavesets later in this chapter indicates, if the second harmonic is greater than 50% of the amplitude of the fundamental, additional zero-crossings appear, which could cause errors in pitch estimation. According to Lent, his method worked well for vocal and piano tones, where the fundamental is usually strong.

Bristow-Johnson (1995) adapted Lent's method for commercial pitch-shifting products marketed by the company Wave Mechanics.

Granular Pitch Shifting with Variable Formants: Gibson's Method

Digital audio effects processing has evolved into an important industry, and commercialization has led to a number of patents for sound granulation processes. On behalf of Digitech and DOD Electronics, Gibson, Jubien, and Roden (1996) obtained a patent describing a granular pitch-shifting circuit with variable formants. A "vocal harmony processor" produced a harmonization of several notes around a singer's fundamental pitch. Gibson's method (as we will call it) is a minor variation of Lent's, which instead of preserving the formant structure of a vocal or instrumental tone, allows variations. The method is a six-stage process:

1. Sample the input signal and store it in memory

2. Determine its pitch

3. Select harmony notes

4. Determine percent of change in sample rate

5. Resample the stored input signal at the desired sampling rate

6. Replicate a portion of the resampled input signal at a rate equal to the fundamental frequency of the desired output signal

The basic difference between Gibson's and Lent's method is that in step 5 the input signal can be resampled to change its timbre (either up or down in frequency), and then window-replicated (step 6) with the window length being the same as the input signal. This produces a tone with an altered timbre but with the same pitch as the input.

It is also possible to shift the pitch while preserving the formant structure of the original. If the desired pitch is above the pitch of the input signal by X semitones, then the algorithm reduces the length of the Hanning window (step 6) by $2^{-X/12}$. Alternatively, if the desired pitch is below the input signal by X semitones, then the algorithm increases the length of the Hanning window by $2^{X/12}$.

Filtering on a Micro Time Scale

The first electrical filters, developed in the early part of the twentieth century, were supratemporal wave-oriented devices, meant to be installed permanently on telephone lines. The familiar term *equalizer* originally referred to such a permanent filter installed in a public address system in order to compensate for the acoustic deficiencies of a hall. Tone controls on radios of the 1940s rolled off the higher frequencies above 2 kHz. Much later, audio engineers included filters operating at fixed frequencies in audio mixing consoles. By the mid-1960s, analog circuit technology allowed for continuously variable or parametric filters, which mixing engineers could control manually by means of rotary knobs.

In the early days of computer music (before 1990), rudimentary digital filters appeared in languages such as Music V, Music-11, Csound, etc., but were tricky to use, owing to their unpredictable output gain and disappointing tone quality. The technology of digital filter design has greatly improved. Stable constant-gain filters are available in real-time synthesis languages, and we can now extend filtering down to the micro time scale.

My recent experiments have shown that filtering on a micro scale can result in lively scintillating sonic textures. Microfiltration couples naturally with granulation. This technique segments a sampled sound into grains, with each grain processed by a unique filter. The filters articulate microvariations by injecting spectral coloration into otherwise static textures. In so doing, they foster heterogeneity inside the sonic fabric.

Experiments with Constant-Q Filters on Grains

In 1997, I wrote a program for granulation, in which every extracted grain passes through a separate filter. This program, GranQ, was written in the SuperCollider 1 language, an interactive sound processing environment for MacOS computers (McCartney 1996). GranQ inserts a bandpass or bandreject filter of variable or constant Q into the granulation routine. Each filter has its own center frequency and bandwidth, selected randomly within limits stipulated by the user. The number of filters corresponds to the density of grains per second, which may be a large number ($>$100/sec).

The most interesting experiments used constant Q filters. The Q of a bandpass filter can be defined as the ratio of the center frequency to the spread of its -3 dB point (cutoff point) bandwidth:

$$Q = \frac{f_{center}}{f_{high} - f_{low}}$$

where f_{center} is the filter's center frequency, f_{high} is the upper cutoff frequency, and f_{low} is the lower cutoff frequency. Notice that when the center frequency is constant, adjusting the Q is the same as adjusting the bandwidth. A constant Q filter, on the other hand, adjusts the bandwidth according to the center frequency, keeping the ratio the same. For example, suppose that we set the Q to be a constant value of 2. When the center frequency is 250 Hz, the bandwidth is 125 Hz. When the center frequency is 2500 Hz, the bandwidth is 1250 Hz. Constant Q filters have the advantage that they sculpt the same musical interval regardless of their center frequency.

GranQ has eleven parameters that greatly affect the output, and which can be adjusted in real-time as the sound is being processed:

1. Pitch—shifts the input to this pitch
2. Pitch Variation—amount of random deviation in the pitch
3. Pitch Quantization—rounds the pitch to a multiple of this value, causing the pitch variation to jump to only a few pitches
4. Time Rate—rate of scanning through the input sound file
5. Time Dispersion—amount of random deviation in the time rate
6. Time Quantization—rounds the time to a multiple of this value, causing the granulation to scan only a few time points in the file

7. Grain Duration

8. Grain Overlap or Density

9. Amplitude

10. Filter Q—constant over a range of 0.1 to 20

11. Filter Range—upper and lower limits, from 20 Hz to 20 kHz

When the filter Q and density are high, the granular stream has a liquid quality. One can disintegrate any sound into a torrent of filtered particles.

GranQ is one of my staple treatments for sound. I applied the program in creating the second movement of my composition *Half-life* (1999), the source material for which consisted of a series of sound files generated by pulsar synthesis (see chapter 4). I processed these files with GranQ at variable densities and grain sizes, creating the cascading clouds heard in the second movement, *Granules*. (See description, chapter 7.)

Dynamics Processing on a Micro Time Scale

Dynamics processing affects the amplitude of audio signals. Such operations include compression of the envelope amplitude of a sound, limiting, expansion, and noise gating (Roads 1996). In typical applications, sound engineers apply these effects on the macro time scale to an entire track or piece. Compression is common in popular music, film and video soundtracks, and broadcasts. It constrains the amplitude of signals to remain within a specific range, allowing the sound engineer to boost the apparent loudness of the treated signal. The compression characteristics of a radio or television station may be set once and then applied to the broadcast signal for years at a time. This is an extreme example of the supratemporal wave-oriented approach to musical signal processing.

Digital techniques let us alter the dynamics of a signal on a short-term basis in order to articulate microfluctuations in amplitude. An example of this type of processing appears in the SoundHack program (MacOS) under the rubric of "Spectral Dynamics" (Erbe 1995). This group of operations applies dynamics processing to the frames of windowed spectrum analysis (see chapter 6). Each frame represents a microsound, a time-slice of the Gabor matrix. Spectral dynamics processing applies dynamics processing (gating, ducking, expansion, compression) individually to each time-slice and spectral band. Depending on how the parameters are adjusted, this articulates the microstructure of a given sound.

Parameters of Spectral Dynamic Processing

The Spectral Dynamics effect in SoundHack offers threshold detection for each band. This means that one frequency band can have the dynamics process active, while other bands are inactive. One can select whether to affect sounds above or below a specified amplitude threshold. One can set the threshold level to one value for all bands, or to a different value for each band by reading in and analyzing a sound file. The spectrum of this sound file can set the thresholds for each band.

Other parameters let users set the amount of gain or reduction for the bands that are past a specified threshold. For compression and expansion, it allows one to set the gain ratio. When affecting sounds below the threshold, the compressor and expander hold the highest level steady and affect lower levels (this is also known as *downward expansion* or *compression*). When affecting sounds above the threshold, the compressor and expander hold the lower threshold level steady and compress or expand upwards.

The attack and decay parameters are important for the manipulation of microsound structure. These set the time window for each band to open or close. When this value is a large time constant, the algorithm ignores transients. If the time constant is a small duration, then the effect tends to modulate the sound file on the time scale of the window within the affected bands.

Waveset and Wavecycle Distortions

Several years ago the British composer Trevor Wishart developed a family of eccentric sound transformations based on a sound particle that he called a *waveset*. He defined a waveset simply as the "distance from one zero-crossing to a third zero-crossing" (Wishart 1994, appendix 2, p. 50). For a pure sinusoidal signal, a waveset is equivalent to one wave period or *wavecycle*. For a more complicated signal with multiple zero-crossings, segmentation by wavesets breaks the signal into fragments, whose size depends on the signal's partial structure. One can use the waveset as a unit of sound transformation, sometimes subdividing it into *half-wavesets*, which span the distance between two zero crossings.

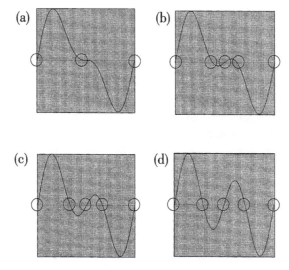

Figure 5.4 Formation of wavesets. The circles indicate zero crossings. (a) Sine wave plus second harmonic in a 1 : 0.5 mix. (b) Sine wave plus second harmonic in a 1 : 0.7 mix. (c) Sine wave plus second harmonic in a 1 : 1 mix. (d) Sine wave plus second harmonic in a 0.5 : 1 mix.

Waveset Formation

What types of signals have multiple zero-crossings? Beginning with a sinusoid, one can add an arbitrary number of partials without crossing zero more than once within the wave period. The classic sawtooth and square waves are examples of single-cycle waveforms with an arbitrary number of partials, limited only by the sampling frequency of the synthesis system.

In any sound with a strong fundamental frequency, waveset manipulations are equivalent to operations on individual cycles. Thus waveset time-stretching produces no artefacts when the signal has a strong and steady fundamental period. But as figure 5.4 shows, wavesets form when the ratio of the amplitude of the fundamental to any of the upper partials dips below 1 : 0.5. In speech, multiple wavesets appear in sounds such as whispering, where the fundamental drops out.

Experiences with Waveset and Wavecycle Distortions

Table 5.1 summarizes Wishart's catalog of distortions based on wavesets and wavecycles. The primary documentation of these distortions is a series of

Table 5.1   Waveset and wavecycle transformations in the Composer's Desktop Project software

Waveset transformations	
Waveset transposition	Substitutes N copies of a waveset in the place of M wavesets, for example 2 in the space of 1, or 1 in the space of 4, for doubling and quartering of frequency, respectively
Waveset reversal	Reverses individual wavesets while retaining their order; reversals can be of each individual waveset or collections of N wavesets at a time
Waveset shaking	Alternates between compressing (in time) and expanding (in time) successive wavesets
Waveset inversion	Inverts the phase of all wavesets in a signal; in Wishart's diagram half-wavesets are inverted
Waveset omission	Deletes every Nth waveset, leaving silence in its place; controlled by initial and final density from 0 to 100%
Waveset shuffling	Permutes collections of wavesets. A simple shuffle of successive wavesets starting with (a, b, c, d) becomes (b, a, d, c); shuffling by pairs of wavesets makes (d, c, a, b)
Waveset distortion	Distorts a signal by squaring and cubing the signal; the example given in Wishart does not indicate how it is tied to waveset boundaries
Waveset substitution	Replaces wavesets by a stipulated waveform of the same amplitude, frequency, and time span as the original waveset
Waveset harmonic distortion	Superimposes N harmonics on the waveset fundamental with a scaling factor M relative to the previous harmonic
Waveset averaging	Creates a signal containing N new wavesets that are the average duration and the average amplitude and time function of the N original wavesets; the overall duration of the signal is unchanged
Waveset enveloping	Applies an envelope to 1 to N wavesets at a time
Waveset transfer	Substitutes the waveform of the wavesets in signal A into the time frames of the wavesets in signal B
Waveset interleaving, method 1	Substitutes wavesets from signal A into alternate wavesets of signal B; applied either to individual wavesets or groups
Waveset interleaving, method 2	Interleaves wavesets from signal A with wavesets of signal B, thus lengthening the output signal; applied either to individual wavesets or groups
Waveset time-stretching	Repeats each waveset N times
Waveset time-shrinking	Retains only the first of every N wavesets or retains only the loudest of every N wavesets
Waveset normalizing	Normalizes every N wavesets above a stipulated amplitude threshold, thus a 10% threshold has a greater effect than a 90% threshold.

Table 5.1   (continued)

Wavecycle transformations

Distort average	Average the waveshape over N wavecycles
Distort cyclecnt	Count wavecycles in soundfile
Distort delete	Time-compress file by deleting wavecycles
Distort divide	Distortion by dividing wavecycle frequency
Distort envel	Impose envelope over each group of N wavecycles
Distort filter	Time-compress sound by filtering out wavecycles
Distort fractal	Superimpose miniature copies of source wavecycles onto themselves
Distort harmonic	Harmonic distortion by superimposing "harmonics" onto wavecycles
Distort interact	Time-domain interaction of sounds
Distort interpolate	Time-stretch file by repeating wavecycles and interpolating between them
Distort multiply	Distortion by multiplying wavecycle frequency
Distort omit	Omit A out of every B wavecycles, replacing them by silence
Distort pitch	Pitch warp wavecycles of sound
Distort repeat	Time-stretch file by repeating wavecycles
Distort replace	Strongest wavecycle in each group replaces others
Distort reform	Modify shape of wavecycles
Distort reverse	Cycle-reversal distortion, wavecycles reversed in groups
Distort shuffle	Distortion by shuffling wavecycles
Distort telescope	Time-compress by telescoping N wavecycles to 1

diagrams in his book. The descriptions in table 5.1 are my interpretations of these sketches.

My own experiments with waveset and wavecycle distortions involved the SoundMaker editor with its SoundMagic FX plug-in effects (Ricci 1997; Norris 1997). The operations in this package include harmonic distortion, interleaving, omission, reversal, time stretch, and normalizing. Additional operations apply to the shorter wavecycles. For example, wavecycle substitution substitutes a user-stipulated waveform for every wavecycle in the input signal.

Assessment of Waveset and Wavecycle Distortions

Waveset operations are bounded on zero-crossings. This does not exclude disjoint transients in the results; it merely guarantees that the transient does not occur between waveset boundaries. Certain operations cause transients at every waveset boundary, so the signal accumulates considerable broadband noise. The results often resemble the jagged waveforms produced by the waveform segment synthesis techniques proposed by G. M. Koenig, H. Brün, and P. Berg (Roads 1996; Berg 1978).

As a unit of sound transformation, a waveset does not seem significantly different from a wavecycle unless a fundamental frequency is weak or absent. Wishart justified its use on the following grounds:

The technique is very fast to compute but often introduces strange, signal-dependent artefacts. (It can therefore be used as a process of constructive distortion in its own right!) (Wishart 1994, p. 30)

A compact disc supplied with his book contains sound examples of waveset distortions. The examples of waveset inversion applied to a speaking voice sound similar to band-shifted radio distortion. Waveset omission creates noise-infused textures, with temporal gaps as the proportion of omitted wavesets increases. In waveset substitution, the timbre changes according to the substituted waveform. For example, when sine waves substitute for wavesets, the result is—not surprisingly—more sinusoidal in quality. Waveset time-stretching, in which each waveset repeats N times, has a distinctly artificial quality.

The more extreme waveset distortions destroy the identity of the source signal, turning it into a chain of arbitrary waveform fragments. As the composer observes, the results are often unpredictable in their detail:

In general, the effects [of waveset time-stretching] produced will not be entirely predictable, but they will be tied to the morphology (time-varying characteristics) of the original sound. (pp. 40–1)

Although [waveset averaging] appears to be similar to the process of spectral blurring, it is in fact quite irrational, averaging the waveset length and the wave shape in perceptually unpredictable ways. (p. 42)

In general, waveset and wavecycle distortions tend to make a signal sound more "electronic," and should probably be applied with this in mind.

Convolution of Microsounds

Increased processor speeds make it possible to realize previously exotic and computationally intensive techniques on personal computers. *Convolution* is one such technique. A fundamental operation in signal processing, convolution "marries" two signals (Rabiner and Gold 1975). Convolution is also implicit in signal processing operations such as filtering, modulation, excitation/resonance modeling, cross-filtering, spatialization, and reverberation. By implementing these operations as convolutions, we can take them in new and interesting directions. This section reviews the theory and presents the results of systematic experimentation with this technique. Throughout it offers practical guidelines for effective musical use of convolution, and later presents the results of new applications such as transcription of performed rhythms and convolutions with sonic particles. Parts of this text derive from Roads (1992b, 1993a, 1996, and 1997).

Status of Convolution

The theory of convolution may remain unfamiliar to most musicians, but to signal processing engineers it is fundamental: the foundation stone of linear system theory. Signal processing textbooks often present it tersely, reducing it to a handful of generalized mathematical clichés. Since these texts are not aimed at a musically-inclined reader, the audio significance of convolution is barely touched upon. Hence engineers are not always aware of the range of convolution effects in the audio domain (an exception is Dolson and Boulanger 1985).

Listeners are familiar with the effects of convolution, even if they are unaware of its theory. Convolution may disguise itself under more familiar terms such as filtering, modulation, and reverberation. Newer software tools running on personal computers unbundle convolution, offering it as an explicit operation, and allowing any two sampled files to be convolved (MathWorks 1995; Erbe 1995; Pranger 1999). Such tools provide a stable basis for musical exploration of convolution, and prompt a need for more universal under-standing of its powers. We begin this task here. Those already familiar with the theory of convolution may want to skip to the section "Musical Significance of Convolution."

Impulse Response and Cross-Synthesis

The definition of a filter is very broad (Rabiner et al. 1972). Virtually any sys-tem that accepts an input signal and emits an output is a filter, and this cer-tainly applies to convolution. A good way to examine the effect of a filter is to see how it reacts to test signals. One of the most important test signals in signal processing is the *unit impulse*—an instantaneous burst of energy at maximum amplitude. In a digital system, the briefest possible signal lasts one sample period. Since short-duration signals have broad bandwidths, this signal contains energy at all frequencies that can be represented at the given sampling frequency. The output signal generated by a filter that is fed a unit impulse is the *impulse response* (IR) of the filter. The IR corresponds to the system's *amplitude-versus-frequency response* (often abbreviated to *frequency response*). The IR and the frequency response contain the same information—the filter's response to the unit impulse—but plotted in different domains. That is, the IR is a time-domain representation, and the frequency response is a frequency-domain representation.

Convolution serves as the bridge between the time-domain and the frequency-domain. Any filter convolves its impulse response with the input signal to produce a filtered output signal. The implications of convolution in audio engineering are vast. One can start from the measured IR of any audio-frequency system (microphone, loudspeaker, room, distortion, delay effect, equalizer, modulator, etc.), and through convolution, impose the characteristics of this system on any audio signal.

This much is understood in the engineering community. By generalizing the notion of impulse response, however, one arrives at quite another set of possibilities. Let us consider any sequence of samples as the impulse response of a hypothetical system. Now we arrive at a new and musically potent application of convolution: cross-synthesis by convolution of two arbitrary sound signals. In musical signal processing, the term *cross-synthesis* describes a number of different techniques that in some way combine the properties of two sounds into a single sound. This may involve shaping the spectrum, time, or spatial pattern of one sound by the other.

What then precisely is convolution? The next section presents an intuitive review of the theory.

Review of Convolution Theory

To understand convolution, let us examine the simplest case: convolution of a signal *a* with a unit impulse, which we call *unit*[*n*]. A unit impulse is a digital sequence defined over *n* time points. At time $n = 0$, *unit*[*n*] = 1, but for all other values of *n*, *unit*[*n*] = 0. The convolution of *a*[*n*] with *unit*[*n*] can be denoted as follows:

output[*n*] = *a*[*n*] ∗ *unit*[*n*] = *a*[*n*]

Here the sign "∗" signifies convolution. This results in a set of values for *output* that are the same as the original signal *a*[*n*]. Thus, convolution with the unit impulse is said to be an *identity operation* with respect to convolution, because any function convolved with *unit*[*n*] leaves that function unchanged.

Two other simple cases of convolution tell us enough to predict what will happen at the sample level with any convolution. If we scale the amplitude of *unit*[*n*] by a constant *c*, we can write the operation as follows:

output[*n*] = *a*[*n*] ∗ (*c* × *unit*[*n*])

The result is simply:

output[*n*] = *c* × *a*[*n*]

In other words, we obtain the identity of *a*, scaled by the constant *c*.

In the third case, we convolve signal *a* by a unit impulse that has been time-shifted by *t* samples. Now the impulse appears at sample *n* − *t* instead of at *n* = 0. This can be expressed as follows:

output[*n*] = *a*[*n*] ∗ *unit*[*n* − *t*]

The result of which is:

output[*n*] = *a*[*n* − *t*]

That is, *output* is identical to *a* except that it is time-shifted by the difference between *n* and *t*.

Putting together these three cases, we can view any sampled function as a sequence of scaled and delayed unit impulse functions. They explain the effect of convolution with any IR. For example, the convolution of any signal *a* with another signal *b* that contains two impulses spaced widely apart results in a repetition or echo of *a* starting at the second impulse in *b*. When the impulses in *b* move closer together, the scaled repetitions of *b* start to overlap.

Thus, to convolve an input sequence *a*[*n*] with an arbitrary function *b*[*n*], we place a copy of *b*[*n*] at each point of *a*[*n*], scaled by the value of *a*[*n*] at that point. The convolution of *a* and *b* is the sum of these scaled and delayed functions. Clearly convolution is not the same as simple multiplication of two signals. The multiplication of one signal *a* by another signal *b* means that each sample of *a* is multiplied by the corresponding sample in *b*. Thus:

output[1] = *a*[1] × *b*[1]

output[2] = *a*[2] × *b*[2]

etc.

In contrast, with convolution *each* sample of *a* is multiplied by *every* sample of *b*, creating an array of samples of length *b* for every sample of *a*. The convolution is the sum of these arrays. Compare convolution by the unit impulse (discussed previously) with multiplication by the unit impulse. The multiplication of *a*[*n*] by the unit impulse *unit*[*n*] results in all values of *output*[*n*] being set to zero except for *output*[0], where *unit*[*n*] equals 1.

Mathematical Definition of Convolution

A mathematical definition of the convolution of two finite sequences of samples *a* and *b* is as follows:

$$a[n] * b[n] = output[k] = \sum_{m=0}^{N-1} a[n] \times b[n-m]$$

where *N* is the length of the sequence *a* in samples and *m* ranges over the entire length of *b*. In effect, each sample of *a*[*n*] serves as a weighting function for a delayed copy of *b*[*n*]; these weighted and delayed copies all add together. The conventional way to calculate this equation is to evaluate the sum for each value of *k*. This is *direct convolution*. At the midpoint of the convolution, *n* copies are summed, so the result of this method of convolution is usually rescaled (i.e., *normalized*) afterward.

Convolution lengthens inputs. The length of the output sequence generated by direct convolution is:

length(*output*) = length(*a*) + length(*b*) − 1

In the typical case of an audio filter (lowpass, highpass, bandpass, bandreject), *a* is an IR that is very short compared to the length of the *b* signal. For a broad smooth lowpass or highpass filter, for example, the IR lasts less than a millisecond.

The Law of Convolution

A fundamental law of signal processing is that the convolution of two waveforms is equivalent to the multiplication of their spectra. The inverse also holds, that is, the multiplication of two waveforms is equal to the convolution of their spectra. Another way of stating this is as follows:

Convolution in the time domain is equal to multiplication in the frequency domain, and vice versa.

The law of convolution has profound implications. In particular, the convolution of two audio signals is equivalent to filtering the spectrum of one sound by the spectrum of another sound. Conversely, multiplying two audio signals (i.e., performing amplitude modulation or ring modulation), is equal to convolving their spectra. Convolution of spectra means that each point in the discrete frequency spectrum of input *a* is convolved with every point in the spectrum of *b*. Convolution does not distinguish whether its input sequences represent samples or spectra. To the convolution algorithm they are both just discrete sequences.

Another implication of the law of convolution is that every time we reshape the envelope of a sound, we also convolve the spectrum of the envelope with the spectrum of the reshaped sound. In other words, every time-domain transformation results in a corresponding frequency-domain transformation, and vice versa.

Relationship of Convolution to Filtering

Convolution is directly related to filtering. The equation of a general *finite-impulse-response* (FIR) filter is as follows:

$$y[n] = (a \times x[n]) \pm (b \times x[n-1]) \pm \cdots (i \times x[n-j])$$

We can think of the coefficients $a, b, \ldots i$ as elements in an array $h(i)$, where each element in $h(i)$ is multiplied by the corresponding element in array $x[j]$. With this in mind, the general equation of an FIR filter presented earlier can be restated as a convolution:

$$y[n] = \sum_{m=0}^{N-1} h[m] \times x[n-m]$$

where N is the length of the sequence h in samples, and n ranges over the entire length of x. Notice that the coefficients h play the role of the impulse response in the convolution equation. And, indeed, the impulse response of an FIR filter can be taken directly from the value of its coefficients. Thus, any FIR filter can be expressed as a convolution, and vice versa.

Since an *infinite-impulse response* (IIR) filter also convolves, it is reasonable to ask whether there is also a direct relation between its coefficients and its impulse response. In a word, the answer is no. There exist, however, mathematical techniques that design an IIR filter to approximate a given impulse response. See Rabiner and Gold (1975).

Fast and Instant Convolution

Direct convolution is notoriously intensive computationally, requiring on the order of N^2 operations, where N is the length of the longest input sequence. Thus it is rarely used to implement narrow band filters or reverberators (both of which have long impulse responses) when simpler methods suffice.

Many practical applications of convolution use a method called *fast convolution* (Stockham 1969). Fast convolution for long sequences takes advantage of the fact that the product of two N-point Fourier transforms is equal to the Fourier transform of the convolution of two N-point sequences. Fast convolution means that direct convolution can be replaced by FFTs, which are dramatically quicker for large values of N. In particular, fast convolution takes on the order of $N \times \log_2(N)$ operations. Speedups begin to occur as soon as N exceeds sixty-four samples. Consider, for example, the direct convolution of a pair of two-second sounds sampled at 48 kHz. This requires about $96,000^2$ or 9.2 billion operations. Fast convolution with the same two sounds requires less than 1.5 million operations, a speedup by a factor of 6100. Put another way, a microprocessor that can perform a fast convolution of a pair of two-second sounds in real time would take three hours and twenty-two minutes to calculate their direct convolution.

Aldo Piccialli applied the concept of *instant convolution* to maximize the efficiency of a pitch-synchronous granular analysis/resynthesis system (De Poli and Piccialli 1991). Instant convolution is a sleight-of-hand that takes advantage of the fact that the convolution of a signal S with a unit impulse is an identity operation. That is, the convolution of any finite-duration signal S with a series of impulses reduces to a series of additions of S. In Piccialli's system S was a grain template that imposed a timbre onto the pitch determined by the impulse train.

Real-Time Implementation of Convolution

In the *block-transform implementation* of fast convolution, the spectrum multiplication occurs only after a block of input samples has been collected in memory and analyzed. Depending on the length of the input signals, this may involve a significant delay. Direct convolution has no such delay, but can require an enormous amount of computation. Fortunately for real-time applications where immediate output is needed, it is also possible to implement fast convolution in *sections*, that is, a few samples at a time. Sectioned and non-sectioned convolution generate equivalent results. Rabiner and Gold (1975) and Kunt (1981) present techniques for sectioned convolution and real-time implementations. Gardner (1995) describes a novel technique that combines direct and sectioned convolution to eliminate processing delays.

Musical Significance of Convolution

A veritable catalog of sonic transformations emerges out of convolution: cross-filters, spatialization, modulation, models of excitation and resonance, and time-domain effects. Indeed, some of the most dramatic effects induced by convolution involve temporal transformations: attack smoothing, multiple echoes, room simulation, time smearing, and reverberation. The type of effect achieved depends entirely on the nature of the input signals. Pure convolution has no control parameters.

The following sections spotlight each type of transformation. A mark (■) in front of an indented section indicates a practical guideline.

Cross-Filtering

One can implement any filter by convolving an input signal with the impulse response of the desired filter. In the usual type of FIR audio filter, the IR is typically less than a few dozen samples in length. The impulse response of a bandpass filter is precisely a grain with a sinusoidal waveform. The longer the grain, the stronger is the effect of the filter.

By generalizing the notion of impulse response to include signals of any length, we enter into the domain of *cross-filtering*; mapping the time-varying spectrum envelope of one sound onto another.

■ If both signals are long in duration and one of the input signals has a smooth attack, the main effect of convolution is a spectrum alteration.

Let us call two sources *a* and *b*, and their corresponding analyzed spectra *spectrum_a* and *spectrum_b*. If we multiply each point in *spectrum_a* with each corresponding point in *spectrum_b* and then resynthesize the resulting spectrum, we obtain a time-domain waveform that is the convolution of *a* with *b*.

■ If both sources are long duration and each has a strong pitch and one or both of the sources has a smooth attack, the result will contain both pitches and the intersection of their spectra.

For example, the convolution of two saxophone tones, each with a smooth attack, mixes their pitches, sounding as though both tones are being played simultaneously. Unlike simple mixing, however, the filtering effect in convolution accentuates metallic resonances that are common in both tones.

Convolution is particularly sensitive to the attack of its inputs.

- If either source has a smooth attack, the output will have a smooth attack.

Listening to the results of cross-filtering, one sometimes wishes to increase the presence of one signal at the expense of the other. Unfortunately, there is no straightforward way to adjust the "balance" of the two sources or to lessen the convolution effect.

Spatiotemporal Effects

Spatiotemporal effects constitute an important class of transformations induced by convolution. These include such staples as echo, time-smearing, and reverberation.

Any unit impulse in one of the inputs to the convolution results in a copy of the other signal. So if we convolve any brief sound with an IR consisting of two unit impulses spaced one second apart, the result is a clear echo of the first sound.

- To create a multiple echo effect, convolve any sound with a series of impulses spaced at the desired delay times. For a decaying echo, lower the amplitude of each successive impulse.

Time-smearing occurs when the pulses in the IR are spaced close together, causing the convolved copies of the input sound to overlap. If, for example, the IR consists of a series of twenty impulses spaced 10 ms apart, and the input sound is 500 ms in duration, then multiple copies of the input sound overlap, blurring the attack and every other temporal landmark.

The IR of a room contains many impulses, corresponding to reflections off various surfaces of the room—its echo pattern. When such an IR is convolved with an arbitrary sound, the result is as if that sound had been played in that room, because it has been mapped into the room's echo pattern.

- If we convolve sound *a* with the IR of an acoustic space, and then mix this convolution with *a*, the result sounds as if *a* is within the acoustic space.

We hear reverberation in large churches, concert halls, and other spaces with high ceilings and reflective surfaces. Sounds emitted in these spaces are reinforced by thousands of closely-spaced echoes bouncing off the ceiling, walls, and floors. Many of these echoes arrive at our ears after reflecting off several surfaces, so we hear them after the original sound has reached our ears; the myriad echoes fuse into a lingering acoustical "halo."

From the point of view of convolution, a reverberator is nothing more than a particular type of filter with a long IR. Thus we can sample the IR of a reverberant space and then convolve that IR with an input signal. When the convolved sound is mixed with the original sound, the result sounds like the input signal has been played in the reverberant space.

Importance of Mixing

For realistic spatial effects, it is essential to blend the output of the convolution with the original signal. In the parlance of reverberation, the convolved output is the *wet* (i.e., processed) signal, and the original signal is the *dry* or unprocessed signal.

- It is typical to mix the wet signal down −15 dB or more with respect to the level of the dry signal.

Noise Reverberation

When the peaks in the IR are longer than one sample, the repetitions are time-smeared. The combination of time-smearing and echo explains why an exponentially-decaying noise signal, which contains thousands of sharp peaks in its attack, results in reverberation effects when convolved with acoustically dry signals.

- If the amplitude envelope of a noise signal has a sharp attack and a fast exponential decay, the result of convolution resembles a natural reverberation envelope.
- To color this reverberation, one can filter the noise before or after convolving it.
- If the noise has a slow logarithmic decay figure, the second sound appears to be suspended in time before the decay.
- If the noise signal has an exponentially increasing envelope, the second sound gives the impression of being played in reverse.

Modulation as Convolution

Amplitude and ring modulation (AM and RM) both call for multiplication of time-domain waveforms. The law of convolution states that multiplication of two waveforms convolves their spectra. Hence, convolution accounts for the sidebands that result. Imagine that instead of impulses in the time-domain, convolution is working on line spectra in the frequency-domain. The same rules apply—with the important difference that the arithmetic is that of complex numbers. The FFT, for example, generates a complex number for each spectrum component. Here, the main point is that this representation is symmetric about 0 Hz, with a replica of each component (halved in amplitude) in the negative frequency domain. This negative spectrum is rarely plotted, since it has significance only inside the FFT. But it helps explain the positive and negative sidebands generated by AM and RM.

Excitation/Resonance Modeling

Many vocal and instrumental sounds can be simulated by a two-part model: an *excitation* signal that is filtered by a *resonance.* The excitation is a nonlinear switching action, like the pluck of a string, the buzz of a reed, or a jet of air into a tube. The resonance is the filtering response of the body of an instrument. Convolution lets us explore a virtual world in which one sound excites the resonances of another.

Through a careful choice of input signals, convolution can simulate improbable or impossible performance situations—as if one instrument is somehow playing another. In some cases (e.g., a chain of bells striking a gong), the interaction could be realized in the physical world, others (e.g., a harpsichord playing a gong), can only be realized in the virtual reality of convolution.

- To achieve a plausible simulation, the excitation must be a brief, impulse-like signal, (typically percussive), with a sharp attack (or multiple sharp attacks). The resonance can be any sound.

Rhythm Input

We have seen that a series of impulses convolved with a brief sound maps that sound into the time pattern of the impulses. A new application of convolution is the precise input of performed rhythms. To enter a performed rhythm, one need only tap with drumsticks on a hard surface, and then convolve those taps with other sounds.

- The convolution of a tapped rhythmic pattern with any sound having a sharp attack causes each tap to be replaced by a copy of the input sound.

This is a direct method of mapping performed rhythms to arbitrary sounds. Since convolution aligns the sounds to the rhythm with a time resolution of the sampling rate, this approach is much more precise than a MIDI percussion controller with its temporal resolution of several milliseconds. One can also layer convolutions using different patterns and input sounds. After prepositioning each tap in stereo space, convolution automatically distributes them spatially.

Convolution and Pulsar Synthesis

The slower the flow of time colors, the greater the clarity with which they can represent themselves ... as rhythms.   (Koenig 1962)

Chapter 4 discussed pulsar synthesis which generates a stream of microsonic events at a continuously variable rate, from the audio range down to the infrasonic frequency domain. Thus it traverses what G. M. Koenig called the "time-color" continuum spanning the durations corresponding to timbre ($<$ $\sim$200 µsec), pitch ($\sim$200 µsec to $\sim$33 ms), and rhythm ($>$ $\sim$33 ms).

The combination of pulsars with convolution is a potent one. Each pulsar, when convolved with an arbitrary sampled sound, acts as the impulse response of a filter. The pulsar imposes its temporal profile, spatial position, and spectrum onto the sampled sound. If the same sampled sound convolves with every pulsar, timbral variations derive from two factors: (1) the filtering effect imposed by the spectrum of each pulsar, and (2) the time-smearing effects caused by convolution with pulsar trains whose period is shorter than the duration of the sampled sound.

This technique requires two collections of sound files: a collection of pulsar trains, and a collection of sampled sounds. Since convolution is highly sensitive to attack shape, only objects with sharp attacks preserve the time structure of precise rhythmic patterns. Long sound objects or those with smooth attacks lead to time-smearing effects which blur the rhythmic pattern, creating rippling continua rather than brief time-discrete events.

In pulsar synthesis, the parameters of rhythm, pitch, and timbre can all be manipulated independently. The technique can generate not only individual sound objects but also rhythmic sequences—allowing sound composition to pass directly from microstructure to mesostructure.

Assessment of Convolution with Microsounds

It is likely that convolution techniques will play an increasing role in sound transformation, particularly as real-time convolvers such as spatializers and reverberators become more generally available.

A word of caution is in order: Convolution is a powerful transformer, and when applied to two arbitrary input signals, it can easily destroy the identity of both sources. Many convolutions that first appear to be interesting musical ideas can result in amorphous sound blobs. An understanding of a convolution's musical implications will save the composer much time spent searching for interesting results.

Spatialization of Sound Particles

When a small box s is situated, relatively at rest, inside a hollow space of a larger box S, then the hollow space of s is a part of the hollow space of S, and the same "space," which contains both of them, belongs to each of these boxes. When s is in motion relative to S, however, the concept is less simple. One is inclined to think that s encloses always the same space, but a variable part of S. It then becomes necessary to apportion to each box its particular space, not thought of as bounded, and to assume that these two spaces are in motion with respect to each other. Before one has become aware of this complication, space appears as an unbounded medium or container in which material objects swim about. But it must now be remembered that there is an infinite number of spaces in motion with respect to one another. The concept of space as something existing objectively and independent of things belongs to prescientific thought.... The subtlety of the concept of space was enhanced by the discovery that there exist no completely rigid bodies. All bodies are elastically deformable and alter in volume with changes in temperature.... In this connection atomism must be borne in mind and its concept of finite divisibility. Spaces of subatomic extension cannot be measured. Atomism compels us to give up the idea of sharply and statically defining bounding surfaces of solid bodies. (Einstein 1952)

The starting point of quantum theory is a wave function that describes all the possible various possible states of a particle. For example, imagine a large, irregular thundercloud that fills up the sky. The darker the thundercloud, the greater the concentration of water vapor and dust at that point. Thus by simply looking at a thundercloud, we can rapidly estimate the probability of finding large concentrations of water and dust in certain parts of the sky. The thundercloud may be compared to a single electron's wave function. Like a thundercloud, it fills up all space. Likewise, the greater its value at a point, the greater the probability of finding the electron there. Similarly, wave functions can be associated with large objects, like people. As I sit in my chair in Princeton, I know that I have a Schroedinger probability wave function. If I could somehow see my own wave function, it would resemble a cloud very much in the shape of my body. However, some of the cloud would spread out all over space, out to Mars and even beyond the solar system, although it would be vanishingly small there. This means that there is a very large likelihood that I am, in fact, sitting here in my chair and not on the planet Mars. Although part of my wave function has spread even beyond the Milky Way galaxy, there is only an infinitesimal chance that I am sitting in another galaxy. (Kaku 1995)

All our experiments indicate that quarks and bosons interact as points with no spatial dimensions, and so are fundamental, like the leptons. If the fundamental particles are really dimensionless points with mass, flavor, color, charge, and other quantum properties, occupying no volume, then the nature of matter appears quite bizarre. The four interactions [strong force, weak force, gravitational force, electromagnetic force] give matter shape. Matter itself is empty. (Lederman and Schramm 1995)

Spatialization of sound particles takes two different approaches. First, in synthesis and granulation, we can articulate the particle texture by scattering individual particles in different spatial locations and at different spatial depths. Second, through the magic of granulation, convolution, and intermodulation, the particles can be deployed as spatializers for other sounds.

Virtual Spaces

Sound may be choreographed by positioning sources and animating their movement. Spatialization has two facets: the virtual and the physical. In the studio, we can spatialize sounds by imposing electronic delays, spectral filters, panoramic motions, and reverberation—giving the illusion of sounds emerging from imaginary environments. In the concert hall, a composer can project sound through a multichannel or *pluriphonic* sound system (Roads 1998a, 2000). These two facets are complementary.

Virtual environments can take on characteristics that would be impossible to realize in physical architecture, such as a continuously changing echo pattern, or the simultaneous presence of different qualities of ambience. Through techniques such as convolution (Roads 1992b, 1993a, 1997), we can take a sound portrait of an existing space, such as a concert hall, and impose its spatial characteristics onto any sound object, creating the illusion of the sound object playing in the portrayed space. Indeed each sound object may appear to emerge from its own virtual space. This leads to spatial counterpoint—the choreography of sounds in an interplay between fixed and moving positions and between foreground and background elements. An electronic work that does not take advantage of these possibilities may suffer from a "spatial sameness" (Vaggione 1996a). We hear this in, for example, compositions where the voices remain fixed in space and submerged in a constant global reverberation.

Scattering Particles in Virtual Spaces

To spatialize microsound means to assign an independent spatial position to every sonic particle. Spatial position is a function of the particle's amplitude in two or more channels, as well the amount of reverberation in which it is immersed. Here we concentrate on the question of position in a pluriphonic (multichannel) environment. The next section deals with reverberation.

Two sound particles may share a spatial position, but it is also possible for each particle in a complex sound object to occupy a unique location. This situation creates a vivid "three-dimensional" sound picture, an effect that is enhanced by loudspeakers with good imaging characteristics.

When the particle density is relatively sparse, it is possible to position each particle manually in a sound editor or mixing program, through the manipulation of the amplitudes and panning curves of the individual tracks. But when densities are relatively high, we design automatic scattering algorithms to assign a position to each of thousands of particles in virtual space. These algorithms obey high-level tendencies stipulated by the composer on a larger time scale. To cite an example, the Cloud Generator program (described in the appendix) offers four scattering options in a stereo field:

1. Stationary spatial position for all grains in a cloud

2. Panoramic motion from one position to another over the duration of a cloud

3. Panoramic motion from a fixed position to a random position, or vice versa

4. Random spatial position for each grain in the cloud

As pluriphonic sound diffusion becomes more commonplace, we will see new spatial scattering algorithms. With an eight-channel source, for example, an alternative approach to spatialization is to control the density of particles per channel. Pluriphonic sound systems that surround the audience suggest circular and elliptical trajectories. The immersive projection spaces associated with virtual reality demand spherical scattering algorithms.

Per-Grain Reverberation

We can deepen the spatial image by adding highly selective reverberation to the spatial algorithm. That is, the spatialization algorithm sets the depth of reverberation of each grain individually. This can be accomplished in several ways.

By controlling the amplitude of a signal sent to a global reverberator, the amount of reverberation is controlled, and so the sound's depth. Thus an efficient way to individuate the grains is to send each grain to at least two outputs. One of the outputs is unreverberated or dry, while the other passes through a global reverberator that is common to all grains. This is the wet signal. The spatialization algorithm can derive the wet/dry ratio for each grain according to a probability function. In a multichannel system, one can generalize this to N global reverberators, where N is the number of output channels. Alberto de Campo tested such a design at CREATE, Santa Barbara, in the octophonic Varèse Studio in the spring of 2000.

A more elaborate design is to create a bank of distinct reverberators. Some have very short decay times, while others have long decay times. Some are dark in color, others brighter, and so on. Probability functions determine to which reverberator a grain is sent.

Per-grain reverberation is most striking at low densities. At high densities, the individual reverberations fuse into a continuous background reverberation, not much different from global wave reverberation.

Spatialization by Modulation with Particles

A simple way to spatialize a source sound is by modulation with particles. Starting by generating a pattern of synthetic particles which are distributed among two or more channels, we extract the amplitude envelope of each channel of particles then impose it on another source signal. Figure 5.5 shows the operation applied to one channel. Here it converts a speech sound to a granular texture. Granulation achieves a similar effect.

Convolutions with Clouds of Sonic Particles

The rolling of thunder has been attributed to echoes among the clouds; and if it is to be considered that a cloud is a collection of particles of water ... and therefore each capable of reflecting sound, there is no reason why very [loud] sounds should not be reverberated ... from a cloud. (Sir John Herschel, quoted in Tyndall 1875)

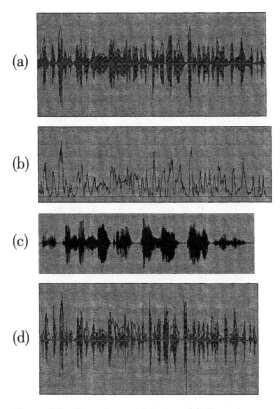

(a)

(b)

(c)

(d)

Figure 5.5 Granular modulation. (a) Granular sound. (b) Extraction of its amplitude envelope. (c) Speech sound. (d) Speech sound modulated by the granular envelope in (b).

A class of powerful sound transformations involves convolutions of arbitrary source sounds with clouds of sonic particles. The particles may be Gabor grains, expodec or rexpodec grains, pulsars, trainlets, or others. The results of such convolutions vary greatly, depending on the particles and their organization in time.

Earlier in this chapter, we showed how an accurate means of simulating the reverberation of a given space is to convolve the impulse response of the space with a source signal to be reverberated. A reverberator is a type of filter, where the length in samples of the IR corresponds to the reverberation time of the simulated hall. The IR of a room is captured by recording the room's response to a broadband impulse. This set of samples is then convolved with the source to be reverberated.

In the case of convolutions with an asynchronous cloud of grains, the particles can be thought of as the IR of an unusual virtual environment (Roads 1992b). What is the shape of this environment? I imagine that it resembles a large balloon with many long nipples. Each nipple resonates at a particular grain frequency.

For a brief source, convolution with a sparse cloud of short grains contributes a statistical distribution of echoes. The higher the grain density of the cloud, the more the echoes fuse into an irregular quasi-reverberation effect, often undulating with odd peaks and valleys of intensity, and weird echoes of the original source (figure 5.6). The virtual reflection contributed by each grain splatters the input sound in time. That is, it injects multiple delays spaced at irregular time intervals. If each grain was a single-sample pulse, then the echoes would be faithful copies of the original input. Since each grain may contain hundreds of samples, however, each echo is locally filtered and time-smeared.

Time-smearing effects fall into two basic categories, depending partly on the attack of the input sound. If the source begins with a sharp attack, each grain generates an echo of that attack. If the cloud of grains is not continuous, these echoes are spaced irregularly in time. If the source has a smooth attack, however, the time-splattering itself is smoothed out into a kind of strange colored reverberation. The "color" of the reverberation and the echoes is determined by the pitch and spectrum of the grains, which are a factor of the frequency, duration, envelope, and waveform of each grain (figure 5.7). See chapter 3 for more details on grain parameters.

For low-density synchronous clouds (<10 particles/second), convolutions result in metrical rhythms resembling tape echo, owing to the repetition of the source. Brief particles produce clear echoes, while long particles accentuate the bandpass filtering effect. At high densities the echoes fuse into buzzing, ringing, or rippling sonorities. The identity of the source may be obfuscated or obliterated.

Effect of Cloud Amplitude Envelope

The amplitude envelope of a cloud plays an important role in sound transformation. If the amplitude envelope of a dense cloud of particles has an exponential decay, then the effect is similar to granular reverberation. If the amplitude envelope of the cloud decreases linearly or logarithmically, the reverberation sustains unnaturally. (Natural reverberation dies out quickly.) An

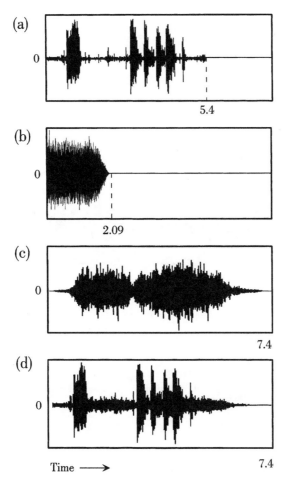

Figure 5.6 Reverberation by granular convolution. (a) Speech input: "Moi, Alpha Soixante." (b) Granular impulse response, consisting of one thousand 9-ms sinusoidal grains centered at 14,000 Hz, with a bandwidth of 5000 Hz. (c) Convolution of (a) and (b). (d) Mixture of (a) and (c) in a proportion of 5:1, creating reverberation around the speech.

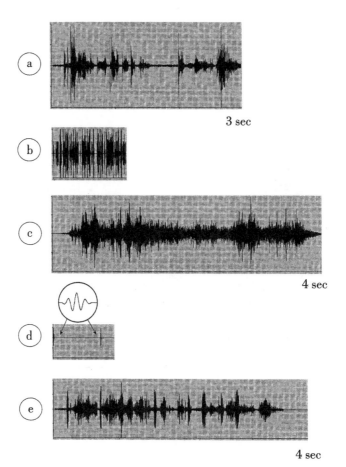

3 sec

4 sec

4 sec

Figure 5.7 Amplitude-versus-time images of convolutions with clouds of grains. (a) Speech signal: "It can only be attributed to human error." (b) Asynchronous cloud of two hundred 10-ms grains spread across the frequency bandwidth from 60 Hz to 12000 Hz. (c) The convolution of (a) and (b) results in the speech being heard amidst an irregular "liquid" echo/reverberation effect. (d) Synchronous cloud of two 10-ms grains at 440 Hz. The circled inset shows the form of the grain in detail. (e) Convolution of (a) and (d) results in a strongly filtered but intelligible echo of (a).

increasing amplitude envelope creates a gradual buildup in echo density over time, unlike any in physical space.

Effect of Particle Envelope

In addition to the amplitude envelope of the entire cloud, the duration and shape of the particle envelopes also determine the time pattern. If each particle was only a single-sample pulse, then echoes of the source would be faithful copies of the original. Since a particle may contain hundreds of sample points, however, each echo is locally time-smeared according to the duration and shape of the particle envelope.

In one experiment, I realized two different convolutions using identical data sets for a dense sound cloud containing over 12,000 particles. In both cases, the scattering algorithm was variable-density asynchronous granular synthesis. The only difference between the two synthetic clouds was the particle envelope. I convolved each of these clouds with a vocal utterance: "Lezione numero undice, l'ora." In the first case (figure 5.8a) the particle envelope is expodec, or an instantaneous attack followed an exponential decay (Weare 1997). In the second case (figure 5.8b) the particle envelope has a Gaussian attack and decay. In theory, the time-smearing introduced by expodec grains should be less pronounced than that of the Gaussian grains, and this was the case. I found that the Gaussian grains not only time-smeared, but they also introduced a churning effect, indicated in figure 5.8b by undulations in different parts of the sonogram.

Effect of Particle Duration

Convolutions with short particles realize time-domain effects, while longer grains accentuate time-smearing and filtering. For example, a stream of 1-ms grains at 440 Hz acts mainly as an echo generator, while a stream of 10-ms grains imposes a sharp bandpass filter. When the input sound has a smooth attack—as in a legato saxophone tone—the result is a time-varying filtering effect on the tone. (See Roads 1993a, 1997 for more details on this technique.)

Effect of Particle Frequency

The internal frequency content of the particles imposes a strong filtering effect, since the convolution calculates the intersection of the input spectrum and the

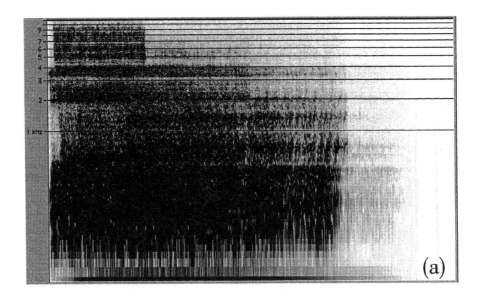

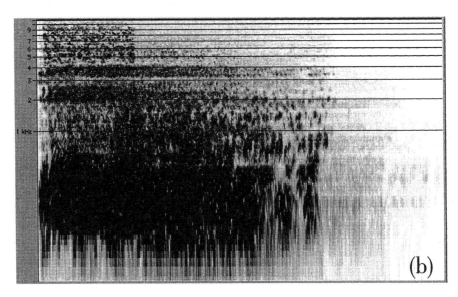

Figure 5.8   Spatialization via convolution with sound particles. These sonograms are the results of convolutions of a vocal utterance with two dense clouds of particles. The sonograms used a 2048-point FFT with a Kaiser-Bessel window. Frequency is plotted logarithmically from 40 Hz to 11.025 kHz. (a) The particle envelope is expodec (sharp attack, exponential decay). (b) The particle envelope has a Gaussian attack and decay. Notice the turgid undulations caused by time-smearing due to the smooth attack.

impulse response spectrum. If the impulse response spectrum is bandlimited, so will be the convolved result.

Effect of Window Type in Sectioned Convolution

Many practical convolution algorithms, such as the one used in the SoundHack program (Erbe 1995), employ sectioned convolution (described previously in this chapter) to preserve memory space. In this technique, the convolution applies to windowed segments of the input source. The results are equivalent to those obtained by non-sectioned convolution, without the need to perform a fast Fourier transform on the entire source, which could consume a great deal of memory space. Sectioned convolution introduces another factor to the transformation, however: the choice of window to use in sectioning the source. Our results show that a rectangular window tends to result in a brighter and more time-determinate convolution, while the bell-shaped Hamming window tends to smooth both the frequency content and the time resolution.

Particle Pluriphony in Physical Spaces

The physical architecture of a concert hall and its sound system complements the virtual acoustics of an electronic music composition. Stereophony, quadraphony, and octophony position sounds in a symmetrical lateral array in front of or around the listener. Periphony extends this scheme to the vertical dimension (Gerzon 1973). Beginning in 1973, a new type of pluriphonic or multiloudspeaker system appeared in the form of the GMEBaphone. Designed by Christian Clozier and Jean-Claude Le Duc, the GMEBaphone (or Cybernéphone as the newest version is called) proposed an orchestra of loudspeakers onstage, along with a complement of supporting loudspeakers surrounding the audience. Conceived for the spatial diffusion of electronic music, the system operated under the control of a composer operating a sound-mixing console configured for spatial projection (Clozier 1998). This idea caught on quickly in France, and has since spread all around the world (Bayle 1989, 1993; Roads 2000).

In contrast to the typical mixdown, in which many input channels reduce to a small number of output channels, the task of pluriphonic spatial projection is to take in a small number of inputs and distribute them to many outputs. One can extend the notion of pluriphony to the projection of sounds from a variety of positions above, below, and even within the audience. The art of pluriphony rests on four fundamental principles:

1. The experience of an electronic music composition is greatly enhanced by a spatial performance realized in the concert hall by the composer. The presence of a performer adds a virtuoso and dramatic aspect to the concert.

2. The sound projection system should offer a variety of contrasting spatial images through the arrangement of multiple loudspeakers placed around the auditorium, around the front stage, vertically, and, if possible within and below the audience. Not all loudspeakers are in use at all times. The composer/performer makes selective use of particular spatial images to highlight certain aspects of the work. For ensemble effects, the use of multiple loudspeakers onstage makes it possible to project a sound-image rivaling in complexity that of an orchestra.

3. Advantage should be taken of the particularities of certain loudspeakers. Different loudspeakers can integrate into the system because they each offer a particular voicing that may be useful in articulating a specific musical texture.

4. The illusion of stereophony, in which sound sources appear to be emerging from between two loudspeakers, is very fragile in a large performing space. Pluriphony seeks to replace the illusion of phantom sources with the physical reality of many loudspeakers. Unlike illusory sources, the location of physical sources is evident from any position in the hall.

The artistic possibilities of a pluriphonic spatial performance system are most attractive. Since 1997, we have engaged in the development of such a system at the Center for Research in Electronic Art Technology (CREATE) at the University of California, Santa Barbara (Roads, Kuchera-Morin, and Pope 1997). The first version of the Creatophone (ten audio output channels, twenty loudspeakers) was inaugurated in a concert featuring Luc Ferrari in October of that year. We have since greatly expanded the capabilities of the system.

Assessment of Spatialization on a Micro Time Scale

The real world is pluriphonic on every time scale. We enrich our music by taking this into consideration. As a phrase unfolds, the position of each object traces a varying topography. Spatialization imposes a curvature on an otherwise flat perspective. Functional oppositions between stationary and moving objects articulate contrapuntal relations.

In the early years of electronic music, the spatial aspect of most compositions was fixed for the entire piece. This was a macrospatial perspective. As composers discovered new techniques, their spatial aesthetic became more refined. Simultaneously, the technology of recording, editing, and mixing of sound became more sophisticated. This made it possible to associate specific localization patterns with different tracks or phrases.

The digital audio workstation, introduced in the late 1980s, extended the time scale of spatial transformations down to the level of individual sound objects.

Through new particle scattering algorithms, micromodulation, per-grain reverberation, and convolution, we have now extended spatialization down to the level of microsound. When we project these microspatial effects in a physical space over widely separated loudspeakers, these tiny virtual displacements appear far larger, and the sounds dance.

Summary

Our principal metaphor for musical composition must change from one of architecture to one of chemistry. We may imagine a new personality combing the beach of sonic possibilities, not someone who selects, rejects, classifies and measures the acceptable, but a chemist who can take any pebble, and, by numerical sorcery, separate its constituents, and merge the constituents from two quite different pebbles . . . (Wishart 1994)

In the first half of the twentieth century, Russolo (1916), Cahill (1897, 1914, 1917, 1919), Cage (1937), and Varèse (1971) extended the borders of music, allowing previously excluded sounds into the territory of composition. Mechanical noise instruments, electrodynamic tone wheels, and electronic circuits produced these sounds. Magnetic tape recording, introduced in the 1950s, made possible another shift in musical practice. Composers could store sounds on tape, which opened up all the possibilities of montage.

Previously transformed sounds are another rich source for the composer. Recursive processing, in which a transformed sound is again transformed, often provides interesting musical evolutions. This principle of recursive variation applies on multiple time scales. The conventional musical practice of variations involves permutations and combinations of discrete notes: repetition, changing the meter, changing the order of the notes, adding or omitting intervals, filling intervals with ancillary notes, inverting the harmony, substituting chords, transposing a melody, and so on. In contrast, sound transformation leads to morphological changes in sound color and spatial position as well as pitch and rhythm. Pitch and rhythm changes introduced by recursive variation may be continuous, rather than discrete.

By the 1980s, software made it possible to begin to develop a catalog of new digital transformations. Automatic segmentation of sound material into micro-temporal particles is the first step in many of these techniques. Recently we have reached a fortunate stage where many transformations operate in real time on inexpensive computers. Besides increasing the efficiency of studio work, this means that powerful sound transformations can be performed in a virtual or physical concert hall.

Circuit speed is less of a limiting factor, but no matter how fast computers become, certain transformations will always be too difficult for a human being to manipulate effectively in real time (Vaggione 1996c). Musical interfaces that offer control through envelopes, presets, and other automation functions will assist composers in planning detailed and elaborate transformations.

6 Windowed Analysis and Transformation

Our attention is clearly attracted by transients and movements as opposed to stationary stimuli, which we soon ignore. Concentrating on transients is probably a strategy for selecting important information from the overwhelming amount of data recorded by our

senses. Yet, classical signal processing has devoted most of its efforts to the design of time-invariant and space-invariant operators, that modify stationary signal properties. This has led to the indisputable hegemony of the Fourier transform, but leaves aside many information-processing applications. The world of transients is considerably larger and more complex than the garden of stationary signals. The search for an ideal Fourier-like basis that would simplify most signal processing is therefore a hopeless quest. Instead, a multitude of different transforms and bases have proliferated.
—Stéphane Mallat (1998)

The stream of samples that form a digital audio signal is merely one representation of a microsound. To convert this signal from the time-domain to the frequency-domain requires a stage of analysis. The analysis seeks evidence of periodicities of a specific waveform. In the case of Fourier analysis, for example, the waveform basis is sinusoidal. Once analysis transforms the signal into a frequency-domain representation, a large family of sonic transformations become possible. In the frequency-domain, the signal exists as a combination of periodic functions.

What interests us here are transformations that issue from the analysis of brief windows of sound. This chapter examines the short-time Fourier transform, the phase vocoder, the vector oscillator transform, wavelet transforms, and the Gabor transform. Some of the explanatory material appeared in my 1996 book *The Computer Music Tutorial*. It appears here revised and updated. The reports on experiments in sound transformation are new.

Overview of Windowed Spectrum Analysis

Though mathematically the Fourier theorem is beyond reproach, even experts could not at times conceal an uneasy feeling when it came to the physical results obtained by this method. After having for the first time obtained the spectrum of a frequency modulated wave, Carson (1922) wrote: "The foregoing solutions, though unquestionably mathematically correct, are somewhat difficult to reconcile with our physical intuitions, and our physical concepts of such 'variable frequency' mechanisms, as, for example, the siren." The reason is that the Fourier-integral method considers phenomena in an infinite interval, sub specie aeternitas, and this is very far from our everyday point of view. The terminology of physics has never completely adapted itself to this rigorous mathematical definition of "frequency." (Gabor 1946)

Analysis in music traditionally has referred to the study of form, phrasing, and note relationships within a score. Digital audio technology lets us take analysis to the level of sonic microstructure—inside the note. The first step in analysis is windowing, or segmenting a continuous sound into discrete particles. The window limits the duration of the analyzed signal, while imposing an envelope on it.

Windowing is akin to synchronous granulation (see chapter 5). The use of the term *window*, however, usually implies that a form of spectrum analysis will follow. By concentrating on one grain or window of sound at a time, the analysis can focus on local or short-time spectra. Like the frames of a motion picture, a series of windowed analyses yields a portrait of the spectrum evolution over time. The pertinence to the creative musician is that windowed operations let us extend composition technique down to an unprecedented level of sonic detail.

The field of spectrum analysis has grown rapidly in the past three decades. Analyzers have evolved from finicky instruments of acoustical study to sophisticated tools of musical production. They have emerged from institutional laboratories into the hands of musicians working in home studios. To create musically interesting effects, we modify the data generated by the analysis, which results in variants of the original sound. This is *analysis-resynthesis* (Risset 1989b).

Methods of Windowed Spectrum Analysis

Many spectrum analysis methods are variations on the basic technique of Fourier analysis of component frequencies. A practical form of Fourier analysis on digital audio signals is the *short-time Fourier transform* (STFT). This method analyzes a sound by extracting successive segments (shaped by a window function) and applying a bank of filters to the selected segment. The output of each filter indicates the amplitude and the phase of the spectrum at that particular frequency. A series of these STFTs captures a time-varying spectrum. At the core of the STFT is the *fast Fourier transform* or FFT, a computationally efficient implementation of Fourier analysis (Cooley and Tukey 1965; Rabiner and Gold 1975).

The phase vocoder (PV) (Flanagan and Golden 1966; Portnoff 1976, 1978, 1980, 1981; Moorer 1978; Dolson 1983, 1985, 1986) deserves special mention, as it is a popular method of sound analysis-resynthesis. The PV converts a sampled input signal into a time-varying spectral format. Many interesting sound transformations can be achieved by editing and resynthesizing PV data.

Wavelet analysis is another type of windowed spectrum analysis. As opposed to short-time Fourier analysis, with its uniform time-frequency regions, wavelet analysis divides the time-frequency plane into nonuniform regions. Wavelet techniques were first applied to audio signals in the 1980s (Grossman, et al. 1987; Kronland-Martinet, et al. 1987). Today there is a significant body of research on applications of wavelets to audio, with notable successes in the domain of transient detection and data reduction.

The theories of Dennis Gabor (see chapter 2) were the precursors of windowed spectrum analysis. As we show later, Gabor analysis has been recast recently in terms of the abstractions of wavelet theory.

Models for Spectrum Analysis

There does not seem to be any general or optimal paradigm to either analyze or synthesize any type of sound. One has to scrutinize the sound—quasi-periodic, sum of inharmonic components, noisy, quickly or slowly evolving—and also investigate which features of the sound are relevant to the ear. (Risset 1991)

No single method of spectrum estimation is ideal for all musical applications. Fourier analysis—the most prevalent approach—is actually a family of different techniques that are still evolving. A variety of non-Fourier methods continue to be developed (see Roads 1996).

Every sound analysis technique should be viewed as fitting the input data to an assumed model. Methods based on Fourier analysis model the input sound as a sum of harmonically related sinusoids—which it may or may not be. Other techniques model the input signal as an excitation signal filtered by resonances, as a sum of exponentially damped sinusoids or square waves, as a combination of inharmonically related sinusoids, as a set of formant peaks with added noise, or as a set of equations that represent the mechanical vibration of a traditional instrument. Innumerable other models are conceivable. Variations in performance among the different methods can often be attributed to how well the assumed model matches the process being analyzed. Hence it is important to choose the appropriate analysis method for a particular musical application.

Spectrum and Timbre

Spectrum and timbre are related concepts, but they are not equivalent. Spectrum is a physical property that can be characterized as a distribution of energy as a function of frequency. How to measure this energy precisely is a matter of ongoing debate. Psychoacoustics uses the term "timbre" to denote perceptual mechanisms that classify sound into families. By this definition, timbre is at least as concerned with perception as it is with sound signals. It is certainly easiest to discuss timbre in the realm of traditional instrument and vocal tones, where almost all past research has focused. Only a few attempts have been made to classify the universe of sound outside of this area, the most heroic being the studies of Pierre Schaeffer (1977; see also Schaeffer, Reibel, and Ferreyra 1967).

A common timbre groups tones played by an instrument at different pitches, loudnesses, and durations. We can tell when a piano is playing, for example, no matter what notes it plays. Human perception separates each instrument's tones from those of other instruments played with the same pitch, loudness, and duration. A single instrument may of course emit many timbres, as in the range of sonorities obtained from saxophones blown in various ways.

Numerous factors inform timbre perception. These include the amplitude envelope of a sound (especially the attack shape), undulations due to vibrato and tremolo, formant structures, perceived loudness, duration, and the time-varying spectral envelope (Schaeffer 1977; Risset 1991; McAdams and Bregman 1979; McAdams 1982; Grey 1975).

Amplitude and duration influence the perception of timbre. A soft flute tone at 50 dB for example, may have the same spectrum profile as one amplified to 120 dB, but we hear the latter only as a piercing blast. Similarly, a toneburst that lasts 10 ms may have the same periodic waveshape as a tone that lasts 10 seconds, but a listener may find it difficult to determine that they come from the same source.

The point is that spectrum is not the only clue to perceived timbre. By examining the time-domain waveform carefully, one can glean much about the timbre of a sound without subjecting it to a detailed spectrum analysis.

Data Packing and Data Reduction in Windowed Spectrum Analysis

Windowed spectrum analysis, contrary to the expectations of some of its inventors, generates an "information explosion" (Risset and Wessel 1982). That is, the analysis data may occupy much more memory space than the original input signal. Adjusting certain parameters of the analysis can make a great difference to the size of the analysis file. For example, a high-resolution analysis with overlapping analysis windows greatly increases the amount of data. In techniques such as the tracking phase vocoder (discussed later), the amount of data depends partly on the complexity of the input sound. The analysis data associated with a thick noisy texture, for example, is much more voluminous than the analysis data for a simple sinusoidal melody. Another factor in the data explosion is the internal representation used by the analysis program, including the word length of the numerical data.

For many reasons, there is great interest in reducing the storage requirements of sound data. Many companies compete in the arena of digital audio encoding schemes, which fall, broadly, into two areas: *lossless packing* and *lossy data reduction.*

Lossless packing does not involve spectrum analysis. It makes use of redundancies in the numerical sample value to reformat it in a more memory-efficient form. Thus it reduces storage while preserving the full integrity of the audio data. See Craven and Gerzon (1996), or Meridian (1998) for details.

Lossy data reduction does involve windowed spectrum analysis. It dissects sounds into a data-reduced form according to a resynthesis model, while discarding large amounts of "nonessential" data. In effect, it reduces sounds to a set of control functions. It presumes the existence of a resynthesis system that can properly interpret these control functions to reconstitute an approximation of the sound.

Lossy data reduction schemes are built into consumer audio products such as the Mini-Disc system, the DVD surround sound format, MP3 (MPEG 1, Layer 3) audio, and other popular Internet audio file formats. MP3, for example, offers a *variable bit rate* (VBR) method (Kientzle 1998). According to the theory of VBR, "simple" sound demands a low bit rate, while "complex" sound demands a higher bit rate. VBR encoding uses windowed spectrum analysis and other techniques to estimate the "complexity" of the signal. In essence, an MP3 audio bitstream specifies the frequency content of a sound and how that content varies over time. It splits the input signal into thirty-two subbands, each of which contains eighteen frequency bands, for a total of 576 frequency bands. (See Brandenburg and Bosi 1997 for details.) An MP3 player resynthesizes the audio signal from its data-reduced form. Many points of compromise are exploited by MP3 encoders. For example, in the interest of speed, MP3 decoders may use integer arithmetic, which sacrifices audio accuracy. The encoding of stereo information is often crude. MP3's "joint-stereo" mode plays the same track through both channels but with the intensity differences of the original tracks.

Data reduction discards information. The losses may be insignificant when the original audio program is already bandlimited, compressed in amplitude, spatially flat, distorted, and designed to be played back over a mediocre audio system, as is the case with much popular music. But such losses are evident in musical material that exploits the full range of a fine audio system. It is not difficult to generate signals that reveal the weaknesses of the commercial coding models. The degradation is more pronounced when these signals are "copied" (or to be more precise, recoded) or further manipulated.

For creative purposes, we prefer data reductions that leave the analysis data in editable form. The literature of computer music includes a large body of research work on data reduction, including pioneering studies by Risset (1966), Freedman (1967), Beauchamp (1969, 1975), and Grey (1975). Techniques that have been used in computer music include line-segment approximation, principal components analysis, spectral interpolation synthesis, spectral modeling synthesis, and genetic algorithms.

Theory of Fourier Analysis

In order to comprehend many of the transformations presented later in this chapter, it is important to have a basic understanding of the theory of Fourier analysis. This section presents a capsule history and the essential points of the theory.

History of Fourier Analysis

In the early eighteenth century, the French engineer and aristocrat Jean-Baptiste Joseph, Baron de Fourier (1768–1830), formulated a theory stating that arbitrary periodic waveforms could be deconstructed into combinations of simple sine waves of different amplitudes, frequencies, and phases. Through the middle of the nineteenth century, Fourier analysis was a tedious task of manual calculation. In the 1870s, the British physicist Lord Kelvin and his brother built the first mechanical harmonic analyzer (Marple 1987). This elaborate gear-and-pulley contraption analyzed handtraced waveform segments. The analyzer acted as a mechanical integrator, finding the area under the sine and cosine waves for all harmonics of a fundamental period. The Michelson-Stratton harmonic analyzer (1898) was probably the most sophisticated machine of this type. Designed around a spiral spring mechanism, it could resolve up to eighty harmonics. It could also act as a waveform synthesizer, mechanically inverting the analysis to reconstruct the input signal.

In the twentieth century, mathematicians refined Fourier's method. Engineers designed analog filter banks to perform simple types of spectrum analysis. Following the development of stored-program computers in the 1940s, programmers created the first digital implementations of the *Fourier transform* (FT), but these consumed enormous amounts of computer time—a scarce commodity in that era. Finally, in the mid-1960s, a set of algorithms known as the *fast Fourier transform* or FFT, described by James Cooley at Princeton University and John Tukey at Bell Telephone Laboratories, greatly reduced the voluminous calculations required for Fourier analysis (Cooley and Tukey 1965).

Fourier Series

Fourier showed that a periodic function $x(t)$ of period T can be represented by the infinite summation series:

$$x(t) = C_0 + \sum_{n=1}^{\infty} C_n \cos(n\omega t + \phi_n)$$

That is, the function $x(t)$ is a sum of harmonically related sinusoidal functions with the frequency $\omega_n = n\omega = 2\pi/T$. C_0 is the offset or DC component; it shifts the waveform up or down. The first sinusoidal component C_1 is the *fundamental*; it has the same period as T. The numerical variables C_n and ϕ_n give the magnitude and phase of each component.

A Fourier series summation is a formula for reconstructing or synthesizing a periodic signal. But it does not tell us how to set the coefficients C_n and ϕ_n for an arbitrary input sound. For this, we need the analysis method called the Fourier transform.

Fourier Transform

This section takes advantage of the complex exponential representation of a sine wave at a given phase. This representation is based on these identities:

$$\cos(2\pi f + \phi) = \cos(2\pi f) + j \sin(2\pi f) = e^{j2\pi f}$$

So, a cosine at a given frequency and phase can also be represented as a complex number, or a complex exponential function. (See Roads 1996, appendix A.)

Suppose that we wish to analyze a continuous-time (analog) signal $x(t)$ of infinite extent and bandwidth. Fourier's theory says that $x(t)$ can be accurately reconstructed with an infinite number of pure sinusoidal waves of different amplitudes, frequencies, and initial phases. These waves make up the signal's Fourier transform spectrum. The FT spectrum represents all frequencies from 0 Hz (a constant) to infinity (∞) Hz, with a mirror image in the negative frequencies.

The formula for the FT or *Fourier integral* is as follows:

$$X(f) = \int_{-\infty}^{\infty} x(t)e^{-j2\pi ft}\, dt$$

This says that the FT at any particular frequency f is the integral of the multiplication of the input signal $x(t)$ by the pure sinusoid $e^{-j2\pi ft}$. Intuitively, we could surmise that this integral will be larger when the input signal is high in amplitude and rich in partials. $X(f)$ represents the magnitude of the Fourier transform of the time-domain signal $x(t)$. By magnitude we mean the absolute value of the amplitude of the frequencies in the spectrum. The capital letter X denotes a Fourier transform, and the f within parentheses indicates that we are now referring to a frequency-domain signal, as opposed to the time-domain signal $x(t)$. Each value of $X(f)$ is a complex number.

The magnitude is not a complete picture of the Fourier transform. It tells us just the amount of each complex frequency that must be combined to synthesize $x(t)$. It does not indicate the phase of each of these components. One can also plot the *phase spectrum*, as it is called, but this is less often shown.

The magnitude of the Fourier transform $X(f)$ is symmetric around 0 Hz. Thus the Fourier representation combines equal amounts of positive and negative frequencies. This is the case for any real-valued input signal. This dual-sided spectrum has no physical significance. (Note that the inverse Fourier transform takes a complex input signal—a spectrum—and generates a real-valued waveform as its output.)

The Discrete Fourier Transform

The one kind of signal that has a discrete frequency-domain representation (i.e., isolated spectral lines) is a periodic signal. A periodic signal repeats at every interval T. Such a signal has a Fourier transform containing components at a fundamental frequency $(1/T)$ and its harmonics and its zero everywhere else.

A periodic signal, in the precise mathematical sense, must be defined from $t = -\infty$ to $t = \infty$. Colloquially, one speaks of signals as periodic if $x(t) = x(t + T)$ for an amount of time that is long relative to the period T. We can construct this kind of periodic signal by replicating a finite-length signal. Imagine that we infinitely replicate the finite-length signal $x(t)$ backwards and forwards in time. In the discrete-time (sampled) domain, this produces a periodic signal $x[n]$. The use of brackets rather than parentheses indicates that the signal is discrete, rather than continuous.

The frequency-domain representation of this replicated periodic signal $x[n]$ is called its *discrete Fourier transform* (DFT). The DFT provides a sampled look at both the magnitude and phase of the spectrum of $x[n]$, and is a central tool in musical signal processing. In effect, the DFT sets up a one-to-one correspondence between the number of input samples N and the number of frequencies that it resolves.

The Short-Time Fourier Transform

To adapt Fourier analysis to the practical world of sampled time-varying signals, researchers molded the FT into the short-time Fourier transform or STFT (Schroeder and Atal 1962; Flanagan 1972; Allen and Rabiner 1977; Schafer and Rabiner 1973).

Windowing the Input Signal

As a preparation for spectrum analysis, the STFT imposes a window upon the input signal. A window is nothing more than a simple amplitude envelope. Windowing breaks the input signal into a series of segments that are shaped in amplitude by the chosen window function and bounded in time according to the length of the window function. In audio applications, the duration of the window is usually in the range of 1 ms to 100 ms, the window envelope is bell-shaped, and the segments usually overlap. By analyzing the spectrum of each windowed segment separately, one obtains a sequence of measurements that constitute a time-varying spectrum.

Unfortunately, windowing has the side effect of distorting the spectrum measurement. This is because the spectrum analyzer is measuring not purely the input signal, but rather, the product of the input signal and the window.

The spectrum that results is the convolution of the spectra of the input and the window signals. We see the implications of this later.

Operation of the STFT

Adopting Dolson's (1986) notation, the equation for a DFT of an input signal $x[m]$ multiplied by a time-shifted window $h[n-m]$ is as follows:

$$X[n,k] = \sum_{m=-\infty}^{\infty} \{x[m]h[n-m]\}e^{-j(2\pi/N)km}$$

Thus the output $X[n,k]$ is the Fourier transform of the windowed input at each discrete time n for each discrete frequency band or bin k. The equation says that m can go from minus to plus infinity; this is a way of saying "for an arbitrary-length input signal." For a specific short-time window, the bounds of m are set to the appropriate length. Here, k is the index for the frequency bins, N is the number of points in the spectrum. The following relation sets the frequency corresponding to each bin k:

$$f_k = (k/N) \times f_s$$

where f_s is the sampling rate. So for a sampling rate of 44.1 kHz, an analysis window length N of 1024 samples, and a frequency bin $k = 1$, f_k is 43 Hz. The windowed DFT representation is particularly attractive because the fast Fourier transform or FFT can calculate it efficiently.

A discrete STFT formulation indicating the *hop size* or time advance of each window is:

$$X[l,k] = \sum_{m=0}^{M-1} h[m]x[m+(lH)]e^{-j(2\pi/N)km}$$

where M is the number of samples in the input sequence, $h[m]$ is the window that selects a block of data from the input signal $x[m]$, l is the *frame index*, and H is the hop size in samples (Serra 1989).

Each block of data generated by the STFT is called a *frame*, by analogy to the successive frames of a film. Each frame contains two spectra: (1) a magnitude spectrum that depicts the amplitude of every analyzed frequency component (figure 6.1c), and (2) a phase spectrum that shows the initial phase value for every frequency component (figure 6.1d). We can visualize each of these two spectra as histograms with a vertical line for each frequency component along the abscissa. The vertical line represents amplitude in the case of the magnitude

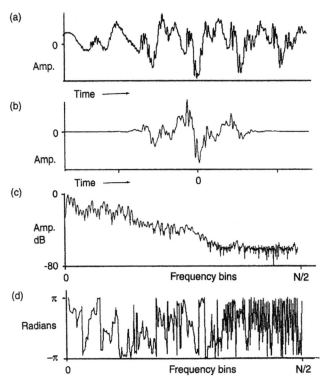

Figure 6.1   Magnitude and phase spectra. (a) Input waveform. (b) Windowed segment. (c) Magnitude spectrum plotted over the range 0 to −8 dB. (d) Phase spectrum plotted over the range −π to π. (After Serra 1989.)

spectrum, and the starting phase (between −π and π) in the case of the phase spectrum. The magnitude spectrum is relatively easy to read, the phase spectrum less so. When normalized to the range of −π and π it is called the *wrapped phase* representation. For many signals, it appears to the eye like a random function. An *unwrapped phase* projection may be more meaningful visually. (See Roads 1996, appendix A.)

To summarize, applying the STFT to a stream of input samples results in a series of frames that make up a time-varying spectrum.

Justifications for Windowing

Theory says that we can analyze a segment of any length and exactly resynthesize the segment from the analysis data. For example, we can analyze in one pass Stravinsky's *Le sacre du printemps* using a thirty-minute-long window, and reconstruct the entire piece from this analysis. This being the case, why bother to break the analysis into overlapping windows on a micro time scale?

The reasons are several. The analysis of a thirty-minute monaural sound sampled at 44.1 kHz would result in a spectrum of over seventy-nine million points. A visual inspection of this enormous spectrum would eventually tell us all the frequencies that occurred over a half hour, but would not tell us when they occurred. This temporal information is embedded deep in the mathematical combination of the magnitude and phase spectra, hidden to the eye. Thus the first thing that windowing helps with is the visualization of the spectrum. By limiting the analysis to micro segments (typically less than a twentieth of a second), each analysis plots fewer points, and we know more accurately when these frequencies occurred.

A second reason for using short-time windows is to conserve memory. Breaking the input into micro segments makes it easy to calculate the FFT in a limited memory space.

A third reason for short-time windows is that one obtains results more quickly. For *Le sacre du printemps* one would have to wait up to thirty minutes just to read in the input signal, plus however long it takes to calculate an FFT on a seventy-nine million point input signal. Windowing the input lets one obtain initial results quickly—after reading just a few milliseconds of the input. This opens up applications for real-time spectrum analysis.

Analysis Frequencies

One can think of the STFT as the application of a bank of filters at equally spaced frequency intervals to the windowed input signal. The frequencies are spaced at integer multiples (i.e., harmonics) of

$$\frac{sampling\ frequency}{N}$$

where N is the size of the analyzed segment. (As we will later see, the value of N is usually greater than the actual number of sound samples analyzed; for now we will assume they are the same length.) Thus if the sampling frequency is 50 kHz and the window length is one thousand samples, the analysis frequencies are spaced at intervals $50,000/1000 = 50$ Hz apart, starting at 0 Hz. The analyzer at 0 Hz measures the direct current or DC offset of the signal, a constant that can shift the entire signal above or below the center point of zero amplitude.

Audio signals are bandlimited to half the sampling rate (25 kHz in this case) and so we are concerned with only half of the analysis bins. The effective frequency resolution of an STFT is thus $N/2$ bins spread equally across the audio bandwidth, starting at 0 Hz and ending at the Nyquist frequency. In our example, the number of usable audio frequency bins is five hundred, spaced 50 Hz apart.

Time-Frequency Uncertainty

The knowledge of the position of the particle is complementary to the knowledge of its velocity or momentum. If we know the one with high accuracy we cannot know the other with high accuracy. (Heisenberg 1958)

All windowed spectrum analyses are hampered by a fundamental uncertainty principle between time resolution and frequency resolution. This is directly analogous to a principle first recognized by quantum physicists such as Werner Heisenberg in the early part of the twentieth century. The *linear resolution principle* (Masri, et al 1997a) states that if we want high resolution in the time-domain (i.e., we want to know precisely when an event occurs), we sacrifice frequency resolution. In other words, we can tell that an event occurred at a precise time, but we cannot say exactly what frequencies it contained. Conversely, if we want high resolution in the frequency-domain (i.e., we want to know the precise frequency of a component), we sacrifice time resolution. This means that we can pinpoint frequency content only over a long time interval. It is important to grasp this fundamental relationship in order to interpret the results of Fourier analysis.

Fourier analysis starts from this abstract premise: if a signal contains only one frequency, then that signal must be a sinusoid that is infinite in duration. Purity of frequency—absolute periodicity—implies infinitude. As soon as one limits the duration of this sine wave, the only way that Fourier analysis can account for it is to consider the signal as a sum of many infinite-length sinusoids that just happen to cancel each other out in such a way as to result in a limited-duration sine wave! While this characterization of frequency neatens the mathematics, it does not jibe with our most basic experiences with sound. As Gabor (1946) pointed out, if the concept of frequency is used only to refer to infinitely long signals, then the concept of changing frequency is impossible.

Figure 6.2 shows the effects of time-frequency (TF) uncertainty at the juncture of an abrupt transition between two pure tones. Figure 6.2a portrays the actual spectrum of the signal fed into the analyzer. Figure 6.2b is the measured short-time Fourier transform of this signal. Notice the band-thickening and blurring, which are classic symptoms of TF uncertainty.

Time-Frequency Tradeoffs

The FFT divides the audible frequency space into $N/2$ frequency bins, where N is the length in samples of the analysis window. Hence there is a tradeoff between the number of frequency bins and the length of the analysis window. For example, if N is five hundred and twelve samples, then the number of frequencies that can be analyzed is limited to two hundred and fifty-six. Assuming a sampling rate of 44.1 kHz, we obtain two hundred and fifty-six bins equally spaced over the bandwidth 0 Hz to the Nyquist frequency 22.05 kHz. Increasing the sampling rate only widens the measurable bandwidth, it does not increase the frequency resolution of the analysis.

If we want high time accuracy (say 1 ms or about forty-four samples), we must be satisfied with only 44/2 or twenty-two frequency bins. Dividing the audio bandwidth from 0 to 22.05 kHz by twenty-two frequency bins, we obtain 22,050/22 or about 1000 Hz of frequency resolution. That is, if we want to know exactly when events occur on the scale of 1 ms, then our frequency resolution is limited to the gross scale of 1000-Hz-wide frequency bands. By sacrificing more time resolution, and widening the analysis interval to 30 ms, one can spot frequencies within a 33 Hz bandwidth. For high resolution in frequency (1 Hz), one must stretch the time interval to 1 second (44,100 samples)!

Because of this limitation in windowed STFT analysis, researchers are examining hybrids of time-domain and frequency-domain analysis, multiresolution analysis, or non-Fourier methods to try to resolve both dimensions at high resolution.

Frequencies in between Analysis Bins

The STFT knows only about a discrete set of frequencies spaced at equal intervals across the audio bandwidth. The spacing of these frequencies depends on the window size. This size corresponds to the "fundamental period" of the analysis. Such a model works well for sounds that are harmonic or quasi-harmonic where the harmonics align closely with the bins of the analysis. What

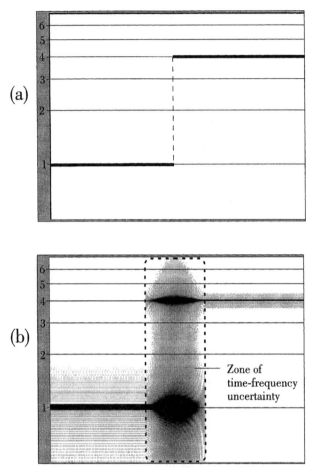

Figure 6.2   Time-frequency uncertainty in short-time Fourier analysis. (a) Idealized spectrum of the signal fed to the analyzer, consisting of a tone at 1000 Hz followed immediately by a tone at 4000 Hz. (b) Analysis sonogram. The blurring indicates the zone of time-frequency uncertainty. Both images are plotted on a logarithmic frequency scale from 500 Hz to 7000 Hz.

happens to frequencies that fall in between the equally spaced analysis bins of the STFT? This is the case for inharmonic sounds such as gongs or noisy sounds such as snare drums.

Let us call the frequency to be analyzed f. When f coincides with the center of an analysis channel, all its energy is concentrated in that channel, and so it is accurately measured. When f is close to but not precisely coincident with the center, energy leaks into all other analysis channels, but with a concentration remaining close to f. The leakage spilling into all frequency bins from components inbetween bins is a well-known source of unreliability in the spectrum estimates produced by the STFT. When more than one component is in between bins, *beating effects* (periodic cancellation and reinforcement) may occur in both the frequency and amplitude traces. The result is that the analysis shows fluctuating energy in frequency components that are not physically present in the input signal.

Significance of Clutter

If the signal is resynthesized directly from the analysis data, the extra frequency components and beating effects pose no problem. These effects are benign artifacts of the STFT analysis that are resolved in resynthesis. Beating effects are merely the way that the STFT represents a time-varying spectrum in the frequency-domain. In the resynthesis, some components add constructively and some add destructively (canceling each other out), so that the resynthesized result is a close approximation of the original.

Beating and other anomalies are harmless when the signal is directly resynthesized, but they obscure attempts to inspect the spectrum visually, or to transform it. For this reason, the artifacts of analysis are called *clutter*. Dolson (1983) and Strawn (1985) assayed the significance of clutter in analysis of musical instrument tones. Cross-term clutter is common in *higher-order analysis*, which can extract detailed phase and modulation laws embedded in the spectrum analysis (Masri, et al. 1997a, 1997b).

The Phase Vocoder

The *phase vocoder* (PV) uses the STFT to convert an audio signal into a complex Fourier representation. Since the STFT calculates the frequency domain representation of the signal on a fixed frequency grid, the actual frequencies of the partial bins have to be found by converting the relative phase change between two STFT outputs to actual frequency changes. The term "phase" in phase vocoder refers to the fact that the temporal development of a sound is contained in its phase information, while the amplitudes denote that a specific frequency component is present in a sound. The phase contains the structural information (Sprenger 1999). The phase relationships between the different bins reconstruct time-limited events when the time-domain representation is resynthesized. The phase difference of each bin between two successive analysis frames determines that bin's frequency deviation from its mid frequency. This provides information about the bin's true frequency, and makes possible a resynthesis on a different time basis.

Phase Vocoder Parameters

The quality of a given PV analysis depends on the parameter settings chosen by the user. These settings must be adjusted according to the nature of the sounds being analyzed and the type of results that are expected. The main parameters of the PV are:

1. Window size (also called frame size)—number of input samples to be analyzed at a time.
2. FFT size—the actual number of samples fed to the FFT algorithm; usually the nearest power of two that is double the window size, where the unit of FFT size is referred to by *points*, as in a "1024-point FFT."
3. Window type—selection of a window shape from among standard types.
4. Hop size or overlap factor—time advance from one window onset to the next.

Next we discuss each parameter in turn. Later we give rules of thumb for setting these parameters.

Window Size

The window size (in samples) determines one aspect of the tradeoff in TF resolution. The larger the window is, the greater the number of frequency bins, but the lower the time resolution, and vice versa. If we are trying to analyze sounds in the lower octaves with great frequency accuracy, we cannot avoid a large window size. Since the FFT computes the average spectrum content within a given window, the precise onset time of any spectrum changes within the span of the window is lost when the spectrum is plotted or transformed. (If the signal is simply resynthesized, the temporal information is restored.) For high-frequency sounds, small windows are adequate, which are also more accurate in time resolution.

FFT Size and Hop Size

The FFT size is typically the nearest power of two that is double the window size. For example, a window size of 512 samples would mandate an FFT size of 1024. The other 512 samples in the FFT are set to zero—a process called *zero-padding*.

The *hop size* is the number of samples that the analyzer jumps along the input waveform each time it takes a new spectrum measurement. The shorter the hop size, the more successive windows overlap. This improves the resolution of the analysis, but requires more computation. Some PVs specify hop size as an overlap factor that describes how many analysis windows cover each other. An overlap of four, for example, means that one window follows another after 25% of the window length. Regardless of how it is specified, the hop size is usually a fraction of the window size. A certain amount of overlap (e.g., eight times) is necessary to ensure an accurate resynthesis. More overlap may improve accuracy when the analysis data is going to be transformed, but the computational cost is proportionally greater.

Window Type

A spectrum analyzer measures not just the input signal but the product of the input signal and the window envelope. The law of convolution, introduced in chapter 5, states that multiplication in the time-domain is equivalent to convolution in the frequency-domain. Thus the analyzed spectrum is the convolution of the spectra of the input and the window signals. In effect, the window modulates the input signal, and this introduces sidebands or clutter into the analyzed spectrum.

A smooth bell-shaped window minimizes the clutter. Most PVs let the user select a window from a family of standard window types, including Hamming, Hanning (or Hann; see Marple 1987), truncated Gaussian, Blackman-Harris, and Kaiser (Harris 1978; Nuttall 1981). All are bell-shaped, and all work reasonably well for general musical analysis-resynthesis. Each one is slightly different, however, so it may be worth trying different windows when the results are critical. The one window to avoid is the rectangular or Dirichelet, which introduces a great deal of clutter or extraneous frequency components into the analyzed spectrum.

Typical PV Parameter Settings

No parameter settings of the PV are ideal for all sounds. Within a certain range, however, a variety of traditional instrumental sounds can be analyzed and resynthesized with reasonable fidelity. Here are some rules of thumb for PV parameter settings that may serve as a starting point for more tuned analyses:

1. Window size—large enough to capture four periods of the lowest frequency of interest. This is particularly important if the sound is time-stretched; too small a window size means that individual pitch bursts are moved apart, changing the pitch, although formants are preserved.
2. FFT size—double the window size, in samples.
3. Window type—any standard type except Dirichelet.
4. Hop size—Time advance of the analysis window. If the analysis data is going to be time-distorted, the recommended hop size is an eighth of the frame size, in samples (i.e., eight times overlap). The minimum technical criterion is that all windows add to a constant, that is, all data is equally weighted. This typically implies an overlap at the -3 dB point of the particular window type chosen, from which can be derived the hop size.

Any given setting of the window size results in an analysis biased toward harmonics of the period defined by that window size. Frequency components that fall outside the frequency bins associated with a given window size will be estimated incorrectly. Some analyzers try to estimate the pitch of the signal in order to determine the optimal window size. This is called *pitch-synchronous analysis* (Mathews, Miller, and David 1961). Pitch-synchronous analysis works well if the sound to be analyzed has a basically harmonic structure.

Resynthesis Techniques

Resynthesis constructs a time-domain signal from the analysis data. If the analysis data has not been altered, then the resynthesis should be a close simulacrum of the original signal. If the analysis data has been altered, the resynthesized sound will be transformed. A variety of resynthesis techniques have been invented. Some are more efficient, some are more accurate, some are more robust under transformation, some are adapted for real time operation. This section presents three techniques. The first two appear in commonly available phase vocoders. The third is more experimental, but gives an idea of the optimizations that can be made.

Overlap-Add Resynthesis

To resynthesize the original time-domain signal, the STFT can reconstruct each windowed waveform segment from its spectrum components by applying the *inverse discrete Fourier transform* (IDFT) to each frame. The IDFT takes each magnitude and phase component and generates a corresponding time-domain signal with the same envelope as the analysis window. Then by overlapping and adding these resynthesized windows, typically at their half power or −3 dB points, one obtains a signal that is a close approximation of the original. This is called the *overlap-add* (OA) method of resynthesis.

We use the qualification "close approximation" as a way of comparing practical implementations of the STFT with mathematical theory. In theory, resynthesis from the STFT is an identity operation, replicating the input sample by sample (Portnoff 1976). If it were an identity operation in practice, we could copy signals through an STFT/IDFT any number of times with no generation loss. However, even good implementations of the STFT lose a small amount of information. This can be verified by a careful comparison between the input and output waveforms. The loss may not be audible after one pass without transformation through the STFT.

Many microsonic transformations manipulate the analysis frames before resynthesizing the sound with the OA method. The OA process, however, is designed for cases where the windows sum perfectly to a constant. As Allen and Rabiner (1977) showed, any additive or multiplicative transformations that disturb the perfect summation criterion at the final stage of the OA cause side effects that will probably be audible. Time expansion by stretching the distance between windows, for example, may introduce comb filter or reverberation effects, depending on the window size used in the analysis. Using speech or singing as a source, some transformations result in voices with robotic or ringing artifacts. One way to lessen unwanted artifacts is to stipulate a great deal of overlap among successive windows in the analysis stage. In selected cases, the distortion introduced by OA resynthesis can be exploited as a sonic effect.

Oscillator Bank Resynthesis

Oscillator bank (OB) resynthesis differs from the overlap-add approach. In contrast to the OA model, which sums the sine waves at each frame, OB resynthesis converts the analysis data from all analyzed frames into a set of amplitude and frequency envelopes for multiple oscillators. In effect, the envelopes convert the analysis data from the micro time scale to the time scale of the analyzed sound.

The advantage of OB resynthesis is that envelopes are much more robust under musical transformation than the spectrum frames. The perfect summation criterion of the OA model does not apply in OB resynthesis. Within broad limits, one can stretch, shrink, rescale, or shift the envelopes without worrying about artifacts in the resynthesis process. Another strength is that the OB representation facilitates graphical editing of the spectrum. A disadvantage of OB is that it is not as efficient computationally as OA methods.

Analysis-by-Synthesis/Overlap-Add Resynthesis

Analysis-by-synthesis/overlap-add (AS/OA) is an adaptive method designed for improved resolution and more robust transformations. AS/OA incorporates an error analysis procedure (George and Smith 1992). This procedure compares the original signal with the resynthesized signal. When the error is above a given threshold, the procedure adjusts the amplitudes, frequencies, and phases in the analysis frame to approximate the original more closely. This adaptive process can occur repeatedly until the signal is more-or-less precisely reconstructed. As a result, the AS/OA method can handle attack transients, inharmonic spectra, and effects such as vibrato with greater accuracy than the OA method. It also permits more robust musical transformations. Another method called the tracking phase vocoder, presented later in the chapter, has similar benefits.

Assessment of the Phase Vocoder

Present methods of windowed spectrum analysis owe a debt to Dennis Gabor's pioneering work (1946, 1947, 1952; see also chapter 2). The frames of the STFT are analogous to his acoustical quanta. The projection of the time-frequency plane onto the sonogram is analogous to a visual representation of the Gabor matrix.

The phase vocoder has emerged from the laboratory to become a popular tool. It is packaged in a variety of widely distributed musical software. The compositional interest of the PV lies in transforming the analysis data before resynthesis, producing variations of the original sound. What the composer seeks in the output is not a clone of the input, but a musical transformation that maintains a sense of the source's identity.

The weaknesses of the STFT and the PV as representations for sound are well known. The uncertainty principle pointed out by Gabor is embedded deeply within the STFT. Time-frequency information is smeared. Overlapping windows mean that it is impossible to modify a single time-frequency atom without affecting adjacent atoms. Such a change will most likely lead to a discontinuity in the resynthesized signal. Many transformations sound "blurry" or "sinusoidal" in quality, a common artifact of Fourier techniques in general. The tracking phase vocoder, described later, is a more secure transformation tool, but it has its own imperfections.

On the positive side, the PV is powerful. Good implementations of the PV offer the possibility of modifying pitch, time, and timbre independently.

Sound Transformation with Windowed Spectrum Operations

Inside a windowed spectrum analyzer is a granulated time-frequency representation of sound. By manipulating this representation, we can obtain many transformations that are difficult or impossible to achieve with time-domain procedures, including high-quality pitch-time changing, frequency-domain filtering, stable and transient extraction, multiband dynamics processing, cross-synthesis, and many other exotic effects. This section explores these techniques, many of which are implemented within phase vocoders.

Pitch-Time Changing

One of the most common windowed spectrum transformations is the altering of a signal is duration whilst maintaining its original pitch. Inversely, one can change pitch without altering duration. For these effects, the phase vocoder often achieves better sound quality than can be obtained with the time-domain granulation algorithms described in chapter 5.

In a PV with overlap-add resynthesis, the time stretching/shrinking algorithm moves the onset times of the overlapping frames farther apart (when stretching) or closer together (when shrinking) in the resynthesis. For the smoothest transpositions, the PV should multiply the phase values by the same constant used in the time base changing (Arfib 1991).

Pitch-shifting alters the pitch without changing the time base. Pitch-transposition is a matter of scaling the frequencies of the resynthesis components. For speech signals in particular, however, a constant scale factor changes not only the pitch but also the formant frequencies. For upward shifts of an octave or more, this reduces the speech's intelligibility. Thus Dolson (1986) suggested a correction to the frequency scaling that reimposes the original spectral envelope on the transposed frequency spectrum. If the original spectrum had a formant at 2 kHz, for example, then so will the transposed version.

Frequency-Domain Filtering

Spectrum filters operate in the frequency domain by rescaling the amplitudes of selected frequency bins. Some of their controls are similar to traditional time-domain filters, such as center frequency, bandwidth, and gain or boost in dB.

Other controls apply to the windowed analysis, such as the window size, FFT size, and overlap factor. These controls affect the efficiency and quality of the analysis-resynthesis process. For example, longer windows and FFTs generally result in more pronounced filtering effects.

Differences between time-domain filters and spectral filters show up when the bandwidths are narrow and the filter Q is high. The spectral filter breaks down a broadband signal into individual sinusoidal components. A tell-tale "breebles" artefact may be heard, as individual components pop in and out. Breebles are characteristic of manipulations on windowed Fourier analyses in general, and appear in a number of other PV transformations.

Another approach to frequency-domain filtering provides a graphic interface, in which the user sees a sonogram display of the sound. The software provides a palette of drawing tools that let users erase or highlight selected regions of the sonogram image. The sound is then resynthesized on the basis of the altered sonogram image. (See the later section on sonographic transformations.)

Stable and Transient Extraction

This is a class of transformations that sorts audio waveforms on a micro time scale into two categories: stable and transient. Spoken vowels, for example, are relatively stable frequencies compared to the transient frequencies in consonants. Once these frequencies are separated, the signals can be further manipulated individually.

In Erbe's (1995) implementation of stable and transient extraction, the user specifies:

1. Number of bands in the analyzer
2. Number of frames to analyze at a time
3. Frequency threshold for the transient part of the signal
4. Frequency threshold of the stable part of the signal

For example, the transient part could be specified as changing more than 30 Hz per frame, while the stable part is specified as changing less than 5 Hz per frame. Erbe's extraction algorithm takes the average of the change in instantaneous frequency over several FFT frames. If this average is greater than the stipulated value for transient information, the amplitude and phase from the source is assigned to the transient spectrum. Similarly, if the average change is less than the stipulated value for stable information the amplitude and phase from the source is assigned to the stable spectrum. Note that if the transient and stable thresholds are not identical, this leaves behind a part of the spectrum that is between the two—neither stable nor transient.

Another approach to stable and transient extraction is via *spectral tracing* (Wishart 1994; Norris 1997). Spectral tracing analyzes a sound and retains only the loudest or softest $N\%$ of the partials in the spectrum. To extract the transient part of a spoken voice, one retains only the softest 1% of the analyzed spectra. The sound quality of this 1% after the result is high-pass filtered, is like noisy whispering.

Dynamic Range Manipulations

Spectrum analysis makes it possible to manipulate the dynamic range of selected frequency bands. The reader is referred to the discussion of dynamics processing on a micro time scale in chapter 5.

Cross-Synthesis: Vocoding, Spectral Mutation, and Analysis-Based Formant Filtering

Cross-synthesis extracts characteristics from the spectrum of one signal and uses them to modify the spectrum of another signal. This can take a variety of forms, including, among others, vocoding, spectral mutation, and formant filtering.

Vocoding (as opposed to phase vocoding) analyzes one signal to adjust a bank of filters (or subbands) that are applied to a second signal. Its operation is relatively simple, meaning that it can be computed in real time. First, it extracts the amplitude envelope of the input signal coming through each filter. This is typically accomplished by rectification and lowpass filtering. The signal from which the amplitude is extracted is called the modulator; the signal that is affected is called the carrier. It then applies the amplitude envelopes from the modulator to a second filter bank through which the carrier is passing. In a typical vocoder, there are a relatively small number of filters (<50) and the center frequency of each of the filters is fixed. These constraints give the effect its characteristic sound quality.

An example of a vocoder is found in Arboretum's Hyperprism program (MacOS). This 26-band real-time vocoder performs an FFT on successive windows of the modulator signal. It adjusts the amplitude of its filter bands to match the spectrum of the incoming signal. That is, the modulating signal sets the gain for each of the filters. It then applies the 26-band filter bank to the carrier signal.

Another type of cross-synthesis involves mutations from one set of spectral data to another. The spectral mutation operations in the SoundHack program (MacOS) interpolate the sign or magnitude of a source set of spectral frames into the sign or magnitude of a target set (Polansky and Erbe 1996). The mutation functions operate on the phase and amplitude data of each analyzed frequency band. A single frame spans a microtemporal duration that is usually between 10 and 90 milliseconds. The degree of mutation is called Ω, which takes a value between 0 (source) and 1 (target). The software offers five mutation functions, some of which move linearly from one the source to the target, while others scramble the two.

A third possibility is creating a new spectrum by taking the intersection of two source spectra. This can be achieved in a variety of ways. One of the spectra, for example, might be derived from an analysis based on linear predictive coding or LPC (Roads 1996). LPC analysis calculates an overall spectrum envelope. One could use the LPC spectrum of one sound to shape the detailed spectrum of another sound, where the detailed analysis was derived by a phase vocoder (Serra 1997). U&I Software's MetaSynth program (MacOS) takes another approach to this cross-synthesis (Wenger and Spiegel 1999). Its Formants Filter effect uses a 128-band filter bank to find the formant peaks in the spectrum of one signal. It then applies this bank to boost the same formant regions in another signal. The effect thus emphasizes the frequencies that the two sounds have in common.

Other Operations on the Time-Frequency Plane

Over the past decade, an extensive catalog of transformations based on windowed spectrum analysis has been developed. Many of these were originally implemented in the Composer's Desktop Project (CDP) software package for Windows computers (Endrich 2000). Trevor Wishart's book *Audible Design* (1994) describes many of these effects using evocative drawings. Table 6.1 is a list of spectrum-based operations available in the CDP package, grouped into fourteen categories. Some of the operations are utilitarian, and do not transform the sound.

For those working on MacOS computers, at least a dozen software packages provide spectrum analysis and resynthesis capabilities. Many of the CDP spectrum operations, for example, were made available as plugins by Michael Norris (1997) and Alex Yermakov (1999) within the SoundMaker program (Ricci 1997).

Sonographic Transformations

A *sonogram, sonograph,* or *spectrogram* is a well-known spectrum display technique. It represents a sound signal as a two-dimensional display of time versus "frequency + amplitude." That is, the vertical dimension depicts frequency (higher frequencies are higher up in the diagram) and shades of gray (or color) indicate the amplitude within a given frequency band.

The first sonogram was Backhaus's (1932) system. In the 1950s, the Kay Sonograph was a standard device for printed sonograms which combined a bank of narrow bandpass analog filters with a recording system that printed dark traces on a roll of paper. The bars grew thicker in proportion to the energy output from each filter.

Today, the STFT is at the core of sonogram analysis. The sonogram can be applied on various time scales (figure 6.3). A sonogram of the meso time level (figure 6.3a) portrays general features such the onset of notes or phonemes, their pitch, formant peaks, and major transitions. See Cogan (1984) for an example of using sonograms in the analysis of musical mesostructure. A sonogram of a single note (figure 6.3b) reveals its pitch and spectrum. A sonogram of a single particle (figure 6.3c) is a coarse indicator of spectrum, since frequency resolution is poor on a micro time scale.

Table 6.1   Typical spectrum operations in the Composer's Desktop Project software

---

1. Blur analysis data

Blur avrg—Average spectral energy over *N* adjacent channels

Blur blur—Blur spectral data over time

Blur chorus—Add random variation to amplitude or frequency in analysis channels

Blur drunk—Modify sound by a drunken walk (a probabilistic process) along analysis windows

Blur noise—Add noise to spectrum

Blur scatter—Thin the spectrum in a random fashion

Blur shuffle—Shuffle analysis windows according to a specific scheme

Blur spread—Spread spectral peaks

Blur suppress—Suppress the most prominent channel data

Blur weave—Weave among the analysis windows in a specified pattern

2. Combine analysis data from two or more files

Combine cross—Replace spectral amplitudes of first file with those of second

Combine diff—Find (and retain) the difference between two spectra

Combine leaf—Interleave (groups of) windows of several spectra

Combine make—Generate an analysis file from data in a formant data file and a pitch data file

Combine max—Retain loudest channel components per window amongst several spectra

Combine mean—Generate the mean of two spectra

Combine sum—Add one spectrum to another

3. Focus on features of analysis data

Focus accu—Sustain each spectral band, until louder data appears in that band

Focus exag—Exaggerate the spectral contour

Focus focus—Focus spectral energy onto the peaks in the spectrum

Focus fold—Octave-transpose spectral components into a specified frequency range

Focus freeze—Freeze the spectral characteristics in a sound, at given times, for specified durations

Focus step—Step-frame through a sound by freezing the spectrum at regular time intervals

4. Formant operations

Formants get—Extract evolving formant envelope from an analysis file

Formants getsee—Get formant data from an analysis file and write as a file for viewing

Formants put—Impose formants in a formant data file on the spectrum in an analysis file

Formants see—Convert formant data in binary formant data file to a file for viewing

Formants vocode—Impose spectral envelope of one sound onto another sound

---

Table 6.1   (continued)

5. Highlight features of analysis data

Hilite arpeg—Arpeggiate the spectrum

Hilite band—Split spectrum into bands and process these individually

Hilite bltr—Time-average and trace the spectrum

Hilite filter—Highpass, lowpass, bandpass, and notch filters, on spectral data

Hilite greq—Graphic equalizer filter on the spectrum

Hilite pluck—Emphasize spectral changes (e.g., use with Hilite arpeg)

Hilite trace—Highlight N loudest partials, at each moment (window) in time

6. Morph smooth transitions between sounds

Morph bridge—Make a bridging interpolation between two sound spectra by interpolating between two time-specified windows in the two input files

Morph glide—Interpolate linearly between two single analysis windows extracted with Spec grab

Morph morph—Morph between one spectrum and another, where the spectra may be time-varying

7. Pitch operations

Pitch alt—Delete alternate harmonics

Pitch chord—Superimpose transposed versions of the spectrum within the existing spectral envelope

Pitch chord2—Superimpose transposed versions of a sound on the original sound

Pitch oct—Octave transpose without a formant shift

Pitch pick—Retain channels that might hold specified partials

Pitch shift—Shift pitch of (part of) the spectrum

Pitch tune—Replace spectral frequencies by harmonics of specified pitch(es)

8. Retrieve pitch information

Pitchinfo info—Display information about pitch data in pitchfile

Pitchinfo hear—Convert binary pitchfile to analysis test tone file (resynthesize to hear pitch)

Pitchinfo see—Convert binary pitchfile or transposition file to a pseudo-soundfile, for viewing

Pitchinfo write—Convert a binary pitch data file to a time frequency breakpoint text file

Pitchinfo zeros—Display whether a pitch file contains uninterpolated zeros (unpitched windows)

9. Phase vocoder analysis and resynthesis of sounds

Pvoc anal—Convert soundfile to spectral file

Pvoc extract—Analyze, then resynthesize sound with various options

Pvoc synth—Convert spectral file to soundfile

Table 6.1   (continued)

10. Repitch pitch-related data

Repitch approx—Make an approximate copy of a pitchfile

Repitch combine—Generate transposition data from two sets of pitch data, or transpose pitch data with transposition data, or combine two sets of transposition data to form new transposition data, producing a binary pitch data file output

Repitch combineb—Generate transposition data from two sets of pitch data, or transpose pitch data with transposition data, or combine two sets of transposition data to form new transposition data, producing a time value breakpoint file output

Repitch cut—Cut out and keep a segment of a binary pitch data file

Repitch exag—Exaggerate pitch contour

Repitch getpitch—Extract pitch from spectrum to a pitch data file

Repitch impose—Transpose spectrum (spectral envelope also moves)

Repitch imposef—Transpose spectrum, but retain original spectral envelope

Repitch invert—Invert pitch contour of a pitch data file

Repitch quantize—Quantize pitches in a pitch data file

Repitch randomize—Randomize pitch line

Repitch smooth—Smooth pitch contour in a pitch data file

Repitch transpose—Transpose pitches in a pitch data file by a constant number of semitones

Repitch vibrato—Add vibrato to pitch in a pitch data file

11. Spectrum operations

Spec bare—Zero the data in channels that do not contain harmonics

Spec clean—Remove noise from phase vocoder analysis file

Spec cut—Cut a section out of an analysis file, between starttime and endtime (seconds)

Spec gain—Amplify or attenuate the spectrum

Spec grab—Grab a single analysis window at time point specified

Spec limit—Eliminate channel data below a threshhold amplitude

Spec magnify—Magnify (in duration) a single analysis window and time time to duration dur

12. Retrieve spectrum information

Specinfo channel—Returns phase vocoder channel number corresponding to specified frequency

Specinfo frequency—Returns center frequency of phase vocoder channel specified

Specinfo level—Convert (varying) level of analysis file to a file, for viewing

Specinfo octvu—Text display of time varying amplitude of spectrum, within octave bands

Specinfo peak—Locate time varying energy center of spectrum (text display)

Specinfo print—Print data in an analysis file as text to file

Specinfo report—Text report on location of frequency peaks in the evolving spectrum

Specinfo windowcnt—Returns the number of analysis windows in input file

Table 6.1 (continued)

---

13. Strange operations

Strange glis—Create glissandi inside the (changing) spectral envelope of the original sound

Strange invert—Invert the spectrum

Strange shift—Linear frequency shift of (part of) the spectrum

Strange waver—Oscillate between harmonic and inharmonic state

14. Stretch time or frequency data

Stretch spectrum—Stretch or compress the frequencies in the spectrum

Stretch time—Stretch or compress a sound in time without changing the pitch

---

Sonogram Parameters

The parameters of the modern sonogram are the same as those of the STFT, except for the display parameters. Adjustments to these parameters make a great difference in the output image:

1. Range of amplitudes and the type of scale used, whether linear or logarithmic.

2. Range of frequencies and the type of scale used, whether linear or logarithmic.

3. Window size (number of samples to analyze) and the size of the FFT; the resolution of time and frequency depend on these parameters.

4. Time advance of the analysis window (hop size) in samples or window overlap factor. This determines the time distance between successive columns in the output display.

5. Number of frequency channels to display, which determines the number of rows in the graphical output and is related to the range and scale of the frequency domain; this cannot exceed the resolution imposed by the window size.

6. Window type—see the previous discussion in the section on the phase vocoder.

The window parameters (3) have the most dramatic effect on the display. A short window results in a vertically oriented display, indicating the precise onset time of events but blurring the frequency reading. A medium length window resolves both time and frequency features fairly well, indicating the presence of

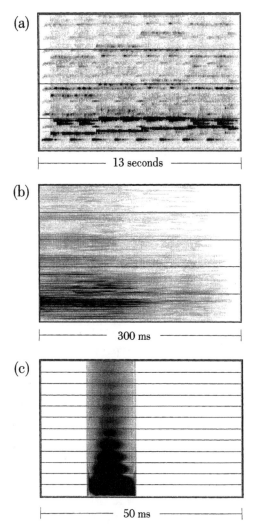

Figure 6.3   Sonograms on three time scales. (a) Meso time scale. 13-second sonogram of a J. S. Bach suite transcribed for recorder, played in a reverberant environment. The frequency scale is linear to 4 kHz. (b) Sound object time scale. 300-ms tone played on an Ondioline, a vacuum tube electronic music instrument (Jenny 1958). The frequency scale is linear to 5 kHz. (c) Micro time scale. 50-ms view on a pulsar particle. The frequency scale is linear to 12 kHz.

formant frequencies. A long window generates a horizontally oriented display, as individual frequency bands come into clear view, but their position in time smears along the horizontal axis.

Sonogram Filtering

A sonogram is a projection of the Gabor time-frequency matrix. So to manipulate the sonogram image is to manipulate the sound. We looked at sonographic synthesis in chapter 4. To draw on the sonogram is to inscribe sound directly, correspondingly, to erase part of a sonogram is to filter the sound. A pioneering program with this capability was Gerhard Eckel's SpecDraw (Eckel 1990).

Today a variety of programs allow for manipulation of the sonogram image. For example, the Ircam AudioSculpt (MacOS) application (Serra 1997) lets users extract or erase spectra with graphical drawing tools. One can inscribe an arbitrary polygon on the time-frequency plane, and stipulate a boost or attenuation of the selected frequencies in that region (see figure 8.1). Users can also boost or erase with a pen tool.

Applications like U&I Software's MetaSynth provide a palette of brushes and graphical operations for manipulating the sonogram image (table 6.2). Going further, one can import and export sonogram images in standard graphics file formats, and then alter them with image processing software, such as Adobe PhotoShop with its many plugin effects. This opens up vast possibilities of sonographical treatments.

Assessment of Sonographic Transformations

Sonograms trace a sound's morphology—its internal shape in frequency and time, making them powerful musical resources in sound transformation. Moreover, a sonogram is an intuitive musical interface. It is easy to learn to draw and erase a sonogram image. This apparent ease of use can be deceptive, however; as with any other musical tool, it takes practice to achieve good results with sonographic transformations. A pretty image does not necessarily correspond to an interesting sound. A sonogram is the projection of a mathematical transform and does not correspond exactly to what we hear. What we perceive as a fused sound object often shows up as a splintered branch of separate frequency components. The ear is quite sensitive to details within this branch, including the frequency ratios and the relative strength of each component. A similar drawing would not necessarily produce a similar sound.

Table 6.2   Sonographic transformations in MetaSynth

Sonographical brushes (the sizes of the brushes are variable)

Pen—Hard-edged rectangular brush

Air brush—Round-edge brush with translucent edges

Filter brush—This brush acts as a multiplier, brightening or darkening depending on the selected color

Harmonics brush—Paints a fundamental and up to five harmonics

Attack brush—Paints a sharp left edge and then a soft decay

Smoothing brush—Smooths the pixels over which it passes

Spray brush—Sprays a cloud of grains

Decay brush—Extends existing pixels to the right to elongate their decay

Note brush—Leaves a trail of discrete notes, aligned to the brush grid interval

Line brush—Paints a harmonic line across the width of the canvas

Smear brush—Smears existing pixels

Smear brighter brush—Smears existing pixels with a brighter gradient than the smear brush

Clone brush—Captures pixels under the brush when the mouse button is pressed and then paints with the captured pixels

Sonographical transformations on the time-frequency grid

Cut, copy, paste selected part of sonogram image

X-Y scaling—Time stretch or compress, frequency stretch or compress

Shift up or down—Transpose all frequencies

Rotate—Change the direction of all frequency trajectories

Contrast and luminence—Removes low-level frequencies, or amplifies noise

Octave transpose—Shift the image (and sound) down by an octave

Smooth—Blur the image so that the sound becomes more sinusoidal

Invert—White becomes black, etc.; a sound becomes a silence in a noise field

Max pict—Paste the PICT clipboard into the selected area, treating the clipboard's black pixels as transparent. Where there are coincident pixels, the brightest one is kept. (Note: PICT is a MacOS bitmap graphics format.)

Min pict—Paste the PICT clipboard into the selected area. Where there are coincident pixels, the one of lowest amplitude one is kept. If either image has black, the result is black.

Add pict—Combine the luminosities of two images

Subtract pict—Subtract the contents of the PICT clipboard from the selected area

Multiply pict—Multiple the selected region by the contents of the PICT clipboard

Merge pict—Merge the PICT clipboard with the selected region using a 50% blend

Crossfade pict—Crossfade the PICT clipboard with the selected region left to right

Expand—Vertically expand the pixel spacing

Fade in out pict—Fade the PICT clipboard in then out while also fading the selected region out then in

---

Table 6.2 (continued)

Contract—Vertically contract the region between the pixels
Triangle filter—A "solarization" effect where luminence above 50% is changed to black
Emboss left or right—Emphasize the leading or trailing edges of shapes
Trace edges—Sharpen the image, making the time-frequency structure more clear
Sonographical transformations on the time grid
mBlur—Smooth transients, remove short pixels
Quantize—Force notes to start and end at the positions determined by the current grid interval
Echo—Repeat pixels to the right with decreasing brightness
Pre-echo—Repeat pixels to the left with decreasing brightness
Reverb—Simulate reverberation by extending and fading the duration of all pixels in the selected region
Repeat—Repeat pixels identically across the region according to the stipulated grid
Reverse—Reverse the region
Pulse—Remove pixels according to the stipulated grid interval
Saw—Similar to pulse, but fades out rather than cuts
Shorten—Shorten the duration of the pixel lines
Attacks—Sharpen the attacks of all notes

Furthermore the tools provided with sonographic interfaces are not always precise, making it difficult to achieve predictable results. To edit on a micro level, we may want to zoom in to the sonogram image. When we do so, however, the image pixellates into large blocks. This simply reflects the hard fact that a sonogram is intrinsically limited in time-frequency resolution.

The Tracking Phase Vocoder

Certain implementations of the PV are called tracking phase vocoders (TPVs) because they follow or track the most prominent peaks in the spectrum over time (Dolson 1983; McAulay and Quatieri 1986; Serra 1989; Maher and Beauchamp 1990; Walker and Fitz 1992). Unlike the ordinary phase vocoder, in which resynthesis frequencies are limited to harmonics of the analysis window, the TPV follows changes in frequencies. The result of peak tracking is a set of amplitude and frequency envelopes that drive a bank of sinusoidal oscillators in the resynthesis stage.

The tracking process follows only the most prominent frequency components. For these components, the result is a more accurate analysis than that done with an equally spaced bank of filters (the traditional STFT implementation). Another benefit is that the tracking process creates frequency and amplitude envelopes for these components, making them more robust under transformation than overlap-add frames. A disadvantage is that the quality of the analysis depends more heavily on proper parameter settings than in the regular STFT. It may take multiple attempts to tune the analysis parameters for a given sound.

Operation of the TPV

A TPV carries out the following steps:

1. Compute the STFT using the frame size, window type, FFT size, and hop size specified by the user.
2. Derive the squared magnitude spectrum in dB.
3. Find the bin numbers of the peaks in the spectrum.
4. Calculate the magnitude and phase of each frequency peak.
5. Assign each peak to a frequency track by matching the peaks of the previous frame with those of the current frame (see the description of peak tracking later).
6. Apply any desired modifications to the analysis parameters.
7. If additive resynthesis is requested, generate a sine wave for each frequency track and sum all sine wave components to create an output signal; the instantaneous amplitude, phase, and frequency of each sinusoidal component is calculated by interpolating values from frame to frame (or use the alternative resynthesis methods described earlier).

Peak Tracking

The tracking phase vocoder follows the most prominent frequency trajectories in the spectrum. Like other aspects of sound analysis, the precise method of peak tracking should vary depending on the sound. The tracking algorithm works best when it is tuned to the type of sound being analyzed—speech, harmonic spectrum, smooth inharmonic spectrum, noisy, etc. This section briefly explains more about the tracking process as a guide to setting the analysis parameters.

The first stage in peak tracking is peak identification. A simple control that sets the *minimum peak height* focuses the identification process on the most significant landmarks in the spectrum. The rest of the algorithm tries to apply a set of *frequency guides* which advance in time. The guides are only hypotheses; later the algorithm will decide which guides are confirmed frequency tracks. The algorithm continues the guides by finding the peak closest in frequency to its current value. The alternatives are as follows:

- If it finds a match, the guide continues.
- If a guide cannot be continued during a frame it is considered to be "sleeping."
- If the guide does not wake up after a certain number of frames—which may be specified by the user—then the tracker deletes it. It may be possible to switch on *guide hysteresis*, which continues tracking a guide that falls slightly below a specified amplitude range. Guide hysteresis alleviates the audible problem of "switching" guides that repeatedly fade slightly, are cut to zero by the peak tracker, and fade in again (Walker and Fitz 1992). With hysteresis the guide is synthesized at its actual value instead of at zero amplitude.
- If there is a near match between guides, the closest wins and the "loser" looks for another peak within the *maximum peak deviation*, a frequency band specified by the user.
- If there are peaks not accounted for by current guides, then a new guide begins.

Windowing may compromise the accuracy of the tracking, particularly in rapidly moving waveforms such as attack transients. Processing sounds with a sharp attack in time-reversed order helps the tracking algorithm (Serra 1989). This gives the partial trackers a chance to lock onto their stable frequency trajectories before meeting the chaos of the attack, which results in less distortion. The data can be reversed back to its original order before resynthesis.

Accuracy of Resynthesis

In contrast to the myth of "perfect reconstruction" which pervades the mathematical theory of signal processing, the actual quality of all analysis-resynthesis methods is limited by the resolution of the input signal and the numerical precision of the analysis procedures. Distortions are introduced by numerical roundoff, windowing, peak-tracking, undersampling of envelope functions, and other aspects of the analysis. Compact disc quality audio (16-bit samples, 44.1

kHz sampling rate) poses a priori limits on the frequency response and dynamic range of the analysis. The fast Fourier transform on a 16-bit signal has a limited dynamic range, and the TPV reduces this further by discarding spectral information below a certain threshold. Any modification that changes the frequency characteristics will likely result in aliasing. Any reduction in amplitude caused by enveloping reduces the bit resolution. The resynthesized result may have lost a large portion of its dynamic range, and artefacts such as amplitude gating, distortion, aliasing, and graininess are not uncommon.

In a well-implemented nontracking phase vocoder, when the analysis parameters are properly adjusted by a skilled engineer and no modifications are made to the analysis data, the error is perceptually negligible. The TPV, on the other hand, discards information that does not contribute to a track. If the TPV parameters are not adjusted correctly, the sifting of low-level energy may discard significant portions of the sound, particularly noisy, transient energy. This can be demonstrated by subtracting an analysis of the resynthesized signal from an analysis of the original signal to yield a *residual* (Serra 1989). One can consider this residual to be analysis/resynthesis error. It is common to refer to the resynthesized, quasi-harmonic portion as the "clean" part of the signal and the error or noise component as the "dirty" part of the signal. For many sounds (i.e., those with fast transients such as cymbal crashes), the errors are quite audible. That is, the clean signal sounds unnaturally sanitized or sinusoidal, and the dirty signal, when heard separately, contains the missing grit.

TPV Computation and Storage

TPV analysis consumes large quantities of computer power even though the inner core is implemented using the efficient FFT algorithm. It can also generate a large amount of analysis data, often ten times greater than the size of the sample data being analyzed. The size of the analysis depends on many factors, however. Low-level narrowband sounds require fewer tracks. Different settings of the analysis parameters can greatly affect the analysis file size.

Sound Transformation with the TPV

The TPV's representation of sound—a bank of hundreds of oscillators driven by amplitude and frequency envelopes—is a robust one that lends itself to many evocative transformations.

Editing the Analysis Data

Certain TPV implementations let one directly edit the analysis data—the frequency, amplitude, and phase curves (Moorer 1978; Dolson 1983). This laborious process is aided by automatic data reduction procedures and graphical editors. For example, Lemur Pro (MacOS) provides a two-dimensional (time-frequency) spectrum editor that lets users modify the characteristics of individual frequency tracks or groups of tracks (Walker and Fitz 1992; Fitz, et al. 1995).

TPV Spectrum Filtering

When the TPV is coupled with a graphical interface for zooming in and selecting tracks, one can alter the amplitude of specific tracks. It may also be possible to cut or extract certain tracks. Cutting removes them from the spectrum, while extracting removes everything but the selected tracks. Such alterations have the effect of filtering the spectrum.

A single sound object may contain hundreds of closely-spaced tracks (figure 6.4). So the question becomes how to select tracks to filter. Keep in mind that an operation on an individual track makes little difference, it is only when a band of frequencies are operated on that the effect becomes noticeable.

Selecting tracks manually is a labor-intensive way to filter a sound. The key to efficiency in TPV editing is to use other strategies.

Selecting tracks by their length, for example, leads to potentially interesting transformations on a micro scale. One interesting transformation is based on eliminating all tracks greater than a threshold of, say, 70 ms, leaving only the microtemporal tracks. This has the effect of removing pitch information, so that a speaking voice becomes wheezing and whispering. Selecting and boosting all tracks less than 10 ms produces a gravely sounding voice.

Another way to select tracks is by amplitude, so that only tracks over or under a given threshold are selected. In combination with the length criterion, this can be used to granulate a sound file in time and frequency. Note that the tracking algorithm in TPV analysis is already a filter. By tuning the parameters so that the analysis rejects low-amplitude frequency components, for example, the analysis data is strongly filtered. One imagines that more sophisticated track selection principles will become available in the future, such as selecting harmonically related tracks.

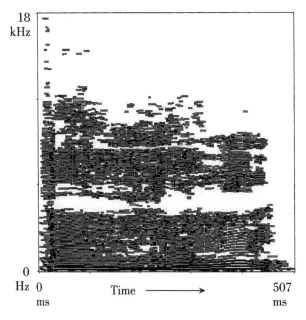

18
kHz

0
Hz 0   Time ⟶   507
    ms   ms

Figure 6.4 This figure shows the profusion of tracks associated with even a single sound, in this case, the French word *payons* (we pay).

TPV Timbre Morphing

One type of cross-synthesis is called *timbre morphing* or just *morphing*. The term "morphing," like the term "cross-synthesis," is not a precise one. It describes a variety of processes that combine the properties of two sounds. Morphing combines the characteristics of two analyzed files to create a new file with an intermediate timbre. For instance, if a long loud tone with a fast and narrow vibrato is morphed with a short quiet tone with a slow and wide vibrato, the ideal morphed result might be a medium length, medium loudness tone with an intermediate vibrato speed and width. (But as the phrase has it: "Actual results may vary.")

A TPV morphing algorithm averages the amplitude envelopes and frequency envelopes of corresponding tracks of the two analyzed files to be morphed. It matches by looking for tracks in each of the analysis files in which the ratio of analyzed frequency to that file's fundamental frequency is approximately equal.

Morphing clearly differs from simply mixing two sources. In practice, some morphs are more convincing than others. Two tones with a common pitch tend to morph more naturally than two tones with different pitches, for example.

TPV Pitch-Time Changing

By altering the position or extent of the tracks, one can shift the pitch or alter the duration of the sound (Portnoff 1978). For example, to stretch the duration, the TPV interpolates new points between existing points in the amplitude and frequency arrays. To shrink the duration by a factor of n, The TPV uses every nth value in reading the amplitude and frequency arrays. In effect, this shifts the sampling rate. To shift the pitch of a sound but not change its duration, one multiplies the frequency values assigned to each of the frequency functions by the desired factor. For example, to shift a sound up a major second, the TPV multiples each frequency component by 11.892%.

Disintegration and Coalescence in the Gabor Matrix

The QuickMQ program (Berkely 1994) reads TPV analysis files generated by the Lemur Pro program. It lets users alter this data through a number of algorithms. The Granny algorithm is especially interesting. Granny pokes holes in the Gabor matrix of a sound, producing a kind of granular disintegration or decomposition. The parameters of granular decomposition are as follows:

1. Maximum percentage of zeroing [0, 100]
2. Entropy rate—rate of decomposition [1, 10]
3. Distribution [random, loud tracks first, soft tracks first]
4. Rest in peace (RIP) switch [on, off]

The maximum percentage of zeroing determines how many zero magnitudes can be written to a track once it is chosen for decomposition. The percentage refers to the total number of frames in the analysis file. If the file has three hundred frames, for example, and the user enters a maximum percentage of zeroing of 50%, then any track selected for decomposition may be zeroed with between zero and one hundred and fifty frames of zero magnitude. The entropy rate determines how quickly maximum decomposition settings occur in the file. Lower values result in more immediate decomposition. The distribution setting lets the user specify whether louder or softer tracks should be decomposed first, or if tracks should be picked at random for decomposition. The RIP switch directs the algorithm not to decompose tracks that have already been decomposed. In practice, RIP mitigates against the decomposition process.

My experiments show that a disintegration effect can be achieved with the following ranges:

1. Maximum percentage of zeroing: 30–80%

2. Entropy rate: 3–7

3. Distribution: loud tracks first

4. RIP switch: off

The effect is imperfect, suffering from unwanted transient artifacts. Tracks suddenly recommence where a zeroed out segment stops. This can be ameliorated by manually editing these transients on a micro time scale. Clearly this granular decomposition algorithm could benefit from a "windowed zeroing" that allows tracks to fade in and out over a few milliseconds instead of cutting in and out abruptly.

This same decomposition algorithm creates its inverse, a coalescence effect, by simply time-reversing the input file before submitting it to the algorithm, and then time-reversing the output after processing.

Deterministic Plus Stochastic TPV

The TPV handles static or smoothly changing tones best. TPVs can also analyze and resynthesize many inharmonic sounds, including bird songs and tuned percussion tones. Since the TPV is based on Fourier analysis, however, it must translate noisy and inharmonic signals into combinations of periodic sinusoidal functions. For noisy signals particularly this can be costly from a storage and computational standpoint; to synthesize a simple noise band requires an ever-changing blend of dozens of sine waves. Storing the control functions for these sines fills up a great deal of memory space—more than ten times as many bytes as the original sound samples. Resynthesizing the sines demands a great deal of computation. Moreover, since the transformations allowed by the TPV are based on a sinusoidal model, operations on noisy sounds often result in clusters of sinusoids which have lost their noisy quality.

Researchers have extended the TPV to make it more effective in handling noisy signals. Xavier Serra (1989) added filtered noise to the inharmonic sinusoidal model in *spectral modeling synthesis* or SMS (Serra and Smith 1990).

SMS reduces the analysis data into a *deterministic* component (prominent narrowband components of the original sound) and a *stochastic* component. The deterministic component tracks the most prominent frequencies in the spectrum. SMS resynthesizes these tracked frequencies with sine waves. SMS also analyzes the *residue* (or *residual*), which is the difference between the deterministic component and the original spectrum. After analyzing the residual SMS approximates this stochastic component through a collection of simplified spectrum envelopes. The resynthesis passes noise through a set of filters controlled by these envelopes.

Musicians can modify the stochastic part through graphical operations on envelopes. However, the perceived link between the deterministic and stochastic parts is delicate; editing them separately may lead to a loss of recognizable connection.

Experiences with TPV Transformations

My experience with the TPV has been with the MacOS programs Lemur Pro, QuickMQ, PAST, and MarcoHack, which share a common file format. Lemur Pro performs the TPV analysis and resynthesis for all the programs, letting the user adjust the analysis parameters, including the window and FFT size, hop size, bandwidth of the analyzing filter, and sidelobe attenuation of the Kaiser window. Once the analysis is done, Lemur Pro offers operations such as track editing (select, delete), time-scale modification, spectrum multiplication and addition (shifting), and track-based amplitude modification.

The PAST program is based on a model of auditory perception. It extracts additional information from the Lemur analysis data, and generates control functions for fourteen features: amplitude, spectral envelope, onset spectral envelope, spectral density, onset asynchrony, spectral distribution, amplitude modulation range, amplitude modulation rate, onset amplitude modulation range, onset amplitude modulation rate, frequency modulation range, frequency modulation rate, onset frequency modulation range, and onset frequency modulation rate (Langmead 1995). Users can then edit envelopes for these features and resynthesize the altered sound.

QuickMQ also reads Lemur analysis data and offers a number of modifications, including granular decomposition in the time-frequency plane, brightness enhancement, spectral rotation, track smoothing, gain changing, dynamic rotate above and below a specific frequency, spectrum expansion, falling or rising spectra, spectral inversion, "scrunch" spectrum, transpose spectrum, and vibrato spectrum. QuickMQ is unfortunately restricted to the older, much slower, Macintosh Quadra processors. While this discouraged casual experimentation, I was able to achieve good results through systematic testing.

MarcoHack (Pranger 1999) implements spectral shaking, stretching, and tracing (Wishart 1994). Spectral shaking adds random deviations to the amplitude and frequency traces of a TPV analysis file. Spectral stretching multiplies the analyzed frequencies by a constant or variable quantity, and, in this implementation, spectral tracing discards low-amplitude tracks in the analysis.

Assessment of the TPV

The tracking phase vocoder converts the analysis data from the cells of the Gabor matrix to a set of time-varying tracks. An operation on one track does not affect other tracks. Manipulations of short tracks, or the segmentation of long tracks into shorter ones by granular decomposition, result in microsonic transformations.

Setting the parameters of the analysis is more critical in the TPV than in the regular PV. This makes planning and experimentation mandatory. Certain operations, like time-stretching of an instrumental tone, may not require all of the TPV's flexibility and the ordinary PV will work well. The plain TPV is limited to a sinusoidal model, which is unsatisfactory for noisy short-time musical signals. For these, however, extensions such as stochastic and transient analysis-resynthesis add to the TPV's promise.

The Vector Oscillator Transform

The *vector oscillator transform*, or VOT, is part of the ancient Turbosynth program (1988, MacOS) by Digidesign. The operation is worth citing, however, for its intuitive graphical interface. In Turbosynth, the VOT appears in a menu as "Convert To Oscillator." It applies a series of windowed spectrum analyses to a sampled sound, each of which covers a short frame of time. The result is a series of analyzed waveforms read in sequence by a *vector oscillator* (Roads 1996). A vector oscillator scans not just a single wavetable, but a sequence of wavetables, crossfading from one to another. The frequency of the playback oscillator is adjustable.

Figure 6.5 shows a vocal fragment and various forms of its VOT. The user can click on any of the wavetables to edit them in either the time-domain or the

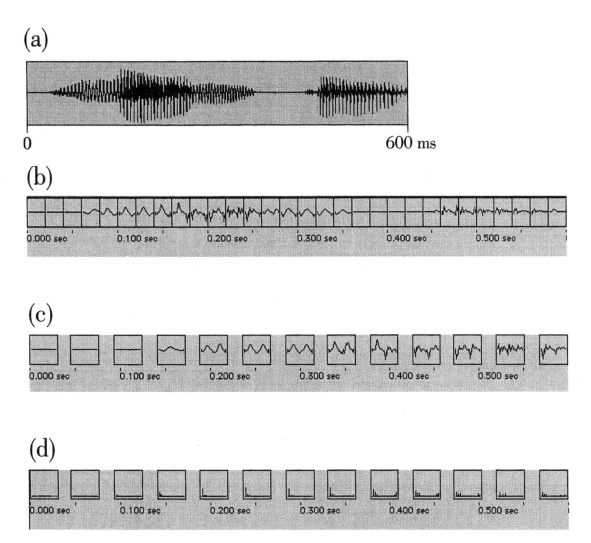

Figure 6.5 Vector oscillator transform. (a) First 600 ms of the waveform of the spoken Italian phrase *Nient'altro*. We see only "Nient'alt." (b) VOT of this phrase with wavetable extracted at at 20 ms intervals. This turns it from samples into a series of thirty wavetables read by an oscillator at a stipulated fundamental frequency. (c) The same set of wavetables stretched in time by a factor of 2.5. In effect, the oscillator takes longer to crossfade between waveforms. (d) A click on a button converts the waveform view into a frequency-domain view, with sixty-four harmonics per wavetable.

frequency-domain. The conversion from time-domain to frequency-domain and back is instantaneous. The temporal distance between the wavetables can be made longer or shorter. A longer distance means that the sound sustains longer on a given wavetable and crossfades more slowly. Users can rearrange the order of the wavetables arbitrarily, leading to scrambling effects.

Assessment of the VOT

The sound quality of the resynthesis produced by the VOT is marked by buzzy or resonating artifacts. This is not surprising given that it is not a phase vocoder but more of a "frequency-domain granulator." The VOT's strong point is its interface with the microtemporal domain. Although developed in the 1980s, its capacity to edit each frame remains unique to this day. The openness of the editing (one can insert any waveform or short-time spectrum into a frame) is exemplary. One could imagine a similar interface for the Gabor transform, where each cell or groups of cells in the Gabor matrix could be edited. Sonographic synthesis systems approach this ideal.

Wavelet Analysis and Resynthesis

Wavelet analysis measures a signal's frequency content within a window of time. As opposed to the Gabor matrix and the STFT, with their uniform time-frequency regions (figure 6.6a), wavelet analysis divides the TF plane into nonuniform regions (figure 6.6a). Low-frequency regions may be long in time and narrow in frequency range, while high-frequency regions may be short in time and wide in frequency range. So a cymbal crash remains invisible to a "slow" (low-frequency) wavelet, but will be detected by a burst of "fast" wavelets. Prior to wavelet analysis, a family of methods called *constant Q analysis* also implemented filter banks in which the bandwidth varied proportionally with frequency (see Roads 1996). In recent years, however, the wavelet transform has largely supplanted research in traditional constant Q techniques.

Wavelet analysis associates each region of the TF plane with a time-domain signal (the *wavelet*) which can be thought of as the impulse response of a bandpass filter (Vetterli and Herley 1992). Wavelets, scaled in duration and frequency and translated in time, form an analysis *basis* for the analyzed signal. When they are added together in prescribed amounts, certain classes of signals can be reconstructed.

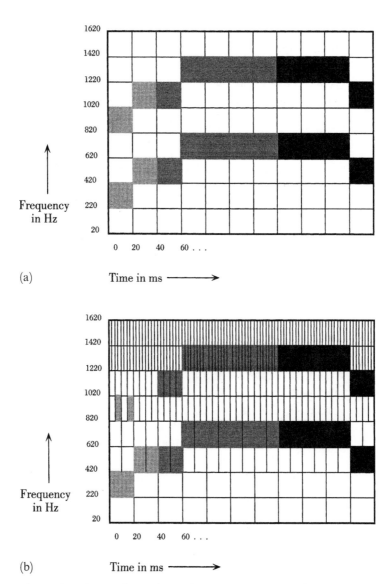

Figure 6.6 Comparison of Fourier and wavelet time-frequency grids. (a) Uniform Gabor matrix/STFT grid. (b) Nonuniform wavelet grid.

The *wavelet transform* (WT) is a multiresolution representation. That is, it decomposes a signal by successive approximation, starting from a coarse version and adding time-frequency details on multiple scales. The WT maps sounds onto a time-frequency grid. The center of each grid is the mean time of occurrence and the spectral centroid. In music analysis with the WT, one sets up the grid according to the goals of the analysis and distorts the grid according to the goals of the resynthesis.

Musical applications often use the Morlet wavelet, which happens to have a Gaussian envelope. Thus the wavelet is similar to the grain discussed in chapter 3, and to the windowed segments of the STFT discussed earlier in this chapter. Unlike a grain, however, no matter what frequency a wavelet contains, it always encapsulates a constant number of cycles. This implies that the size (duration) of the wavelet window stretches or shrinks according to the frequency being analyzed, referred to in the literature as *dilation* and *contraction*. The implication of a variable window size is that the WT trades frequency resolution for time resolution at high frequencies, and trades time resolution for frequency resolution at low frequencies.

History of Wavelet Analysis

The term "wavelet" and its French equivalent "ondelette" were used in early twentieth century physics to describe the packets of energy emitted by atomic processes (Crawford 1968). Modern wavelet theory brings together a cluster of ideas imported from pure mathematics, computer vision, image processing, and signal processing (Torresani 1989). Yves Meyer (1994) has traced seven different origins for modern wavelet theory.

The modern WT was originally developed in 1983 by Jean Morlet, a geophysicist working for Elf Aquitaine, in collaboration with Alex Grossmann of the Centre Nationale de Recherche Scientifique (CNRS) in Marseille (Meyer, Jaffard, and Rioul 1987; Risset 1999). It was applied immediately to problems in acoustics and image processing (Dutilleux, Grossmann, and Kronland-Martinet 1988; Kronland-Martinet and Grossmann 1991; Boyer and Kronland-Martinet 1989; Kronland-Martinet 1988). The wavelet transform was a slow and computationally intensive operation until 1985, when S. Mallat and I. Daubechies presented a recursive algorithm for what is called the *fast wavelet transform* or FWT (Mallat 1988, 1989, 1998). Meanwhile, engineers and physicists elaborated the mathematics of the WT, and found additional applications

(Strang 1989; Evangelista 1991; Kussmaul 1991; Vetterli and Herley 1992). Today wavelet theory is one of the most extensively researched subjects in all of signal processing.

Operation of Wavelet Analysis

A casual reference to "measurable functions" and $L^2(\mathrm{R})$ can be enough to make an aspiring pilgrim weary. (Kaiser 1994)

Wavelet theory is buried in mathematics. Part of the difficulty for the non-mathematician is that its foundations are expressed in terms of linear algebra, mappings between vector spaces, and the theory of generalized functions. A large portion of the literature is devoted to projecting the extent of wavelet theory and its abstract relationships to other branches of mathematics. These abstractions are far removed from applications in musical signal processing. Only the most basic tenets of wavelet theory can be explained using simple mathematical concepts.

The Grossmann-Morlet wavelet equation (Meyer, et al. 1987; Kronland-Martinet and Grossmann 1991) centered on point b in time, can be defined as:

$$\Psi_{a,b}(t) = \frac{1}{\sqrt{a}} \psi\left(\frac{t-b}{a}\right), \quad a > 0, b \in R$$

The variable a is the scale factor. The wavelet function $\Psi_{a,b}(t)$ oscillates at the frequency $1\sqrt{a}$. When the scale is very small, the first factor in the equation, $1/\sqrt{a}$, tends toward 1, while the time interval contracts around b as $(t-b)/a$ tends toward $t-b$.

The wavelet transform is:

$$S(a,b) = \int \bar{\psi}_{a,b}(t)s(t)\,dt = \frac{1}{\sqrt{a}} \int \bar{\psi}\left(\frac{t-b}{a}\right)s(t)\,dt$$

where $\bar{\psi}$ represents the complex conjugate. In effect, the WT multiplies the input signal $s(t)$ by a grid of analyzing wavelets, bounded by frequency on one axis and by time scale factor on the other. This multiplication process is equivalent to convolving with a bandpass filter's impulse response. Dilation of this impulse response corresponds to an inverse frequency scaling. Thus, the duration of each wavelet corresponds to the center frequency of a filter. The longer the wavelet, the lower is its center frequency. The output of the WT is a two-part spectrum, with one part representing the modulus or magnitude at a given frequency and the other part representing phase.

The frequency scale of the analysis grid can be logarithmic. This means that the frequency of each analyzing wavelet is related to the others by a logarithmic musical interval such as a fifth or a third, depending on the way the system is set up. The use of a logarithmic scale is not mandatory, however, since the WT can be aligned on an arbitrary frequency scale. In many papers on wavelets, the analyzing grid is assumed to be *dyadic*, which can be interpreted as constant Q filtering with a set of octave-band filters (Vetterli and Herley 1992).

Wavelet Resynthesis

In terms of matrix algebra, the inverse wavelet transform is the transpose of the analysis. In practical terms, wavelet resynthesis can be carried out in two ways: overlap-add and oscillator-bank additive (Boyer and Kronland-Martinet 1989). Each method lends itself to certain types of transformations. In the case of the overlap-add (the so-called *granular*) method, one needs as many oscillators as there are overlapping wavelets. In additive resynthesis, the number of oscillators is constant, since each frequency component is assigned its own oscillator.

Basis Functions

A time-domain signal can be represented as a family of impulses at successive time points, while a frequency-domain signal can be represented by a family of sinusoids of varying frequency. In both domains there is an orthogonal family of functions that represent any arbitrary signal; these are the *basis functions*. One of the main points of wavelet theory is that any signal can be decomposed by means of different basis functions. Theory imposes only a few constraints on this choice. For example, the wavelets must have finite energy and have no DC bias. Each family of wavelets determines a particular type of analysis on an audio signal.

In the time domain, an audio signal can be represented by a pair of basis functions that generates a series of scaled impulses $\delta(t)$

$$x(t) = \sum_t a_t \delta(t)$$

In the Fourier frequency domain, the same signal can be represented by a pair of basis functions that generate a sum of scaled sinusoids:

$$x(t) = \sum_f a_t \cos(2\pi f t)$$

Wavelet theory represents signals by the weighted sum of a family of basis functions that are dilations, contractions, and translations of an initial wavelet function $\Psi(t)$.

$$x(t) = \sum_{j,k} b_{jk} \Psi(2^j t - k)$$

where b is a scaling function, Ψ is a wavelet function, j is the scale factor, and k is the time translation or delay.

In the terminology of wavelet theory, the *support* of a wavelet is the region over which it is nonzero. Wavelets that are nonzero over a narrow range are said to have a *compact support* or finite length (Vetterli and Herley 1992). One can also stipulate a family of wavelets that is nonzero for all k; such a family has *extended support* or infinite length. If the support of a wavelet family is compact, it is straightforward to compute the WT.

The Fast Wavelet Transform (FWT)

Direct evaluation of the wavelet transform is computationally intensive. In 1985, S. Mallat and I. Daubechies presented a recursive algorithm for the fast wavelet transform (FWT). It can calculate the forward and inverse wavelet transform of a signal in a time period that is of the order $n \times \log_2(n)$, where n is the number of samples analyzed. At each level of recursion, the algorithm extracts the details at that level of resolution, and constructs a coarser (less detailed) version of the signal for analysis at the next level. This process repeats on successively coarser representations of the signal, until only the average value of the signal remains. The inverse transform works in reverse. It adds detail to the signal's coarse representation from higher and higher levels of resolution.

The FWT is a subset of a more general transform, the wavelet packet transform (WPT), developed by R. Coifman. In the FWT, the sampled data passes through lowpass and highpass filters with complementary bandwidths. The highpass output is the *detail*, and the lowpass output is the *approximation*. The output of the approximation filter, decimated by a factor of two, can be fed to another pair of wavelet filters, identical to the previous pair, to yield yet another set of detail and approximation coefficients. This process of multiscale analysis can continue until only a small unit data set is left.

Wavelet Display

A byproduct of research in wavelet analysis is the evocative display method developed by scientists affiliated with the Centre Nationale de Recherche Scientifique (CNRS) in Marseilles. This visualization tool can be thought of as a traditional spectrum plot projected in time and flipped on its side. In the modulus display, time projects horizontally, and frequency projects vertically with the low frequencies on the bottom and the high frequencies on the top. The difference between the sonogram plot and this wavelet plot is their pattern of time localization. Short wavelets detect brief transients, which are localized in time, sitting at the apex of a triangle. Kronland-Martinet et al. (1987) shows the wavelet plot of a delta function; its wavelet display clearly projects a triangle on the frequency-versus-time plane, pointing to the locale of the impulse. Long wavelets detect low frequencies; they sit at the base of the triangle, spread out (blurred) over time.

The triangle of the delta function is the wavelet's domain of influence in time. The domain of influence for frequencies is a constant horizontal band, as in the spectrogram. The darker the band, the stronger the magnitude within that frequency range. Using a log scale for the dilation axis allows a greater range of scales to be observed, important in audio applications where frequencies can vary over several orders of magnitude.

A *voice* is a set of transform coefficients with fixed dilation parameters. Thus a voice in some ways corresponds to a frequency band in an equalizer. If the frequency grid is aligned to a musical interval, the modulus projects a strong dark indicator when the input signal contains that interval.

A plot of the phase spectrum is sometimes referred to as the *scalagram*. The scalagram yields interesting details about the phase transitions within a given signal, such as the onset of transients and the nature of the modulations within the signal (Kronland-Martinet, et al. 1987; Kronland-Martinet, et al. 1997).

Transformation of Sounds Using Wavelets

Once a sound signal has been analyzed with the WT, one can alter the analysis data in order to transform the original signal. This section describes the various transformations.

Substituting a New Synthesis Wavelet

One possibility offered by the WT is that of substituting a different wavelet function for the resynthesis than was used for the analysis. Using Mallat's smooth wavelet for the analysis, for example, and substituting Haar's boxcar wavelet for the synthesis introduces a noisy distortion effect. From a technical standpoint, this is a straightforward operation.

Wavelet Filtering

Another direct transformation is to filter by suppressing certain frequency channels in the resynthesis. Since wavelet representations involve both translation and scale parameters, one can impose amplitude envelopes at different scales, so that the frequency content of the signal changes with time. The logarithmic spacing of the voices makes it possible to extract chords from the sound by setting all but a few voices in each octave to zero (Boyer and Kronland-Martinet 1989). When this technique is applied to the speaking voice, for example, it gives the impression of a person talking "harmonically." Cross-synthesis possibilities are also suggested by this transformation. Kronland-Martinet notes that cross-synthesis can be achieved by resynthesizing from the modulus of one sound and the phase of another.

Pitch-Time Changing with the Wavelet Transform

Pitch-time changing with the WT can be accomplished using complex-valued signals and wavelets, since it involves stretching the grid of scale and translation values to achieve the desired duration, and then multiplying the phase of the values so that the resulting pitch is unchanged. To shift pitch by a constant factor, one multiplies the phase values of the analyzed wavelets by this constant. To dilate or contract the timebase while keeping the pitch the same, one can expand or compress the point of overlap of the wavelets in resynthesis.

Comb Wavelet Separation of Noise from Harmonic Spectrum

The comb wavelet transform, developed at the University of Naples «Federico II,» sorts transients, unpitched sounds, and pitch changes from quasiperiodic signals (Evangelista 1992, 1997; Piccialli et al. 1992). The comb WT starts from a windowed segment of sound. The algorithm estimates the fundamental pitch period, and fits a comb filter to the segment with peaks aligned on the harmonics of the fundamental. The comb filter sifts out the energy in the harmonic spectrum. The algorithm then performs a wavelet analysis on this "clean" harmonic signal. When the inverse WT is subtracted from the original signal, the residual or "dirty" part of the signal remains. The dirty part includes the attack transient and the details that give the sound its identity and character. Once the clean and dirty part are separated, one can perform a kind of cross-synthesis by grafting the dirty part of one sound into the clean part of another. This type of separation is similar in concept—though not in implementation—to the technique used in the spectral modeling synthesis of Serra (1989).

Evangelista and Cavaliere (1998) extended the comb wavelet technique to handle the case of inharmonic partials, warping the frequencies of the analysis to adapt the pitch-synchronous comb wavelet filters to unequally spaced partials. With this technique they were able to resolve separately the hammer noise and the resonant components of a piano tone. Frequency warping also allows for transformations such as detuning the microintervals within a complex sound.

Other Wavelet Transformations

Other transformations include altering the geometry of the frequency grid, such as multiplying by or adding a scaling factor to all the frequencies in resynthesis. Cheng (1996, 1997) described an application of wavelets to make a spectral "exciter" effect in which high frequencies are boosted and an additional octave of high frequency information is extrapolated from existing lower frequencies. According to the author, this algorithm worked best on broadband transient percussion sounds, but was not well adapted to speech, where the added frequencies were perceived as artificial.

Experiences with Wavelets

Wavelet-based software for audio applications is rare at present. For the MacOS platform there is WaveLab, a library for the Matlab environment developed at the Department of Statistics at Stanford University and the National Aeronautics and Space Administration. WaveLab was designed for wavelet analysis, wavelet-packet analysis, cosine-packet analysis, and matching pursuit. It also provides a library of data files, including artificial signals as well as images and a few brief sampled sounds. As is, however, the WaveLab package is not well suited for musical experimentation. A great deal of additional programming would be required for serious experimentation in musical sound transformation.

Soniqworx Artist by Prosoniq is an audio editor with signal processing effects for MacOS. The effects, written by Stephan Sprenger, include wavelet-based transformations. One of these, wavelet signal reduction, discards all but a stipulated percentage of the analysis wavelets, leaving only the strongest components. It is conceptually analogous to the spectral tracing effect described in the section on the phase vocoder. Instead of sinusoidal basis functions, however, it uses wavelet basis functions. Owing to the change in basis function from a sinusoid to the jagged Daubechies second wavelet, the sonic effect is quite different from spectral tracing (figure 6.7).

Synthetic Wavelets

One could synthesize a stream of wavelets without an analysis of an existing sound. Malvar wavelets (Meyer 1994), for example, bear a strong resemblance to the FOF particles and to the grains with a quasi-Gaussian envelope. My grainlet technique (described in chapter 4), produces grains whose duration is a function of frequency, like the usual wavelet families. Wickerhauser (1994) proposed that a single wavelet packet generator could replace a large number of oscillators. Through experimentation, a musician could determine combinations of wavelet packets that produce especially interesting sounds. It could also be possible to reproduce the sounds of traditional instruments by decomposing an instrumental sound into wavelet packet coefficients. Reproducing the note would then require reloading those coefficients into a wavelet packet generator and playing back the result. Transient characteristics such as attack and decay could be controlled separately (for example, with envelope generators), or by using longer wave packets and encoding those properties into each note.

Assessment of the Wavelet Transform

Almost every author seems to have a favorite basis function, depending on their area of interest and background. (Navarro et al. 1995)

Traditional Fourier methods measure the average energy across a window whose duration remains constant, no matter what frequency component is being analyzed. This tends to delocalize the view of the onset time of high-

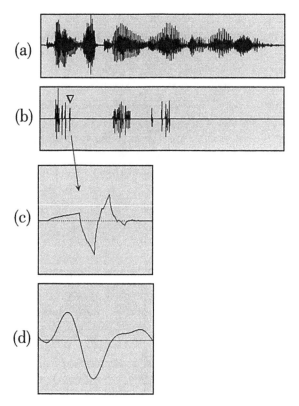

Figure 6.7 Wavelet signal reduction compared with spectral tracing. (a) Original waveform of spoken voice saying "pulse code modulation." (b) Resynthesized waveform after 90% of the weaker wavelets have been discarded. (c) The fluctuation indicated by the ∇ symbol in (b) blown up. It has the shape of the second Daubechies wavelet, which was the basis function of the analysis. (d) The same region of the sound file covered by (c) but resynthesized after spectral tracing, which discarded all but the strongest 1% of sinusoidal components.

frequency transients. In contrast, the WT offers a multiresolution view of a musical signal, since fine temporal analysis is resolved with short, high-frequency wavelets, while long, low-frequency wavelets resolve fine frequency differences. Thus the WT is well suited for the study of transients or onset times in musical signals, because it exhibits remarkable time sensitivity at high frequencies (Dutilleux, Grossmann, and Kronland-Martinet 1988). In the past, FFT-based methods had a computational advantage over wavelet methods. By now, engineers have developed optimizations for many types of wavelet transforms (Shensa 1992).

Torrésani (1995) pointed out how group theory operations (translation, expansion, compression, rotation) can be applied to signals in the wavelet domain. As Arfib noted in 1991, however, an arbitrary geometrical transformation of a time-frequency analysis is not guaranteed to produce an interesting sonic result. Meijer has argued:

Unless the mathematical properties of an exact lossless and/or orthogonal mapping and its inverse reconstruction are considered essential, there is no convincing reason to use wavelets in sound synthesis and analysis. For instance, in auditory perception almost nothing is exact, even though the localization properties in time and frequency are very important. There is also no reason why the resonance properties of the basilar membrane would be best described using wavelets, since the constant-Q property approximates only part of the membrane. Constant bandwith, as suited to fixed-width time windowing, better approximates the admittedly often less important low-frequency part.... Furthermore the human hearing system is known to be nonlinear in a number of ways, so even without knowing how to exploit that one can argue that a linear mapping is not going to be an optimal mapping for human auditory scene analysis. (Meijer 1998)

At present, the vast majority of wavelets in audio are not concerned with artistic transformations of sound. The principle applications are utilitarian:

- Audio data reduction—for transmission in broadcast and network media. Wannamaker and Vrscay (1997) report compression ratios of 3:1 with "generally satisfactory reconstruction." The results do not preserve high fidelity. Barnwell and Richardson (1995) criticize wavelet techniques for audio compression, particularly the dyadic wavelet grids based on octave-band filter banks. (See also Erne 1998.)

- Denoising—removal of broadband noise from an audio recording, with "faint birdy noise" remaining as an epiphenomenon of the denoising process (Ramarapu and Maher 1997).

- Detection and classification of transient signals in background noise—for example, detection and classification of underwater acoustic signals generated by whale clicks, or scratches in vinyl recordings (Grossmann et al. 1987; Learned and Willsky 1993).

- Display of spectrum features—using the properties of the wavelet technique to isolate specific features of audio signals and project them visually (Kronland-Martinet, et al. 1987; Newland 1994).

- Detection and display of internal modulations (Arfib and Delprat 1993, 1998; Delprat et al. 1990; Kronland-Martinet, et al. 1997).

- Analysis of turbulence and chaos—the wavelet transform can serve as an alternative to the Fourier decompositions in analyzing turbulence (Liandrat and Moret-Bailly 1990).

- Analysis of performed rhythms—Tait (1995) applied wavelets to the display of rhythmic patterns in jazz.

- Sound texture matching—Bar-Joseph et al. (1999) analyzed stationary or statistically constant sound textures (rain, waterfalls, crowds of people, machine noises, etc.) using a multiresolution wavelet approach. They could then synthesize similar textures using granular synthesis.

The mathematical conditions that must be satisfied to create a wavelet function are "weak" or relatively unconstrained. This offers great freedom in the choice of wavelet. Specific wavelet functions can be devised to detect special features in an audio signal. Kronland-Martinet, et al. (1997) imagined the decomposition of a signal in order to detect a specific word pronounced with different pitches and durations. This flexibility is seen in some of the analysis applications just mentioned. The musical potential of feature-based searching could be great, especially when coupled with selection and transformation.

Wavelets have been proposed as a component in the modeling of *weak turbulence* or *deterministic chaos* (Arneodo et al. 1995). In certain forms of chaos, the pattern of turbulence is similar (but not identical) on different time scales. Since wavelets offer a multiscale representation, they can be combined with *multifractals*. These are mathematical models of intermittence in the small scale of turbulence. This combination could create multilevel models of deterministic chaos. Fractal systems can model the degree of regularity at each scale, leading to the concept of a *spectrum of singularities* (irregularities). This is a rich territory of scientific exploration which may well have artistic potential. (See Robindoré 1996a.)

The wavelet paradigm has generated great interest since its introduction in the 1980s. In the larger context of the past several decades of signal processing, however, wavelets and multiresolution filter banks have offered a limited range of musical applications. Fourier and Gabor techniques remain dominant, and powerful applications such as fast convolution have stayed within the Fourier camp. Masri, et al. (1997a) suggest that the logarithmic frequency scale of the wavelet transform is an advantage in detecting pitch, but that the linear frequency scale of the Fourier and Gabor transform is an advantage in analyzing linear-space harmonics. Nevertheless, it seems clear that the full scope of wavelet techniques has not yet been exploited in the musical domain.

Gabor Analysis

Expansion into elementary signals is a process in which Fourier analysis and time description are two special cases.   (Gabor 1946)

As chapter 2 recounts, in the 1940s, Dennis Gabor proposed a comprehensive approach to the analysis of sound, authoring a series of important scientific papers combining insights from quantum physics and psychoacoustics with practical experiments (Gabor 1946, 1947, 1952). In these papers, he suggested that the representation of a signal purely in terms of its time series (e.g., the sequence of samples of a discrete signal) or purely in terms of its frequency content (Fourier expansion) were both extreme cases of a wide range of signal expansions. They show high locality (precision) in one domain, but no locality at all in the other. For the analysis and manipulation of sound, good locality in both time and frequency is desirable. Gabor showed that any sound could decompose into a combination of elementary acoustical quanta. A plot of the analysis data on a time-versus-frequency rectangular grid is the Gabor matrix or lattice. Each quantum has a finite extent in time and in frequency. Gabor proposed a smooth Gaussian window for the quantum, a natural choice since the spectrum of a Gaussian window resembles a similar bell-shaped curve. In this case, a locality in the time domain corresponds to the locality in the frequency domain.

Theory of the Gabor Transform

Gabor's design for sound analysis was similar to the short-time Fourier transform (STFT) which applies a sequence of localized Fourier transforms on fixed-duration windowed segments of a source signal. The STFT emerged out of research in speech analysis and resynthesis in the 1960s and 1970s at the Bell Telephone Laboratories. During this period, Gabor's pioneering work was neglected.

Gabor's papers described an iterative approximation method to calculate the matrix. By 1966, Helstrom had shown how to recast Gabor's analysis and resynthesis approximation into an exact identity by turning the elementary signals into orthogonal functions. Bacry, Grossman, and Zak (1975) and Bastiaans (1980, 1985) verified these results, and developed analytic methods for evaluating the matrix.

The analysis procedure that results in this time-frequency representation is the *Gabor transform* (GT). At the core of the GT is the *gaboret* (Arfib and Delprat 1993), a complex exponential signal limited in duration by a Gaussian window. The GT multiplies the gaboret at different frequencies by a succession of windowed segments of the input signal. These multiplications generate the Gabor matrix, also known as the modulus of the GT (figure 6.8). Since the gaborets are complex, the GT also produces a representation of phase, called the *phasogram*. Researchers have used this representation to reveal phase periodicities—indicators of modulation laws hidden in the input signal (Kronland-Martinet et al. 1997). See Arfib 1991 for a discussion of the differences between the phase vocoder and the GT.

A drawback of Gabor's original design was the lack of pure orthogonality. This is because of the smoothness of the Gaussian window, which does not trail perfectly to zero at its extrema, leaving a small DC component. When using the same window in the resynthesis, the result is unstable, leading to spikes in the output. Researchers have spent great effort on the construction of biorthogonal or dual functions, a set of compensating windows that correct for the lack of orthogonality of the Gaussian window (Helstrom 1966; Bacry, Grossman, and Zak 1975; Bastiaans 1980, 1985; Navarro et al. 1995a). Bastiaans and Geilen (1996) showed how the discrete Fourier transform, in conjunction with the discrete Zak transform, can calculate the discrete Gabor transform in a sum-of-products form, which leads to fast algorithms.

The flowering of wavelet theory since the 1980s has had a strong influence on the modern theory of the Gabor transform, leading to a new characterization of the gaborets, also called the *Gabor wavelets* or *gaborettes* (Torresani 1995). This has led to a reformulation called the *multiresolution* or *discrete Gabor transform* (DGT). In the DGT, the complex spectrogram of a signal is defined as the Fourier transform of the product of the signal and the shifted and complex

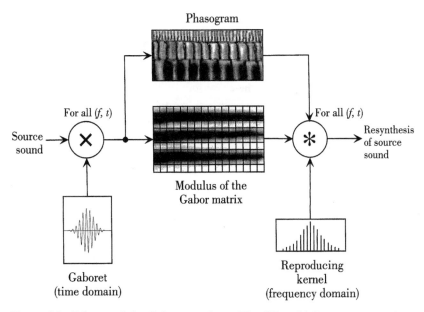

Figure 6.8 Schema of the Gabor transform. The GT multiplies a segment of a source signal by a complex Gaboret, translated in frequency and time according to the resolution of the Gabor matrix. The energy occupies cells in the modulus of the GT, and the phase information appears in the phasogram. To resynthesize the source, each cell of the matrix is convolved with the reproducing kernel, the dual of the complex Gaboret.

conjugated version of a window function. The complex spectrogram is determined by its values on the points of the Gabor lattice. In recent years, mathematicians have pushed the theory of the GT beyond the Gaussian gaborets to account for larger classes of particles: general subgroups on the TF plane (Torrésani 1995).

Properties of the Gaussian Window Used in the GT

Harris (1978) compared the properties of twenty-three different window shapes, including the Gaussian window used in the GT. According to Harris, two properties of a window are paramount in spectrum analysis. One is its *highest side lobe level* or HSSL. To maximize frequency detectibility, this should be low relative to the central lobe. The other is its *worst case processing loss*. The WCPL indicates the reduction in output signal-to-noise ratio as a result of windowing and worst case frequency location. It should, therefore, be low, or the quality of the analysis will be compromised.

The HSSL of the rectangular Dirichelet window is only -13 dB, a poor figure that results in noise-cluttered spectral analysis. The WCPL of the Dirichelet window is 3.92 dB. In comparison, the Gaussian window is considerably more selective, with a highest side lobe level of -42 to -69 dB, depending on the peakedness of the envelope. Its WCPL ranges from 3.14 to 3.73 dB.

Other windows outperform the Gaussian window in these properties. A narrow Kaiser-Bessel window has an HSSL of -82 dB, while a wide Hanning window has a WCPL of 3.01 dB. These cases are somewhat opposite to each other, however, and the Gaussian window remains a good compromise between the two.

Musical Applications of the Gabor Transform

Daniel Arfib, working at the Laboratoire de Mécanique et d'Acoustique (Centre Nationale de Recherche Scientifique, Marseilles), was the first to apply a digital Gabor transform to the analysis and resynthesis of musical sounds (Arfib 1990, 1991; Risset 1992). He was soon joined by his colleague Nathalie Delprat. One of their first results was a robust time compression and expansion operation in which pitch remains constant. They also applied the GT to other musical applications including frequency transposition, phase manipulations, cross-synthesis of speech with other sounds, and modifying the vibrato of a sung vocal tone while keeping other characteristics intact. They also separated the noisy, inharmonic parts of a sound from the harmonic parts (Arfib 1990, 1991; Arfib and Delprat 1992, 1993, 1998).

Kronland-Martinet et al. (1997) combined the Gabor transform with the innovative display techniques developed for the wavelet transform in Marseilles. Their plots show the phase structure of signals, which is normally hidden from view. According to the authors, this phase information can be used to make frequency estimations more accurate. They also applied the GT to the estimation of the amplitude and frequency modulation laws of musical instrument tones. (See also Delprat et al. 1990.) This work may lead to a more complete analysis of musical tones, one that quantifies the energy at each point in the time-frequency plane, but that also accounts for its internal modulations. This separation opens up the possibility of modifying the energy distribution independent of the modulation, or vice versa, which is impossible with standard Fourier techniques.

Leigh Smith (1996) proposed a Gabor wavelet representation of performed rhythms (pulsations between 0.1 to 100 Hz in frequency) as a model for the human perception of musical phrase groupings. The analyzer indicated the locations of accents, and could infer musical phrase structure from these cues.

Assessment of the Gabor Transform

Advances in the theory of the Gabor transform proceed in two directions. The first direction consists of elaborations on the plane of pure mathematics: newer theorems, higher abstractions, and more far-flung links to other branches of mathematics. Here the signal is quite secondary in importance, indeed, there may be no signal. The second direction extends the range of applications of the GT in the analysis and transformation of sound. For musicians, the first direction is of interest only insofar as it may foster the second.

Like the short-time Fourier transform and the wavelet transform, the GT is limited in resolution by a fundamental uncertainty principle. The sponge of the reproducing kernel blurs any manipulation of the Gabor matrix.

As Jean-Claude Risset (1992) has observed, the GT and the wavelet transform have many points in common. They are both concerned with elementary functions limited in time and in frequency. They each offer modification of the analysis data using an arbitrary function applied to the reproducing kernel. They both allow the possibility of resynthesis from a discrete analysis grid. In musical applications, Risset has noted:

[The Gabor transform] can produce excellent results in the processing of hyperbaric speech and in slowing down a spoken recording by a factor of more than 100 whilst preserving intelligibility (on the condition of only slowing down the vocalized parts of the signal). (Risset 1999b)

It is clear that the GT is a potent means of sound transformation. The work of the Marseilles group has been especially important in adapting wavelet concepts to the GT. Fortunately for us, their focus is on acoustical problems. Hopefully this research will eventually be made into widely available software tools.

Summary

Where the telescope ends, the microscope begins. Which has the grander view? (Victor Hugo 1862)

By allowing noise to make inroads into musical sound, Varèse accelerated a trend toward the shattering of traditional musical language. Together with the inadequacy of neoserialism, this resulted in a fragmentation of musical language and a consequent proliferation of composition techniques, very far from a possible theoretical unification. On the other hand, the increase in methods of acoustic analysis created a situation analogous to the physics of the microcosmos—an imagined unity of sonic phenomena. Here began an opposition to the continuous wave theory of sound, a granular atomism that was capable of representing any chaotic state of sound material and was also effective on the plane of synthesis. (Orcalli 1993)

Beginning in the 1950s, a handful of visionary scientists, acoustical engineers, and musicians such as Gabor, Meyer-Eppler, Xenakis, and Stockhausen proposed new theories of sound organization based on microsonic particles. Critics attacked them on the basis that sound quanta were divisible and therefore not fundamental, thereby missing the point. While there are no fundamental sound particles, any sound can be decomposed into an innumerable number of different particles, depending on the chosen basis functions. Each such decomposition makes possible myriad sound transformations. The catalog of transformations based on window spectrum analysis undoubtedly will continue to proliferate.

7 Microsound in Composition

Scientific tests help us estimate the potential of a technique of synthesis or sound transformation. They may even suggest how to compose with it, but the ultimate test is artistic. The aesthetic proof of any signal processing technique is its use in a successful composition. The first part of this chapter presents early experiments in digital granular synthesis, the middle section examples of microsound in my own compositions, and the final section examples of microsound in compositions by other composers.

Experiments in Digital Granular Synthesis

Gabor carried out the first experiments in sound granulation using opto-electronic parts from film projectors (see chapter 2). Several others, including Schaeffer's colleague Jacques Poullin, built conceptually similar devices based on magnetic tape technology. In 1959, Iannis Xenakis completed a short granular synthesis study, *Analogique B*, realized by splicing together hundreds of analog tape fragments. (See the description in chapter 2.) These heroic, labor-intensive experiments gave a glimpse of what might eventually be achieved with digital technology.

Klang-1: Study in Digital Granular Synthesis

My first study in digital granular synthesis was *Klang-1*, realized in December of 1974. Chapter 3 described the technical environment: a large mainframe computer running the Music V synthesis language. *Klang-1* was a technical test of three parameters of granular synthesis: (1) the grain envelope, (2) the grain duration, and (3) the density of grains in time. To prepare, I graphed on paper two time-varying curves, which indicated the frequency and density of the grains. From these, I designed a detailed score that specified the starting times and frequencies of seven hundred and sixty-six grains over a 30-second period. I then typed this numerical data onto punched cards, one grain per card. The Music V instrument was a simple sine generator with a Gaussian test envelope. Music V interpreted each grain as a NOTE statement which fed numbers of the synthesis instrument.

The duration of every grain was fixed at 40 ms, a figure derived from Xenakis's theory (1992, p. 54). The density of the grains ranged from zero to a maximum of twenty-five grains per second. The converter hardware fixed the sampling rate at 20 kHz. Grain frequencies in the *Klang-1* étude varied from 16.11 Hz to 9937.84 Hz. Between this range, I calculated a 1000-tone scale, which divided each whole tone into twenty-four subdivisions (Roads 1975), and approximated the *just-noticeable-difference* (JND) thresholds for pitch (Moles 1966).

I did not intend *Klang-1* to be anything more than a technical experiment. Yet I recall vividly the magical impression that the granular sound had on me as it poured forth from the computer for the first time.

Prototype: **Study in Automated Granular Synthesis**

The *Prototype* study incorporated refinements derived from the *Klang-1* experiment. More than a technical test, it was also a preliminary attempt to compose with granular sound. The technical refinements included:

1. Automated grain generation from high-level cloud specifications
2. Use of a quasi-Gaussian grain envelope, with a smooth attack and decay and an extended sustain, also known as a *cosine taper* or *Tukey window* (Harris 1978)
3. Shorter grain durations (20 ms)
4. Increased grain density

Prototype is an eight-minute granular study, written in April of 1975. The composition followed a set of systematic procedures that I worked out by hand. Later, I incorporated these procedures into a larger program for algorithmic composition (Roads 1976, 1987).

The first task that I confronted was automating the grain generator. Integral to Xenakis's conception of granular synthesis was the notion of global stochastic control.

For a macroscopic phenomenon, it is the massed total result that counts ... Microsounds and elementary grains have no importance [in themselves] on the scale that we have chosen. Only groups of grains and the characteristics of these groups have any meaning. (Xenakis 1992)

To realize *Prototype*, I wrote PLFKLANG, a program in Algol to generate thousands of grain specifications from seven high-level cloud parameters. PLFKLANG implemented asynchronous granular synthesis (as described in chapter 3) with a grain waveform that could vary between a sine wave and bandlimited pulse.

Compositional Logic of **Prototype**

Prototype is the result of systematic compositional procedures. Involving interaction among fourteen synthesis parameters. These parameters described the global properties of a sound cloud filled with grains: begin time, duration, center frequency, center frequency slope (increasing or decreasing), spectral bandwidth, spectral bandwidth slope (increasing or decreasing), rate of spatial change, amount of reverberation, and grain density of a set of granular clouds.

Any number of synthesis parameters could interact, meaning that as a "master" parameter varied, another parameter linked to it would mirror these variations. The connection between the parameters was not a simple linear scaling function, however, but rather a linkage between their degree of order or disorder. This meant that if a master parameter remained stable (ordered) over the course of calculating several clouds, then all parameters linked to it would also remain stable, and vice versa. Another possibility was an inverse link between parameters. In this case, a stable master parameter would cause parameters inversely linked to it change rapidly (disordered).

This type of compositional logic encourages entropic contrasts. By keeping some synthesis parameters stable, one imposes continuity between successive sound clouds, while letting other parameters vary more freely.

Behind *Prototype* are twenty different configurations for parameter linkages, each corresponding to a specific section of the piece. I drew these as a set of twenty interconnection digraphs. (A digraph, or directed graph, consists of a set of nodes connected by lines with arrowheads on each line.) Figure 7.1 shows the first four of these digraphs. Each digraph corresponded to a specific section of the piece.

This procedure resulted in an "Entropy Chart" that indicated the degree of order or disorder associated with each parameter in each section. I interpreted the tendencies indicated by the chart, and developed specifications for one hundred and twenty-three clouds. I typed these numerical specifications on punched cards. The PLFKLANG program read them. A typical specification was:

BEG	DUR	MU	BETA	DEN	DELTA	MUSL	BESL	DESL
SV1	0	1.0	100	90	87	99	0	−30	0

where BEG is begin time of a cloud, DUR is cloud duration, MU is the initial center frequency of a cloud, BETA is the initial bandwidth of cloud, DEN is the grain density, DELTA is the initial amplitude of a cloud, and MUSL, BESL, DESL represent the time-varying slopes of the MU, BETA, and DELTA parameters over the course of the cloud, respectively. I then prepared a graphic score, which plotted each cloud over time. The graphic score also shows variations in reverberation and spatial panning, which I added later.

I divided the sample calculations into eight one-minute sections. The entire synthesis process involved sixty-three steps of compilation, calculation, data transfer, and digital-to-analog conversion over a period of weeks. After assem-

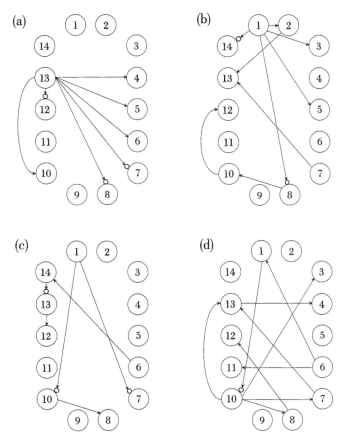

Figure 7.1 The first four digraphs of *Prototype*. The arrows indicate parameter linkages (see the text).

bling the eight sound fragments on analog tape, I took this tape to the Village Recorder—a sound studio in West Los Angeles—for the final mixdown on a Quad-Eight mixing console. There I added electronic plate reverberation (EMT reverberator with a 2.5 second reverberation time) and spatial panning according to the graphic score.

I played this étude to a number of friends and colleagues as a demonstration of granular synthesis, and once in a concert in May 1975 at UCSD. Around the same time, David Cloud, host of the new music program Zymurgy, broadcast *Prototype* on the radio station KPFK-FM in Los Angeles. I can hardly imagine the effect this strange experiment must have had on the unsuspecting listener.

Microsound in Compositions by the Author

Four of the compositions that I made between 1980 and 1999 used microsound techniques. This section describes these works. Since 1995 I have also realized a large number of experiments and particle studies. At the time of this writing (2001), I am assembling this material into new compositions.

Polychromatic Timbre in *nscor* and *Field*

Granular synthesis appears briefly in two compositions I made in the early 1980s: *nscor* (1980) and *Field* (1981). An article on the realization of *nscor* appears in (Roads 1985a, 1985b), so this description will be concise. *nscor* was realized in the Experimental Music Studio at the Massachusetts Institute of Technology (MIT). The starting point was a collection of tapes of source material that I had produced over the previous five years at different studios. I wanted to create a new work in which quite different sounds could all function. This was a deliberate attempt to go beyond the monochromatic approach, or the use of a single synthesis technique. The goal was to try to expand the range of sound color toward a polychromatic palette.

To convert, store, and mix dozens of sound files—as we do now so easily—was not possible at the MIT studio during that era. (Chapter 3 describes the computing environment.) The only practical way to realize the piece was to assemble it with analog technology. This meant using the studio's mixing console, and the four-track and two-track tape recorders. I mixed and spliced *nscor* in the late night hours between March and August of 1980. It premiered at the 1980 International Computer Music Conference in New York, and appeared on a compact disc released by Wergo in 1987 (Wergo 2010–50).

Granular synthesis appears in three parts of *nscor*. In the first appearance at 0:39 sec, a half-second burst of high-frequency grains, sounding like the asynchronous ringing of a small metal bell, concludes a rapid phrase produced by a Vosim generator at the Institute of Sonology, Utrecht. Immediately thereafter, at 0:41 to 0:44, a scintillating cloud of grains in the same register ends the introductory section. The second appearance is a granular explosion midway through the work, which is the primary crescendo of the composition. This explosion begins gradually as a sparse scattering of grains at 4:29. It builds with increasing density and broadening of bandwidth to a sustained peak at 4:36 that abruptly ends at 4:41. Finally, between 5:06 and 5:40, a section constructed entirely out of thirteen granular clouds serves as a transition between two additive synthesis textures (figure 7.2).

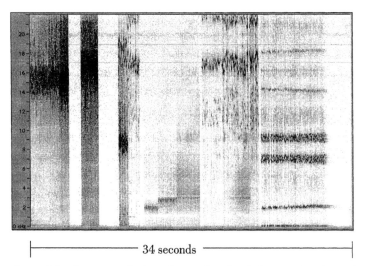

├─────────────── 34 seconds ───────────────┤

Figure 7.2 Spectrum display of granular clouds in *nscor* by the author, from 5:06 to 5:40. The frequency scale is linear.

Composed in the winter of 1980–81, *Field* is another polychromatic composition, in which granular synthesis serves as one instrument in a larger orchestra. *Field*, like *nscor*, formed from the ground up, starting with the assembly of sound objects, building larger structures as the composition continued. Again, I realized the montage with analog equipment. A major difference between *nscor* and *Field* was the number of tracks that I had to work with. I now had the use of a 24-track recorder at a studio in Boston (thanks to a grant from the MIT Council for the Arts), making it much easier to create an effective montage. The crossfading flow of musical shapes in *Field* reflects this. The composition premiered on New Year's Eve 1981, as part of Boston's First Night Festival. In 1985, *Field* appeared on a compact disc sponsored by Sony and produced by the MIT Media Laboratory as part of its inaugural. This CD was reissued in 1999.

Granular synthesis appears only once in *Field*, in the form of a granular explosion at 3:38–3:43. This explosion is the climax of the piece, dividing its two major sections.

Clang-Tint

Clang-Tint (1994) is not built exclusively from microsounds, but it is a work in which microsounds are integrated with other sounds. Its point of origin traces back to a sunny late afternoon, 9 December 1990, following a visit to an exhibition of photographic works by the Starn brothers at the Akron Museum of Art (Ohio, USA). These works combine prints and large transparencies with wood, tape, metal pipes, and other media to create three-dimensional sculptures. I was intrigued by the mixture of "sampled" imagery in conjunction with idiosyncratic methods of construction. Inspired by the exhibition, I imagined a structure for a new composition. Shortly thereafter I received a commission from the Kunitachi Ongaku Daigaku (Kunitachi College of Music, Tokyo) and the Bunka-cho (Japanese Ministry for Cultural Affairs). The title *Clang-Tint* refers to the notion of "sound-color." The composition starts from sampled sounds, cut and framed in myriad ways, spatialized throughout, and mixed with unusual synthetic sounds.

Parts of the work were composed during residencies in Tokyo (1991 and 1994), as well as at my studio in Paris and at Les Ateliers UPIC. At the Kunitachi school, I was fortunate to have access to the Gakkigaku Shirôkan (musical instrument museum). There I recorded forty-five instruments, some two millennia old, some as modern as the Ondes Martenot—a vacuum-tube electronic instrument. These recording sessions resulted in a database of ten hours of sound.

I conceived the composition in four sections: *Purity, Filth, Organic,* and *Robotic.* Each section takes its identity from the sound materials and organizational principles used in it. For example, *Purity* explores a simple musical world of sinusoidal waves and harmonies derived from a microtonal scale created for this composition.

The second movement, entitled *Organic,* focuses on expressive phrasing. It combines bursts of insect, animal, and bird calls with pulsar synthesis. Pulsars appear throughout the composition in different forms: pulsating blips, elongated formant tones, and clouds of asynchronous pulsars. For the latter, I first generated multiple infrasonic pulsar trains, each one beating at a different frequency in the range of 6 to 18 Hz. I then mixed these together to obtain the asynchronous pulsar cloud.

"Dirty" sounds make up the sound material of *Filth*: a morass of crude waveforms, raw transients, irregular globs and grains, industrial noises, and distorted tones. Most of the synthetic particles appear in its first section. After an intense climax, the final section consists of soft sounds in layers. Running throughout most of the section is a recording of burning embers of wood. I filtered and ring-modulated these natural particles to narrow their bandwidth to a specific range in the middle part of the spectrum then extensively edited the sound file on a micro time scale to emphasize certain rhythms. I removed or displaced many transients, for example, to decrackle the texture and articulate more important transient bursts.

The sound world of *Robotic* is percussive. It begins with acoustic percussion hits, many of which were pitch-shifted, filtered, or modulated to make variations on the original sounds recorded in the studio. As it progresses, more and more synthetic tones appear, produced by pulsar synthesis, transient drawing, and other methods.

Clang-Tint premiered at Kunitachi in 1994, and has since been performed around the world.

Half-life

Half-life, composed in 1998 and 1999, explores the birth, replication, mutation, and decay of sound particles. The composition divides into two parts, *Sonal atoms* and *Granules*, with a total duration of six minutes. Work on the piece began after experimentation with pulsar synthesis. (See chapter 4.). Shortly after writing a pulsar synthesis program in the SuperCollider 1 language, I wrote a separate program for sound file granulation. In this granulation program, a constant-Q bandpass filter modifies each sampled grain. The frequency of the filter varies randomly within stipulated limits. (See the description of microfiltration in chapter 5.)

The source material of *Half-life* consisted of about forty-five minutes of stereo sound of two types. The first type were raw pulsar trains with many internal variations. The second consisted of granular filtrations of the first. Whereas the pulsar trains tended to be pointillist in texture, the filtrations were more continuous and churning. The sound material in *Sonal atoms* is of the first type, while the material in *Granules* is of the second.

A period of dedicated editing followed the synthesis of the source material. Much of the composition was assembled on the micro time scale, editing and filtering individual particles. By lining up the particles in rapid succession, I could induce the illusion of tone continuity. (See the description of particle cloning synthesis in chapter 4.) Particle cloning shifted the perceived time scale of a particle from the micro to the sound object level. I also introduced new particles by transient drawing. (See the description of transient drawing in chapter 4.) As a result, the tendency toward recycling and repetition, which is still present in the work, was somewhat broken up. At the end of the day, many particles in the piece were singularities—unique events appearing once only.

Figure 7.3 Concert hall of the Australian National Conservatory, Melbourne, prior to the performance of the premiere of *Half-life*, May 1998. View from the stage. A loudspeaker is suspended at the center.

Half-life received its world premiere in May 1998 at the Next Wave Festival in Melbourne, Australia, with sound projection over twenty-eight loudspeakers (figure 7.3). The revised version premiered at the SuperCollider Night School at the Center for New Music and Audio Technologies (CNMAT), University of California, Berkeley in July 1999.

Tenth vortex and *Eleventh vortex*

On the night of 20 October 2000, I performed eleven "sound cloud vortices." These consisted of real-time granulations of a single sound file: a train of electronic impulses emitted by the PulsarGenerator program. Granulation expanded the time base of the original by a factor of up to six, while also filtering each grain and scattering it to a random point in space. The swirling combination of thousands of individual grains makes up the vortex.

I chose the tenth and eleventh performances for further treatment. I cut the *Tenth vortex* into four pieces, then nine more pieces, tuning and tweaking on a micro time scale. The work proceeded rapidly. I linked the parts into the final version on Christmas Eve 2000. *Eleventh vortex* (2001) called for more non-linearity in the macrostructure. I divided it into over eighty fragments, which resulted in a much more complicated compositional puzzle, and a more idio-syncratic structure, alternating between coalescence and disintegration. Both vortices premiered at Engine 27 in New York City in February 2001.

Microsound Techniques in Works by Various Composers

This section, which presents examples of works by various composers, cannot hope to be exhaustive. The goal is to indicate how microsonic techniques are being used by others.

Barry Truax

Several years after my article on the implementation of digital granular syn-thesis (Roads 1978a), the technique began to evoke interest for other compos-ers. The Canadian Barry Truax developed the first of several implementations in 1986. His implementations are notable for their emphasis on real-time oper-ation. Real-time synthesis is inevitably stream-oriented, and the musical aes-thetic explored by Mr. Truax reflects this orientation. Since the mid-1980s, he has applied granular synthesis as a central technique in his oeuvre. His primary emphasis is on the real-time granulation of sampled sounds, where he intro-duced many innovations. He has documented these in numerous articles (Truax 1986, 1987, 1988, 1990a, 1990b, 1991, 1992, 1994a, 1994b, 1995, 1996a, 1996b).

Truax was the first composer to explore the gamut of effects between syn-chronic and asynchronic granular synthesis, which he employed effectively in a series of compositions. In *Riverrun* (1986, Wergo WER 2017–50), from 5:40 to 6:50, he generated a series of synchronic "steps" consisting of overlapping grains that simultaneously drift apart and lengthen, forming a melodic line. *Wings of Nike* (1987, Cambridge Street Records CSR CD-9401, also *Perspec-tives of New Music* CD PNM 28) was the first granular piece to use a sampled sound as its source. The entire work is derived from two 170-ms phonemes, magnified by the composer into a twelve-minute opus (Truax 1990b). Mixed from an eight-track master, the work explores evolving streams of synchro-nic and asynchronic grains which become increasingly dense and merge into massive droning rivers of sound—up to eight thousand grains per second by the end of the work. *Tongues of Angels* (1988, Centrediscs CMC CD-4793) features pulsating grains that widen in spectrum as their duration shrinks. *Beauty and the Beast* (1989, Cambridge Street Records CSR-CD 9601) was the first composition to employ the process of real-time granulation of continuously sampled sound, pioneered by the composer.

Much of Truax's output promotes the notion of *soundscape*, a sound portrait of an environmental ambiance (Schafer 1977; Truax 1984). An early example of soundscape music is Luc Ferrari's opus *Presque rien, numéro 1*, composed between 1967 and 1970 (Robindoré 1998). Here is Truax's description of soundscape composition:

The soundscape composition is a form of electroacoustic music, characterized by the presence of recognizable environmental sounds and contexts, the purpose being to invoke the listener's associations, memories, and imagination related to the soundscape. At first, the simple exercise of 'framing' environmental sound by taking it out of context, where often it is ignored, and directing the listener's attention to it in a publication or public presentation, meant that the compositional technique involved was minimal ... This 'neutral' use of the material established one end of the continuum occupied by soundscape compositions, namely those that are the closest to the original environment, or what might be called 'found compositions.' Other works use transformations of environmental sounds ... with an inevitable increase in the level of abstraction. However, the intent is always to reveal a deeper level of signification inherent within the sound and to invoke the listener's semantic associations without obliterating the sound's recognizability. (Truax 1996b)

It is in the transformational vein that Barry Truax worked in his soundscape composition *Pacific* (1990, Cambridge Street Records CSR CD-9101). The piece starts with four sound sources: ocean waves, boat horns, seagulls, and a Dragon Dance recorded on the Chinese New Year. All sounds are heard at their original pitch but are time-stretched through granulation, with up to twelve stereo layers producing a chorus effect. Similarly, *Pacific Fanfare* (1996) contains ten "soundmarks" recorded in the Vancouver area in the early 1970s and the 1990s, reflecting the changing soundscape of the city. The signals appear both in their original state and granulated with resonance filtering and time-stretching.

Horacio Vaggione

As early as the 1970s, Horacio Vaggione explored a musical aesthetic based on the generation of a dense fabric of microsonic events. *La Maquina de Cantar*

(1978) for example, applied an IBM computer to control a Moog synthesizer, generating up to ten sounds per second in each of four voices (Bvdón 2000). His output in the 1980s can be seen a bridge period. Examples from the 1980s involving microsonic techniques and multiscale perspectives (using Music-*N* computer languages for synthesis and transformation) are *Thema* (1985, Wergo WER 2026-2), realized at IRCAM, and *Tar* (1987, Le Chant du Monde LCD 278046/47), realized at the Technische Universität Berlin Elektronisches Studio, also *Kitab* (1992, Centaur CRC 2255), for bass clarinet, piano, contrabass and computer-processed sound.

As noted in chapter 5, Horacio Vaggione's 1995 composition *Schall* for tape, commissioned by the Institut International de Musique Electroacoustique in Bourges, is an outstanding example of the use of creative granulation. It represents a considerable refinement of technique. The sound material of *Schall* consists of tens of thousands of sound particles derived from sampled piano notes.

The music is focused on a limited collection of objects of different sizes, which appear in diverse perspectives, all along the process. The work plays essentially with contrasts between textures composed of multiple strata, as an expression of a concern with a detailed articulation of sound objects at different time scales. (Vaggione 1999)

What makes *Schall* unique is its brilliant use of switching between different time scales: from the microscopic up to the note-object level and down again into the microscopic. Of course, the shorter the notes, the more broadband the texture, as in the noisy section between 2:10 and 2:28, or the final thirty seconds of the work. Thus the interplay is not just between durations, but also between pitch and noise.

Of the composition process, which involved interactive sound editing and mixing software, the composer says:

Considering the handcrafted side, this is the way I worked on Schall *(along with algorithmic generation and manipulation of sound materials): making a frame of 7 minutes and 30 seconds and filling it by "replacing" silence with objects, progressively enriching the texture by adding here and there different instances (copies as well as transformations of diverse order) of the same basic material.* (Vaggione 1999)

In his studio, the composer demonstrated to me some of the micromontage techniques used to make *Schall*. These involved arranging microsounds using a sound mixing program with a graphical time-line interface. He would load a catalog of pre-edited microsounds into the program's library then select items and paste them onto a track at specific points on the timeline running from left to right across the screen. By pasting a single particle multiple times, it became a sound entity of a higher temporal order. Each paste operation was like a stroke of a brush in a painting, adding a touch more color over the blank space of the canvas. In this case, the collection of microsounds in the library can be thought of as a palette. Since the program allowed the user to zoom in or out in time, the composer could paste and edit on different time scales. The program offered multiple simultaneous tracks on which to paste, permitting a rich interplay of microevents.

With *Nodal* (1997), Vaggione has taken the materials used in *Schall* several steps further, while also opening up his sound palette to a range of percussion instruments. The identity of these instruments is not always clear, however, since they articulate in tiny particles. The composition lasts 13:06, and divides into three parts, with part I lasting until 5:46, and part II spanning 5:49 to 9:20. The strong opening gesture establishes immediately the potential force of the granular texture, and sets up a dramatic tension. Although the continuously granulating texture that follows is often quiet in amplitude, one senses that the floodgates could burst at any moment. This effect is enhanced by "creaking" sounds that give the impression of reins being strained.

Part II begins with a warm fluttering texture that turns into a chaotic noise. While the ear tracks this low-frequency rumbling, at 6:18 a distinct mid-high crotale "roll" with a sharp resonance at 1600 Hz sweeps across. The overall texture becomes unpredictably turgid and chaotic, until at 7:11 the composer introduces an element of stasis: a rapidly repeating piano tone during which the granulation background briefly lets up. This leads to a section of almost tactile noise, soft like a wet snowstorm. At 8:46 another wood tapping appears. Part II ends on an incongruous major chord from what sounds like a toy piano. Part III introduces a resonant tom-tom-like tone. The background texture is high in frequency, sounding like rain on a thin roof. The density of the texture gradually builds, as new bursts and resonances sweep into view. The texture ebbs at 11:35, letting up until 12:09. The penultimate texture (a low-frequency rumbling that also concludes *Agon*), is a long 39-second fade out. This texture continues (at a low amplitude) for several seconds after the final gesture of the piece, a concluding three-event percussive tag ending.

The electroacoustic work *Agon* (1998) further elaborates the processes and materials heard in *Nodal*. It opens with a continuously "grinding" band in the range between 6 kHz and 16 kHz. The rate of the grinding modulation is in the range of 10 Hz to 20 Hz. The continuity of the high-frequency band is broken by various colored explosions. It is as if different percussive sounds are being

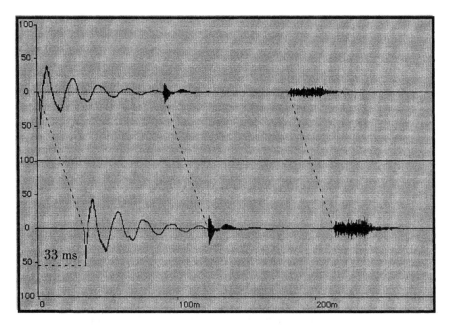

Figure 7.4 A time-domain view of the final gesture in Horacio Vaggione's *Agon*, a triple-stroke "tom-click-hiss."

dropped into a gigantic granulator, to be instantaneously mulched into bits of microsound.

Upon first hearing, *Agon* appears to be a continuous stream of new material. Repeated listening reveals that the work recycles material in an efficient manner. For example, the penultimate gesture of the work—a swirling mid-low frequency band—has already been heard in the first thirty-five seconds. The final gesture of the work, a triple stroke "tom-click-hiss," appears first at 2:59 and again at 3:08 (figure 7.4). Two other distinctive timbres are a small metal bell, and a tom-tom stroke. The bell is first heard forty seconds into the piece, resonating at about 750 Hz; at fifty-nine seconds it shifts up to 1080 Hz (approximately an augmented fourth). The tom-tom is first heard in a burst of strokes at thirty-four seconds. Both the bell and the tom-tom reappear at many points. A shimmering cymbal sound interweaves throughout—a component of the high-frequency band that streams through most of the piece. A piano tone-cluster, first heard at 2:01, signals the end of a quiet zone at 5:54, and marks a turning point of the finale at 8:10.

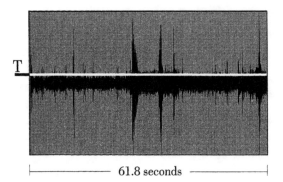

├─────────── 61.8 seconds ───────────┤

Figure 7.5 The amplitude envelope of the first 61.8 seconds of *Agon* by Horaciio Vaggione. The line marked T indicates the amplitude threshold between the foreground peaks and the background granulations.

Microsound as a Foreground/Background Texture

A fascinating aspect of style in *Schall, Nodal,* and *Agon,* is the use of continuously granulating textures, composed of dense agglomerations of short-duration grains. These scintillating, sometimes crackling or frying textures serve as a stationary element in the mesostructure of the pieces, holding the listener's attention. By keeping these granulations low in amplitude, their background role is evident. The composer sustains the low-level textures for ten to twenty seconds or more at a time, keeping the listener engaged while he sets up the next burst or explosive release (figure 7.5).

Musical Examples by Other Composers

This section offers capsule profiles of pieces by other composers who have used microsound synthesis and transformation. The techniques are now widespread, and new compositions are appearing regularly. This survey, then, is little more than a sampling of a larger body of work. The order of the descriptions is roughly chronological.

Henri Pousseur's pioneering work *Scambi* (1957) applies serial principles to "the finest particles of the musical-acoustical material," which in this case consisted of dense sequences of aleatoric pulses, resulting in white noise (Acousmatrix 4, compact disc BVHAAST 9010).

As Michelangelo specified shape by chipping at his block of marble with a chisel, so Pousseur specified crisp, clear, and pitched sounds by chipping at his block of white noise with an electronic chisel called a filter.   (Chadabe 1987)

The 1969 *Chants de Maldoror* by Reiner Riehn (Deutsche Grammaphon 137011) is a fascinating example of the use of microsonic materials in musical synthesis. The sound material of this analog electronic work, composed at the Institute of Sonology in Utrecht, consists of many thousands of filtered impulses.

The second movement of Paul Lansky's *As If* (1982) for string trio and computer-synthesized sounds (Centaur CRC 2110) features quasi-granular textures, which appear to be the result of echoes. The composer is also one of the pioneers of micromontage, which he employed skillfully in a series of compositions including *Idle Chatter* (1985, Wergo 2010–50), in which the raw material consists of vocal phoneme fragments of about 80 ms in duration scattered metrically with a constantly shifting accent pattern. His subsequent pieces *just_more_idle-chatter* (1987) and *Notjustmoreidlechatter* (1988) continue along the same line, with strong emphases on articulation of meter and tonal harmonic progressions.

The technical environment of the 1970s and early 1980s made everything to do with computer music rather laborious. Trevor Wishart's opus *VOX 5*, for example, was conceived in 1979, but could not be realized until 1986, when the technical climate was more beneficent. *VOX 5* is based on the phase vocoder described in chapter 6. Although the utility of the phase vocoder was proven by experiments in the mid-1970s (Portnoff 1976; Moorer 1978), it was not available to musicians until a decade later. This was first possible with the CARL software package from the University of California, San Diego (Moore 1982; Dolson 1983, 1985, 1986). In *VOX 5*, Wishart creates a "supervoice" at center stage, whose utterances metamorphose into natural events: crowds, bells, trees, and less specific granular complexes. Another of Wishart's piece to combine vocalisms with particle processing is *Tongues of Fire*, composed in 1995, about which the composer has written:

I have newly invented many of the processes employed for this work. These include: Spectral Tracing—a process in which a windowed Fourier analysis of the sound is made using the phase vocoder; the sound is then reconstructed on a window-by-window basis using only the N loudest components, the process itself is time-variable. Waveset Distortion—the time domain signal is divided into elements at each even zero-crossing, and these elements are manipulated in a variety of ways: for instance, each is repeated N times to produce a strongly colored form of time-stretching which generates pitched "beat streams" within the sound; or N elements are replaced by just one of their number, extended in length to span the entire set of N. The "fireworks" transformation is produced by this procedure, etc. Another process that is used, although less radically, is Sound Shredding, a technique related to Brassage. In this process a fixed length of sound is cut into arbitrary length segments which are reordered at random, and this process is then repeated many times. The progressive application of this process is heard in the voices to "water"-like transformation from 13 m 20 s to 14 m 40 s.   (Wishart 1996)

Jean-Claude Risset made use of granular time expansion in *Attracteurs étranges*. In this work, the clarinetist Michel Portal recorded a number of scored musical phrases and sound effects. The composer transformed these segments in various ways, including sequences speeded up or slowed down using the Gabor grains (Risset 1992, 1998). In *Sud* (1984) and *Elementa* (1998), both of which rely largely on field recordings, Risset employed granular time-shuffling. For *Invisible* for soprano and tape, he used the Gabor grains as implemented in the Sound Mutations program for MacOS (Arfib and Delprat 1992).

Some of the earliest and most intensive use of phase vocoder transformations is by the Santa Barbara composer JoAnn Kuchera-Morin. She has radically altered the time, pitch, and spectrum structure of instrumental and vocal sounds in a number of compositions including *Dreampaths* (1989), *Cantata* (1989), *Concerto for Clarinet and Clarinets* (1991), and more recently *Paleo* (2000) for double-bass and tape. A typical use would be to stretch the first thirty seconds of a sampled instrumental part into a three-minute layer. Another technique is shrinking the duration of a melodic line from several seconds down to a few hundred milliseconds, then expanding the duration of the shrunk line back to the original length to emphasize the artifacts of the process. Using Trevor Wishart's library of phase vocoder spectral operations, Kuchera-Morin also made musical use of such advanced processes as morphing between two sounds and spectral glissandi. Her work has involved three generations of phase vocoders. The first was Mark Dolson's pioneering implementation in the UCSD CARL package with Wishart's library of transformations, the second was the MixViews program developed by Douglas Scott at UCSB, the third a variety of phase vocoders for MacOS.

Stéphane Roy, in his 1992 composition *Mimetismo* (Empreintes Digitales IMED 9630), explored a particulated world of microsounds based on the plucked attacks of an acoustic guitar. The vocabulary of *Mimetisimo* relies heavily on granulose manipulations. The work delights in the sensuous flutter of acoustic vibrations on the eardrum.

Feuillages (1992) was composed by Philippe Schoeller for fourteen instruments and eight channels of electronic sound. The electronic part of this work uses an "acoustic pixel" technique developed by the composer and his technical assistant, R. G. Arroyo. The acoustic pixels (whose waveforms may be sampled or synthesized) were generated in multiple streams (*chemins stratifiés*), which often overlap. The team then filtered the streams to create a "liquid" quality.

The Neapolitan composer Giancarlo Sica's *En Sueño* (*Dreaming*), realized in 1996, strives for a continuous transition from the comprehensible to the incomprehensible. He achieves this through asynchronous granulation of the Spanish word *sueño* sung by a tenor and repeated like an evocation. The granulation techniques were mixed with an additive synthesis texture that combined thirty-two sine waves according to time-varying envelopes. The composition was realized using the Csound language.

The Paris-based composer Gérard Pape has employed granular techniques in combination with convolution in *Makbénach* (1997) for saxophone and tape.

In Makbénach, *I worked with samples of various extended techniques for the saxophone, developed and played by the saxophonist Daniel Kientzy. These were chained together to make "timbre paths." These timbre paths were composed as an alternative to isolated "sound effects." That is, the paths involve a chaining together of isolated extended techniques to emphasize an overall timbral transformation, from simplicity to complexity, purity to noise richness, harmonicity to inharmonicity, etc.* (Pape 1998)

Pape used two programs to transform the timbre paths. First, he produced a series of grains (using Cloud Generator) that followed a particular trajectory. He used these as impulse responses to be convolved (using SoundHack) with saxophone samples. The saxophone was transformed according to the path of the grains. He also used Cloud Generator to create a series of evolving granulations of the saxophone samples, establishing a new timbre path for the saxophone, with the choppy rhythms of the grains.

Granular and phase vocoder techniques are central to certain compositions of the German composer Ludger Brümmer. His pieces scatter volcanic eruptions in a barely audible sea of sound. *La cloche sans vallées* (on Cybele CD 960.101) was realized in 1993 at the Stanford University studios in California. The piece tends toward sparse, low-level textures, punctuated by "explosive interruptions" (program notes). *The Gates of H.* (1993) expands a brief fragment of a folk melody sung by a female choir into an 18-minute composition. After an explosive opening gesture, from about 1:10 to 2:07 the only sound is a low-level reverberation which fades in and out of perception. A sharp burst signals the start of the next section. The rest of the composition follows the

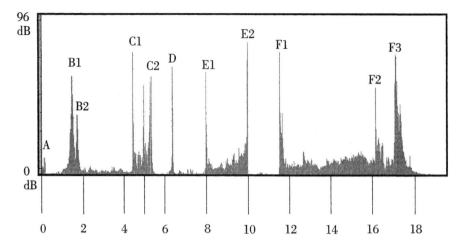

Figure 7.6 The amplitude envelope of the 19-minute, 28-second composition *Cri* by Ludger Brümmer. The letters indicate crescendi sections. Note that the peak between C1 and C2 reflects a momentary increase in low-mid-frequency energy (four pulsations). It is not a crescendo.

same logic: sudden crescendo interjections follow long near-silent spaces. The composer realized *Dele!* (1995, Cybele CD 960.102) at the studios of the Academy of Arts in Berlin. It begins with samples of children shouting. These were then time-stretched, pitch-shifted, and filtered using phase vocoders. *Cri* (Edel 0014522TLR) employs the same materials and phase vocoder techniques. As in his other compositions, dramatic gestures cause sounds to sweep into view and then quickly disappear. For example, after a climax at 10:00 (E2 in figure 7.6), the composition drops in amplitude by approximately 50 decibels and drifts in and out of an inaudible zone for another minute-and-half. This near-silence is broken by a dramatic flourish (F1 in figure 7.6).

The Franco-American composer Brigitte Robindoré has also employed the Cloud Generator program in a number of pieces. She has also developed techniques with microarcs on the UPIC system. Her *Comme étrangers et voyageurs sur la terre* (1995) is a prime example of this latter technique. The mesostructure consists of dense layers of sound masses that smoothly cross-fade into a constantly evolving flow. These are derived from samples of gamelan instruments from the composer's own recordings, filtered with a variety of convolution impulses. The piece combines these processed sounds with UPIC microarc synthesis. The UPIC system generated multiple types of musical structures:

grain clouds using fifteen different envelopes simultaneously, repetitive poly-rhythmic arc clusters based on sample extractions placed in infrasonic frequencies, and long sequences of superimposed sine waves that produce beating effects in the range of 40 to 120 Hz. In these works, microsonic techniques serve an aesthetic of emergent symbolism. In the composer's words:

Deeply embedded ideas slowly attain the threshold of perception and, at the right moment, brim over into conscious thought. (Robindoré 1996b)

In his 1999 doctoral dissertation, Manuel Rocha describes his three granular synthesis compositions: *Transiciones de Fase* (1993), *SL-9* (1994), and *Móin Mór* (1995), which was realized with the Granular Synthesis Toolkit (Eckel, et al. 1995). *Móin Mór* is based on an eighth century Irish poem and other, contemporary, poems in Gaelic. These poems mix with recordings made during the composer's trip to Ireland in 1993, as well as sounds recorded by Italian journalist Antonio Grimaldi from Bloody Sunday (1972) in Londonderry. *Móin Mór* begins with a granulated voice reciting the poems, using only consonant sounds. The rest of the piece consists of multiple layers of granulated textures, including phoneme fragments, over which the composer superimposes recognizable "scenes" from the Irish soundscape.

The media artist Kenneth Fields realized a compelling soundtrack for an interactive science-education CD-ROM entitled *Life in the Universe* (1996). Realized at CREATE, University of California, Santa Barbara, it featured resonant wood-like grains and granulations of the computer synthesized voice of the physicist Steven Hawking. According to the composer:

It was an appropriate metaphor, I thought, to use granular synthesis techniques for a project having to do with the properties and history of the universe, particle and wave physics, and the possibility of finding intelligent life in the universe beyond the Earth. Hawkings' synthesized narration for the CD-ROM was recorded on tape and sent to me. The piece has three parts, corresponding to three terrains we used as an organizational/ navigational strategy: the cosmological, biological, and mathematical terrains. Original materials were derived both from sampled and synthesized (Csound) sources, then processed with Gerhard Behles's real-time Granular program Stampede II (Behles, Starke, and Röble 1998). The music for the CD-ROM then, is a multiple path composition, dependent on the user's navigational choices. (Fields 1998)

Jon Christopher Nelson's granular opus *They Wash Their Ambassadors in Citrus and Fennel* (Nelson 1996) was awarded a prize at the Bourges Festival in 1996. This piece uses granular textures as a background accompaniment to an extended vocal performance by soprano Joan La Barbara.

Damián Keller, a student of Barry Truax, developed a suite of programs for producing granular sounds on models of such physical processes as bouncing, breaking, scraping, and filling (Keller and Truax 1998). The results were made available on an enhanced compact disc entitled *touch 'n' go* (Keller 1999; earsay productions es–99002), which combined the text of these programs with original music compositions.

Natasha Barrett composed *Little Animals* in 1997. It appears on the 1998 *Computer Music Journal* compact disc. This composition, labeled "acousmatic" by the composer, employs fine granulations and particulations as a primary strategy. According to the composer:

In Little Animals *sound material rich in connotation opens the work, and then throughout the last six minutes progressively fragments into pitch-textures.... The composition of* Little Animals *began by recording source material already containing an allusive potential (through mimetic approximation), which could be emphasized by straightforward editing techniques (such as cutting, pasting and mixing). After establishing these allusions in the composition, fragmentation techniques obscured the allusive aspect, revealing musical qualities. The next transformation stage mainly involved filtering, spectral stretching and fragmentation techniques. The fragmentation aspect is the most important as it serves to concentrate the ear on the relationship between fragments, as opposed to the allusive content and the physical resonant properties of the original sound. This method allowed the investigation of musical potentials without overt concern for the sounds' acoustic properties.* (Barrett 1998)

In her doctoral dissertation Barrett described the work in detail, focusing on the different listening strategies it tends to elicit (see also Barrett 1999).

The Italian composer Agostino Di Scipio has employed granular techniques in a series of nine compositions, beginning with the tape work *Punti di tempo* (1988) and extending to the ensemble and electronics piece *Texture-Multiple* (2000). His approach emphasizes algorithmic control of microsound synthesis:

The task of microcompositional strategies can be described as one of letting global morphological properties of musical structure emerge from the local conditions in the sonic matter ... The fundamental point in such approaches lies in the fact that algorithms implementing a model of sound material also implement ideas concerned with musical form. (DiScipio 1994)

In his *Sound & Fury*, Di Scipio performs on a Kyma system (developed by the Symbolic Sound company), effecting time expansion and frequency scaling on an ensemble of acoustic instruments by using faders to control parameters such as the time expansion, frequency, grain rate, and the spacing between grains (Di Scipio 1997b).

The developer of the Kyma system, the Illinois composer Carla Scaletti, used it to time-stretch sounds from a telephone in an interactive installation called *Public Organ:*

I used granular time stretching on the voices of installation participants who picked up a telephone (with a high-quality microphone installed in place of the original telephone microphone) and either left a "voice mail message" or were speaking with another instal- lation participant over the net via CUSeeMe. I captured fragments of their voices and then played them back a short time later time stretched. These time-stretched fragments were stored on disk and became part of the sounds made by the installation in its other states, long after the people had left. (Scaletti 1996)

Kim Cascone's *Pulsar Studies 1–20* (1999) is an MP3 release (Internet: fals.ch). The composer calls it "a new exploratory collection of one-minute studies composed using ... pulsar synthesis." The sound material originated from an early version of the PulsarGenerator program developed by Alberto de Campo and me (see chapter 4).

Finally, Thom Blum's *Five Haiku* (2000) decomposes the soundscapes of San Francisco into a swirling stream of sound particles, the sonic interpretation of poems by the composer and Matsuo Basho (1644–1694).

Summary

[Of the Nobel prize winning physicist, J. J. Thomson, the discoverer of the electron] ... His early mathematical work was not outstandingly important. He was not skillful in the execution of experiments. His talent—one that is for both theorists and experimentalists the most important—lay in knowing at every moment what was the next problem to be attacked. (Weinberg 1983)

The synthesis and transformation of microsound has already affected the music of our time. Viewing sound as a particulate substance opens up new approaches to composition. Variations on the micro scale provoke changes in musical tex- ture on higher time scales. Manipulations of particle density let coalescence and evaporation function as event articulators, as they bring sound into and out of being. Particle density also serves as the bridge between pulse and pitch, be- tween rhythm and timbre. The plasticity of the sound, which is inherent in its particle substrate, allows mutation to play an important compositional role, since every sound object is a potential transformation.

Do we intend such operations to reduce compositional practice exclusively to the level of microacoustical fluctuations? No. They merely add this stratum to the rest of the known layers of composition, thereby enriching the field. When the microsonic layers interact with the higher layers, they tend to articulate each other's specificity. We see this in the opposition of a long note underneath a sparse cloud of impulses. But the situation is more complex, since we can make any continuous sound evaporate at will. This introduces a fresh element of dramatic tension to the unfolding of musical structure.

In the early years of digital synthesis, the musical possibilities inherent in microsound were untested. This chapter shows that the situation is changing and that important compositions employ these techniques. Utilizing microsound will require less justification in the future, it has already proved itself in the most important arena, the domain of music composition.

8   Aesthetics of Composing with Microsound

Aesthetics seems to thrive on controversy, even to demand it; on the conflict, typically, of new and old, of simplicity and complexity.
—Edward Lippman (1992)

If styles and genres did not suffer exhaustion, there would be only one style, one genre in each art.
—Jacques Barzun (1961)

An encounter with aesthetic philosophy is unavoidable in composition. To pick up a gold-tipped fountain pen and inscribe a treble clef and key signature on onionskin staff paper is to import a system of composition. It entails a selection from an enormous range of possible approaches to making music, a palette of sounds, their combinations, a mode of performance, and even the audience. Every subsequent compositional decision further articulates the chosen aesthetic.

No less a decision is taken in launching a program for granular synthesis, which implies another context for creation, performance, reception, and evaluation of the resulting work. The differences between these choices, which are but two out of innumerable others, are differences of aesthetic philosophy. An aesthetic philosophy is nothing more than a collection of ideas and preferences that inform the artist's decision-making. This collection does not determine every artistic decision, but it guides the general direction. Nor is it static. Music is in a constant state of change. The aesthetic sensibility of the creative artist is continually evolving.

The purpose of this chapter is to try to identify the main aesthetic issues raised by composition with microsonic materials. It is a worthwhile exercise for a composer to formulate an aesthetic philosophy. Such reflection forces one to think through issues that may have been taken for granted. Reflection upon aesthetic ideas may lead to compositional ideas, and vice versa.

No matter how deliberately one composes, the aesthetic ramifications of a piece escape total control by the composer, who often has no power over the theatrical presentation and the acoustical environment in which a work is performed. Even more important is the listener's mood, a narrow filter imposed on the sonic sensation.

Before continuing, I should state that I do not mean to prescribe my aesthetics for others. My goal is simply to explain preoccupations that have guided my own musical experiments.

Aesthetic Premises

> *Every doctrine of aesthetics, when put into practice, demands a particular mode of expression—in fact, a technique of its own.* (Stravinsky 1936)

The present practice of electronic music composition rests on a foundation of aesthetic premises. Some are old, others have emerged only recently. This section presents several of these premises.

The Philosophy of Organized Sound

Edgard Varèse opened up a new path of exploration of musical sound when he proposed, in the 1920s, a philosophy of "organized sound." He was encouraged by the early advances in music technology in electronic instruments such as the Telharmonium, the Thereminovox, and the Ondes Martenot (Cahill 1897; Rhea 1972, 1984; Chadabe 1997; Weidenaar 1989, 1995). For a time, Varèse also championed the experimental performances of the Futurist musicians, builders of "noise instruments." The Futurists wrote an emotional manifesto, *The Art of Noises*, in which Luigi Russolo observed:

> *Musical sound is too limited in its variety of timbres. The most complicated orchestras can be reduced to four or five classes of instruments in different timbres of sound: bowed instruments, brass, woodwinds, and percussion. Modern music flounders within this tiny circle, vainly striving to create new varieties of timbre. We must break out of this limited circle of sounds and conquer the infinite variety of noise-sounds!* (Russolo 1916)

The philosophy of organized sound extended the boundaries of accepted musical material, and hence the scope of composition, to a wider range of acoustic phenomena. (See also Cowell 1930; Cage 1937.) Creative musicians sought beauty not only in the traditional, but also in the strange, in the formerly overlooked:

> *I insist upon the charm of combinations of noise instruments. But to appreciate this quality, the most absolute silence is necessary in the concert hall. No one can imagine what charm is attained with harmonic modulations and held chords produced, for example, by the blend of low and medium howlers, low whistler, and hummer. What a marvelous contrast results if a high crackler suddenly enters above this group to inflect a theme, or a gurgler to hold some notes or point up the rhythm! It is an effect that is completely unknown in orchestras, since no orchestra but that of the noise instruments can produce this sensation of excited and pulsing life, exalted through the intensity and rhythmic variety found in the combination of [the noise instruments].* (Russolo 1916)

What critics dismissed as unmusical noise is now a potent element in the composer's palette. Broad acceptance of this was slow in coming and Varèse encountered much rejection (Chou Wen-Chung 1966; Stuckenschmidt 1969). After World War II, the musical avant-garde embraced him, though the general public did not. Criticism and controversy surrounded his final projects, *Déserts* (1954, orchestra and tape), and *Poème électronique* (1958, electronic tape). Varèse died in 1965.

Many post-WWII-generation composers sensed a great aesthetic crisis in music. The twelve-tone ideas of Schoenberg and his followers had contributed to the feeling that traditional methods of harmonic and rhythmic organization were nearly exhausted:

The history of music and of musical thought is the story of artificial systems, their inception, bloom, and decline, their absorption or replacement by other artificial systems.... Recent developments in the field of musical composition have shown that the limited and conditioned system of musical elements, considered musical material for several hundred years, has now entered the administrative stage, where all possible permutations will no longer possess any new meaning. (Brün 1970)

Simultaneous with this sense of crisis, new types of music were emerging out of new musical materials. These included Pierre Schaeffer's musique concrète, and electronic music based on impulses, sine waves, noise generators, and eventually, computer-generated sounds.

The aesthetic of organized sound places great emphasis on the initial stage of composition—the construction and selection of sound materials. This may involve synthesis, which often begins with microsounds, furnishing the elementary components used in the assembly of higher-level sound objects. Just as the molecular properties of wood, thatch, mud, steel, and plastic determine the architectural structures one can construct with them, so sonic microstructure inevitably shapes the higher layers of musical structure.

The middle layers of musical structure—mesostructure—arise through interaction with the material. That is, to sculpt sonic material into gestures or phrases involves mediation between the raw waveforms and the will of the composer. This mediation is not always immediately successful, which is part of the struggle of composition. If the initial result is unsatisfactory, the composer has two choices. The first is to develop new materials that will more easily fit a preconceived phrase mold. The second choice is to abandon the mold, which means following the "inner tensions"—to use Kandinsky's phrase—of the sonic material (Kandinsky 1926). In this case, the material suggests its own mesostructures. Later, the composer may intervene to reshape these structures from the vantage point of another time scale.

These interrelationships between sound and structure confirm what musicians have known all along: material, organization, and transformation work together to construct a musical code. It is in this context that a given sound accrues meaning and beauty.

Expansion of the Temporal Field

Music theorists have long acknowledged a multiplicity of time scales in compositions. Today we can extend this awareness to the micro time scale. The call for an expanded temporal field was first issued in the 1930s by composers such as Henry Cowell and John Cage, who said:

In the future ... the composer (or organizer of sound) will be faced not only with the entire field of sound but also with the entire field of time. The "frame" or fraction of a second, following established film technique, will probably be the basic unit in the measurement of time. No rhythm will be beyond the composer's reach.   (Cage 1937)

By the 1950s, electronic devices had opened paths to the formerly inaccessible territories of microtime. In electronic music studios, one could assemble complex sounds by splicing together fragments of magnetic tape. Composers such as Stockhausen and Xenakis began to explore the temporal limits of composition using these tape splicing techniques where, at a typical tape speed of 38 cm/sec, a 1 cm fragment represented a time interval of less than 27 ms.

The analog signal generators of the 1950s let composers create for the first time sequences of impulses that could be transposed to different time scales by means of tape speed manipulations. Designed for test purposes, the analog signal generators were not meant to be varied in time but favored a timeless wave approach to sound. Their multiple rotary knobs and switches did not allow the user to switch instantly from one group of settings to another. Because of the weakness of their temporal controls, these devices imposed strict practical limits, which, with assistance and a great deal of labor, one could work. (The creation of Stockhausen's *Kontakte* comes to mind.)

By the 1970s, voltage-controlled analog synthesizers had become available, manufactured by Moog, Arp, Buchla, and other small companies. Analog synthesizers offered control through low-frequency oscillators, manual keyboards, and analog sequencers, but they could not provide for fine control at the micro time scale. Neither was analog tape an ideal medium for organizing microsonic compositions, owing to its inherent generation loss, linear access, and razor-blade splicing. It was only with the dawn of computer synthesis and digital audio techniques that a micro approach to sound could be explored in depth. (See chapter 2.)

Illusions of Continuity and Simultaneity

If events are absolutely smooth, without beginning or end, and even without modification or perceptible internal roughness, time would find itself abolished. It seems that the notions of separation,... of difference, of discontinuity, which are strongly interrelated, are prerequisites to the notion of anteriority. In order for anteriority to exist, it is necessary to be able to distinguish entities, which would then make it possible to "go" from one to the other.... Time, in a smooth continuum, is illegible. (Xenakis 1989)

Science has taken thousands of years to determine that the fine structure of matter, space, and even time, is discontinuous and quantified (Hawking and Penrose 1996). Human sensory organs set strict limits on our ability to perceive the discontinuity beneath the apparently hard surface of all phenomena.

Discontinuous variations on the micro time scale of music melt the frozen abstractions of traditional music theory such as pitch, instrumental timbre, and dynamic marking. Even such sacred notions as tone continuity and simultaneity reveal themselves to be illusions. The micro time scale defrosts these frozen categories into constantly evolving morphologies.

Continuity of tone is an auditory illusion. The mechanics of human hearing smear streams of discrete events into an illusion of continuum. (See the section on "Perception of Microsound" in chapter 1.) When we examine apparently continuous tones under a microscope, we see gaps scattered throughout, like the spaces between the threads of a blanket. These silent spaces—on the order of milliseconds—are not perceived as temporally discrete events but as fluctuations of a continuous tone. When two identical tones desynchronize on the same time scale we perceive only a "phase shifting" effect, if anything at all.

A related illusion in music is simultaneity. As Xenakis (1989) observed, a measurement as to whether two events occur simultaneously (or occupy the same spatial position) depends entirely on the scale of observation. A detailed analysis of onset times for supposedly simultaneous attacks in musical performance might reveal asynchronisms on the order of dozens of milliseconds.

A Multiscale Approach to Composition

A multiscale approach to composition allows for compositional intervention on every time scale. The power of this approach comes from the fact that different temporal zones interconnect. Operations on one time scale generate structures which may be perceived on other time scales. This suggests the possibility of working on the micro time scale in order to generate high-level musical structure. Iannis Xenakis predicted such an approach:

Suppose that each point of these [granular] clusters represents not only a pure frequency ... but an already present structure of elementary grains, ordered a priori. We believe that in this way a sonority of a second, third, or higher order can be produced. (Xenakis 1960)

Interaction between the microtemporal scale and higher time scales is especially intriguing. To cite a simple example; a gradual change in particle durations results in timbre variations on a higher time scale. Certain signals cross from one time scale to another, such as a descending glissando that crosses the infrasonic threshold, turning from tone to rhythm.

For some composers, part of the attraction of composing with microsound is the way it blurs the levels of musical structure:

The task of microcompositional strategies can be described as one of letting global morphological properties of musical structure emerge from the local conditions in the sonic matter. (Di Scipio 1994)

In an approach that favors "emergent properties" or second-order sonorities, sound objects emerge from a composer's manipulations of microstructural processes (Di Scipio 1997a). This is also known as a bottom-up compositional strategy, since the composition takes its shape from microsonic interactions. This stands in contrast to a top-down strategy in which a composer fills in a preplanned form (e.g., sonata).

The bottom-up strategy can be fascinating, partly because its results cannot always be predicted in advance. On the other hand, why limit the scope of compositional decisions to a single time scale? To navigate the widest possible zone of creativity, the creative composer wants to float freely across time scale boundaries. To insert, delete, rearrange, or mold sounds on any time scale, this is the multiscale approach to composition.

Differences Between Time Scales

In the 1950s, a few serial composers tried to invent a system of composition that could uniformly apply to any time scale. Their aim was for a kind of ideal logical coherence. This did not take into account the nonlinearities of musical perception. As chapter 2 indicates, a main lesson of Stockhausen's 1957 essay "How time passes" is precisely how awkward it can be to apply a proportional series developed for one time scale (e.g., pitch periods) to another time scale (e.g., note durations). (Specifically, it does not make much sense to transpose the intervallic relations of the chromatic scale into the domain of note durations). Little music corresponds to a geometrically pure and symmetric hierarchical model. As Vaggione has stated:

The world is not self-similar. . . . Coincidences of scale are infrequent, and when one thinks that one has found one, it is generally a kind of reduction, a willful construction. The ferns imitated by fractal geometry do not constitute real models of ferns. In a real fern there are infinitely more accidents, irregularities and formal caprices—in a word—singularities— than the ossification furnished by the fractal model.   (Vaggione 1996a)

Strictly hierarchical and symmetrical note relations are not necessarily perceived as such (Vaggione 1998). Gyorgy Ligeti (1971) pointed out the difficulty of organizing all time scales according to a unitary scheme, owing to a lack of correlation with human perception. The musicologist Carl Dahlhaus (1970) adopted a similar tack in his critique of serial pitch rule applied to the organization of microstructure.

Sound phenomena on one time scale may travel by transposition to another time scale, but the voyage is not linear. Pertinent characteristics may or may not be maintained. In other words, the perceptual properties of a given time scale are not necessarily invariant across dilations and contractions. A melody loses all sense of pitch, for example, when sped up or slowed down to extremes. This inconsistency, of course, does not prevent us from applying such transpositions. It merely means that we must recognize that each time scale abides by its own rules. A perfect hierarchy is a weak model for composition.

Density, Opacity, Transparency

The expansion of sonic possibilities adds new terms to the vocabulary of music. We can now shape sonic matter in terms of its particle density and opacity. Particle density has become a prime compositional parameter. Physics defines density as the ratio of mass to volume. In music this translates to the ratio of sound to silence. Through manipulations of density, processes such as coalescence (cloud formation), and evaporation (cloud disintegration) can occur in sonic form. Opacity correlates to density. If the density of microsonic events is sufficient, the temporal dimension appears to cohere, and one perceives a continuous texture on the sound object level. Thus by controlling the density and size of sound particles we have a handle on the quality of sonic opacity. Co-alescence takes place when particle density increases to the point that tone

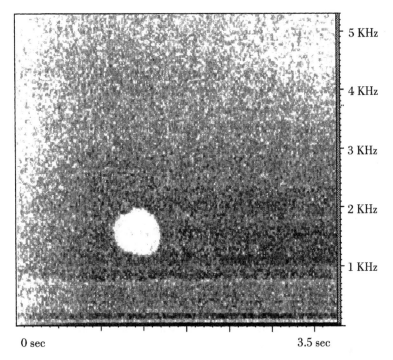

5 KHz

4 KHz

3 KHz

2 KHz

1 KHz

0 sec   3.5 sec

Figure 8.1 A hole in a broadband sound, sculpted by a sonogram filter. We can carve time-frequency gaps on different time scales.

continuity takes hold. An opaque sound tends to block out other sounds that cross into its time-frequency zone.

Going in the opposite direction, we can cause a sound to evaporate by reducing its particle density. A sparse sound cloud is transparent, since we can easily hear other sounds through it. A diaphanous cloud only partially obscures other sounds, perhaps only in certain spectral regions. For example, by means of sonogram filtering we can create transparent holes in the spectrum of a sound (figure 8.1) which might provide a window onto another layer of sound beneath.

Stationary, Stochastic, and Intermittent Textures

Many complex musical textures resemble what statistics calls *stationary processes*. A stationary process exhibits no trend. The texture has a fixed mean value and fluctuates around the mean with a constant variance. A stationary process is not necessarily static in time, but its variations remain within certain limits, and are therefore predictable. We see these characteristics in many sound-mass textures created with particle synthesis. Consider a dense cloud of grains scattered over a broad zone of frequencies. It scintillates while never evolving, and is therefore a stationary texture.

Stationary textures are fertile material for composition. One can place them at low amplitude in the background layer, where they lend depth to the musical landscape. Positioned in the foreground, their constant presence introduces dramatic tension and sets up an expectation of change. The ear notices any change as a deviation from the stationary.

Changes in texture appear as slow trends or sudden intermittencies. To impose a trend is to gradually change the texture. This may take place over time periods associated with the meso time scale (i.e., many seconds). A trend converts a stationary texture into a *weighted stochastic texture*. One can introduce a trend by opening or closing the bandwidth of a cloud, by altering its center frequency, by filtering, or by any other perceptible time-varying operation.

Sudden changes create intermittent texture. The intermittencies break up the stationary texture by injecting loud particles or silent micro-intervals. This latter technique—composing with silence—remains largely unexplored, but can be effective. The idea is to begin with a multichannel stationary texture and introduce silent intervals into it, working like a sculptor, carving rhythmic and spatial patterns by subtraction.

Composition Processes on the Microsonic Level

Interactive digital sound editing originated in the 1970s (Moorer 1977a, 1977b), but did not become widely available until the 1990s. It seems so taken for granted today, I am not sure that musicians recognize its profound impact on the art of electronic music composition. The possibility of editing sound on any time scale has opened up a vast range of transformations. For example, through selective gain adjustment it is possible to magnify a tiny subaudio fluctuation into an intense microsonic event (see the description of transient drawing, chapter 4). We can shape the event through microsurgery or filtering on a micro time scale (chapter 5). By replicating the event on the micro time scale, it can be transformed into a pitched sound object (see the description of particle cloning synthesis in chapter 4). Through time-stretching it can be magnified into a long, slowly unfolding texture (pitch-time changing chapter 5, and sound transformation with the phase vocoder, chapter 6). Then through granulation we can decompose it once again into small particles, "from dust to dust" (granulation, chapter 5).

Such manipulations open up a catalog of new compositional processes:

- Variations (contrasts, increases, and decreases) of particle density
- Coalescence (cloud formation) and evaporation (cloud disintegration)
- Time stretching to extend a microstructure into a large-scale event
- Time shrinking large events into microsounds
- Hierarchical variations of the same event structure on multiple time scales
- Lamination of a cloud through multiple layers with microtemporal delays
- Particle spatialization (scattering particles in space)
- Granular reverberation
- Precise polymetric pulsations in space, created by superimposing multiple metrical streams
- Multiple formant streams, each with its own frequency and spatial trajectory
- Spectrum evolution via manipulation of particle envelopes
- Microsurgery on the Gabor matrix to extract the chaotic, harmonic, loudest, softest, or other selected particles within a sound and reassemble it with alterations

Such operations change the practice of composition, and mandate a rethinking of compositional strategy and architecture. This cultural process has only just begun.

Heterogenity and Uniqueness of Sound Materials

In the 1950s, certain composers began to turn their attention toward the composition of sound material itself. In effect, they extended what had always been true at the phrase level down to the sound object level. Just as every phrase and macro form can be unique, each sound event can have an individual morphology. This creates a greater degree of diversity—of heterogeneity in sound material—without necessarily losing continuity to other objects. Chapter 3 showed how we can extend the concept of heterogeneity even further, down to the level of microsound, where each sound particle may be unique. The microstructure of any sound can be decomposed and rearranged, turning it into a unique sound object.

Simultaneous with this shift in musical thinking, certain researchers have shifted their focus from the analysis of periodicities to the analysis of singularities (Arneodo et al. 1995). They have turned from the analysis of continuous signals to the analysis of intermittencies, that is, from stationary and homogeneous emissions to nonstationary and nonhomogeneous distributions of energy.

The variety of sound opened up by electronic music comes at a high price: the loss of note homogeneity and with it, the foundation of traditional abstract musical language. To adopt the universe of heterogeneous sound objects is to be cast into a strange new land without conventional language. The terrain of this land is nonhomogeneous, pocked by fractured disjunctions (intermittencies) and nonlinear transitions from one perceived state to another. A simple linear change may trigger such a percept, such as a pulse train whose frequency is smoothly increasing from 5 to 50 Hz. In the midst of this change, listeners perceive a series of rhythmic pulsations passing through an ambiguous zone between rhythm and pitch into a continuous tone. An asynchronous cloud of grains cross the threshold (from discontinuity to continuity) as the density increases from five to one hundred grains per second. Many other examples of nonlinear thresholds could be cited.

Aesthetic Oppositions

It seems inevitable that we seek to define and understand phenomena by positing their opposite. High cannot be understood without the concept of low, and so with near and far, big and small, etc. A given aesthetic tendency can be seen as confronting its opposite. The question is whether such a simplification can lead to a clarification. This section explores certain aesthetic oppositions raised in composing with microsound.

Formalism versus Intuitionism

In composing with microsound, we face an ancient conflict: formalism versus intuitionism. Formal models of process are natural to musical thinking. As we listen, part of us drinks in the sensual experience of sound, while another part is setting up expectations—hypotheses of musical process. To the envy of the other arts, notation and logical planning have been part of music-making for centuries. As Schillinger (1946) demonstrated, we can make a music generator out of virtually any mathematical formula. Lejaren Hiller's pioneering experiments with automated composition in the 1950s proved that the computer could model arbitrary formal procedures (Hiller and Isaacson 1959). Computer programs sped up the time-consuming labor associated with systematic composition. This led to a surge of interest in applying mathematical procedures to composition (Hiller 1970).

Since the start of music notation, it has been possible to manipulate musical materials as symbols on paper, separated from the production of sound in time. Herein lies a fundamental dichotomy. Because formal symbols can be organized abstractly, such manipulations have been closely identified with the organization of sound material. Music, however, is more than an abstract formal discipline. It must eventually be rendered into sound and heard by human beings. Thus it remains rooted in acoustical physics, auditory perception, and psychology.

One cannot escape formal control when working with a computer. Every gesture translates into an intervention with a formal system. This system is encoded in the logic of a programming language and is executed according to the algebra of the machine hardware. The question is at what level of musical structure do such formalisms operate? The pianist practicing on a digital piano is interacting with a computer music system. She is not concerned that her performance is triggering a flurry of memory accesses and data transfers. The familiarity of the keyboard and the sampled piano sounds makes the interaction seem direct and natural. This is a great illusion, however. With a change of formal logic, the same equipment that produces the piano tones could just as well synthesize granular clouds, as we saw with the Creatovox (chapter 5).

Applied at different strata of compositional organization, formal algorithms can be a powerful means of invention. An algorithm for spawning sound particles can handle enormous detail in a fraction of a second. Other algorithms can iterate through a collection of variations quickly, offering the composer a wide range of selections from which to choose. Interactive performance systems try to balance preprogrammed automation with spontaneous decisions.

While formal algorithms enable interaction with a machine, formalism in composition means imposing constraints on one's self. The formalist composer follows a logical system from beginning to end. This logic exists only in an ideal conceptual plan. The plan must ultimately be translated into the real world of acoustics, psychoacoustics, and emotional response. It is in this translation that the game is often lost.

Coherence versus Invention

Coherence must bear some relation to the listener's subconscious perspective. But is this its only function? Has it not another of bringing outer or new things into wider coherence? (Ives 1962)

In academic theory, formal coherence is one of the most vaunted characteristics of musical composition. In general, coherence signifies "logical integration and consistency." This quality is not always easy to measure in practice. In its most obvious form, coherence manifests itself as a limitation in the choice of compositional materials and a consistency in the operations applied to those materials.

One can easily place the organization of microsound under the regime of a formal system. In this case, the operations that produce the composition ensure that it always remains within the boundaries of the formal rules. Such an approach makes for a tidy package, free from anomalies and logical inconsistencies. The compositions it produces can be proven to be "coherent" in a formal sense, even if they are dull or incomprehensible.

The problem here, as we have stated before, is that music is not a purely logical system. Rigor is not synonymous with perceived musical coherence. Music is rooted in acoustics, auditory perception, and psychology. Musical coherence seems to be a poorly understood psychological category. It is one of those ubiquitous terms in aesthetic discourse that everyone uses subjectively and no one has ever studied from a scientific viewpoint.

As Horacio Vaggione (1997) observed, by convention, a "rule" must necessarily be followed many times. But the artist can invoke a rule only once! Thus we might focus our attention on other criteria in the way that we compose with microsound. Inventiveness, I would suggest, is at least as important as coherence.

Spontaneity versus Reflection

We find in electronic music new examples of a venerable opposition in music-making, pitting the immediate spontaneity of improvisation in performance against the careful, reflective process of studio-based composition. This confrontation is particularly sharp in the case of real-time systems that spawn a constant swarm of sound particles. To control this flow in such a way as to make interesting musical gestures is not easy. The musician's interface can either help or hinder this process.

Barry Truax's granular synthesis programs GSX and GSAMX (Truax 1988) incorporated several types of controls:

low-level grain parameters—center frequency, frequency range, average duration, duration range, delay (density)

presets—groups of stored grain parameter settings

ramps—patterns of change in grain parameters, stored in a ramp file

tendency masks—graphic control shapes that are translated into ramps and presets, stored in a tendency mask file

The composer could override any of these stored parameters in performance, intermingling planned functions with spontaneous gestures.

Our Creatovox instrument (chapter 5) takes another approach to the problem of particle synthesis in real time. Designed as a solo instrument for virtuoso performance, it is played using a traditional keyboard, with additional joystick, fader, and foot pedal controllers. In the Creatovox, each keystroke spawns a cloud of grains, whose parameters can be varied with the real-time controllers.

PulsarGenerator (chapter 4) was not intended for the concert-hall, although we anticipated that it would be used in this way, because it could be operated in real time. We wanted a program which would allow improvisation as a fast way to explore the wide range of pulsar textures, but which also allowed for careful planning through control by envelopes and stored presets.

Despite the attractions of real-time music-making, the studio environment is the ultimate choice for the musician who seeks the maximum in creative freedom:

- The possibility of editing allows any previous decision to be revised or retracted in the light of reflection.

- Rehearsal of all gestures permits refinement.

- In contrast to real-time improvisation, where the focus tends to be local in scope, studio decision-making can take into account the entire range of time scales.

- An arbitrary number of independent musical threads can be superimposed carefully via mixing.

- The sound structure can be monitored and manipulated on a particle-by-particle basis, which is impossible in real time.

A potential hazard in studio work is over-production. An over-elaborate montage may result in a stilted and contrived product.

Intervals versus Morphologies

Atomism compels us to give up the idea of sharply and statically defining bounding surfaces of solid bodies. (Einstein 1952)

Linked to a wave-oriented view of sound is a classical aesthetic—dating back to the Greeks—that assigns great value to works of art that conform to certain numerical proportions and intervals. This aesthetic imprints itself throughout the history of music, particularly in the domain of pitch relations. It is also implicit in the treatment of metrical rhythms, with its scale of durational values based on duple and triple divisions of the beat.

Intertwined with intervallic thought is the notion of scales. As Karlheinz Stockhausen indicated (1957, 1962), any continuous musical parameter (spatial position, filter setting, etc.) can be subdivided into an arbitrary scale and then manipulated in terms of intervallic relations. The twentieth century saw the introduction of serial, spectral, and minimalist aesthetic theories, all of which were intervallic. The main differences between them concern which intervals and which scales are most important.

Acoustic and perceptual reality stand in contrast to the simplications of intervallic thought. The momentary frequency of most acoustic instruments is constantly changing. Noise is ubiquitous. Difference thresholds limit all aspects of perception. Masking and other nonlinear effects complicate perception. Training and mood strongly influence musical hearing.

To think in terms of microsonic materials and procedures is to shift the aesthetic focus away from sharply defined intervals toward curvilinear and fuzzy morphologies. Just as it has become possible to sculpt habitats from fiberglass foam, the flowing structures that we can create with microsound do not necessarily resemble the usual angular forms of musical architecture. On the contrary, they tend toward droplike, liquid, or cloudlike structures.

Sound particles dissolve the solid notes into more supple materials which cannot always be measured in terms of definite intervals. As a result, sound objects may have "fuzzy edges," that is, ambiguous pitch and indefinite starting and ending times (owing to evaporation, coalescence, and mutation). Microvariations melt the frozen abstractions of traditional music theory such as continuous tone, pitch, instrumental timbre, and dynamic marking, reducing them to a constantly evolving stream of particle morphologies. Intervals may emerge, but they are not an indispensable grid, there is instead an interplay between intervallic and nonintervallic material.

Within these flowing structures, the quality of particle density—which determines the transparency of the material—takes on prime importance. An increase in density induces fusion. It lifts a cloud into the foreground, while a decrease in density causes evaporation, dissolving a continuous sound band into a pointillist rhythm or vaporous background texture. Keeping density constant, a change in the characteristics of the particles themselves induces mutation, an open-ended transformation.

Smoothness versus Roughness

The shapes of classical geometry are lines and planes, circles and spheres, triangles and cones. They inspired a powerful philosophy of Platonic harmony.... [But] clouds are not spheres.... Mountains are not cones. Lightning does not travel in a straight line. The new geometry models a universe that is rough, not rounded, scabrous, not smooth. It is the geometry of the pitted, pocked, and broken up, the twisted, tangled, and intertwined.... The pits and tangles are more than blemishes distorting the classical shapes of Euclidean geometry. They are often the keys to the essence of the thing. (Gleick 1988)

Microsonic synthesis techniques contain a dual potential. On the one hand, they can create smooth and pitch-stable continua, characteristic of the formants of the voice and resonant instruments. On the other hand they can create intermittent particles and nonstationary textures, which in the extreme tend toward chaotic noise bands.

The determinants of pitched continua are stable waveforms, round envelopes, and long particle durations. In contrast, the determinants of noisy signals are irregular waveforms, jagged envelopes, and brief particle durations. The opposition between smooth and rough textures can serve as an element of tension in composition, akin to the tension between *consonance* and *dissonance*, with transitions between these two extremes acting as a bridge.

Attraction versus Repulsion in the Time-Domain

Astronomers from the Paris Observatory have detected the densest mass of galaxies that is visible in the southern hemisphere, which may constitute the central element of the Great Attractor. Predicted in 1987, the Great Attractor would be an enormous concentration of galaxies that attracts other galaxies in its environment—including our own—at speeds on the order of 500 to 600 km per second. (Associated Press France 1997)

The universal principle of attraction and repulsion governed the primal cosmological explosion of the Big Bang as well as the inner structure of atomic particles. It manifests itself in physical biology as the experience of pleasure and pain, and in the psychological experience of love and hate, of lust and disgust. It rules over individual human relationships as much as relationships between tribes and cultures.

The principle of attraction and repulsion also plays a role in music. For example, Igor Stravinsky used attraction as a means of organizing the time structure of a composition:

Composing leads to a search for the ... center upon which the series of sounds ... should converge. Thus if a center is given, I shall have to find a combination that converges on it. If, on the other hand, an as yet unoriented combination has been found, I shall have to find a center towards which it will lead. (Stravinsky 1947)

Edgard Varèse thought that it might be possible to adapt the principle of repulsion as an organizing principle:

When new instruments will allow me to write music as I conceive it, taking the place of the linear counterpoint, the movement of sound-masses, or shifting planes, will be clearly perceived. When these sound-masses collide, the phenomena of penetration or repulsion will seem to occur. (Varèse 1971)

Temporal attraction takes three forms: *attraction to a point*, *attraction to a pattern*, and *attraction to a meter*.

Attraction to a point refers to when numerous particles gravitate toward a specific time point, and the clustering results in a climactic explosion. Its conceptual opposite is emptiness or silence, or the repulsion of sound objects away from a central point. I have applied these concepts in my piece *Clang-tint*, where points of attraction control the density of sonic events (see chapter 7).

Attraction to a pattern refers to a strong tendency toward reoccurrence of a given rhythmic motive. The isorhythms of ancient music exemplify this phenomenon. Repulsion from a pattern refers to the absence or avoidance of regularity in motivic figuration.

Attraction to a meter means alignment to a regular pulsation. A strong metric beat attracts a metric response. It is easy to synchronize multiple layers on top of a regular pulse. The opposite of metric attraction is metric repulsion, found in the rich realm of ametric (or aleatoric) rhythms. It is difficult to overdub synchronously on top of an ametric rhythm. An ametric rhythm is not the same as syncopation; syncopation reinforces meter by emphasizing various of its subdivisions.

Parameter Variation versus Strategy Variation

In electronic music, every technique of synthesis is controlled by a number of parameters. This invites a process of composition based on parameter variation. Consider the technique of frequency modulation synthesis (Chowning 1973). The timbre of many computer music pieces of the 1970s and 1980s relied on variations of essentially two parameters: the index of modulation and the carrier-to-modulator ratio. In granular synthesis, variations in grain spacing and grain density lead to time-stretching and time-shrinking effects, while variations in grain duration lead to spectrum transformations. A prime example of parameter variation is Barry Truax's composition *The Wings of Nike* (*Perspectives of New Music* 28 compact disc, 1990). Here two phonemes, each about 170 milliseconds in length, iterate over a 12-minute composition, a repetition-expansion by a factor of four thousand.

As a compositional strategy employed to the exclusion of others, parameter variation reflects an obsession with consistency. It can take the form of a preoccupation with deriving every sound from the previous one, or from a source sample. If this is carried out only through variation of a single algorithm, it may lead to a monochromatic timbral palette. It may also result in a restricted range of gestures, since no morphological developments can occur that are not derived from parameter variation.

Alternatively, the compositional strategy can itself be the subject of variations. Even a simple change, such as switching to a different synthesis technique, alters the parameters. Another strategic change is a step up or down to a different level of structure. Juxtaposition refreshes the brain, breaking the cycle of closed permutations and combinations.

Simplicity versus Complexity in Microsound Synthesis

The synthesis instruments presented in chapters 3 and 4 are simple in structure, reflecting my own approach to the synthesis of microsound. Certain basic sounds, like the magical sine wave, can be made expressive with only a touch of vibrato and tremolo, and perhaps a dash of reverberated ambiance. Most other interesting sounds, however, are more complicated in their time-varying behavior.

From the standpoint of the composer who is also a programmer, the question is whether to embed such complex behavior within a synthesis instrument, or whether to separate the behavior from the instrument. My tendency is towards the latter. Rather than designing a latter-day Wurlitzer organ controlled by dozens of parameters, I prefer to build a library of small distinct instruments, each with its own articulators and modes of performance. In this approach, the score serves as the primary point of control. Therefore, the score is the source of synthesis complexity. As in the traditional practice of orchestration, it is by selecting and combining different instruments that one achieves a broad palette of timbral colors. The score interweaves these colors in detail. In electronic music, of course, the score does not necessarily take the form of a five-line staff. It can be a collection of sound events and envelopes, as in the note lists of the Music *N* languages, or the graphical regions of a sound mixing program (e.g., Digidesign's Pro Tools).

When particles assemble into sound objects, it is their combination *en masse* that forms the morphology of the sound. By controlling this combination from a high level, we shape the sound's evolution. High-level controls imply the existence of algorithms that can interpret a composer's directives, translating them into, potentially, thousands of particle specifications. An early example of such an algorithm is my 1975 grain generator program PLFKLANG, described in chapter 7. This trend is now re-emerging in the form of high-level generators of microsonic behavior. A recent example is the program Cmask (Bartetzki 1997a, 1997b). This is a stochastic event generator which works in conjunction with the Csound synthesis language. The program reads a composer-specified parameter file and generates a score file that Csound can immediately read. For every parameter of an event, Cmask selects a random value from a time-varying tendency mask. CMask also provides other methods of parameter generation, including cyclic lists, oscillators, polygons, and random walks. A different method may generate each parameter of an event.

James McCartney's SuperCollider language provides another set of high-level event generators, called Spawn, Tspawn, OverlapTexture, and XFade-Texture which generate a variety of behaviors that can be edited and adjusted by the user. For example, OverlapTexture creates a series of overlapped sounds, where the sounds are generated by a user supplied synthesis instrument. By adjusting the parameters of the OverlapTexture, and randomizing some of them within specific limits, one can create a wide variety of ambient textures.

To conclude, a synthesis technique is a means to an end. In my work, synthesis is the starting point for sound design, which is itself only the beginning of composition. I inevitably edit (cut and paste) and alter raw sound material with a variety of transformations. This editing involves trial-and-error testing and refinement. Because of this, it would be impossible to bundle into a synthesis algorithm.

Code versus Grammar

If played and heard often enough, every musical gesture is prone to be interpreted by musicians and listeners, as a gesture of musical speech. As the gesture becomes familiar, and thus recognized by society, the composed structure, in which the context generates the meaning of its components, will be misunderstood, instead, as one in which the components give meaning to their context. (Brün 1983)

Traditional western music is characterized by a familiar—yet fundamentally incomplete and ambiguous—musical grammar. This grammar describes the materials employed in pieces (pitches and timbres) as well as many aspects of their organization. In contrast, in new music, particularly pieces that employ microsonic synthesis, the audience does not necessarily know the grammar in advance. Here, it is the task of each new piece to establish its own code, with perhaps only a few symbols inherited from the past. The term "code" distinguishes the provisional nature of the communication protocol, as opposed to a more established language with its grammar.

When we can recognize a familiar unit of musical structure, we might say that it is a cliché. The popular understanding of "cliché" is that it is equivalent to "overly familiar." Yet frequency of exposure seems to have little to do with the issue; lovers of Mozart never tire of their hero's recognizable sound. Cliché is a pejorative in colloquial English, where it is a synonym for "hackneyed." Its meaning is more neutral in its original French, where it may also refer to a template—an original from which many instances can be derived.

The danger of clichés, in the narrow, popular sense, is omnipresent. The naive presentation of trite formulas (as if they retained any freshness) creates a negative impression. The definition of what is fresh and what is trite is subjective, however, and varies with fickle artistic fashion. Music history shows a constant struggle between progressive and reactionary trends, in which the ascendence of each alternates every few years. As progressive movements stop evolving, they become reactionary, while trends that formerly seemed hackneyed, seem suddenly fresh or even daring in comparison. (A classic example is the rise of simple tonal music in the 1970s and 1980s after the peak of serialism.)

In artificial intelligence research, the term "cliché" has been used with another meaning, and it is this sense that I would like to emphasize here. In this context, a cliché is a unit of knowledge that corresponds to a formal structure such as a *semantic network* (Winston 1984). Semantic networks offer a formal structure for capturing the essential properties of a known class of objects or situations, enabling programs to recognize instances of them. If, for example, we define a table as an object with a flat surface supported by one or more legs, a program should be able to classify all such objects, in many shapes and sizes, as instances of a single cliché. David Cope (1996) uses the term "signature" in a manner similar to my use of "cliché."

The notion of cliché or signature in music refers to memorable units of musical structure, and implies a process of recognition on the part of the listener. It is important that the cliché be memorable. Given enough of the cliché we can "fill in the blanks" and substitute missing pieces. As with the table example, we can spot a cliché in many guises.

Naturally, to spot a musical cliché requires sensitivity and erudition. Neophytes cannot spot clichés as readily as experts and some clichés are stronger or easier to recognize than others. But the ability to recall entire pieces of music from fragments of as few as two or three notes—more or less instantaneously—reminds us of how human perception is attuned to cliché (Buser and Imbert 1992). Perhaps the notion of cliché can be applied in a practical agenda to make computers more musically intelligent.

Through the accumulation of clichés over time, understandable codes inevitably emerge from the magma of artistic creation. Strange musical landscapes become more familiar. The vintage sonorities of early electronic music, for example, are no longer novel. The basic textures of granular synthesis are becoming familiar. The practice of composition with microsound must eventually shift from the creation of novel sonic effects to the construction of compelling new musical architectures.

Sensation versus Communication

Within a fraction of a second after the eyes, nose, ears, tongue or skin is stimulated, one knows the object is familiar and whether it is desirable or dangerous. How does such recognition, which psychologists call preattentive perception, happen so accurately and quickly, even when the stimuli are complex and the context in which they arise varies? (Freeman 1991)

Sound waves speak directly to our senses. They can be likened to the immediate perception of touch, if touch could penetrate to the inner ear. The experience of music is a cognitive reaction to a perceptual reaction. It reaches directly toward emotions and associations. Intellectualization is a side effect.

Traditional musical languages abide by familiar grammars. This familiarity acts as a framework for setting up small surprises. In creative electronic music, which attempts to extend musical expression itself, the goal is often the opposite. Since so much is new, little is expected. The surprise comes in finding familiarity.

In this music, the role of the composer is to create a pattern of acoustic sensations in the form of a code that organizes them into a meaningful structure. (I will not attempt to define "meaningful" here.) The intellectual challenges and emotions experienced by the composer in creating this structure may be very profound and intense (or not). In any case, they are independent of those experienced by the listener. The composer cannot hope to account for the mindset carried into the concert hall by the listener. Acoustic sensations are inevitably filtered by the listener through the extremely narrow sieve of subjective mood and personality. These interpretations trigger a reverberant halo of emotions and reflections unique to each person.

The ideal of musical communication would imply a direct transmission of emotional and intellectual experience from composer to listener. This is probably quite rare. Is direct transmission the point? The point seems to be to stimulate the listener with organized sensations. The composer takes the listener on a fantastic voyage. Let each person make up their own mind about what they experience.

Summary

Every work of art aims at showing us life and things as they are in truth, but cannot be directly discerned by everyone through the mist of subjective and objective contingencies. Art takes away the mist. (Schopenhauer 1819)

Art, and above all, music, has a fundamental function ... It must aim ... toward a total exaltation in which the individual mingles, losing consciousness in a truth immediate, rare, enormous, and perfect. If a work of art succeeds in this undertaking, even for a single moment, it attains its goal. (Xenakis 1992)

Art music is designed according to an aesthetic vision. It is formed by a blend of pure sensation and logical organization. The joy of composition derives from the free interplay between goal-driven intellectual and emotionally driven intuitive modes of working. The act of composition cannot avoid expressing philosophical attitudes, even if these are vague (ambiguous) or even contradictory (ironic).

In recent years, the concept of microsound has taken root in the musical world. Readily available software generates and manipulates microsound. This in turn has sparked a great deal of experimentation on the part of musicians. Judging by the number of compositions that have appeared employing granular techniques, one could say that these methods have enjoyed a certain vogue. Is a fascination with the microsonic domain a passing fancy? For some musicians, this is probably the case. Yet as a resource for expressive sounds, the mine of microsound is far from exhausted.

Certain timbres produced by granular synthesis have a recognizable signature. These familiar textures can function as memorable units of musical structure. The manipulation of recognizable elements or clichés is an integral part of composition. Musical material is never entirely new at every level of musical structure. Even the most advanced realms of musical expression eventually accumulate a storehouse of clichés, and this accumulation is a natural historical process of music. It is akin to Herbert Brün's concept of "decay of information," in which familiarity leads to increased legibility at the expense of freshness (Hamlin and Roads 1985). Although Brün warned that "understanding, familiarity, and communicativity" are not necessarily positive aspects, the composer of electronic art music remains in no immediate danger of being smothered by the hazards of social success.

9 Conclusion

More than a half century ago, Gabor observed:

Any signal can be expanded in terms of [elementary acoustical quanta] by a process which includes time analysis and Fourier analysis as extreme cases. (Gabor 1946)

In other words, any sound can be decomposed into constituent particles. Operations on the Gabor matrix let us transform the particles to create striking variations of a given sound. Alternatively, one can synthesize entirely new sounds directly from novel arrangements of elementary particles.

A goal of technology is increased precision and ever-finer control. To make the Hollerith tabulating machine at the turn of the last century, machinists had to manufacture parts to the precision of a millimeter. Semiconductor manufacturers now etch microprocessor features down to less than 0.1 of a micron. The trend toward precision is also reflected in our sound tools, which have passed from wave-oriented to particle-oriented operation, even as the sample grid has shrunk to just over 5 μsec (at a 192 kHz sampling rate).

This book has presented the argument for microsound as a fertile resource in composition. By now, hundreds of compositions employ granular synthesis and other particle techniques. The raw material of this music consists of grains and globules scattered in sonically transparent, diaphanous, or opaque textures. These textures can be molded, stretched, and combined with others into supple morphologies. By means of these materials, musical development can take place not only in the large intervals of pitch and rhythm, but also in micro-variations of amplitude, duration, timbre, density, and spatial position.

Perhaps more important than the particles themselves are the sonic brushes we use to paint them on the canvas of time and frequency. These brushes are computer programs. By connecting these programs with interactive real-time controllers, we have built particle synthesis instruments for virtuoso performance, not only for onstage, but also for studio use.

In computer graphics, three-dimensional animation programs incorporate sophisticated algorithms for scattering particles. These emulate physical models of flow, perturbation, and collision. In the domain of sound, we can also apply physical models to regulate the flow of particles. But we should not be limited to emulations of reality. As stated at the beginning of the book, the computer's artistic power derives from its ability to model fantasies as well as reality.

Creating sonic fantasies begins with recording, letting us "photograph" real sounds and store their images on tape. The techniques of montage—cutting, splicing, and mixing—are essentially manipulations of time structure. As a pioneer in electronic composition once observed:

If there is one dimension of the music totality, one component which originally led composers to the electronic medium, it was and is the temporal domain.... Those who originally turned to electronic tape were obviously attracted to the element of control. After all, the tape was not a source of sound. Tape is for storage. You can, however, control time as a measurable distance of tape. Here we are talking about rhythm in every sense of the word. Not only durational rhythm, but also the time rate of changes of register, of timbre, of volume, and of those many musical dimensions that were unforeseen until we tried to find out how we heard and how we could structure the temporal. (Babbitt 1988)

Discs and semiconductors have largely superseded tape. Mixing and editing software has replaced the splicing block. A fundamental capability of this software is the zooming in and out on multiple time scales. These tools let us work at the limits of auditory phenomena, from microsurgery on individual sample points, to the global rearrangement of sound masses. In the intermediate time scales, we can edit each sound until it has exactly the right duration, density, spectral weight, amplitude envelope, and spatial profile. The timing·of each transition can be adjusted precisely.

Much work remains in rethinking existing signal processing paradigms to take into account the micro time domain. The question is how can researchers integrate windowing, scattering, and density manipulations with other signal processing operations on multiple time scales?

Microacoustic phenomena are still not fully understood. Likewise, in science, the study of granular processes has emerged as a distinct scientific discipline, with a focus on the interaction of granular streams confronted by external forces and objects (Behringer and Harmann 1998). At the same time, we see an emerging science of disordered systems, phase transitions, intermittencies, and particle simulations. These too may serve as fertile analogies for musical processes.

Guidebooks to the sonic territories, including the present one, are incomplete. Few maps exist, and shortcuts are scarce. So we base our composition strategy on a heuristic search for remarkable sound objects, mesostructures, and transformations. It is the job of each composer to discover the interrelations between operations on the micro time scale and their perceptual effects at other time scales.

Listeners are increasingly open to the beauties found in complex transient elements, particularly when they appear in lush combination textures. The acceptance of microsounds also reflects an increasing sophistication in their deployment. When a synthesis technique is first invented, it is not evident how to best compose with it—every new instrument requires practice. Much experience has been gained with microsound, and every composer who touches this resource brings new insights to the puzzle.

Gradually this strange terrain will become familiar as the storehouse of signature gestures accumulates. The understanding shared by only a small circle of composers today will grow more widespread. We need not concern ourselves as to whether electronic music will evolve into a language as formal as common-practice harmony (which is not totally formalized), rather, it is our destiny to enjoy our newfound land, to invent materials and codes, and to revel in creative freedom.

References

Allen, J. B., and L. R. Rabiner. 1977. "A unified approach to short-time Fourier analysis and synthesis." *Proceedings of the IEEE* 65: 1558–1564.

American Technology Corporation. 1998. "HyperSonic sound." Internet: www.atcsd.com.

Apel, K. 1972. *Harvard Dictionary of Music.* Cambridge, Massachusetts: Harvard University Press.

Arfib, D. 1990. "In the intimacy of a sound." In S. Arnold and G. Hair, eds. *Proceedings of the 1990 International Computer Music Conference.* pp. 43–45.

Arfib, D. 1991. "Analysis, transformation, and resynthesis of musical sounds with the help of a time-frequency representation." In G. De Poli, A. Piccialli, and C. Roads, eds. 1991. *Representations of Musical Signals.* Cambridge, Massachusetts: MIT Press. pp. 87–118.

Arfib, D. 1998. "Different ways to write digital audio effects programs." In B. Garau and R. Loureiro, eds. *Proceedings 98 Digital Audio Effects Workshop.* Barcelona: Pompeu Fabra University. pp. 188–191.

Arfib, D., and N. Delprat. 1992. "Sound Mutations, a program to transform musical sounds." In A. Strange, ed. *Proceedings of the 1992 International Computer Music Conference.* San Francisco: International Computer Music Association. pp. 442–3.

Arfib, D., and N. Delprat. 1993. "Musical transformations through modifications of time-frequency images." *Computer Music Journal* 17(2): 66–72.

Arfib, D., and N. Delprat. 1998. "Selective transformation using a time-frequency representation: an application to the vibrato modification." Preprint 4652 (P5–S2). Presented at the 104th Convention. New York: Audio Engineering Society.

Arfib, D., J. Dudon, and P. Sanchez. 1996. "WaveLoom, logiciel d'aide à la création de disques photosoniques." Internet: www.ircam.fr/equipes/repmus/jim96/actes/arfib/waveloom.html.

Arkani-Hamed, N., S. Dimopoulos, and G. Dvali. 2000. "The universe's unseen dimensions." *Scientific American* 283(2): 62–69.

Arneodo, A., F. Argoul, E., J. Elezgaray, and J.-F. Muzy. 1995. *Ondelettes, multifractales, et turbulences.* Paris: Diderot Editeur.

Babbitt, M. 1962. "Twelve-tone rhythmic structure and the electronic medium." *Perspectives of New Music* 1(1). Reprinted in B. Boretz and E. Cone, eds. 1972. *Perspectives on Centemporary Music Theory.* New York: W. W. Norton. pp. 148–179.

Babbitt, M. 1988. "Composition in the electronic medium." In F. Roehmann and F. Wilson, eds. 1988. *The Biology of Music-making.* Saint Louis: MMB Music. pp. 208–213.

Backhaus, J. 1932. "Über die Bedeutung der Ausgleichsvorgänge in der Akustik." *Zeitschrift für technische Physik* 13(1): 31–46.

Backus, J. 1962. "*die Reihe:* a scientific evaluation." *Perspectives of New Music* 1(1): 160.

Backus, J. 1969. *The Acoustical Foundations of Music.* New York: Norton.

Bacry, A., A. Grossman, and J. Zak. 1975. "Proof of the completeness of the lattice states in the *kq* representation." *Physical Review* B12: 1118.

Barlow, C. 1997. "On the spectral analysis of speech for subsequent resynthesis by acoustic instruments." In F. Barrière and G. Bennett, eds. *Analyse en Musique Electroacoustique.* Bourges: Éditions Mnemosyne. pp. 276–283.

Barnwell, T., and C. Richardson. 1995. "The discrete-time wavelet transformation and audio coding." Preprint 4047 (A-2). Presented at the 99th Convention of the Audio Engineering Society. New York: Audio Engineering Society.

Barrett, N. 1997. "Structuring processes in electroacoustic music." Ph.D. thesis. London: City University.

Barrett, N. 1998. "*Little Animals*—compositional ideas, a brief summary." Unpublished manuscript.

Barrett, N. 1999. "*Little Animals:* compositional structuring processes." *Computer Music Journal* 23(2): 11–18.

Bartetzki, A. 1997a. "CMask: ein stochastischer Eventgenerator für Csound." *Mitteilunger* 26. Berlin: DegeM.

Bartetzki, A. 1997b. "Csound score generation and granular synthesis with Cmask." Internet: www.kgw-tu-berlin.de/~abart/CMaskPaper/cmask-article.html.

Barzun, J. 1961. "The request for the loan of your ears." In H. Russcol. 1972. *The Liberation of Sound.* Englewood Cliffs: Prentice-Hall. pp. ix–xii.

Bar-Joseph, Z., D. Lischinski, M. Werman, S. Dubnov, and R. El-Yaniv. 1999. "Granular synthesis of sound textures using statistical learning." In J. Fung, ed. *Proceedings of the 1999 International Computer Music Conference.* pp. 178–181.

Bass, S., and T. Goeddel. 1981. "The efficient digital implementation of subtractive music synthesis." *IEEE Micro* 1(3): 24–37.

Bastiaans, M. 1980. "Gabor's expansion of a signal into Gaussian elementary signals." *Proceedings of the IEEE* 68: 538–539.

Bastiaans, M. 1985. "On the sliding-window representation of signals." *IEEE Transactions on Acoustics, Speech, and Signal Processing* ASSP-33(4): 868–873.

Bastiaans, M., and M. Geilen. 1996. "On the discrete Gabor transform and the discrete Zak transform." *Signal Processing* 49(3): 151–166.

Bayle, F. 1989. "La musique acousmatique ou l'art des sons projetés." Paris: *Encyclopedia Universalis.*

Bayle, F. 1993. *Musique Acousmatique.* Paris: Institut National de l'Audiovisuel/Groupe de Recherches Musicales et Buchet/Chastel.

Beauchamp, J. 1969. "A computer system for time-variant harmonic analysis and synthesis of musical tones." In H. von Foerster and J. Beauchamp, eds. *Music by Computers.* New York: Wiley. pp. 19–62.

Beauchamp, J. 1975. "Analysis and synthesis of cornet tones using nonlinear interharmonic relationships." *Journal of the Audio Engineering Society* 23(10): 718–795.

Beekman, I. 1604–1634. *Journal tenu par Isaac Beekman de 1604 à 1634.* Four volumes. C. de Waard, ed. 1953. The Hague.

Behles, G., S. Starke, and A. Röble. 1998. "Quasi-synchronous and pitch-synchronous granular sound processing with Stampede II." *Computer Music Journal* 22(2): 44–51.

Behringer, R., and H. J. Herrmann, eds. 1998. *Granular Matter.* Volume 1. Berlin: Springer-Verlag. (journal).

Benade, A. 1990. *Fundamentals of Musical Acoustics.* New York: Dover Publications. Originally published 1976.

Bencina, R. 2000. Audiomulch software. Internet: www.audiomulch.com.

Bennett, G., and X. Rodet. 1989. "Synthesis of the singing voice." In M. Mathews and J. Pierce, eds. *Current Directions in Computer Music Research.* Cambridge, Massachusetts: MIT Press. pp. 19–44.

Berg, P. 1978. "A user's manual for SSP." Utrecht: Institute of Sonology.

Berkley, S. 1994. "QuickMQ: a software tool for the modification of time-varying spectrum analysis files." M.S. thesis. Hanover: Department of Music, Dartmouth College.

Blauert, J. 1997. *Spatial Hearing*. Cambridge, Massachusetts: MIT Press.

Bode, H. 1984. "History of electronic sound modification." *Journal of the Audio Engineering Society* 32(10): 730–739.

Boerger, G. 1965. "Die Lokalisation von Gausstönen." Doctoral dissertation. Berlin: Technische Universität, Berlin.

Boulanger, R. 2000. ed. *The Csound Book*. Cambridge, Massachusetts: MIT Press.

Boulez, P. 1960. "Form." Darmstadt lecture, reprinted in P. Boulez, 1986. *Orientations*. London: Faber and Faber. pp. 90–96. Translated by M. Cooper.

Bowcott, P. 1989. "Cellular automation as a means of high level compositional control of granular synthesis." In T. Wells and D. Butler, eds. 1989. *Proceedings of the 1989 International Computer Music Conference*. San Francisco: Computer Music Association. pp. 55–57.

Boyer, F., and R. Kronland-Martinet. 1989. "Granular resynthesis and transformation of sounds through wavelet transform analysis." In T. Wells and T. Butler, eds. *Proceedings of the 1989 International Computer Music Conference*. San Francisco: International Computer Music Association. pp. 51–54.

Brandenburg, K., and M. Bosi. 1997. "Overview of MPEG audio: current and future standards for low-bit-rate audio coding." *Journal of the Audio Engineering Society* 45(1/2): 4–21.

Bristow-Johnson, R. 1995. "A detailed analysis of a time-domain formant-corrected pitch-shifting algorithm." *Journal of the Audio Engineering Society* 43(5): 340–352.

Brün, H. 1970. "From musical ideas to computers and back." In H. Lincoln, ed. *The Computer and Music*. Ithaca: Cornell University Press. pp. 23–41.

Brün, H. 1983. *Compositions*. Program notes with long-play recording Nonsequitur 1–3. Champaign: Non Sequitur Records.

Budón, O. 2000. "Composing with objects, networks, and time scales: an interview with Horacio Vaggione." *Computer Music Journal* 24(3): 9–22.

Bumgardner, J. 1997. *Syd 1.0 User Manual*. Internet: www.jbum.com/jbum.

Buser, P., and M. Imbert. 1992. *Audition*. Cambridge, Massachusetts: MIT Press.

Butler, D. 1992. *The Musician's Guide to Perception and Cognition*. New York: Schirmer Books.

Cage, J. 1937. "The future of music: credo." Lecture reprinted in Cage (1973). pp. 3–6.

Cage, J. 1959. "History of experimental music in the United States." Lecture reprinted in Cage (1973). pp. 67–75.

Cage, J. 1973. *Silence.* Middletown: Wesleyan University Press.

Cahill, T. 1897. U. S. Patent 580, 035.

Cahill, T. 1914. U. S. Patent 1, 107, 261.

Cahill, T. 1917. U. S. Patent 1, 213, 803 and 1, 213, 804.

Cahill, T. 1919. U. S. Patent 1, 295, 691.

Calvet, D., C. Vallée, R. Kronland, and T. Voinier. 2000. "Déscriptif téchnique du Cosmophone à 24 voies." Internet: cosmophone.in2p3.fr/docs/cosmo24.pdf.

Castonguay, C. 1972. *Meaning and Existence in Mathematics.* New York: Springer-Verlag.

Castonguay, C. 1973. "Mathematics and ontology." In M. Bunge, ed. *The Methodological Unity of Science.* Dordrecht: D. Reidel. pp. 15–22.

Cavaliere, S., and A. Piccialli. 1997. "Granular synthesis of musical signals." In C. Roads, S. Pope, A. Piccialli, and G. De Poli, eds. *Musical Signal Processing.* Lisse: Swets & Zeitlinger.

Cavaliere, S., G. Evangelista, and A. Piccialli. 1988. "Synthesis by phase modulation and its implementation in hardware." *Computer Music Journal* 12(1): 29–42.

Cavendish, Margaret Lucas. 1653. *Poems and Fancies.* London.

Chadabe, J. 1997. *Electric Sound.* Upper Saddle River: Prentice-Hall.

Chaitin, G. 1998. *The Limits of Mathematics.* Singapore: Springer-Verlag Singapore.

Chavez, C. 1936. *Toward a New Music.* Reprinted 1975. New York: Da Capo Press.

Cheng, C. 1996. "Wavelet signal processing of digital audio with applications in electro-acoustic music." M.A. thesis. Hanover: Department of Music, Dartmouth College.

Cheng, C. 1997. "High-frequency compensation of low sample-rate audio files: a wavelet-based spectral excitation algorithm." In T. Rikakis, ed. *Proceedings of the 1997 International Computer Music Conference.* San Francisco: International Computer Music Association. pp. 458–461.

Chion, M. 1982. *La musique électroacoustique.* Paris: Presses Universitaires de France.

Chou Wen-Chung. 1966. "A Varèse chronology." *Perspectives of New Music.* Reprinted in B. Boretz and E. Cone, eds. 1971. *Perspectives on American Composers.* New York: Norton. pp. 55–58.

Chowning, J. 1973. "The synthesis of complex audio spectra by means of frequency modulation." *Journal of the Audio Engineering Society* 21(7): 526–534. Reprinted in C. Roads and J. Strawn, eds. 1985. *Foundations of Computer Music.* Cambridge, Massachusetts: MIT Press. pp. 6–29.

Christensen, E. 1996. *The Musical Timespace.* Aalborg: Aalborg University Press.

Clark, M. 1993. "Audio technology in the United States to 1943 and its relationship to magnetic recording." Preprint 3481(H2–1). New York: Audio Engineering Society.

Clarke, M. 1996. "Composing at the intersection of time and frequency." *Organised Sound* 1(2): 107–117.

Clarke, M. 1998. "Extending *Contacts:* the concept of unity in computer music." *Perspectives of New Music* 36(1): 221–239.

Clozier, C. 1998. "Composition-diffusion/interprétation en musique électroacoustique." In F. Barrière and G. Bennett, eds. *Composition/Diffusion en Musique Electroacoustique.* Bourges: Éditions Mnémosyne. pp. 52–101.

Cochran, W. 1973. *The Dynamics of Atoms in Crystals.* London: Edward Arnold.

Coelho, V., ed. 1992. *Music and Science in the Age of Galileo.* Dordrecht: Kluwer Academic Publishers.

Cogan, R. 1984. *New Images of Musical Sound.* Cambridge, MA: Harvard University Press.

Cohen, H. 1984. *Quantifying Music.* Dordrecht: D. Reidel Publishing Company.

Cook, P. 1996. "Physically informed sonic modeling (PhISM): percussive synthesis." In L. Ayers and A. Horner, eds. *Proceedings of the 1996 International Computer Music Conference.* pp. 228–231.

Cook, P. 1997. "Physically informed sonic modeling (PhISM): synthesis of percussive sounds." *Computer Music Journal* 21(3): 38–49.

Cooley, J., and J. Tukey. 1965. "An algorithm for the machine computation of complex Fourier series." *Mathematical Computation* 19: 297–301.

Cope, D. 1996. *Experiments in Musical Intelligence.* Madison: A-R Editions.

Correa, J., E. Miranda, and J. Wright. 2000. "Categorising complex dynamic sounds." Internet: www.nyrsound.com.

Cowell, H. 1930. *New Musical Resources.* New York: A. A. Knopf. Reprinted 1996. Cambridge, England: Cambridge University Press.

Craven, P. G., and M. A. Gerzon. 1996. "Lossless coding for audio discs." *Journal of the Audio Engineering Society* 44(9): 706–720.

Crawford, F. 1968. *Waves.* Berkeley Physics Course Volume 3. New York: McGraw-Hill.

Dahlhaus, C. 1970. "Aesthetische Probleme der elektronischen Musik." In F. Winckel, ed. *Experimentelle Musik.* Berlin: Mann-Verlag.

D'Allessandro, C., and X. Rodet. 1989. "Synthèse et analyse-synthèse par fonctions d'ondes formantiques." *Journal Acoustique* 2: 163–169.

Davies, H. 1964. "*Die Reihe* Reconsidered–1." *Composer* 14: 20.

Davies, H. 1965. "*Die Reihe* Reconsidered–2." *Composer* 16: 17.

de Broglie, L. 1945. *Ondes corpuscules mécanique ondulatoire.* Paris: Albin Michel.

de Campo, A. 1998. "Using recursive diminution for the synthesis of micro time events." Unpublished manuscript.

de Campo, A. 1999. *SuperCollider Tutorial Workshop.* Documentation provided with the program. Austin: AudioSynth.

Delprat, N., P. Guillemain, and R. Kronland-Martinet. 1990. "Parameter estimation for non-linear resynthesis methods with the help of a time-frequency analysis of natural sounds." In S. Arnold and G. Hair, eds. *Proceedings of the 1990 International Computer Music Conference.* pp. 88–90.

De Poli, G., and A. Piccialli. 1988. "Forme d'onda per la sintesi granulare sincronica." In D. Tommassini, ed. 1988. *Atti di VII Colloquio di Informatica Musicale.* Rome: Associazione Musica Verticale. pp. 70–75.

De Poli, G., and A. Piccialli. 1991. "Pitch-synchronous granular synthesis." In G. De Poli, A. Piccialli, and C. Roads, eds. *Representations of Musical Signals.* Cambridge, Massachusetts: MIT Press. pp. 187–219.

de Reydellet, J. 1999. Personal communication.

Desantos, S. 1997. "Acousmatic morphology: an interview with François Bayle." *Computer Music Journal* 21(3): 11–19.

Di Scipio, A. 1990. "Composition by exploration of nonlinear dynamical systems." In S. Arnold and G. Hair, eds. *Proceedings of the 1990 International Computer Music Conference.* San Francisco: International Computer Music Association. pp. 324–327.

Di Scipio, A. 1994. "Formal processes of timbre composition challenging the dualistic paradigm of computer music." *Proceedings of ISEA*, from Internet: www.uiah.fi/bookshop/isea_proc/nextgen/j/19.html.

Di Scipio, A. 1995. "Da *Concret PH* a *GENDY301*, modelli compositivi nella musica elletroacustica de Xenakis." *Sonus—materiali per la musica contemporanea* 7(1–3): 61–92.

Di Scipio, A. 1997a. "The problem of 2nd-order sonorities in Xenakis' electroacoustic music." *Organised Sound* 2(3): 165–178.

Di Scipio, A. 1997b. "Interactive micro-time sound design." *Journal of Electroacoustic Music* 10: 4–8.

Di Scipio, A. 1998. "Scienza e musica dei quanti acustici: l'eredità di Gabor." *Il Monocordo* 3(6): 61–78.

Dodge, C., and T. Jerse. 1997. *Computer Music: Synthesis, Composition, and Performance*. Second edition. New York: Schirmer.

Dolson, M. 1983. "A tracking phase vocoder and its use in the analysis of ensemble sounds." Ph.D. dissertation. Pasadena: California Institute of Technology.

Dolson, M. 1985. "Recent advances in musique concrète at CARL." In B. Truax, ed. Proceedings *of the 1985 International Computer Music Conference*. San Francisco: International Computer Music Association. pp. 55–60.

Dolson, M. 1986. "The phase vocoder: a tutorial." *Computer Music Journal* 10(4): 14–27.

Dolson, M., and R. Boulanger. 1985. "New directions in the musical use of resonators." Unpublished manuscript.

Doughty, J., and W. Garner. 1947. "Pitch characteristics of short tones I: two kinds of pitch thresholds." *Journal of Experimental Psychology* 37: 351–365.

Douglas, A. 1957. *The Electrical Production of Music*. New York: Philosophical Library.

Dudon, J., and D. Arfib. 1990. "Synthèse photosonique." *Actes du 1er congrès d'Acoustique, colloque C2*. Marseille. pp. 845–848

Dutilleux, P., A. Grossmann, and R. Kronland-Martinet. 1988. "Application of the wavelet transform to the analysis, transformation, and synthesis of musical sounds." Preprint 2727 (A–2). Presented at the 85th Convention. New York: Audio Engineering Society.

Eckel, G. 1990. "A signal editor for the IRCAM Musical Workstation." In S. Arnold and G. Hair, eds. *Proceedings of the 1990 International Computer Music Conference*. San Francisco: International Computer Music Association. pp. 69–71.

Eckel, G., M. Rocha-Iturbide, and B. Becker. 1995. "The development of GiST, a granular synthesis toolkit based on an extension of the FOF Generator." In R. Bidlack, ed. *Proceedings of the 1995 International Computer Music Conference*. San Francisco: International Computer Music Association. pp. 296–302.

Eimert, H. 1955. "What is electronic music." *die Reihe* 1:1–10. English edition 1958. Bryn Mawr: Theodore Presser Company.

Einstein, A. 1952. *Relativity: The Special and the General Theory*. Fifteenth edition of the original published in 1916. New York: Three Rivers Press.

Elmore, W., and M. Heald. 1969. *Physics of Waves*. New York: Dover.

Endrich, A., Coordinator. 2000. Composer's Desktop Project. 12 Goodwood Way, Cepen Park South, Chippenham Wiltshire SN14 0SY, United Kingdom. archer@trans4um.demon.co.uk.

Erbe, T. 1995. *SoundHack User's Manual.* Oakland: Mills College.

Erne, M. 1998. "Embedded audio compression using wavelets and improved psycho-acoustic models." In B. Garau and R. Loureiro, eds. *Proceedings 98 Digital Audio Effects Workshop.* Barcelona: Pompeu Fabra University. pp. 147–150.

Evangelista, G. 1991. "Wavelet transforms that we can play." In G. De Poli, A. Piccialli, and C. Roads, eds. 1991. *Representations of Musical Signals.* Cambridge, Massachusetts: MIT Press. pp. 119–136.

Evangelista, G. 1997. "Wavelet representation of musical signals." In Roads, et al. eds. *Musical Signal Processing.* Lisse: Swets and Zeitlinger. pp. 126–153.

Evangelista, G., and S. Cavalière. 1998. "Dispersive and pitch-synchronous processing of sounds." In B. Garau and R. Loureiro, eds. *Proceedings 98 Digital Audio Effects Workshop.* Barcelona: Pompeu Fabra University. pp. 232–236.

Fairbanks, G., W. Everitt, and R. Jaeger. 1954. "Method for time or frequency compression-expansion of speech." *Institute of Radio Engineers Transactions on Audio* AV–2(1): 7–12.

Feichtinger, H., and T. Strohmer, eds. 1998. *Gabor Analysis and Algorithms.* Boston: Birkhäuser.

Fields, K. 1998. Personal communication.

Fitz, K., L. Haken, and B. Holloway. 1995. *Lemur Pro 4.0.1 documentation.* Urbana: Engineering Research Laboratory, University of Illinois.

Flanagan, J. L., and R. Golden. 1966. "Phase vocoder." *Bell System Technical Journal* 45: 1493–1509.

Flanagan, J. L. 1972. *Speech Analysis, Synthesis, and Perception.* New York: Springer-Verlag.

Fletcher, N., and T. Rossing. 1991. *The Physics of Musical Instruments.* New York: Springer-Verlag.

Fokker, A. 1962. "Wherefore, and Why?" *die Reihe* 8. English edition 1968, 68–79.

Fourier, L. 1994. "Jean-Jacques Perrey and the Ondioline." *Computer Music Journal* 18(4): 18–25.

Fraisse, P. 1982. "Rhythm and tempo." In D. Deutsch, ed. *The Psychology of Music.* Orlando: Academic.

Freed, A. 1987. "MacMix: recording, mixing, and signal processing on a personal computer." In J. Strawn, ed. 1987. *Music and Digital Technology.* New York: Audio Engineering Society. pp. 158–162.

Freedman, M. D. 1967. "Analysis of musical instrument tones." *Journal of the Acoustical Society of America* 41: 793–806.

Freeman, W. 1991. "The physiology of perception." *Scientific American* 264(2): 78–85.

Freeman, W. 1995. "Chaos in the central nervous system." In F. Ventriglia, ed. *Neural Modeling and Neural Networks.* New York: Pergamon Press. pp. 185–216.

Gabor, D. 1946. "Theory of communication." *Journal of the Institute of Electrical Engineers* Part III, 93: 429–457.

Gabor, D. 1947. "Acoustical quanta and the theory of hearing." *Nature* 159(4044): 591–594.

Gabor, D. 1952. "Lectures on communication theory." Technical Report 238, Research Laboratory of Electronics. Cambridge, Massachusetts: Massachusetts Institute of Technology.

Galente, F., and N. Sani. 2000. *Musica Espansa.* Lucca: Ricordi LIM.

Galilei, Galileo. 1623. "Parable of Sound." Quoted in V. Coelho. "Musical myth and Galilean science in Giovanni Serodine's *Allegoria della Scienza.*" See V. Coelho (1992).

Gardner, M. 1957. *Fads and Fallacies in the Name of Science.* New York: Dover.

Gardner, W. 1995. "Efficient convolution without input-output delay." *Journal of the Audio Engineering Society* 43(3): 127–136.

Gassendi, P. 1658. *Syntagma Philosophicum.*

George, E., and M. Smith. 1992. "Analysis-by-synthesis/overlap-add sinusoidal modeling applied to the analysis and synthesis of musical tones." *Journal of the Audio Engineering Society* 40(6): 497–516.

Gerrard, G. 1989. "Music4C—A Macintosh version of Music IVBF in C." Melbourne: University of Melbourne.

Gerzon, M. 1973. "Periphony: with-height sound reproduction." *Journal of the Audio Engineering Society* 21(1): 2–10.

Gibson, B., C. Jubien, and B. Roden. 1996. "Method and apparatus for changing the timbre and/or pitch of audio signals." U. S. Patent 5,567,901.

Gleick, J. *Chaos.* 1988. London: Cardinal.

Goeyvaerts, K. 1955. "The sound material of electronic music." *die Reihe* 1: 35–7. English edition 1958. Bryn Mawr: Theodore Presser Company.

Gogins, M. 1991. "Iterated function systems music." *Computer Music Journal* 15(1): 40–48.

Gogins, M. 1995. "Gabor synthesis of recurrent iterated function systems." In R. Bidlack, ed. *Proceedings of the 1995 International Computer Music Conference.* San Francisco: International Computer Music Association. pp. 349–350.

Gordon, J. 1996. "Psychoacoustics in computer music." In C. Roads. 1996. *The Computer Music Tutorial.* Cambridge, Massachusetts: MIT Press. pp. 1053–1069.

Green, D. 1971. "Temporal auditory acuity." *Psychological Review* 78(6): 540–551.

Grey, J. 1975. "An exploration of musical timbre." Report STAN–M–2. Stanford University Department of Music.

Grossman, A., M. Holschneider, R. Kronland-Martinet, and J. Morlet. 1987. "Detection of abrupt changes in sound signals with the help of wavelet transforms." *Inverse Problems: Advances in Electronic and Electronic Physics.* Supplement 19. San Diego: Academic Press. pp. 298–306.

Hamlin, P., with C. Roads. 1985. "Interview with Herbert Brün." In C. Roads, ed. *Composers and the Computer.* Madison: A-R Editions. pp. 1–15.

Harley, J. forthcoming. *The Music of Iannis Xenakis.* London: Harwood Academic Publishers.

Harris, F. 1978. "On the use of windows for harmonic analysis with the discrete Fourier transform." *Proceedings of the IEEE* 66(1): 51–83.

Hawking, S., and R. Penrose. 1996. "The nature of space and time." *Scientific American* 248(7): 60–65.

Heisenberg, W. 1958. *Physics and Philosophy.* New York: Harper.

Helmholtz, H. 1885. *On the Sensations of Tone.* Translated by A. Ellis. New edition 1954. New York: Dover Publications.

Helmuth, M. 1991. "Patchmix and StochGran: Two Graphical Interfaces." In B. Alphonce and B. Pennycook, eds. *Proceedings of the 1991 International Computer Music Conference.* San Francisco: International Computer Music Association. pp. 563–565.

Helmuth, M. 1993. "Granular Synthesis with Cmix and Max." In S. Ohteru, ed. *Proceedings of the 1993 International Computer Music Conference.* San Francisco: International Computer Music Association. pp. 449–452.

Helstrom, C. 1966. "An expansion of a signal in Gaussian elementary signals." *IEEE Transactions on Information Theory* IT–12: 81–82.

Hiller, L., and L. Isaacson. 1959. *Experimental Music.* New York: McGraw-Hill.

Hiller, L. 1970. "Music composed with computers—a historical survey." In H. Lincoln, ed. *The Computer and Music.* Ithaca: Cornell University Press. pp. 42–96.

Hoffmann, P. 1994. *Amalgam aus Kunst und Wissenschaft. Naturwissenschaftliches Denken im Werk von Iannis Xenakis.* Frankfurt: Peter Lang.

Hoffmann, P. 1996. "Amalgamation of art and science: scientific thought in the work of Iannis Xenakis." Abbreviated version of Hoffmann (1994) in English. Unpublished manuscript.

Hoffmann, P. 1997. Personal communication.

Holden, A. 1986. *Chaos.* Princeton: Princeton University Press.

Howard, E. 1996. Personal communication.

Howe, H. S., Jr. 1975. *Electronic Music Synthesis.* New York: Norton.

Hugo, V. 1862. *Les Misérables.* Reprinted 1999. Paris: Gallimard.

Ives, C. 1962. in H. Boatwright, ed. *Essays Before a Sonata and Other Writings.* New York: W. W. Norton. p. 98.

Jenny, G. 1955–56. "Initiation à la luthérie éléctronique." *Toute la Radio* (September 1955): 289–94, (November 1955): 397–404, (December 1955): 455–9, January 1956): 23–6, (February 1956) 67–72.

Jenny, G. 1958. "L'Ondioline: conception et réalisation." *Toute la radio.*

Jones, D., and T. Parks. 1986. "Time scale modification of signals using a synchronous Gabor technique." *Proceedings of the 1986 ASSP Workshop on Applications of Signal Processing to Audio and Acoustics.* New York: IEEE.

Jones, D., and T. Parks. 1988. "Generation and combination of grains for music synthesis." *Computer Music Journal* 12(2): 27–34.

Kaegi, W. 1967. *Was Ist Elektronische Musik.* Zürich: Orell Füssli Verlag.

Kaegi, W. 1973. "A minimum description of the linguistic sign repertoire (part 1)." *Interface* 2: 141–156.

Kaegi, W. 1974. "A minimum description of the linguistic sign repertoire (part 2)." *Interface* 3: 137–158.

Kaegi, W., and S. Tempelaars. 1978. "VOSIM—a new sound synthesis system." *Journal of the Audio Engineering Society* 26(6): 418–426.

Kaiser, G. 1994. *A Friendly Guide to Wavelets.* Boston: Birkhäuser.

Kaku, M. 1995. *Hyperspace.* New York: Anchor Books.

Kaler, J. 1997. *Cosmic Clouds.* New York: Scientific American Library.

Kandinsky, W. 1926. *Point et ligne sur plan.* 1991 edition, Paris: Gallimard.

Kargon, R. H. 1966. *Atomism in England from Hariot to Newton.* Oxford: Clarendon Press.

Keller, D. 1999. *Touch 'n Go.* Enhanced compact disc with synthesis data. ES 99002. New Westminster, British Columbia: Earsay.

Keller, D., and C. Rolfe. 1998. "The corner effect." *Proceedings of the XII Colloquium on Musical Informatics.* Gorizia: Centro Polifunzionale di Gorizia. Also see Internet: www.thirdmonk.com.

Keller, D., and B. Truax. 1998. "Ecologically-based granular synthesis." In M. Simoni, ed. *Proceedings of the 1998 International Computer Music Conference.* San Francisco: International Computer Music Association. pp. 117–120.

Kientzle, T. 1998. *A Programmer's Guide to Sound.* Reading, Massachusetts: Addison-Wesley.

Kling, G., and C. Roads. 2004. "Audio analysis, visualization, and transformation based on the matching pursuit algorithm." Submitted to the Seventh International Conference on Digital Audio Effects (DAFX-04) Naples, Italy.

Koenig, G. M. 1959. "Studium im Studio." *die Reihe* 5. English edition 1961. Bryn Mawr: Theodore Presser Company. pp. 30–39.

Koenig, G. M. 1962. "Commentary on Stockhausen's ... how time passes ... on Fokker's wherefore, and why, and on present musical practice as seen by the author." *die Reihe* 8. English edition 1968. Bryn Mawr: Theodore Presser Company. pp. 80–98.

Koenig, R. 1899. Articles in *Annalen der Physik* 69: 626–660, 721–738. Cited in Miller 1916, 1935.

Koenigsberg, C. 1991. "Stockhausen's new morphology of musical time." Posted June 1996. Internet: www2.uchicago.edu/ns-acs/ckk/smmt.

Krenek, E. 1955. "A glance over the shoulders of the young." *die Reihe* 1: 14–16. English edition 1958. Bryn Mawr: Theodore Presser Company.

Kronland-Martinet, R. 1988. "The wavelet transform for the analysis, synthesis, and processing of speech and music sounds." *Computer Music Journal* 12(4): 11–20.

Kronland-Martinet, R., and A. Grossman. 1991. "Application of time-frequency and time-scale methods (wavelet transforms) to the analysis, synthesis, and transformation of sounds." In G. De Poli, A. Piccialli, and C. Roads, eds. 1991. *Representations of Musical Signals.* Cambridge, Massachusetts: MIT Press. pp. 45–85.

Kronland-Martinet, R., Ph. Guilliman, and S. Ystad. 1997. "Modeling of natural sounds by time-frequency and wavelet representations." *Organised Sound* 2(3): 179–191.

Kronland-Martinet, R., J. Morlet, and A. Grossmann. 1987. "Analysis of sound patterns through wavelet transforms." *International Journal on Pattern Recognition and Artificial Intelligence* 1(2): 273–302.

Kunt, M. 1981. *Traitement numérique des signaux.* Paris: Dunod.

Küpper, L. 2000. "Le temps audio-numérique." In C. Clozier and F. Barrière, eds. *Les actes d'académie de musique électroacoustique.* Bourges: Institute International de Musique Électoacoustique de Bourges. pp. 94–115.

Kussmaul, C. 1991. "Applications of wavelets in music: the wavelet function library." M. A. thesis. Hanover: Dartmouth College.

Langmead, C. 1995. *Perceptual Analysis Synthesis Tool 1.6 Manual.* Hanover, New Hampshire: Dartmouth College.

Learned, R., and A. Willsky. 1993. "Wavelet packet approach to transient signal classification." Technical Report LIDS–P–2199, Laboratory for Information and Decision Systems. Cambridge: MIT

Lederman, L., and D. Schramm. 1995. Second edition. *From Quarks to the Cosmos.* San Francisco: W. H. Freeman.

Lee, F. 1972. "Time compression and expansion of speech by the sampling method." *Journal of the Audio Engineering Society* 20(9): 738–742.

Lee, A. 1995. "Csound granular synthesis unit generator." In *Proceedings of the 1995 International Computer Music Conference.* San Francisco: International Computer Music Association. pp. 230–1.

Leichtentritt, H. 1951. *Musical Form.* Englewood Cliffs: Prentice-Hall.

Lent, K. 1989. "An efficient method for pitch shifting digitally sampled sounds." *Computer Music Journal* 13(4): 65–71.

Lesbros, V. 1995. "Atelier incrémental pour la musique expérimentale." Thèse doctorat en Intelligence Artificielle. Paris: Université Paris 8.

Lesbros, V. 1996. "From images to sounds: a dual representation." *Computer Music Journal* 20(3): 59–69.

Liandrat, J., and F. Moret-Bailly. 1990. "The wavelet transform: some applications to fluid dynamics and turbulence." *European Journal of Mech., B/Fluids* 9: 1–19.

Ligeti, G. 1971. "Fragan und Antworden von mir selbst." *Melos* 12: 509–516.

Lippe, C. 1993. "A musical application of real-time granular sampling using the IRCAM signal processing workstation." In S. Ohteru, ed. *Proceedings of the 1993 International Computer Music Conference.* San Francisco: International Computer Music Association. pp. 190–193.

Lippman, E. 1992. *A History of Western Music Aesthetics.* Lincoln: University of Nebraska Press.

López, S., F. Martí, and E. Resina. 1998. "Vocem: an application for real-time granular synthesis." In B. Garau and R. Loureiro, eds. *Proceedings 98 Digital Audio Effects Workshop*. Barcelona: Pompeu Fabra University. pp. 219–222.

Lorrain, D. 1980. "A panoply of stochastic 'cannons'." *Computer Music Journal* 4(1): 53–81. Reprinted in C. Roads. 1989. *The Music Machine*. Cambridge, Massachusetts: MIT Press. pp. 351–379.

Luce, D. 1963. "Physical correlates of nonpercussive instrument tones." Sc.D. dissertation. Cambridge, Massachusetts: MIT Department of Physics.

Lucretius. 55. *De Rerum Natura*. In J. Gaskin, ed. 1995. *The Epicurean Philosophers*. London: Everyman. pp. 79–304.

Maconie, R. 1989. *Stockhausen on Music*. London: Marion Boyars.

Maher, R., and J. Beauchamp. 1990. "An investigation of vocal vibrato for synthesis." *Applied Acoustics* 30: 219–245.

Malah, D. 1979. "Time-domain algorithms for harmonic bandwidth reduction and time scaling of speech signals." *IEEE Transactions on Acoustics, Speech, and Signal Processing* 27(4): 121–133.

Mallat, G. 1988. "Review of multifrequency channel decompositions of images and wavelet models." Technical Report No. 412. New York: New York University, Department of Computer Science.

Mallat, G. 1989. "A theory for multiresolution signal decomposition: the wavelet representation." *IEEE Transactions on Pattern Analysis and Machine Intelligence* 11(7): 674–693.

Mallat, S. 1998. *A Wavelet Tour of Signal Processing*. San Diego: Academic Press.

Mallat, S. G. 1998. *A Wavelet Tour of Signal Processing*. San Diego: Academic Press.

Marino, G., J.-M. Raczinski, and M.-H. Serra. 1990. "The new UPIC system." In S. Arnold and G. Hair, eds. *Proceedings of the 1990 International Computer Music Conference*. San Francisco: International Computer Music Association. pp. 249–252.

Marple, S. 1987. *Digital Spectral Analysis*. Englewood Cliffs: Prentice-Hall.

Masri, P., A. Bateman, and N. Canagarajah. 1997a. "A review of time-frequency representations, with an application to sound/music analysis-resynthesis." *Organised Sound* 2(3): 193–205.

Masri, P., A. Bateman, and N. Canagarajah. 1997b. "The importance of the time-frequency representation for sound/music analysis-resynthesis." *Organised Sound* 2(3): 207–214.

Mathews, M. 1969. *The Technology of Computer Music*. Cambridge, Massachusetts: MIT Press.

Mathews, M., and J. Miller. 1965. *Music IV Programmer's Manual.* Murray Hill: Bell Telephone Laboratories.

Mathews, M., J. Miller, and E. David, Jr. 1961. "Pitch synchronous analysis of voiced sounds." *Journal of the Acoustical Society of America* 33: 179–186.

MathWorks, The. 1995. *Matlab Reference Guide.* Natick: The MathWorks.

McAdams, S. 1982. "Spectral fusion and the creation of auditory images." In M. Clynes, ed. *Music, Mind, and Brain.* New York: Plenum.

McAdams, S., and A. Bregman. 1979. "Hearing musical streams." *Computer Music Journal* 3(4): 26–44. Reprinted in C. Roads and J. Strawn, eds. 1985. *Foundations of Computer Music.* Cambridge, Massachusetts: MIT Press. pp. 658–698.

McAulay, R., and T. Quatieri. 1986. "Speech analysis/synthesis based on a sinusoidal representation." *IEEE Transactions on Acoustics, Speech, and Signal Processing* ASSP–34: 744–754.

McCartney, J. 1990. Synth-O-Matic version 0.06 software.

McCartney, J. 1994. Synth-O-Matic version 0.45 software.

McCartney, J., 1996. *SuperCollider, A Real-time Sound Synthesis Programming Language.* Austin: AudioSynth.

McCartney, J. 1998. "Continued evolution of the SuperCollider real time synthesis environment." In M. Simoni, ed. *Proceedings of the 1998 International Computer Music Conference.* San Francisco: International Computer Music Association. pp. 133–136.

Meijer, P. 1998. "Auditory wavelets?" Internet: ourworld.compuserve.com/homepages/Peter_Meijer/wavelet.htm.

Meridian. 1998. "Meridian lossless packing: provisional data June 1998." Huntington: Boothroyd-Stuart Meridian.

Mersenne, M. 1636. *Harmonie Universelle.* Reprinted 1957, translated by Roger E. Chapman. The Hague: Martinus Nijhoff.

Meyer, Y. 1994. *Les ondelettes: algorithmes et applications.* Paris: Armand Colin éditeur.

Meyer, Y., S. Jaffard, and O. Rioul. 1987. "L'analyse par ondelettes." *Pour la Science.* September. pp. 28–37.

Meyer-Eppler, W. 1959. *Grundlagen und Aufwendungen der Informationstheorie.* Springer-Verlag: Berlin.

Meyer-Eppler, W. 1960. "Zur Systematik der elektrischen Klangtransformation." *Darmstadter Beitrage zur Neuen Musik III.* Mainz: Schott.

Miller, D. C. 1916. *The Science of Musical Sounds.* New York: MacMillan.

Miller, H. 1945. *The Air-conditioned Nightmare.* New York: New Directions.

Miranda, E. 1998. "Chaosynth: a cellular automata-based granular synthesiser." Internet: website.lineone.net/~edandalex/chaosynt.htm.

Moles, A. 1960. *Les musiques expérimentales.* Zürich: Editions du Cercle de l'Art Contemporain.

Moles, A. 1968. *Information Theory and Esthetic Perception.* Urbana: University of Illinois Press.

Moog, R. 1996. "Build the EM Theremin." *Electronic Musician* 12(2): 86–99.

Moon, F. 1987. *Chaotic Vibrations.* New York: Wiley-Interscience.

Moore, F. R. 1982. "The computer audio research laboratory at UCSD." *Computer Music Journal* 6(1): 18–29.

Moore, F. R. 1990. *Elements of Computer Music.* Englewood Cliffs: Prentice-Hall.

Moorer, J. A. 1977a. "Editing, mixing, and processing digitized audio waveforms." Paper presented at the 57th Convention of the Audio Engineering Society. New York: Audio Engineering Society.

Moorer, J. A. 1977b. "Signal processing aspects of computer music." *Proceeding of the IEEE* 65(8): 1108–1137. Reprinted in *Computer Music Journal* 1(1): 4–37 and in J. Strawn, ed. 1985. *Digital Audio Signal Processing: An Anthology.* Madison: A-R Editions.

Moorer, J. A. 1978. "The use of the phase vocoder in computer music applications." *Journal of the Audio Engineering Society* 26(1/2): 42–45.

Morawska-Büngler, M. 1988. *Schwingende Elektronen.* Cologne: P. J. Tonger.

Morris, R. 1987. *Composition with Pitch-Classes.* New Haven: Yale University Press.

Nahin, P. 1996. *The Science of Radio.* Woodbury: American Institute of Physics.

Navarro, R., A. Tabernero, and G. Cristobal. 1995. "Image representation with Gabor wavelets and its applications." In P. Hawkes, ed. *Advances in Imaging and Electron Physics.* Orlando: Academic Press.

Nelson, G. 1997. "Wind, Sand, and Sea Voyages: an application of granular synthesis and chaos to musical composition." www.timara.oberlin.edu/people/%7Egnelson/papers/Gola/gola.pdf.

Nelson, Jon Christopher. 1996. *They Wash Their Ambassadors in Citrus and Fennel.* On the compact disc *Cultures Electroniques* 9. LCD 278060/61. Bourges: Série Bourges/Unesco/Cime.

Neve, R. 1992. "Rupert Neve of Amek replies." *Studio Sound* 34(3): 21–22.

Newland, D. 1994. "Harmonic and musical wavelets." *Proceedings of the Royal Society of London* A 444: 605–620.

Norris, M. 1997. *SoundMagic 1.0.3 Documentation.* Wellington, New Zealand: Michael Norris.

Nuttall, A. 1981. "Some windows with very good sidelobe behavior." *IEEE Transactions on Acoustics, Speech, and Signal Processing* ASSP–29(1): 84–91.

Nyquist, H. 1928. "Certain topics in telegraph transmission theory." *Transactions of the American Institute of Electrical Engineers* 4.

Olson, H. F. 1957. *Acoustical Engineering.* New York: D. Van Nostrand. Reprinted 1991. Philadephia: Professional Audio Journals.

Oohashi, T., E. Nishina, N. Kawai, Y. Fuwamoto, and H. Imai. 1991. "High frequency sound above the audible range affects brain electric activity and sound perception." Preprint 3207(W–1). Presented at the 91st Convention of the Audio Engineering Society. New York: Audio Engineering Society.

Oohashi, T., E. Nishina, Y. Fuwamoto, and N. Kawai. 1993. "On the mechanism of hypersonic effect." In S. Ohteru, ed. *Proceedings of the 1993 International Computer Music Conference.* San Francisco: International Computer Music Association. pp. 432–434.

Orcalli, A. 1993. *Fenomenologia della Musica Sperimentale.* Potenza: Sonus Edizioni Musicali.

Orton, R., A. Hunt, and R. Kirk. 1991. "Graphical control of granular synthesis using cellular automata and the Freehand program." In B. Alphonce and B. Pennycook, eds. *Proceedings of the 1991 International Computer Music Conference.* San Francisco: International Computer Music Association. pp. 416–418.

Otis, A., G. Grossman, and J. Cuomo. 1968. "Four sound-processing programs for the Illiac II computer and D/A converter." Experimental Music Studios Technical Report Number 14. Urbana: University of Illinois.

Pape, G. 1998. Personal communication.

Piccialli, A., S. Cavaliere, I. Ortosecco, and P. Basile. 1992. "Modifications of natural sounds using a pitch synchronous technique." In A. Piccialli, ed. *Proceedings of the International Workshop on Models and Representations of Musical Signals.* Napoli: Università di Napoli Federico II.

Pierce, A. D. 1994. *Acoustics: An Introduction to Its Physical Principles and Applications.* Woodbury, New York: Acoustical Society of America.

Pierce, J. R. 1983. *The Science of Musical Sound.* New York: W. H. Freeman.

Pines, D. 1963. *Elementary Excitations in Solids.* New York: W. A. Benjamin.

Polansky, L., and T. Erbe. 1996. "Spectral mutation in SoundHack." *Computer Music Journal* 20(1): 92–101.

Pompei, F. J. 1998. "The use of airborne ultrasonics for generating audible sound beams." Preprint 4853 (I–5). New York: Audio Engineering Society.

Pompei, F. J. 1999. "The use of airborne ultrasonics for generating audible sound beams." *Journal of the Audio Engineering Society* 47(9): 726–731.

Pope, S. T. 1997. *Sound and Music Processing in SuperCollider.* Santa Barbara: www.create.ucsb.edu.

Portnoff, M. 1976. "Implementation of the digital phase vocoder using the fast Fourier transform." *IEEE Transactions on Acoustics, Speech and Signal Processing* 24(3): 243–248.

Portnoff, M. 1978. "Time-scale modification of speech based on short-time Fourier analysis." Sc.D. dissertation. Cambridge, Massachusetts: MIT Department of Electrical Engineering and Computer Science.

Portnoff, M. 1980. "Time-frequency representation of digital signals and systems based on short-time Fourier analysis." *IEEE Transactions on Acoustics, Speech, and Signal Processing* 28: 55–69.

Portnoff, M. 1981. "Time-scale modification of speech based on short-time Fourier analysis." *IEEE Transactions on Acoustics, Speech, and Signal Processing* 29(3): 374–390.

Pound, E. 1934. Quoted in R. Murray Schafer, editor, 1977, *Ezra Pound and Music: the Complete Criticism.* New York: New Directions.

Pranger, M. 1999. *MarcoHack Version 1 Manual.* Internet: www.koncon.nl/Marco-Hack.

Quate, C. 1979. "The acoustic microscope." *Scientific American.* Reprinted in 1998, *Science's Vision: The Mechanics of Sight.* New York: Scientific American. pp. 31–39.

Rabiner, L., and B. Gold. 1975. *Theory and Application of Digital Signal Processing.* Englewood Cliffs: Prentice-Hall.

Rabiner, L., J. Cooley, H. Helms, L. Jackson, J. Kaiser, C. Rader, R. Schafer, K. Steiglitz, and C. Weinstein. 1972. "Terminology in digital signal processing." *IEEE Transactions on Audio and Electroacoustics* AU–20: 322–7.

Raczinski, J.-M., and G. Marino. 1988. "A real time synthesis unit." In C. Lischka and J. Fritsch, eds. *Proceedings of the 1988 International Computer Music Conference.* San Francisco: International Computer Music Association. pp. 90–100.

Raczinski, J.-M., G. Marino, and M.-H. Serra. 1991. "New UPIC system demonstration." In B. Alphonce and B. Pennycook, eds. *Proceedings of the 1991 International Computer Music Conference.* San Francisco: International Computer Music Association. pp. 567–570.

Ramarapu, P., and R. Maher. 1997. "Methods for reducing audible artefacts in a wavelet-based broad-band denoising system." *Journal of the Audio Engineering Society* 46(3): 178–190.

Read, O., and W. Welch. 1976. *From Tin Foil to Stereo: Evolution of the Phonograph.* Indianapolis: Howard Sams.

Reder, L., and J. S. Gordon. 1997. "Subliminal perception: nothing special, cognitively speaking." In J. Cohen and J. Schooler, eds. *Cognitive and Neuropsychological Approaches to the Study of Consciousness.* Hillsdale, New Jersey: Lawrence Erlbaum Associates. pp. 125–134.

Reeves, W. 1983. "Particle systems—a technique for modeling a class of fuzzy objects." *ACM Transactions on Graphics* 2(2): 359–376.

Rhea, T. 1972. "The evolution of electronic musical instruments in the United States." Ph.D. dissertation. Nashville: Peabody College.

Rhea, T. 1984. "The history of electronic musical instruments." In T. Darter, ed. 1984. *The Art of Electronic Music.* New York: Quill. pp. 1–63.

Ricci, A. 1997. SoundMaker software. Distributed by MicroMat Computer Systems.

Risset, J.-C. 1966. "Computer study of trumpet tones." Murray Hill: Bell Telephone Laboratories.

Risset, J.-C. 1969. *An Introductory Catalog of Computer Synthesized Sounds (With Sound Examples).* Murray Hill: Bell Laboratories. Reprinted 1995 with the compact disc *The Historical CD of Digital Sound Synthesis,* Computer Music Currents 13, Wergo 2033–2. Mainz: Wergo Schallplatten.

Risset, J.-C. 1985. "Computer music experiments: 1964–..." *Computer Music Journal* 9(1): 11–18. Reprinted in C. Roads, ed. 1989. *The Music Machine.* Cambridge, Massachusetts: MIT Press. pp. 67–74.

Risset, J.-C. 1989a. "Paradoxical sounds." In M. Mathews and J. Pierce, eds. 1989. *Current Directions in Computer Music Research.* Cambridge, Massachusetts: The MIT Press. pp. 149–158.

Risset, J.-C. 1989b. "Additive synthesis of inharmonic tones." In M. Mathews and J. Pierce, eds. 1989. *Current Directions in Computer Music Research.* Cambridge, Massachusetts: The MIT Press. pp. 159–163.

Risset, J.-C. 1991. "Timbre analysis by synthesis: representations, imitations, and variants for musical composition." In G. De Poli, A. Piccialli, and C. Roads, eds. 1991. *Representations of Musical Signals.* Cambridge, Massachusetts: MIT Press. pp. 7–43.

Risset, J.-C. 1992. "Composing sounds with computers." In J. Paynter, T. Howell, R. Orton, and P. Seymour, eds. *Companion to Contemporary Musical Thought.* London: Routledge. pp. 583–621.

Risset, J.-C. 1996. "Définition de la musique électroacoustique." In G. Bennett, C. Clozier, S. Hanson, C. Roads, and H. Vaggione, eds. *Esthétique et Musique Electro-acoustique.* Bourges: Mnemosyne. pp. 82–84.

Risset, J.-C. 1997. "Problèmes d'analyse : quelque clés pour mes premières pieces." In F. Barrière and G. Bennett, eds. *Analyse en Musique Electroacoustique.* Bourges: Editions Mnemosyne. pp. 169–177.

Risset, J.-C. 1998. "Examples of the musical use of digital audio effects." In B. Garau and R. Loureiro, eds. *Proceedings 98 Digital Audio Effects Workshop.* Barcelona: Pompeu Fabra University. pp. 254–259.

Risset, J.-C. 1999a. Personal communication.

Risset, J.-C. 1999b. Overview of research at the Laboratoire de Mécanique et d'Acoustique. Internet: omicron.cnrs_mrs.fr.

Risset, J.-C., and D. Wessel. 1982. "Exploration of timbre by analysis and synthesis." In D. Deutsch, ed. 1982. *The Psychology of Music.* Orlando: Academic. pp. 25–58.

Roads, C. 1975. "Computer music studies 1974–1975." Unpublished manuscript. 44 pages.

Roads, C. 1976. "A systems approach to composition." Honors thesis. La Jolla: University of California, San Diego.

Roads, C. 1978a. "Automated granular synthesis of sound." *Computer Music Journal* 2(2): 61–62. Revised and updated version printed as "Granular synthesis of sound" in C. Roads and J. Strawn, eds. 1985. *Foundations of Computer Music.* Cambridge, Massachusetts: MIT Press. pp. 145–159.

Roads, C. 1978b. "Interview with Gottfried Michael Koenig." *Computer Music Journal* 2(3): 11–15. Reprinted in C. Roads and J. Strawn, eds. 1985. *Foundations of Computer Music.* Cambridge, Massachusetts: MIT Press. pp. 568–580.

Roads, C., ed. 1985a. *Composers and the Computer.* Madison: A-R Editions.

Roads, C. 1985b. "The realization of nscor." In C. Roads, ed. 1985. *Composers and the Computer*. Madison: A-R Editions. pp. 140–168.

Roads, C. 1985c. "Granular synthesis of sound." In C. Roads and J. Strawn, eds. 1985. *Foundations of Computer Music*. Cambridge, Massachusetts: MIT Press. pp. 145–159.

Roads, C. 1985d. "Grammars as representations for music." In C. Roads and J. Strawn, eds. 1985. *Foundations of Computer Music*. Cambridge, Massachusetts: MIT Press. pp. 403–442.

Roads, C. 1987. "Experiences with computer-assisted composition." Translated as "Esperienze di composizione assistata da calculatore." In S. Tamburini and M. Bagella, eds. *I Profili del Suono*. Rome: Musica Verticale and Galzeramo. pp. 173–196.

Roads, C. 1991. "Asynchronous granular synthesis." In G. De Poli, A. Piccialli, and C. Roads, eds. 1991. *Representations of Musical Signals*. Cambridge, Massachusetts: MIT Press. pp. 143–185.

Roads, C. 1992a. "Composition with machines." In J. Paynter, T. Howell, R. Orton, and P. Seymour, eds. *Companion to Contemporary Musical Thought*. London: Routledge. pp. 399–425.

Roads, C. 1992b. "Musical applications of advanced signal transformations." In A. Piccialli, ed. *Proceedings of the Capri Workshop on Models and Representations of Musical Signals*. Naples: University of Naples Federico II, Department of Physics.

Roads, C. 1992c. "Synthulate." Software documentation. Unpublished.

Roads, C. 1992d. "Granulateur." Software documentation. Unpublished.

Roads, C. 1992–1997. "Design of a granular synthesizer." Unpublished design documents.

Roads, C. 1993a. "Musical sound transformation by convolution." In S. Ohteru, ed. *Proceedings of the 1993 International Computer Music Conference*. San Francisco: International Computer Music Association. pp. 102–109.

Roads, C. 1993b. "Organization of *Clang-tint*." In S. Ohteru, ed. *Proceedings of the 1993 International Computer Music Conference*. San Francisco: International Computer Music Association. pp. 346–348.

Roads, C. 1996. *The Computer Music Tutorial*. Cambridge, Massachusetts: MIT Press.

Roads, C. 1997. "Sound transformation by convolution." In C. Roads, S. Pope, A. Piccialli, and G. De Poli, eds. *Musical Signal Processing*. Lisse: Swets & Zeitlinger.

Roads, C. 1998a. "Espace musical : virtuel et physique." In F. Barrière and G. Bennett, eds. *Composition/Diffusion en Musique Electroacoustique. Actes III. Académie Internationale de Musique Électroacoustique*. Bourges: Editions Mnemosyne. pp. 158–160.

Roads, C. 1998b. "The Creatovox synthesizer project." Unpublished manuscript.

Roads, C. 1999. "Synthèse et transformation des microsons." Doctoral thesis. Paris: Department of Music, University of Paris VIII.

Roads, C. 2000. "Notes on the history of sound in space." Presented at the CREATE symposium SOUND IN SPACE 2000, University of California, Santa Barbara. Revised version forthcoming in *Computer Music Journal*.

Roads, C. 2001. "Sound composition with pulsars." *Journal of the Audio Engineering Society* 49(3).

Roads, C., and J. Alexander. 1995. *Cloud Generator Manual*. Distributed with the program Cloud Generator. Internet: www.create.ucsb.edu.

Roads, C., J. Kuchera-Morin, and S. Pope. 1997. "The Creatophone sound spatializer project." Unpublished research proposal.

Robindoré, B. 1996a. "Eskhaté Ereuna: extending the limits of musical thought—comments on and by Iannis Xenakis." *Computer Music Journal* 20(4): 11–16.

Robindoré, B. 1996b. Program notes. *Computer Music Journal* compact disc. Volume 20, 1996.

Robindoré, B. 1998. "Interview with an intimate iconoclast." *Computer Music Journal* 23(3): 8–16.

Rocha, M. 1999. "Les techniques granulaires dans la synthèse sonore." Doctoral thesis. Paris: Université de Paris VIII.

Rodet, X. 1980. "Time-domain formant-wave-function synthesis." In J. G. Simon, ed. 1980. *Spoken Language Generation and Understanding*. Dordrecht: D. Reidel. Reprinted in *Computer Music Journal* 8(3): 9–14. 1984.

Rodet, X., Y. Potard, and J.-B. Barrière. 1984. "The CHANT project: from synthesis of the singing voice to synthesis in general." *Computer Music Journal* 8(3): 15–31. Reprinted in C. Roads, ed. 1989. *The Music Machine*. Cambridge, Massachusetts: MIT Press.

Russolo, L. 1916. *The Art of Noises*. Translated 1986 by Barclay Brown. New York: Pendragon Press.

Scaletti, C. 1996. "Description of *Public Organ*." Internet: www.symbolicsound.com.

Schaeffer, P. 1959. "The interplay between music and acoustics." *Gravensaner Blätter* 14: 61–69.

Schaeffer, P. 1977. *Traité des objets musicaux*. Second edition. Paris: Éditions du Seuil.

Schaeffer, P., and A. Moles. 1952. *À la recherche d'une musique concrète*. Paris: Editions du Seuil.

Schaeffer, P., G. Reibel, and B. Ferreyra. 1967. *Trois microsillons d'exemples sonores de G. Reibel et Beatriz Ferreyra illustrant le Traité des Objets Sonores et présentés par l'auteur.* Paris: Éditions du Seuil.

Schafer, R. M. 1977. *The Tuning of the World.* New York: Knopf.

Schafer, R., and L. Rabiner. 1973. "Design and simulation of a speech analysis-synthesis system based on short-time Fourier analysis." *IEEE Transactions on Audio and Electroacoustics* AU–21: 165–174.

Schillinger, J. 1946. *The Schillinger System of Musical Composition.* New York: Carl Fischer. Reprinted 1978. New York: Da Capo Press.

Schindler, A. 1998. *Eastman Csound Tutorial.* Internet: www.esm.rochester.edu/online-docs/allan.cs.

Schnell, N. 1995. "GRAINY—granularsynthese in Echtzeit." *Beitrage zur Electronischen Musik* 4. Fraz: Institüt für Elektronische Musik, Hochschule für Musik und Darstellende Kunst.

Schoenberg A. 1967. *Fundamentals of Music Composition.* London: Faber and Faber.

Schopenhauer, A. 1819. "Art and the art of music." From *The World of Will and Idea.* Translated by R. Haldane and J. Kemp, reprinted in J. Randall et al. 1946. *Readings in Philosophy.* New York: Barnes and Noble. pp. 246–254.

Schottstaedt, W. 2000. *Common Lisp Music Manual.* Online documentation. Internet: www-ccrma.stanford.edu/CCRMA/Software/clm/clm-manual/clm.html.

Schroeder, M., and B. S. Atal. 1962. "Generalized short-time power spectra and auto-correlation functions." *Journal of the Acoustical Society of America* 34: 1679–1683.

Scott, R., and S. Gerber. 1972. "Pitch-synchronous time-compression of speech." *Proceedings of the IEEE Conference for Speech Communication Processing.* New York: IEEE. 63–65.

Serra, M.-H. 1992. "Stochastic Composition and Stochastic Timbre: Gendy3 by Iannis Xenakis" *Perspectives of New Music* 31.

Serra, M.-H. 1997. "Introducing the phase vocoder." In C. Roads, S. Pope, A. Piccialli, and G. De Poli, eds. *Musical Signal Processing.* Lisse: Swets and Zeitlinger. pp. 31–90.

Serra, X. 1989. "A system for sound analysis/transformation/synthesis based on a deterministic plus stochastic decomposition." Stanford: Center for Computer Research in Music and Acoustics, Department of Music, Stanford University.

Serra, X., and J. Smith. 1990. "Spectral modeling synthesis: a sound analysis/synthesis system based on a deterministic plus stochastic decomposition." *Computer Music Journal* 14(4): 12–24.

Shensa, M. 1992. "The discrete wavelet transform: wedding the à trous and Mallat algorithms." *IEEE Transactions on Signal Processing* 40(10): 2464–2482.

Smalley, D. 1986. "Spectro-morphology and structuring processes." In S. Emmerson, ed. *The Language of Electroacoustic Music.* London: Macmillan. pp. 61–93.

Smalley, D. 1997. "Spectromorphology: explaining sound shapes." *Organised Sound* 2(2): 107–126.

Smith, L. 1996. "Modelling rhythm perception by continuous time-frequency analysis." In L. Ayers and A. Horner, eds. *Proceedings of the 1996 International Computer Music Conference.* San Francisco: International Computer Music Association. pp. 392–395.

Solomos, M. 1997. Program notes to *Xenakis: Electronic Music.* Compact disc CD 003. Albany: Electronic Music Foundation.

Sprenger, S. 1999. "Time and pitch scaling of audio signals." Internet: www.dspdimension.com/html/timepitch.html.

Steiglitz, K. 1996. *A Digital Signal Processing Primer.* Menlo Park: Addison-Wesley.

Steinberg. 1998. "Cubase VST/24 audio recording." Karlsruhe: Steinberg Soft- and Hardware GmbH.

Stevenson, R., and R. B. Moore. 1967. *Theory of Physics.* Philadelphia: W. B. Saunders.

Stockham, T. 1969. "High-speed convolution and convolution with applications to digital filtering." In B. Gold and C. Rader. 1969. *Digital Processing of Signals.* New York: McGraw-Hill. pp. 203–232.

Stockhausen, K. 1955. "Actualia." *die Reihe* 1. English edition. Bryn Mawr: Theodore Presser Company. pp. 45–51.

Stockhausen, K. 1957. "... How time passes ..." *die Reihe* 3: 10–43. English edition translated by Cornelius Cardew. 1959. Reprinted with revisions as "... wie die Zeit vergeht ..." in K. Stockhausen. 1963. *Texte zur elektronischen und instrumentalen Musik.* Band 1. Cologne: DuMont Schauberg: pp. 99–139.

Stockhausen, K. 1961. "Two lectures." *die Reihe* 5. English edition. Bryn Mawr: Theodore Presser Company. pp. 59–82.

Stockhausen, K. 1962. "Die Einheit der musikalischen Zeit." [The unity of musical time.] Translated by E. Barkin as "The concept of unity in electronic music." *Perspectives of New Music* 1(1): 39. Reprinted in B. Boretz and E. Cone, eds. 1972. *Perspectives on Contemporary Music Theory.* New York: Norton. pp. 129–147. German version published in Stockhausen (1963), pp. 211–221.

Stockhausen, K. 1963. *Texte zur elektronischen und instrumentalen Musik.* Band 1. Cologne: DuMont Schauberg.

Strang, G. 1994. *A Friendly Guide to Wavelets.* Boston: Birkhaüser.

Stravinsky, I. 1936. *An Autobiography.* New York: W. W. Norton.

Stravinsky, I. 1947. *Poetics of Music.* Cambridge, Massachusetts: Harvard University Press.

Strawn, J. 1985. "Modelling musical transitions." Ph.D. dissertation. Stanford: Stanford University Department of Music.

Stuckenschmidt, H. H. 1969. *Twentieth Century Music.* New York: McGraw-Hill.

Sturm, B. 1999. "A potential G.U.T. of signal synthesis." Internet: www-ccrma.stanford.edu/~sturm/research.html.

Supper, M. 1997. *Elektroakustische Musik und Computermusic.* Hofheim: Wolke Verlag.

Sussman, G., and Steele, G. 1981. "Constraints: A language for expresssing almost-hierarchical descriptions." A.I. Memo 502A. Artificial Intelligence Laboratory, Massachusetts Institute of Technology, Cambridge, Massachusetts Reprinted in *Artificial Intelligence* 14: 1–39.

Tait, C. 1995. "Audio analysis for rhythmic structure." *Proceedings of the 1995 International Computer Music Conference.* San Francisco: International Computer Music Association. pp. 590–1.

Tempelaars, S. 1976. "The VOSIM oscillator." Presented at the 1976 International Computer Music Conference, MIT, Cambridge, Massachusetts, 28–31 October.

Tempelaars, S. 1977. *Sound Signal Processing.* Translated by Ruth Koenig. Utrecht: Institute of Sonology.

Tempelaars, S. 1996. *Signal Processing, Speech, and Music.* Lisse: Swets and Zeitlinger.

Todoroff, T. 1995. "Real-time granular morphing and spatialization of sounds with gestural control within Max/FTS." In R. Bidlack, ed. *Proceedings of the 1995 International Computer Music Conference.* San Francisco: International Computer Music Association. pp. 315–318.

Torrésani, B. 1995. *Analyse continue par ondelettes.* Paris: InterEditions.

Truax, B. 1984. *Acoustic Communication.* Norwood, New Jersey: Ablex Publishing.

Truax, B. 1986. "Real-time granular synthesis with the DMX-1000." In P. Berg, ed. 1987. *Proceedings of the 1986 International Computer Music Conference.* San Francisco: Computer Music Association. pp. 138–145.

Truax, B. 1987. "Real-time granulation of sampled sound." In S. Tipei and J. Beauchamp, eds. 1987. *Proceedings of the 1987 International Computer Music Conference.* San Francisco: Computer Music Association. pp. 138–145.

Truax, B. 1988. "Real-time granular synthesis with a digital signal processing computer." *Computer Music Journal* 12(2): 14–26.

Truax, B. 1990a. "Time-shifting of sampled sound sound using a real-time granulation technique." In *Proceedings of the 1990 International Computer Music Conference.* San Francisco: Computer Music Association. pp. 104–107.

Truax, B. 1990b. "Composing with real-time granular sound. *Perspectives of New Music* 28(2): 120–134.

Truax, B. 1992. "Composition with time-shifted environmental sound." *Leonardo Music Journal* 2(1): 37–40.

Truax, B. 1994a. "Discovering inner complexity: time-shifting and transposition with a real-time granulation technique." *Computer Music Journal* 18(2): 38–48.

Truax, B. 1994b. "Granulation and time-shifting of sampled sound in real-time with a quad DSP audio computer system." In *Proceedings of the 1994 International Computer Music Association.* San Francisco: Computer Music Association. pp. 335–337.

Truax, B. 1995. "Sound in context: soundscape research and composition at Simon Fraser University." In *Proceedings of the 1995 International Computer Music Conference.* San Francisco: International Computer Music Association. pp. 1–4.

Truax, B. 1996a. "Time-stretching of hyper-resonated sound using a real-time granulation technique. In *Proceedings of the 1996 International Computer Music Conference.* San Francisco: International Computer Music Association. pp. 491–492.

Truax, B. 1996b. "Soundscape, acoustic communication, and environmental sound composition." *Contemporary Music Review* 15(1): 49–65.

Tyndall, J. 1875. *Sound.* Akron: Werner.

Ungeheuer, E. 1992. *Wie de elektronische Musik "erfunden" wurde ...* Mainz: B. Schott's Söhne.

Vaggione, H. 1984. "The making of *Octuor." Computer Music Journal* 8(2): 48–54. Reprinted in C. Roads, ed. 1989. *The Music Machine.* Cambridge, Massachusetts: The MIT Press. pp. 149–155.

Vaggione, H. 1996a. "Autour de l'approche électroacoustique : situations, perspectives." In G. Bennett, C. Clozier, S. Hanson, C. Roads, and H. Vaggione, eds. *Esthétique et Musique Électroacoustique.* Bourges: Éditions Mnemosyne. pp. 101–108.

Vaggione, H. 1996b. "Articulating micro-time." *Computer Music Journal* 20(2): 33–38.

Vaggione, H. 1996c. "Vers une approche transformationelle en CAO." *Actes des JIM 1996.* Les cahiers du GREYC. Caen: CNRS-Université de Caen. Internet: www.ircam.fr/equipes/repmus/jim96/actes/Vaggione/VaggioneTEXT.html.

Vaggione, H. 1997. "Singularité de la musique et analyse: l'espace d'intersection." In F. Barrière and C. Clozier, eds. *Analyse en Musique Éléctroacoustique.* Bourges: Éditions: Mnemosyne. pp. 74–81.

Vaggione, H. 1998. "Transformations morphologiques: quelques exemples." *Actes des JIM 1998.*

Vaggione, H. 1999. Personal communication.

Varèse, E. 1940. "Organized sound for the sound film." Quoted in Miller (1945).

Varèse, E. 1962. From a lecture given at Yale University. Reprinted in Varèse (1971).

Varèse, E. 1971. "The liberation of sound." In C. Boretz and E. Cone, eds. *Perspectives on American Composers.* New York: Norton. pp. 26–34.

Vercoe, B. 1993. *Csound: A Manual for the Audio Processing System and Supporting Programs with Tutorials.* Cambridge, Massachusetts: MIT Media Laboratory.

Vetterli, M., and C. Herley. 1992. "Wavelets and filter banks: theory and design." *IEEE Transactions on Signal Processing* ASSP–40(9): 2207–2234.

Walker, B., and K. Fitz. 1992. *Lemur Manual.* Urbana: CERL Sound Group, University of Illinois.

Wannamaker, R., and E. Vrscay. 1997. "Fractal wavelet compression of audio signals." *Journal of the Audio Engineering Society* 45(7/8): 540–553.

Weare, C. 1997. Personal communication.

Weidenaar, R. 1989. "The Telharmonium: A History of the First Music Synthesizer, 1893–1918." Ph.D. dissertation. New York: New York University.

Weidenaar, R. 1995. Magic Music from the Telharmonium. Metuchen: Scarecrow Press.

Weinberg, S. 1983. *The Discovery of Subatomic Particles.* New York: W.H. Freeman.

Wenger, E., and E. Spiegel. 1999. *MetaSynth Manual.* San Francisco: U&I Software.

Whitehouse, D. 1999. "Haunting sound from the dawn of time." British Broadcasting Company. 23 September 1999. Internet: news.bbc.co.uk/hi/english/sci/tech/newsid_454000/454594.stm

Whitfield, J. 1978. "The neural code." In E. Carterette and M. Friedman, eds. 1978. *Handbook of Perception,* vol. IV, Hearing. Orlando: Academic.

Wickerhauser, V. 1989. "Acoustic signal compression with wave packets." New Haven: Department of Mathematics, Yale University.

Wiener, N. 1964. *I Am a Mathematician.* Cambridge, Massachusetts: MIT Press.

Wiener, N. 1964. "Spatial-temporal continuity, quantum theory, and music." In M. Capek, ed. 1975. *The Concepts of Space and Time.* Boston: D. Reidel.

Winckel, F. 1967. *Music, Sound, and Sensation.* New York: Dover Publications.

Winham, G. 1966. *The Reference Manual for Music 4B.* Princeton: Princeton University Music Department.

Winham, G., and K. Steiglitz. 1970. "Input generators for digital sound synthesis." *Journal of the Acoustical Society of America* 47(2, Part 2): 665–666.

Winston, P. 1984. *Artificial Intelligence.* Second edition. Reading, Massachusetts: Addison-Wesley.

Wishart, T. 1994. *Audible Design.* York: Orpheus the Pantomime.

Wishart, T. 1996. Program notes for *Tongues of Fire.* Internet: www.aec.at/prix/1995/E95gnM-tongues.html.

Xenakis, I. 1960. "Elements of stochastic music." *Gravensaner Blätter* 18: 84–105.

Xenakis, I. 1971. *Formalized Music.* Bloomington: Indiana University Press.

Xenakis, I. 1989. "Concerning time." *Perspectives of New Music* 27(1): 84–92. Reprinted in French as "Sur le temps" in I. Xenakis, 1994, *Kéleütha.* Paris: L'Arche.

Xenakis, I. 1992. *Formalized Music.* Revised edition. New York: Pendragon Press.

Yermakov, A. 1999. *SoundFront documentation.* Internet: www.kagi.com

A   The Cloud Generator Program

Features of Cloud Generator

Start Time and Duration

Density

Bandlimits

Cloud Type

Stereo Location

Grain Duration

Selection Order

Waveform

Text/AIFF Output

This appendix describes Cloud Generator (CG), an interactive MacOS program for granular synthesis and sound file granulation (figure A.1). Since its development, I have taught hundreds of musicians how to operate this easy-to-use software. It appears that CG will soon be obsolete, owing to changes in the underlying operating system. On an appropriate platform, however, the program is still useful for teaching and for experimentation. (See www.create.ucsb.edu for information on our newer program for particle synthesis, PulsarGenerator.)

John Alexander and I wrote Cloud Generator in the C programming language in 1995. At the time, John Alexander was my student at Les Ateliers UPIC (now CCMIX) in Paris. We based CG on a suite of my 1988–1992 programs for granular synthesis. (See description in chapter 3.) These programs were not easy to use, since they required users to operate within environment of a C compiler.

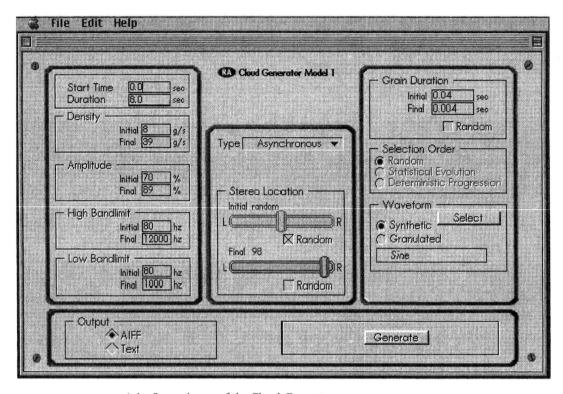

A.1   Screen image of the Cloud Generator program.

CG merged the code from several of these programs into a single stand-alone application. It unified them under a common interface. Our goal was to create a tool for experimentation, teaching, and composition with granular techniques.

We created CG before Power PC microprocessors were generally available for Apple computers. Due to changes in MacOS, it would require considerable effort to update the program for newer processors. Nonetheless, the non-floating-point (NFPU) version runs in emulation mode on any Power Macintosh computer up through the G3/450 MHz running MacOS System 8.6. The performance is acceptable; many clouds compute in faster than real time.

Since we developed CG, I have continued to extend my earlier programs for purposes of experimentation. Since these programs do not depend on interaction with a graphical user interface, they can more easily be programmed to perform operations not in CG. Each program in the suite performs a particular type of granular synthesis or granular transformation. Since 1998, Alberto de Campo and I moved most of the functionality of CG to the Creatovox instrument, which chapter 5 documents.

Features of Cloud Generator

We designed the front panel of CG to look like a laboratory signal generator. The console contains all the parameters that a user needs to control granular synthesis.

CG emits two types of grains: synthetic (which repeat a fixed waveform), and granulated (which extract waveforms from different locations in a sound file). The synthetic grain mode offers a choice of preset grain waveforms, such as sine, square, and sawtooth. Users can also extract any waveform stored in a sound file, including sampled waveforms. Finally, the program provides a graphical editor for drawing grain waveforms manually. High-resolution interpolating oscillators generate the synthetic grains.

In granulation mode, CG accepts a stereo sound file as its input. After loading this file into its memory space, CG extracts sound particles from the soundfile according to random, statistical, or deterministic progression algorithms (described later).

The output of CG is either a synchronous cloud or an asynchronous cloud. In a synchronous cloud, the grains follow one another after a fixed time interval. In an asycnhronous cloud, the grains scatter randomly in time.

As it is calculating, CG displays the formation of the cloud as a plot of time versus frequency. It produces a stereo soundfile output. If desired, it can also produce a textfile, listing the numerical properties of each grain in a cloud. Plotting programs can can read this text. In one, exceptional, case, the composer Mark-David Hosale used CG to produce texts that he transcribed into an instrumental composition.

The next sections explain the meaning of the parameters displayed on the console.

Start Time and Duration

The start time and duration parameters set the temporal boundaries of a cloud, indicated in seconds. The usual start time of a cloud is 0. A positive start time, such as 2.0, creates a sound file containing silence for two seconds, followed by the cloud. This feature could be useful in precisely synchronizing multiple soundfiles in an editing and mixing program. If the output of the program is text, this feature could be used to order multiple clouds in a plotting program.

The duration of a cloud can range from 0.000001 to an upper bound of 47.0 seconds, given sufficient memory. The reason for the upper bound on cloud duration is that the synthesis data is calculated in random-access memory (RAM) before being written to disk. The program preallocates a buffer large enough to accomodate 47 seconds of stereo audio for a synthetic cloud.

Density

Grain density is a function of grains per second. A synchronous cloud generates metrical rhythmic sequences when grain densities are in the range of between two and twenty grains per second. When the initial density is not the same as the final density, this creates an acceleration or deceleration effect.

For asynchronous clouds, a variation between the initial and final density produces an irregular acceleration or deceleration. To create continuous noise sounds, one sets the density to above one hundred grains per second.

Bandlimits

Bandlimits describe the frequencies of the four corners of a trapezoidal region inscribed on the frequency-versus-time plane. The grains scatter within the bounds of this region. To create a line of grains at a fixed frequency, one sets all the bandlimits to the same frequency, for example, 440 Hz. To scatter grains in a rectangular region between 80 Hz and 300 Hz, one sets both high bandlimits to 300, and both low bandlimits to 80. For a cloud that converges to 300 Hz, one would set both final bandlimits to 300. (See figure 3.6.)

Bandlimits apply only in the case of a cloud filled by synthetic grains, where the selected waveform is of the type "Synthetic." They have no meaning when the cloud is a granulated sound file.

Cloud Type

This parameter specifies the temporal distribution of the grains, either synchronous or asynchronous. Synchronous generation means that one grain follows another in series, with the distance between the grain attacks determined by the density parameter. For example, a synchronous cloud with a density of five grains per sec creates quintuplets at a tempo of M.M. 60. The spacing between grain attacks is 200 ms. Asynchronous clouds scatter grains at random time points within the specified boundaries of the cloud, at the specified density. Asynchronous clouds produce aleatoric and explosive effects.

Stereo Location

The stereo location potentiometers provide an intuitive interface for the initial and final position of the sound cloud. By clicking on either the initial or final Random box the grain scatters to a random position in stereo space. This randomization articulates the granular texture of a cloud. It enhances the impression that the cloud is a three-dimensional object in space.

Grain Duration

Grain duration has a strong influence on the timbre of the resulting cloud. Grain duration is a value in seconds. Thus a value of 0.1 equals 100 ms. The initial grain duration applies at the beginning of the cloud. The final grain grain duration applies at the end. If the Random box is checked, the grain duration parameters switch from "Initial" to "Minimum" and from "Final" to "Maximum." In this case, the grain duration is a random function between the specified minimum and maximum values.

Selection Order

The Selection Order parameter applies only to granulated clouds. It determines the order in which grains are selected from the input sound file. Three options present themselves:

1. Random—select input grains from random points in the input sound file.
2. Statistical evolution—select input grains in a more-or-less left-to-right order. That is, at the beginning of the cloud there is a high probability that grains derive from the beginning of the input file; at the end of the cloud there is a high probability that grains derive from the end of the input file.
3. Deterministic progression—select input grains in a strictly left-to-right order.

Option 1 results in a scrambled version of the input. Option 3 preserves the temporal order of the original (we use this mode when time-shrinking or time-stretching the input sound file). Option 2 is a blend of options 1 and 3.

Waveform

The waveform parameter has several controls. The first is a choice between Synthetic or Granulated source waveforms. The name of the chosen waveform appears in the small box below the buttons.

- In a synthetic cloud, an oscillator reads a wavetable containing one period of a waveform at a frequency within the high and low bandlimit boundaries.
- In a granulated cloud, the grains are extracted from a stereo input sound file of any length. The extracted grains are scattered in time without pitch transposition. The bandlimit parameters are not operational in a granulated cloud.

The Select button brings up a dialog box that depends on whether the cloud is synthetic or granulated. If it is synthetic, the dialog box displays five choices:

1. Sine
2. Sawtooth
3. Square
4. User-drawn—one can freely draw in the waveform editor
5. Imported from a sound file. The imported file must be exactly 2048 samples (46 ms) in length. If the waveform is extracted from a sampled sound file, this waveform will repeat at its extracted frequency only if the cloud bandlimits are set to 21 Hz. Any frequency above this transposes the waveform

If the cloud is granulated, the Select button displays an Open File dialog box. The user is invited to select a stereo sound file to granulate.

Text/AIFF Output

This option lets one save the cloud data in the form of numerical text. This text could be read by a plotting program to make a graphical score. Clicking on AIFF creates a sound file as the output of the program's calculations. This is the normal mode.

B   Sound Examples

These sound examples are available for download at **mitpress.mit.edu/microsound**.
They were originally published as a CD packaged with the book.

This recording documents the history of synthesis with microsonic particles and presents artistic excerpts of music compositions realized with these techniques. It also serves as an audio notebook of research experiments in this domain.

Tracks 1 through 3 present the historical examples. Tracks 4 through 13 present musical excerpts. Tracks 14 through 44 present an audio notebook of research experiments in particle synthesis. Tracks 45 through 68 present an audio notebook of experiments in microsonic sound transformation.

Historical Examples

1. Three excerpts of *Analogique A et B* for string orchestra and analog granular synthesis by Iannis Xenakis. The piece was composed in 1958 and 1959. The composition opposes part A for string orchestra, and part B for tape. (a) Tape part alone. (b) Tape with instruments in a busy section. (c) Tape with instruments in a sparse section. Reproduced with the permission of Iannis Xenakis and Éditions Salabert, 22 rue Chauchat, 75009 Paris, France, www.salabert.fr.   [1:03]

2. *Klang-1* (Curtis Roads, December 1974), first granular synthesis experiment by computer. The recording is distorted, due to technical factors.   [0:48]

3. Excerpt of *Prototype* (Curtis Roads, April 1975), first study in automated granular synthesis.   [0:26]

Sound Particles in Music Compositions

4. Excerpt of *nscor* (Curtis Roads, 1980). This excerpt [4:30–5:40] features a granular explosion followed by a passage of granular noise clouds in different frequency bands.   [1:14]

5. Excerpt of *Field* (Curtis Roads, 1981). This excerpt [3:37–4:02] features a granular explosion.   [0:28]

6. Excerpt of *Organic* (Curtis Roads, 1994). This excerpt [1:55–2:49] opens with an asynchronous pulsar cloud. All of the beating and pulsating sounds are pulsars. [0:58]

7. Excerpt of *Half-life* (Curtis Roads, 1999). This excerpt [0:00–1:04] from the first movement, entitled *Sonal Atoms*, consists of a pulsar stream that has been granulated and then extensively edited on a microsonic time scale. [1:09]

8. Excerpt of *Tenth vortex* (Curtis Roads, 2000). This excerpt [0:00–1:29] consists of a constantly evolving cloud of grains produced by my constant-Q granulation program applied to a stream of synthetic pulsars. [1:28]

9. Excerpt of *Eleventh vortex* (Curtis Roads, 2001). The opening of this excerpt [0:00–1:30] features multiple synchronous pulsar streams, each at a separate tempo. The thick stream of particles thins into a series of discrete particles about 40 seconds into the piece. [1:05]

10. Excerpt of *Sculptor* (Curtis Roads, 2001). The source material of *Sculptor* was a driving percussion piece by the group Tortoise, sent to me for processing in August 2000 by John McEntire. I granulated and filtered the material by means of the constant-Q granulator, which disintegrated the beating drums into a torrent of sound particles. Beginning with this whirling sound mass, I articulated the internal morphologies and implied causalities within the current of particles. This meant shaping the river of particle densities, squeezing and stretching the amplitudes of individual particles and particle clouds, carving connected and disconnected frequency zones, and twisting the spatial flow. Over months of intermittent editing on different time scales, I was able to sculpt this material into its current form. The composition was completed in July 2001 in Santa Barbara. [1:31]

11. Excerpt of *Agon* (Horacio Vaggione, 1998). *Agon* is one of a series of works by Horacio Vaggione that explore the concept of composition on multiple time scales. The original sound sources were acoustic percussion instruments, which have been broken down into microsonic particles and reassembled by the composer in a technique of micromontage. [1:08]

12. Excerpt of *Life in the Universe* (Ken Fields, 1997). This excerpt [0:00–1:36] features the granulation of the synthetic voice of physicist Steven Hawking. It appeared on a CD-ROM entitled *Steven Hawking Life in the Universe* that was marketed by Meta-Creations. [1:42]

13. Three excerpts from the electronic part of *Paleo* for double bass and CD. (JoAnn Kuchera-Morin, 2000) demonstrating the use the phase vocoder to time scale sounds. (a) The first 45 seconds of the computer-generated portion of the work. The sound consists of processed double bass and dijeridu string Csound instruments. No time scaling. (b) From the middle section of the work, a passage time-stretched by a factor of 7.9. (c) From the middle section of the work, a passage time-shrunk by a factor of 0.5. [2:36]

Experiments in Particle Synthesis

Synthetic Granular Synthesis

14. A melodic stream of sinusoidal grains, increasing regularly in density over 40 seconds. The frequency band within which the grains are scattered opens up to a high frequency of 5000 Hz and a low frequency of 80 Hz. The pitch is random within this range. The grain duration is also diminishing over time, from 310 ms to 1 ms, resulting in a short pop at the end. Reverberation added.   [0:42]

15. Synchronous granular cloud with a wide bandwidth at a constant density of fifteen grains per second, followed by an asynchronous cloud with the same specifications. Reverberation added.   [0:30]

16. In a synchronous granular cloud, the grain duration and density parameters may be a stronger determinant of pitch than the frequency of the waveform inside the grain. This example presents a synchronous cloud of 10-ms sinusoidal grains with a nominal frequency of 200 Hz. The pitch changes as the density increases from 100 to 200 grains per second. In effect, the onset time of the grains becomes the perceived fundamental pitch.   [0:12]

17. Dense cloud made up of sinusoidal grains. The initial density of 600 grains per second, diminishing to 1. The initial frequency bandwidth is 13 kHz down to 40 Hz, and the final frequency bandwidth is centered at 200 Hz; hence the narrowing frequency band. The duration of the grains is random between 12 ms and 1 ms.   [0:11]

18. Sparse, broadband cloud of very short grains, with durations between 1 ms and 500 μsec. Reverberation added.   [0:11]

19. Metric stream of grains, 30 ms in duration, in a looped pattern. Reverberation added.   [0:25]

20. Real-time granular synthesis performed on the Creatovox synthesizer. A collage of Creatovox sounds originally performed by composer Bebe Barron in Studio Varèse, Center for Research in Electronic Art Technology (CREATE), University of California, Santa Barbara, July 2000. Ms. Barron's musical assistant was Alberto de Campo. The method of synthesis was synthetic granular synthesis. Reverberation was added at the time of recording. This collage was assembled by Curtis Roads in August 2001.   [1:18]

Glisson Synthesis

21. Isolated glissons. (a) Two 250 ms glissons, one sweeping from 1000 Hz to 500 Hz, the other in the opposite direction. (b) Two 56 ms glissons, sweeping from 55 Hz to 1400 Hz and the other in the opposite direction. (c) Two sets of "bird call" glissons.   [0:11]

22. Trains of 6 ms glissons with small frequency deviations centered at 1450 Hz and 400 Hz respectively.   [0:07]

23. Seven glisson clouds. (a) High-density cloud, wide frequency sweep. (b) Long glissons, high density cloud, converging on 550 Hz. (c) Long glissons converging on 1100 Hz. (d) High-density glisson cloud sweeping from 6 to 2000 Hz. (e) Long glissons. (f) Short glissons. (g) High-frequency glissons.   [1:46]

Grainlet Synthesis

Experiments in grainlet synthesis, 1996–1998. These experiments demonstrate linkages between grainlet frequency and grainlet duration. All experiments realize asynchronous (non-metric) clouds. I have added reverberation and some editing effects, primarily particle replication.

24. Sparse cloud in which high frequency grainlets are short, while low-frequency grainlets are long.   [0:10]

25. Four clouds. (a) One cycle (fundamental period) per grainlet. (2) Four cycles per grainlet. (3) Eight cycles per grainlet. (d) Sixteen cycles per grainlet.   [0:33]

26. Medium-density grainlet cloud, with short high frequencies and long low frequencies.   [0:23]

27. A cloud with a frequency pole at 440 Hz, making grainlets around that frequency much longer than low frequency and high frequency grainlets.   [0:13]

28. Three high-density (90 particles per second) grainlet clouds. (a) Two cycles per grainlet. (b) Four cycles per grainlet. (c) Twenty cycles per grainlet.   [0:20]

29. Six high-density grainlet experiments.   [1:06]

Trainlet Synthesis

Experiments in trainlet synthesis, 1999–2000.

30. Individual trainlets. (a) Gbuzz test demonstrating increasing "lowest harmonic." (b) 40 Hz trainlet with 16 harmonics and chroma = 1.0. (c) 600 Hz trainlet with chroma = 1.0. (d) 600 Hz trainlet with chroma = 0.5.   [0:34]

31. Sparse trainlet phrases.   [1:00]

32. Dense trainlet clouds.   [1:02]

Pulsar Synthesis

Experiments in pulsar synthesis, 1991–2001.

33. Cosmic pulsar from the neutron star PSR 0329+54.   [0:07]

34. Pulsar variations. (a) Constant fundamental frequency, three variable formant frequencies. Each formant has an independent trajectory in space. (b) Variable fundamental frequency, three constant formant frequencies (low, mid, high frequency). Each formant has an independent trajectory in space.   [0:49]

35. Pulsar rhythm versus tone. (a) Pulsar rhythm. (b) Pulsar tone, with the same formant envelope as the previous rhythm example.   [0:53]

36. Rhythmic burst masking examples, 8 Hz pulsar rhythm. One second of silence separates each example. (a) No burst masking. (b) 2:1 burst ratio. (c) 4:1 burst ratio. (d) 5:1 burst ratio. (e) 5:5 burst ratio.   [1:03]

37. Tone burst masking, subharmonics, and long tone pulses. 260 Hz pulsar rhythm with the same formant structure as the previous example. The only difference is the fundamental frequency. One second of silence separates each example. (a) No burst masking makes a constant tone. (b) 2:1 burst ratio, subharmonic effect. (c) 4:1 burst ratio, subharmonic effect. (d) 5:1 burst ratio, subharmonic effect. (e) 5:5 burst ratio, resulting in a slow amplitude modulation effect. (f) 5:10 burst ratio, resulting in discrete pulses. (g) 14:N burst ratio, where N is increasing, resulting in long pulses.   [1:06]

38. Stochastic masking in a low-frequency 40 Hz tone. Notice the intermittency in the pulsar stream. The constantly-varying formants are independent of this intermittency.   [0:22]

39. Eight short pulsar trains demonstrating a variety of pulsar sounds, from strong formant streams to rhythms and noise. Some examples have been edited and processed with reverberation.   [3:36]

Graphic and Sonographic Synthesis of Microsound

40. Synthesis of microsound in Phonogramme. This example presents a sparse scattering of microarcs, followed by a more dense cloud of microarcs.   [0:14]

41. Two examples of synthesis of microsound in MetaSynth. A complex cloud painted with MetaSynth's spray jet brush. Each particle is played by a sample playback oscillator. Both examples correspond to the same image score, but are edited afterward so that they have different accent points. (a) Sample playback with mallet instrument samples. (b) Sample playback with percussion instruments.   [0:28]

Synthesis by Transient Drawing and Particle Cloning

42. Synthesis by transient drawing. (a) 4.75 sec of transient waveforms drawn in a sound editor with a stylus tool (Alchemy by Passport Designs). (b, c, d) Beats and tones made by extracting particles from (a) and replicating and transposing them. (e) Six tones made from a single particle, replicated and transposed.   [0:24]

43. Transient transformation, in which a single transient event is extracted from a longer sound and then reshaped into different sounds through editing operations. Each example is separated by two seconds of silence. (a) The original source, a noisy one-second sound recorded by a hydrophone. (b) 125-ms extraction from (a). (c) The same event as (b), pitch-shifted up an octave, cloned ten times, and shaped with an exponential decay envelope. (d) The same event as (b), strongly filtered to create a colored tone. (e) The same event as (b) reversed and re-enveloped into a percussive sound. (f) The same event as (e), pitch-shifted and replicated to form two pitched tones. [0:18]

Physical Models of Particles

44. Examples of Perry Cook's maracas model as realized by J. Bumgartner's SYD program. Each sound object is like a single shake of a maraca. (a) Resonance frequency 100 Hz. (b) Resonance frequency 700 Hz. (c) Resonance frequency 3200 Hz. This is probably closest to the frequency of real maracas. (d) Resonance frequency 3200 Hz, but with a low probability of bean collisions. This models the case of a small number of beans in the maraca. (e) Strong resonance frequency 80 Hz. (f) Strong resonance frequency 600 Hz. [0:24]

Experiments in Sound Transformation with Particles

Micromontage

45. Result of micromontage in a graphical sound editing and mixing program, corresponding to figure 5.1. [0:04]

Granulation

46. Basic granulations. (a) Original spoken Italian utterance. (b) "Robotic" granulation transformation by layering several copies slightly delayed. (c) "Thickening" with increasing delay. (c) "Scrambling" with large grains. (d) Scrambling with medium-sized grains at medium density. (e) Scrambling with tiny grains and high density, going to long grains and low density. (f) Granulation with pitch shifting for a chorus effect. (g) "Graverberation" (granular reverberation) effects realized with the SampleHose by Michael Norris. [1:34]

47. Timbral enrichment by particle envelope manipulation. (a) Edgard Varèse speaking. (b) Change in formant location caused by many overlapping grains. (c) Short grains make the speech noisy. [0:44]

Pitch-Shifting on a Micro Time Scale

48. Experiments with pitch-shifting on a micro time scale. (a) Italian spoken phrase cut into 150 ms grains, each of which is pitch-shifted up to 40% up or down. (b) Same phrase with 50 ms grains and broader range of pitch-shifting. (c) Phrase with ten times grain overlap within a narrow range up and down. (d) Phrase with ten times overlap within a broad range up and down, creating a chorus effect.   [0:25]

Granular Time Stretching and Shrinking

49. Example of granular time-stretching using Cloud Generator. (a) Statement by Iannis Xenakis on "quantum sound synthesis," recorded 1989 by Christian Clozier. (b) Time stretched by a factor of two, with grain density increasing from 10 to 50 grains per second while the grain duration decreases from 100 ms to 50 ms. (c) Time shrunk to one-half the original duration. The grain durations are constant at 75 ms and the density is 50 grains per second. In both examples, the grains are randomly scattered within the stereo field.   [0:36]

Granular Formant Shifting

50. Granular formant shifting. The fundamental pitch and the duration of the sound remain constant. (a) Original Italian phrase. (b) +3 semitones formant shift. (c) +12 semitones formant shift. (d) −3 semitones formant shift. (e) −12 semitones formant shift.   [0:27]

Filtering on a Micro Time Scale

51. Experiment with constant-Q filters on grains. (a) Excerpt of Hopkinson Smith playing the lute composition *Gagliardi 5* from *Libro Primo d'Insta Volatura di Lauto* by G. G. Kapsberger (1580–1651) recorded on Astrée E 8553. (b) Constant-Q granulations of (a), including time scrambling of the grains. Realized in real-time with SuperCollider.   [1:58]

52. Experiment with constant-Q filters on grains. (a) Excerpt of percussion track sent to me by John McEntire, July 2000. (b) Excerpt of *Tsound*, a study made by constant-Q granulation of (a) with additional editing on a micro time scale.   [2:44]

Dynamics Processing on a Micro Time Scale

53. Granular dynamics processing. (a) Original Italian phrase. (b) Compression and expansion of high frequency band above 4000 Hz. (c) Processed with mid-frequency compansion. (d) Processed with extreme compansion focused on a narrow frequency band (452 Hz and its harmonics).   [0:14]

Waveset and Wavecycle Distortions

54. Waveset transformations, realized with the SoundMagic FX package by Michael Norris, a plugin set for SoundMaker. (a) Original Italian phrase. (b) Waveset harmonic distortion. (c) Time-varying waveset omission. (d) Waveset reversal. The waveset size is 60. (e) Waveset time-stretching by a factor of 7.6.   [0:58]

Convolution of Microsounds

Experiments in convolving sound particles with other sounds.

55. Granular convolution examples. (a) Synchronous grain cloud of grains lasting 7 seconds. The grain durations are between 1 and 9 ms. (b) Snare drum rim shot. (c) Convolution of (a) and (b). (d) Convolution of (b) with an asynchronous grain cloud with increasing density up to 90 grains per second. (e) 12-second synchronous cloud of sinusoidal grains at a density of 7 grains per second. (f) Swirling electronic texture lasting 7 seconds. (g) Convolution of (e) and (f), which extends the duration to 19 seconds.   [1:25]

56. Convolutions with a dense cloud of sonic grains to create quasi-reverberation effects. Convolution of Italian spoken phrase "Lezione numero undice, l'ora" with a dense cloud of Gaussian grains. The convolution window is of the Hamming type.   [1:25]

57. Pulsar convolution example. (a) Italian word "qui." (b) Pulsar train. (c) Convolution of (a) and (b).   [0:26]

Sound Transformation with Windowed Spectrum Operations

58. Phase vocoder operations: pitch-shifting with constant duration. (a) Edgard Varèse speaking. (b) Pitch shifting up five semitones. (c) Pitch-shifting down five semitones.   [0:54]

59. Phase vocoder operations: time stretching and shrinking with constant pitch. (a) Edgard Varèse speaking. (b) Time stretching by a factor of two. (c) Time shrinking by a factor of one-half.   [0:37]

60. Exotic spectrum transformations that manipulate the Gabor matrix. These examples were realized with the SoundMagic and SoundFront plugins to the SoundMaker editor. (a) Original Italian phrase. (b) Spectral magnet aligned to a pentatonic scale. (c) Spectral blurring with a 200 ms frame. (d) Spectral filter sweeping up. (e) Spectral randomizer. (f) Two examples of spectral tracing: the softest 1% of the spectrum followed by the loudest 1%, both normalized. (g) Spectral shift, upward sweep. (h) Spectral mirror, inversion around 1 kHz.   [0:47]

61. A classic vocoder transformation. (a) Speaking voice. (b) Fragment of orchestra music (*Sinfonia sopra una canzone d'amore* by Nino Rota, 1947, Fonit Cetra NFCD 2020). (c) Vocoding of (a) and (b), where (a) is the filterbank modulator and (b) is the carrier. The effect was realized with Arboretum HyperPrism.   [0:52]

Sonographic Transformations

62. Sonogram filtering. (a) Voice of Edgard Varèse. (b) Voice filtered by inscribing multiple regions on a sonogram and reducing them by 24 dB.   [0:26]

Transformations Based on the Tracking Phase Vocoder

63. Tracking phase vocoder (TPV) manipulations 1, manipulations based on track amplitudes. (a) Spoken French phrase. (b) Resynthesized from a TPV analysis. (c) Resynthesis after deletion of low-level tracks less than 80 dB down. (d) Resynthesis after deletion of low-level tracks less than 30 dB down. (e) Resynthesis with deletion of all tracks greater than 100 ms in duration. (f) Resynthesis with deletion of all tracks less than 100 ms in duration.   [0:27]

64. TPV transformations 2, spectrum shifting and multiplying. (a) Original Italian phrase. (b) Spectrum frequency shifted by 200 Hz. (c) Spectrum multiplied by 0.8. [0:18]

65. TPV transformations 3, disintegration. (a) Original Italian phrase. (b) Granular disintegration caused by deleting more and more time-frequency tracks (up to 85% by the end).   [0:12]

66. TPV transformations 4, morphing sounds. (a) Flute morphing into a clarinet. (b) Flute morphing into a cello. Examples courtesy of Kelly Fitz.   [0:15]

The Vector Oscillator Transform

67. (a) Spoken Italian phrase. (b) VOT resynthesis with 100 Hz fundamental. (c) VOT resynthesis with 60 Hz fundamental. (d) Time stretched version.   [0:16]

Wavelet-Based Transformations

68. Comb wavelet separation of harmonic and inharmonic components. (a) Violin note. (b) Harmonic part of violin tone. (c) Inharmonic part of violin tone. (d) Low piano tone. (e) Harmonic part of piano tone. (f) Inharmonic part of piano tone.   [0:19]

Name Index

Subject Index